JEAN RACINE

DRAMATIST

JEAN RACINE

DRAMATIST

BY

MARTIN TURNELL

A NEW DIRECTIONS BOOK

First published by New Directions in 1972
Manufactured in Great Britain

New Directions Books are published for James Laughlin
by New Directions Publishing Corporation,
333 Sixth Avenue, New York 10014

CONTENTS

INTRODUCTION

THIS is a book about dramatic experience. A friendly critic once suggested that I was more interested in the 'study' than the 'stalls'. The answer is that both are necessary. Every dramatist's goal is successful production on the stage. It is the only means of communicating his experience to the audience in its entirety. The primary aim of the practical critic is to help his readers to share the dramatist's experience in the theatre. It is obviously impossible to appreciate the work of a major dramatist to the full merely by watching occasional performances of his plays from the 'stalls'. Each play is an experience which is complete in itself. The way must be prepared by a careful study of the text which takes into account every aspect of the experience and the method of presenting it. Professor Raymond Picard said recently that 'Corneille and Racine can be enjoyed in print' and that 'a careful reading may be more rewarding than a poor performance'. This is undoubtedly true, but one thing should always be borne in mind: the plays must be studied as *dramatic* and not as *literary* works.

Racine's tragedies are pure drama in the sense in which we are accustomed to speaking of 'pure poetry'. Their essence is the continual *confrontation* of the characters at the right moment with the right words. The dialogue gives the plays their life. It moves perpetually between two extremes, the duel and the duet: duels between leaders of opposing factions, between rival lovers, between rejected lovers and the beloved; the duets of youthful and usually thwarted lovers or confidants and their masters and mistresses.

The form conditions the poetry. Racine is France's greatest dramatic poet. His poetry is rightly admired for its incantatory power, but is different in kind from much of Shakespeare's. It is a poetry of *situation* and not of *contemplation*. It only achieves its maximum effect when seen in its context, as part of an exchange between individuals. We cannot meditate on it, recite it to ourselves, unless we remember the context and the speaker, which may explain the seemingly pedantic arguments which have taken place in France over the poetic merits of 'l'Orient désert' and 'une flamme si noire' (which anyway was a borrowing from a minor dramatist) when discussed out of context.

Although the dialogue is interspersed like Shakespeare's with confessions and soliloquies, there are no discourses, no meditations or reflections on life in general, as there are in Hamlet's 'To be, or not to be'. Every line in Racine is directly related to the central theme and marks a stage, however slight, in the psychological development of the drama. This is one of the clearest signs of the tightness of structure and the intense compression which contribute largely to the dramatic force of the plays in performance.

When Hamlet or Claudio meditate on death, they introduce another dimension—a metaphysical dimension—which transcends the immediate situation. The metaphysical dimension is something that we do not find in Racine until we come to *Phèdre*, but even in that great masterpiece the new dimension is implicit in the tragedy as a whole and is never given explicit expression by an individual as it is in *Hamlet* and *Measure for Measure*. Phèdre is not 'puzzled' by

> The undiscover'd country from whose bourn
> No traveller returns . . .

She does not see herself

> imprison'd in the viewless winds
> And blown with restless violence round about
> The pendant world . . .

For her the prospect of death is simply a blackout:

> Fuyons dans la nuit infernale.

Words cannot be divorced from a particular character or situation in *Phèdre* any more than in the rest of the plays. These simple words are spoken by Phèdre herself at a critical moment in her downfall and their impact is very great.

I have dwelt on the importance of performance for both the dramatist and his audience. It involves special difficulties so far as the French classics are concerned. The English are better off than the French. The repertoire of the Royal Shakespeare Company is much more extensive than that of the Comédie Française. It is possible to see not only most of Shakespeare within a reasonable period of time, but some of the best plays of his contemporaries. It is far otherwise in France. There is no difficulty about seeing *Andromaque*, *Britannicus*, *Bérénice* and *Phèdre*, but unless one is in the happy position of being able to board a plane for Paris at the drop of a hat, the rest of the tragedies are a matter of luck because they are so seldom performed. I have seen the four plays I have just named about half-a-dozen times each. On one occasion I was researching in Paris in the spring

and saw my only performance of *Mithridate*. On another I had the good
luck to turn up one autumn in a 'flu-ridden Paris and managed to see
Bajazet. It was my only performance of that play, too, but I was more fortunate than the Dutch author of a substantial monograph on it who admitted that he had never seen it performed. And I was just in time to see
Korène in *Athalie*—unfortunately with new music instead of Moreau's—
before she finished her stint at the Comédie Française. *Iphigénie* is the one
secular tragedy of Racine's maturity that I have never seen. It is a pity
that only the more popular of the tragedies are available in full-length
versions on gramophone records and I have had to make do with a record
of selections from *Iphigénie*.

The sixteenth and seventeenth centuries were the great age of European
drama with England, France and Spain in the lead. It seems to me desirable that anyone who specializes in the drama of one of these countries
should have at least a working knowledge of the classics of the other two.
This applies particularly to Spain which today is the most neglected of the
three. It is a sad thing that it was the one major European country which
was not represented at the London World Theatre season until its eighth
year. What seems almost incredible is that the belated offering when it
came was not Lope de Vega or Calderón or even a modern master like
García Lorca, but a Spanish version of Jean Genet's *Les Bonnes*. I therefore make no apology for working in references to the Spanish classics
whenever I saw an opportunity of doing so.

Some readers may be surprised to find a number of references in a book
on Racine to cinematic techniques like 'flashbacks', 'cuts', and in one instance to a 'mix' or 'dissolve'. They are not facile or superficial comparisons. The underlying principle is an important one. There are certain
basic techniques which are common to different media. For obvious
reasons a particular technique is likely to be a good deal more effective in
one medium than another, which is one of the reasons why many distinguished novelists have tried their hands at drama and why some of them
like Robbe-Grillet are now showing signs of going into film not simply as
writers, but as directors. One of the clearest signs that film is an art in its
own right is the fact that we can see in retrospect that certain writers were
feeling for techniques which went beyond their own medium and could
only be fully effective in film. Anyone who wants to understand this cannot
do better than study Flaubert's two major novels. I must confess that I was
personally disappointed to find that the most distinguished film of
Madame Bovary did not exploit its innate cinematic elements in the way
that I had expected. Perhaps the truth is that great novels seldom make
great films and that lesser novels do. Robert Bresson made great films of
two of Bernanos's novels, but was less successful when he turned in *Une
Femme douce* to Dostoyevsky. Again, Buñuel's *Tristana* seems to me to be

artistically superior to the novel that inspired it which is not one of Pérez Galdós's outstanding successes.

I am not, however, concerned here with novelists. The point I want to make is that from time to time Racine and other dramatists use techniques which were to become more effective in film than in any other medium, and that there are scenes in Racine which would gain considerably by the addition of the visual element. It does not require any great effort of imagination to see what a first-rate director could make in filmed versions of the plays of Oreste's madness, Phèdre's confessions or Athalie's dream. In some respects Joad's prophecy is the most interesting example of all. The blend of music and dialogue may look like a move in the direction of opera. There is possibly a deeper motive: an unconscious search for another dimension which given the nature of the vision would have been better satisfied by the visual than any other element.

I sometimes have the impression that the English are allergic to prosody. It is not something that we can afford to neglect in the study of Racine. Very little has been written in English about Racine's versification or, for that matter, about the alexandrine. I have therefore included a section in my last chapter dealing with the basic principles. In discussing the plays I have had to assume a knowledge of these principles, but anybody who is not familiar with them might find it helpful to read this section before going on to the chapters on the individual plays.

I am only interested in Racine as a tragic dramatist. The omission of any discussion of his one comedy is therefore deliberate.

I have to thank the Arts Council of Great Britain for making me a grant in 1969–70 to assist me in the writing of this book. I also wish to thank Mr. Peter Hoy of the Department of Education and Science for his assistance in tracing gramophone records of the plays, and the Editors of *The Southern Review* for permission to include material from an abridged version of the opening chapter which was originally published in that journal.

March, 1971   M.T.

APPROACH TO RACINE

CHAPTER I

APPROACH TO RACINE

I

'OF all our authors', François Mauriac once said, 'Racine is one of the least accessible to the peoples of other countries'.[1]

Racine presents special difficulties for foreigners. They are by no means confined to foreigners. There are at present two generally accepted approaches to the French classic dramatists. You can either wipe away the veneer which has accumulated with the passage of time and obscures the work of the master and try to think yourself back into the seventeenth century, or you can argue that no great writer belongs exclusively to a particular period and insist on the importance of the plays as dramatic *experience*. The first of these approaches is the safer, the second the more rewarding and also the more dangerous.

The dangers are illustrated by a controversy which began in France some fifteen years ago and is perhaps still not ended. In 1955 the Compagnie Madeleine Renaud-Jean-Louis Barrault decided to mount a production of *Bérénice* at the Théâtre Marigny and to mark the event by the publication of a special number of the company's *Cahiers* devoted to Racine. Henry de Montherlant was invited to write the introduction to it. He called his article 'Racine Langouste'. He drew a comparison between the conventions of seventeenth-century drama and the lobster's shell. If you scrape and prod long enough and hard enough, you may get a few tasty morsels from the animal. In the same way you may extract a few fragments of poetry from Racine—Montherlant put the aggregate at twenty-seven lines for the twelve plays—if you are prepared to spend your time 'painfully and interminably removing the shell'.[2]

Four years later Jean Vilar, who had consistently opposed all attempts to persuade him to add Racine to the repertoire of the Théâtre National Populaire on the grounds that he was not suitable for 'popular' consumption, yielded to public pressure and produced *Phèdre* with Maria Casarès in the name part. It was Roland Barthes' turn to enter the lists. In an article published in *Théâtre Populaire*, the TNP's own journal, he declared that the production was a misfortune for Casarès who 'had risked a lot and lost a lot'. The dramatist did not escape. If we go to see *Phèdre*, said Barthes, 'it is on account of a particular actress, a certain number of felicitous lines, some famous *tirades* set against a background of obscurity and boredom. We tolerate the rest.' 'I do not know,' he concluded, 'whether it is still possible to perform Racine today. It may be that on the stage his work is three-quarters dead.'[3]

3

Jean Dutourd was still more forthright. 'The couple Bajazet-Atalide is impossible', he wrote in a review of a 1966 production of *Bajazet*. 'Those alexandrines of Racine's are quite absurd: they are 99 per cent rhetoric and 1 per cent poetry.'[4]

Even the greatest writers suffer periodically from changing fashions and the fickleness of public taste. In the case of the French classic dramatists the productions of the national theatres do not always help. If you question a Frenchman about a current production of Racine, you can be pretty sure that he will murmur something about the *distribution*. Racine of course makes enormous demands on his casts. If they are not adequately met, the production inevitably leaves us cold and makes even the dramatist's most ardent admirers wonder whether it is worth while going to see him performed. I must confess that though I have seen masterly performances of some of the leading roles, it is only on rare occasions that I can recall seeing a wholly satisfactory production. Either one of the principals was not up to the job, or the supporting artists did not give the right support.

These things may explain the temporary eclipse of a master. They do not explain the recent controversy which somebody called a 'mauvaise aventure'.[5] It cannot be too often repeated that the true test of a dramatist is his effectiveness, or his continuing effectiveness, on the stage. Racine's critics were not suggesting that owing to a lean period among the *sociétaires* of the Comédie Française Racine should be given a rest. They were saying that though he had undoubted merits as a poet, the plays themselves were no longer actable, that they should be removed permanently from the theatre to the study, that Racine should in fact be treated like Robert Garnier, the great sixteenth-century writer, whose works are almost certainly no longer actable because they are dramatic poems rather than plays.

The thesis I am going to defend is that when properly performed, Racine is still the greatest French tragic dramatist and that the pronouncements of the critics from Montherlant to Barthes and Dutourd are perfect examples of Mauriac's problem of *access*.

2

One way of tackling the problem is to take a look at Racine's imagery. The setting of eight of the tragedies is a palace. In *Athalie* it is a temple with a palace not far away; in *Alexandre* and *Iphigénie* a military camp. This means that at the start of nine of the tragedies we, the public, find ourselves metaphorically speaking outside a stately building, separated by a formidable array of masonry from a world which, as one critic put it, does seem 'far from us'.[6] Our job is to secure 'access' to the palaces and the temple, to find out what is going on behind those walls and to merge ourselves in palace life. Racine himself provides a clue—we might almost call it a 'pass'—in the opening scenes of three of the plays.

In *Bérénice* Antiochus says to his confidant:

> Arrêtons un moment. La pompe de ces lieux,
> Je le vois bien, Arsace, est nouvelle à tes yeux.

In *Bajazet* the vizir asks his confidant to follow him into the palace and report on the mission he has just completed. The confidant replies:

> Et depuis quand, Seigneur, entre-t-on dans ces lieux
> Dont l'*accès* était même interdit à nos yeux?

Finally, in *Esther* the queen's confidant says to her mistress:

> De ce palais j'ai su trouver l'entrée.
> O spectacle! O *triomphe* admirable à mes yeux,
> Digne en effet du bras qui sauva nos aïeux!

In each of the plays a person who knows the way round introduces a confidant or servant into a palace which is totally unknown to him or her. Their reactions are different. In *Bérénice* the accent falls on novelty and grandeur; in *Bajazet* on the difficulties and dangers of 'access'; in *Esther* on the staggering sight which greets the confidant's eyes.

In every case it is an ordinary person who is admitted or finds a way into the palace and is confronted by what seems an entirely new mode of life. That is the position of the audience. It is not enough to watch a production of Racine as though it were a faintly remote spectacle and cavil at the way in which it is mounted. We have to identify ourselves with the newcomer, follow him into the palace, listen to the explanation that the guide offers, which is Racine's exposition, and then see for ourselves.

The moment we enter we are conscious of a marked change of atmosphere. We have somehow been translated to a different plane. On the surface everything looks, sounds, feels different from the world we know. Next, we have the contradictory feeling that life in the palace has a strange dualism about it. It is at once very unlike and very like our world: unlike because of the setting; like because of the human frailty of its occupants. We are aware from the first of an almost suffocating tension in the air combined with a desperate effort to maintain some sort of control which frequently breaks down. The tension is pervasive; it is also contagious. It is the atmosphere which produces fascinating and frightening revelations about human nature—about ourselves. It is only by surrendering to it that we gain psychological as well as physical access to Racine's world and that we come to share his vision.

* * *

The palaces vary considerably in style. Three are Greek, two Roman, three oriental. They have one thing in common. There is something of the prison about them. We have the impression that the community is somehow confined within their walls, that while 'access' may be difficult, once you are in it is almost impossible to get out again. The sense of confinement is partly psychological, but in some of the palaces we shall find that one or two members of the community are literally prisoners. Some of the palaces are more disturbing than others. They are huge, dark, claustrophobic. They give the occupants the alarming impression that they are constantly being watched, that their lives are in danger and that disaster may overtake them at any moment.

The situation of the palaces is important. Four of them stand by the sea; most of the others are within reasonable distance of it. One of the palaces looks out on a sunlit sea which seems, tantalizingly, to beckon to the prisoners, inviting them to abandon their troubles, to leave the claustrophobic palace and enjoy freedom in the open air—to live instead of to languish. In another we hear the waves beating, a trifle ominously, against the walls of the building. In still another the waves merely 'lap' against the palace walls. The occupants of most of the palaces are acutely aware of the proximity of the sea. They mention it repeatedly in their conversation; their language contains what on the face of it appears to be a surprising number of nautical images. There are references to storms at sea, to shipwrecks, to people flinging themselves or being flung into the sea and drowning, and in one instance to a phenomenal calm at sea which actually determines the unfolding of the drama. At the same time their attitude is decidedly ambivalent. The sea does, indeed, offer a prospect of escape from their prison and their troubles, but in their heart of hearts they know that it is an illusion, that the hope will never be realized, or if it is their escape will turn out to be not freedom but separation from the loved one, or they themselves will be dead by the time their henchmen, who have survived a palace massacre, make a bolt by way of the sea.

If the prospect of escape is an illusion, there is nothing illusory about the threat from the sea. It is in a sense a two-way traffic. For practical purposes the outward journey is never accomplished; the inward journey from the sea invariably is. It is the sea which brings all sorts of people to the palace who have a dangerous and disrupting effect on life inside: the outsider posing as an ambassador who provokes disaster; the return a of tyrannical father, reported missing believed dead; the murderous slave who stabs nearly every occupant of the palace to death.

It is time to turn from the buildings to their inmates.

3

The palaces are royal in every sense. The inhabitants are for the most part kings, queens, princes, princesses, and their retainers. The structure of society is a simple one. There are strictly speaking only two classes: masters and servants, the rulers and the ruled, royalty and 'the people'. Yet the combination of the two, as we shall see, plays an important part in the development of the drama.

We are not merely inside a palace; we are at court. The court is a small one. There are two or three people belonging to the same family. They are joined on occasion by some one from outside: a prince seeking the hand of one of the royal daughters, or a princess who is betrothed to a member of the family as well as by the dangerous outsiders and unwanted relatives who arrive by sea.

The protocol plays a large and important part in the life of the court. The members know one another intimately, but their deportment strikes the visitor as curious. Parents, to be sure, address their children familiarly except when a monarch loses his temper and switches from 'enfant' to 'Prince'. So do brothers and sisters. In a moment of euphoria a young man may call his girl 'Belle Monime!' Or an angry woman may scrap all titles and simply call the man who has rebuffed her by his name. In most other cases, whether they are husband and wife, engaged couples or simply servants speaking to masters and mistresses, they use, or begin by using, the standard form of address: 'Seigneur', 'Madame', 'Prince', 'Princesse'.

This sounds at first like mere convention. In these palaces it is a good deal more. It is a sign of the occupants' status certainly; it is also a sign of their state of mind from moment to moment. It serves to some extent as a safety device. As long as the standard forms of address are in use the speakers retain some degree of control over their emotions. When they go, everything goes. They are in fact the life line. The life line snaps. This produces the tragedy.

It is obvious from the moment we enter the building that this is no ordinary day in the life of the palace, that we have arrived in the middle of a major crisis. As we watch the expressions on the faces of the occupants and listen to what they are saying, we realize that they are intelligent, civilized, sensitive, perceptive, but that they are also incredibly highly strung, 'touchy' in the extreme. They are visibly making prodigious efforts to control themselves, to maintain some sort of balance, but the artificial restraint does nothing to diminish the growing tension. It simply intensifies to an almost unheard of degree the violence of the outbursts and the final explosions when they come.

* * *

There are only two people in the room: a young prince and his father's middle-aged confidant. The prince is telling the confidant that he has just heard that the army of the king, his father, has been routed by the Romans and the king himself killed in the battle. He goes on to speak of his bad relations with his half-brother who is suspected of plotting a sell-out to Rome. It is the first news of the family feud which is characteristic of palace life. Then comes the most serious thing of all which the prince describes, significantly, as his 'secret'. He is deeply in love with his father's youthful fiancée and believes that the treacherous half-brother is after her too. The prince suddenly catches sight of the fiancée and hurriedly dismisses the confidant. She has in fact come to enlist his help against his half-brother who is 'importuning' her. This is too much for the prince who plunges into a declaration of love. The half-brother joins them. The argument begins. Then the fiancée's confidant rushes breathlessly into the room with the worst news of all. The king is not dead. He had just landed at the port—'come in from the sea'. All three are badly shaken. The fiancée and her confidant depart, leaving the half-brothers to discuss the situation. The potential traitor proposes a pact. He gets no response. They leave. The fiancée returns with her confidant and proceeds to disclose her 'secret'. She is in love with the young prince. They leave. The king makes his entry with his two sons. He sends them away and remains alone with his confidant. He explains that he is still desperately in love with his betrothed. He is suspicious of his sons' attitude and questions the confidant. The confidant ducks. The fiancée reappears. During our day at the palace we shall find that after several meetings the king very basely tricks her into revealing her 'secret'.

This sets the pattern and the pace. The word 'secret' is on everybody's lips. Nearly everyone has something to hide from some one else. The 'secrets', as we can see, are concerned with love and politics. They divide the community into factions, into pursuers and pursued, aggressors and victims.

The attempts of one party to hide and the other to discover its 'secrets' determine the pace of palace life. The palace is a hive of activity. The occupants are perpetually on the move. There are continual comings and goings: meetings, encounters, separations. Racine's casts are small. It is unusual for more than three of the principal characters to be present at the same time and this only happens occasionally. For the most part the activity consists of a rapid succession of couples, sometimes with and sometimes without their confidants: unhappy meetings of thwarted lovers; stormy encounters between pursuers and pursued; furious clashes between 'rivals'. They are interspersed with conversations between individuals and their confidants. Voices drop to a murmur as a problem is debated by a young man and a young woman, or by lovers and their confidants. Suddenly a voice rises in anguish or ends in a scream. With every meeting the crisis gathers momentum.

Although there is nothing comparable to the conferences which take place in the Cornelian palaces with most of the court assembled, some meetings are rather more formal than others. A king is receiving an ambassador or outlining plans for a military campaign. On other occasions a speaker makes highly provocative or even deeply wounding remarks, but though the people to whom they are addressed may be twitching with rage the situation is governed by the protocol. They do not interrupt; they hear him out and hold their fire until he has had his say.

These occasions bring home to the visitor one important point. There is a basic language which is common to all the inhabitants of the palaces. It is simple, measured, dignified or, to borrow an expression used by Valbuena Prat of one of the Spanish seventeenth-century dramatists, it is the 'sober, elevated palace style'.[7] It provides a background which underlines and throws into relief the contrast between the formal meetings and those scenes in which disappointed lovers and angry rivals let their hair well and truly down. For the meetings between the couples are usually highly emotional. That is the crux of the matter. It is not only what people say that counts; it is the tone in which it is said: the voice that goes straight to the heart and does more than almost anything to involve the visitor in the life of the palace. And here one might interject that one of the most important qualifications for the Racinian actor or actress is a rich, strong, vibrant voice. The content of the speech naturally determines the tone, but speaking for myself it is the tone that finally 'gets' me.

The palaces are massive; there are long winding corridors with innumerable rooms leading off them. But we, the visitors, are only admitted to a single room. The whole of the drama is concentrated inside it. In that one room every major decision is taken or, if not, it is duly reported there. Equally, almost every word of importance is spoken in our hearing and before our eyes. The drama is an internal one. What interests us most is what is happening inside the occupants' minds and comes out in their speech. Except for an occasional suicide, there is properly speaking no action in the room: no duels or only furious verbal duels and threats; no lovemaking; simply word and gesture. At the same time, we are aware that the room, or more accurately, the palace, is a world within a world which it is trying to dominate. We hear people talking about 'the empire', 'the world' and even 'the universe'. Messengers come hurrying in and deliver terrifying reports of actions taking place in the outside world or in a distant part of the palace. A king has been assassinated; a lover has been done to death in a different room, or a mistress has committed suicide on the steps of an altar where her lover married a rival; rebellion by the army or the people is imminent. The message is nearly always: 'All is lost'.

Confinement to a single room contributes enormously to the claustrophobic atmosphere and greatly increases the tensions. There is no relaxation, or if there is it is illusory and a prelude to a vast storm. There is no escape either from pursuers who have a nasty way of turning up at precisely the wrong moment and finding a 'rival' slumped at the girl's feet. When they have discovered, or think they have discovered, the other party's 'secret' they denounce their behaviour in the most violent terms. This is the signal for an explosion.

The explosions are frequent, sudden, complete. The protocol goes by the board, producing an extraordinary contrast between past dignity and present violence. The last vestiges of civilized deportment vanish. There are no titles, only savage denunciation or agonized protest, or both. The Words 'perfide', 'infidèle', 'traître' and 'barbare' echo and re-echo all over the palace. There are switches from the polite 'vous' to the bitingly contemptuous 'tu'. The language of the courtier is replaced by the harangues of the fishwife. The ferocious denunciation turns into a verbal battle which will end in murder or suicide. The aggressors, who are not invariably male, behave like wild beasts determined to drag the victims into bed, or failing that, to tear them to pieces. The victims of the male aggressors are distraught women staggering through the rooms of the palace or falling to the ground and describing themselves as 'égarées' and 'éperdues'.

The contrast between the outward dignity of palace life and the ferocious passions unleashed is so extraordinary, the ending with reports of violent deaths pouring in and the sight of principals who have poisoned or stabbed themselves to death, intensified in one instance by the ranting of a madman, that we feel slightly dazed, wondering how it could all have happened, how people could have got themselves into quite such a mess. It is not difficult to explain. At the root of most of the trouble is the erotic instinct. A loves B who is in love with C who returns his or her love. This form of triangle is basic in palace life. We can anticipate by saying that A is usually the aggressor, B and C the victims. A father, as we have seen, returns defeated from the wars to find that not one, but both his sons are in love with his betrothed. An emperor is sick of his unexciting wife whom he was forced to marry against his will for political reasons, and is carried away by his half-brother's fiancée. He murders the half-brother and the fiancée takes the veil. A sultana is tired of being bedded by a lecherous sultan and is madly in love with the sultan's half-brother who is in love with his childhood sweetheart. She has the man murdered, is murdered herself by the sultan's slave and the girl commits suicide. Another father returns from a womanizing expedition to discover after endless misunderstandings that his wife has tried unsuccessfully to seduce her stepson and is nearly mad with jealousy because the stepson, too, has fallen for another girl. In still another case A loves B who is in love with C, but is prevented from marrying him by Roman law. This does for the lot of them as completely as the dagger or the poison cup.

Although the origins of several of the tragedies are sexual there is a close connection between public and private interests. Royalty are never free agents. They have naturally enough a public as well as a private role and their private actions have public repercussions. Unless the individual is subordinated to the public personage, there is bound to be trouble. The union of A and B or B and C may be open to moral, political or legal objections, or to all three. When the objections are disregarded, as they usually are, the consequences are catastrophic. They create divisions in public and private life. There is a danger of uprisings by the army or the people and of the awakening of homicidal impulses in the family, producing the family feud. War is often in the air. In one case the enemy is actually advancing on the capital in order to capture the monarch and probably to burn his palace to the ground. The sexual rivalry of a father and son leads to civil war with father and son on opposite sides. In another play there is a danger of a war which was supposed to be over and done with breaking out afresh, or of a preventive civil war to put a stop to it. In still another a sultan has defeated a foreign enemy and is on his way back home in order to put down a palace revolution only to find, on arrival, that the family feud has done the job for him.

It is evident that the crisis is caused mainly by the fact that, whatever the cost and even if it means that everybody will perish in the process, A is absolutely determined to get B. That is where the confidants come in.

Racine's confidants have been sweepingly dismissed as faceless individuals only fit to run errands, deliver messages and try to comfort masters and mistresses. This might be a possible comment on Corneille for the simple reason that his protagonists are usually too tough morally to need the sort of help confidants can offer. It cannot be accepted without considerable reservations in the case of Racine. It is true that some of his confidants are nonentities, but others have an important role. Although they are all born into the same class there are sub-divisions. A number have risen from the ranks, become commanders, governors or advisers to their masters. A few are more complex than the rest and look like projections of their masters' and mistresses' good and bad impulses. The bad confidants encourage the protagonists' weaknesses and hasten the disaster. The good ones adopt a much more positive attitude. They are simple people partly no doubt because the structure of the tragedies does not leave room for the elaborate characterization of confidants even if it were desirable, but mainly because what Racine needed in these parts were simple, honest, clearsighted, down-to-earth people. The right kind of

confidant is the one who is class-conscious in a wholly laudatory sense,
who sees himself as the representative of 'the people' and does his best to
protect their interests against the vagaries of royalty. These confidants
stand for common sense; they take an objective view of the situation; they
weigh the pros and cons; they know which path the master ought to take
and do everything they can to convince him of it. The fact that they nearly
always fail is immaterial. It is they who help to provide a balance—the
balance found in a single individual in Corneille—and enable us to see the
actions of the protagonists in their true perspective.[8]

We can perhaps summarize the function of the palaces in this way. They
are not simply impersonal buildings which provide a setting for the tragedy
or mere status symbols of the occupants. They represent a particular
order. The drama centres round the fortunes of this order. It is in control
at the beginning of the play, but its fate varies from one play to another
and is of critical importance. In some plays it is preserved; in others it is
destroyed. In others still there is a conflict between two orders which ends
in the destruction of one and its replacement by the other.

The drama centred on order naturally has an immediate impact on the
inmates of the palace and is largely responsible for dividing them into
parties or factions: those who are trying to maintain the existing order and
those who are trying to escape from its clutches or replace it by another
order. I have said that there is something of the prison about the palaces,
that their effect is partly physical and partly psychological. The inmates
not only suffer from a sense of confinement; the palaces often isolate, and
in some cases insulate, them from everyday life, cut them off from 'the
people'. That is why many of them get their values so badly wrong and
why I have emphasized the importance of the confidants.

The occupants are continually using a group of words expressing their
sense of confinement: 'captif', 'captive', 'esclave', 'dompter', 'fers', 'lier',
'piège', 'joug', 'noeud'. They are the 'prisoners', 'captives' or 'slaves' of an
order or a régime. In many cases they are equally the 'captives' or 'slaves'
of their own impulses or the impulses of other people. They get caught in
'traps', are forced to submit to a 'yoke', are bound by 'fetters' or a 'knot'.
Release is impossible unless they manage to dodge the 'trap', shed the
'yoke', or cut the 'knot'.

This shapes the action which on occasion takes the form of a palace intrigue or a palace revolution. 'Secret' is also one of a recurring group of
words: 'cacher', 'dissimuler', 'déguisement', 'feindre', 'tromper', 'artifice',
'stratagème'. The drama is taken up with the attempts of the aggressors to
wrest their victims' 'secrets' from them and the victims' efforts to safeguard their rights by preserving their 'secrets'. In order to do so they are
obliged at times to resort to the same subterfuges—the 'artifices' and

'stratagèmes'—as the aggressors. This adds up to a desperate attempt to shed the 'yoke', cut the 'knot' or simply to 'escape'. 'Fuir' and its variants are used 165 times in the plays.[9] They usually stand for frustration and failure. And that spells death and disaster, or at best a refuge in the sanctuary of the Vestal Virgins after the aggressor has poisoned your beloved.

4

I want to take a closer look at what I have called the erotic instinct. I was once scolded by an academic for speaking of the references to 'bed' in Racine. The truth of the matter is that he is a sexier writer than appears on the surface. He suffered from the inhibiting effect of the *bienséances* which left French dramatists with much less freedom than their English and Spanish contemporaries or even than contemporary French authors of prose fiction. It applies particularly to Spanish dramatists who did not mind a rape or two or a stepmother actually bedding her stepson though the penalties admittedly were devastating. It would no doubt be an exaggeration to describe *Bajazet* as Racine's X Certificate play, but he came as near in it as he dared to writing a sex play. He was still a long way off as we can see by comparing it with one of his sources—the novelist Segrais' story, 'Floridon ou L'Amour imprudent'. And whatever Louis XIV's relations with Marie Mancini, I always goggle at the idea of that five years' courtship in *Bérénice* without a single go!

Discussion of the erotic instinct brings us to some of the differences between Corneille and Racine. Corneille, as we know, was a pupil of the Jesuits, Racine a pupil of the Jansenists. There is a tendency at present to play down the influence of Jansenism on Racine's work. This seems to me to be a mistake. Jansenism was much more a matter of atmosphere than of doctrine. The Jesuits laid great stress on free-will. Jansenist teaching was strongly coloured by the Lutheran teaching on original sin. The Fall had led to the complete ruin of human nature which was incapable of any good action without the direct intervention of divine grace. The Jansenists also leaned towards the doctrine of predestination. This added to the gloom, but it fitted in quite neatly with the conception of destiny in those of Racine's plays which were Greek in inspiration.[10]

Corneille's protagonists are fighters. They use their will power to the full in withstanding the ravages of original sin. When faced with a moral dilemma they stand back, take stock and decide on the right course of action. Even if they lose their lives in the process they end up as better men than they started. They have experienced the moment of truth: the transcendental moment when they see what they must do and know that they have the moral strength to do it. In Corneille the conflict is purgatorial: in Racine it is plain hell. The drama opens with the proverbial *coup de foudre*. A man catches sight of a girl or a girl of a man. The damage is done. They are predestined to disaster from that very moment. They at once become the victims of an irresistible impulse which sends them down the dizzy slope to destruction. The dagger or the poison cup which ends their lives is no more than consummation on the *physical* plane of the total ruin which has already taken place on the *psychological* plane.

This has sometimes created the impression that the conflict in Racine is not a moral conflict, but simply a clash of personalities who are determined to batter the beloved into submission or smash a rival. The short answer is that if this were so Racine would not be the master that he is. Violence is endemic in his work; there are times when will power scarcely seems to exist and his principal characters are certainly people of extremes. It does not mean that they are unaware of what they are doing or are devoid of all moral scruples. It depends on the nature of the erotic impulse.

We can best approach it by way of Corneille's celebrated pronouncement in the dedication of *La Place Royale*:

> It was from you that I learnt that the love of a decent man (*honnête homme*) should always be voluntary; that we must never let things reach a stage at which we cannot stop loving; that if we go as far as that love becomes a tyranny whose yoke must be cast off; and that lastly, the person whom we love has much more reason to be grateful for our love when it is the result of our choice and her merit than when it comes from blind inclination (*inclination aveugle*).

Although the dedication was published two years before Racine was born, our reaction is obvious. It sounds, we say, like a commentary on Racine. It is a forthright statement of the 'rules' of love. Corneille's own greatness depends on the fact that his finest characters never fail to keep them; Racine's on the fact that his seldom fail to break them. We must, however, distinguish. I have spoken so far as though there were only one kind of love in Racine. This is not so. There is the frantic passion of the aggressors and the moderate and reasonable love of the victims. For simplicity therefore I shall call the first 'passion' and the second 'love'.

With this reservation, we may fairly describe the dedication as an intriguing account of Racinian passion. A number of phrases leap to the eye: 'voluntary', 'tyranny', 'cast off the yoke', 'blind inclination', as well as the references to 'choice' and the 'merit' of the loved one. In Racine passion is never 'voluntary'; it is always 'tyrannical'; the characters never manage to 'cast off the yoke'; it is invariably a 'blind inclination' which is never the result of reasoned 'choice' or the 'merit' of the beloved. Corneille's characters announce the victory of 'reason' over 'inclination'; Racine its total defeat. This is Corneille:

Une femme d'honneur peut avouer sans honte
Ces surprises des sens que la raison surmonte;
Ce n'est qu'en ces assauts qu'éclate la vertu,
Et l'on doute d'un coeur qui n'a point combattu.

(*Polyeucte*, I, 3)

Ma raison, il est vrai, dompte mes sentiments;
Mais quelque autorité que sur eux elle ait prise,
Elle n'y règne pas, elle les tyrannise;
Et quoique le dehors soit sans émotion,
Le dedans n'est que trouble et que sédition.

(*Polyeucte*, II, 2)

This is Racine:

Puisqu'après tant d'efforts ma résistance est vaine,
Je me livre en aveugle au destin qui m'entraîne.

(*Andromaque*, I, 1)

Je me suis engagé trop avant.
Je vois que la raison cède à la violence.

(*Phèdre*, II, 2)

There are people who regard the moral conflict in Corneille with a certain degree of scepticism. What I want to stress here is its power and its authenticity. There is nothing facile or mechanical about it, no conventional adulation of 'reason'. In Corneille 'reason' is the faculty which imposes order and preserves the unity of the person. For Pauline its workings are decidedly painful as we can see from the contrast between the verbs 'régner' and 'tyranniser'. She is outwardly calm, but her mind is in a state of turmoil. In the present context—she is speaking to Sévère—'trouble' has a sexual undertone, but it is widely used and is a comparatively mild word. It is followed by the strong word, 'sédition', which matches 'tyrannise'. It will be observed that Pauline sees the conflict in political terms as a conflict between public and private interest. 'Reason' has to operate 'tyrannically' and repress by force an uprush of the senses which in moral terms are trying to violate the rights of the husband in favour of a rival and are therefore 'seditious'. The accent falls finally on words signifying victory: 'surmonte' and 'dompte'. In the passages from *Andromaque* and *Phèdre* the words 'livre', emphasized by 'aveugle' and 'cède', are the sign not merely of defeat, but of a rout.[11] Corneille's characters accept 'reason' as a necessary discipline however painful its operation: the attitude of Racine's is usually one of unqualified hostility:

Pylade, je suis las d'écouter la raison.

Tant de raisonnements offensent ma colère.

(*Andromaque*, III, 1; IV, 3)

Although Racine's characters are inclined to treat 'reason' as an exasperating obstacle which keeps them out of the beloved's bed, it will be apparent that in both Racine and Corneille the conflict is basically the same: a conflict between public and private interests or between personal inclination and the rights of another human being. The difference lies in the result and there it is absolute.

The position becomes clearer still when we look at two other sets of words. They are 'trouble', 'agité', 'inquiet', 'transport', 'désordre', 'égaré', 'éperdu' and their opposites: 'repos', 'tranquillité', 'douceur', 'clarté', 'bornes', 'ordre'. They represent the two ways of life which offer themselves to the protagonists. For Corneille once again they are a positive goal. The use of the verbs 'surmonter', 'dompter', and in another place 'vaincre', show that it is not only attainable, but has been attained. In Racine the first set of words is the reality, the second the mirage.[12]

Two of the lines I have quoted from *Polyeucte* deserve a second look:

> Ce n'est qu'en ces assauts qu'éclate la vertu,
> Et l'on doute d'un coeur qui n'a point combattu.

In spite of its painfulness, Pauline welcomes the conflict because it puts her to the test and demonstrates her integrity. This explains the difference in the moral weight of the words 'vertu', 'honneur' and 'gloire' in the two dramatists. In Corneille the victory of 'vertu' is a sign of 'honneur' or personal integrity which leads to 'gloire' or a public reputation for moral integrity. Except when used of victory on the battlefield, Racine's 'gloire' is a much more personal and much less moral affair, really amounting to little more than self-esteem. Racine's characters are very sensitive to their reputations which means that on occasion they are prepared to sacrifice 'vertu' to something which is no more than keeping up appearances, however deceptive. So we have Oenone's advice to Phèdre:

> pour sauver notre honneur combattu,
> Il faut immoler tout, et même la vertu.

When we come to *Bérénice*, we shall find that even when reason or will power appears to triumph, the effects are destructive. We are back at the formula I once used in another place. Corneille's characters are people *qui se construisent*, Racine's people *qui se défont*. Corneille's moment of truth is matched in Racine by the moment of disintegration when the character begins to have doubts about his identity.[13]

I have drawn a distinction between the 'passion' of the protagonists and the 'love' of the young couples who are sometimes known as the *jeunes premiers*. Although their love is doomed to disaster through the intervention of the protagonists, they stand for a virtuous and a balanced love which if satisfied would bring happiness without harming the rights of anybody. They have an obvious and a close link with the more impressive confidants. They provide perspective and contrast; they show that tragedy could have been avoided if the protagonists had possessed the same restraint, the same respect for the given word as themselves.

The reason why innocent love is only satisfied in two or the plays is explained by the word 'tyranny'. The protagonists, too, are convinced that success in love will bring them happiness, but their obsession has reached such an extreme degree that they are faced with the choice between union with the victim of their passion or death. Their peculiar helplessness in the throes of a passion which has turned into a malady is evident in one of Pyrrhus's pronouncements:

> Je meurs si je vous perds, mais je meurs si j'attends.

The tyranny is twofold. The protagonists suffer from the tyranny of a passion which they are powerless to resist. It is because of their anguish that they themselves become tyrants. The word 'blackmail' has been used by more than one critic. In five of the plays A, whether a man or a woman, is a tyrant who is determined to blackmail B into breaking off relations with C and marrying him or her. The blackmailer holds the carrot, usually a crown, in one hand, and the dagger or the poison cup in the other. There is Néron's ultimatum to Junie which is disguised as an offer:

> ne préférez point, à la solide gloire
> Des honneurs dont César prétend vous revêtir,
> La gloire d'un refus, sujet au repentir

And when the unhappy Junie does precisely that Britannicus is handed the poison cup in the guise of a 'loving cup'.

The tragedy is the outcome of impassioned individuals who break all the rules, brush aside morality, the law, the claims of State and the rights of fellow human beings certainly; it is equally the outcome of the determination of the victims to preserve their integrity, to fulfil their pledges, to remain in a literal sense 'faithful unto death'.

5

I must return now to the criticisms that I mentioned at the outset and attempt a more specific assessment of Racine's relevance for the present age. They amount to two main charges, neither of them particularly original. The first is that Racine's tragedies are simply a reflection of seventeenth-century life, that his metaphorically periwigged figures are anachronisms and that his psychology is out of date. The second is that the rules of classical drama were so rigorous and so artificial that even if what he said were relevant, communication, at any rate on the stage, has become impossible.

Nobody doubts any longer that like Corneille Racine was very much a man of his time. One critic has gone to extreme lengths in trying to discover 'originals' for virtually every character in the secular plays except the confidants. There have been others who sought to establish a connection between the action of some of the plays and political events such as the English Revolution. I am not convinced myself that this kind of speculation does much to increase our appreciation of Racine's art, but it helps to situate him. No writer can be indifferent to contemporary events which even in a classical period are bound to leave some impression on his work or possibly provide him with inspiration. We shall see in due course that in some of the plays there are tributes to Louis XIV, and that *Bérénice* probably contains a reference to an early love affair, but we shall also see that the importance of the age is somewhat different.

What seems to me to matter is less the events and personalities than the ethos in which Racine lived and wrote. It is a change of ethos which goes a long way towards explaining the celebrated rivalry between Corneille and Racine and the differences in their work. Corneille's first masterpieces are heroic plays in the strict sense. One of the reasons for the failure, or comparative failure, of the plays of the middle period is that the heroic age was past, and that in trying to go on writing heroic plays Corneille was writing against the grain of the new age. It was a belated recognition of the situation which led to a changed approach, to what is known as 'the eclipse of the hero', in the last plays of all which show a move in the direction of Racine.[14] Now Racine was the product of an unheroic age which is reflected in nearly all his plays from the first one to the last. There are no heroes in them in the Cornelian sense for the simple reason that, as I have said, one of his principal themes is the frailty of human nature. The ruler is always a tyrant; the society is aristocratic; there is a contrast between the polished surface and the internal corruption; the disaster is the result of the predatory designs of the tyrant. This was no doubt an accurate picture of the periods in which the tragedies are set; it is certainly a fair picture of Racine's own age. We may as well call things by their names. Racine lived under an absolute monarchy which was the seventeenth-century equivalent of the modern dictatorship; he moved in aristocratic circles; there was the same startling contrast between the outward splendour of 'the Golden Age' and its inner weaknesses and corruption. It was the century of unhappy love, the *mariage de raison* which so often went wrong with the most unfortunate consequences. Louis XIV himself is a good example. As a young man he was compelled for political reasons to abandon his projected marriage to Marie Mancini. It is a fair inference that if he had been in a position to decide for himself he would have done nothing of the sort, but would have set out to get the girl with the same ruthless determination, the same disregard of everybody else's interests as a Racinian protagonist. This was followed by the spectacle of a neglected queen weeping alone in her room; La Vallière departing in tears to a convent; the arrival of Mme de Montespan, a woman with the mentality of a Roxane; her eventual dismissal and replacement by the prudish Mme de Maintenon. There is one other resemblance between Louis and the Racinian protagonists. The Bourbons were a notoriously highly sexed family. In his later years the king still insisted on two goes a day with his morganatic spouse. She got no comfort when she complained to her confessors about the monarch's 'excessive demand'. They told her bluntly that she was bound to perform her wifely duties in order to prevent her husband from indulging in still more adulterous associations.

The parallels between past and present draw attention to one of the more curious contradictions between the man and the writer. From the first the ambitious young man set out to cultivate the king. When he abandoned the theatre to become one of the royal historiographers, he also became one of the most obsequious of courtiers. Although it was no doubt unconscious, it can hardly have been accidental that four of the plays are attacks on the kind of regime under which he was living. In *Britannicus* a tyrannical order is strengthened; in *Bajazet* it is preserved, and in *Mithridate* it is destroyed. We shall find that in *Athalie* he goes furthest of all. With the help of religion he not only delivers his most vigorous attack on despotism; he exposes the inherent dangers of absolute power.

One of the principal claims made by and for classical periods is *finality*. The writers are convinced that they see humanity *sub specie aeternitatis*, that it is basically unchanging and that what they see remains true for succeeding generations. There is a good deal of substance in the view that it was precisely because Racine was so much a man of his time that he was able to concentrate on aspects which are valid for all time. His contemporaries were right in arguing that his characters were not Greeks or Romans or Turks, but Frenchmen. They were wrong in holding it against him. The greatness of his work depends not only on his findings, but on the way in which they are integrated into their environment, on the matching of the inner and the outer man. Although integration is an artistic essential, we must recognize that the vision of a great writer transcends time. When we look into it, we can see that his interests and the reactions of his characters are remarkably like our own and would be the same if they found themselves in the twentieth century. What he shows bears an uncomfortable resemblance to the happenings of the present age: ruthless dictatorships; the horrors of wars in which all human standards go by the board; conflicts between public and private interests, between the desires of the individual and the rights of a fellow human being which today are consistently leading to murder and suicide; the spread of violence to every walk of life.

We have seen something of the workings of the erotic instinct in his work. Now the French theory of the *femme fatale* is not entirely moonshine. We have to admit, if we are honest with ourselves, that whatever our beliefs or principles, there exists somewhere in the world a man or a woman who would be fatal to *us*, would send us straight off the rails and make us behave in much the same fashion as Racine's protagonists if we had the misfortune to meet him or her as Racine's protagonists always do.

We must take a closer look at what might be called individual psychology. I mean by this, particular characters, the way in which they appear to us and the interpretations we put on them today. We must do so because the claim to universal validity is not restricted to Racine or to France. The criticisms I have been discussing could be, in some cases have been, applied to other dramatists in other countries: to Shakespeare in England, to Lope de Vega and Calderón in Spain.

Although she apparently supports the claim to universal validity, Annie Ubersfeld has observed in an illuminating essay on *Andromaque* that Pyrrhus is a seventeenth-century monarch and Hermione a seventeenth-century princess, and thinks that it would be difficult to envisage them in any other capacity.[15] This was not exactly the view of the great Louis Jouvet. Here is what he said about Junie to one of the girls—her name was Viviane—attending his practical acting course at the Paris Conservatoire in 1939:

> The characters of the classics are whatever one likes to make of them. According to the period, Junie has been a young virgin martyr, a young Christian, a young republican. *A character in one of the classics is a revolving lighthouse.* It all depends where you happen to be standing in relation to the lighthouse; you are caught by certain flashes which light you up. Junie will touch you by flashes which are sensitive and human and which you will receive from the character because you are you, Viviane.[16]

The same might be said of Shakespeare. Hamlet is a seventeenth-century prince, an intellectual, an Elizabethan melancholic whose melancholy incidentally (metaphysics apart) has affinities with Oreste's. Without going so far as the late Ernest Jones, it is not difficult to see him as a twentieth-century neurotic with a touch of the Oedipus complex which wrecks his relations with poor Ophelia. Whichever way we look at him, his soliloquies do not cease to grip. And think of the interest the French took in him in the nineteenth century. What again could be more 'modern' than Shakespeare's Achilles in *Troilus and Cressida*, or more horrifying than the 'stratagem' he uses to defeat the gallant Hector in the field—an all-time dirty trick?

I move over to Spain. Lope de Vega's *Fuenteovejuna* is an early seventeenth century play with a fifteenth-century setting. A randy military commander goes round the village seducing or raping every girl he fancies—and he fancies most of them. He comes up against a tough one. He takes her by force. She organizes reprisals. The men of the village, accompanied by the womenfolk, seek out the seducer and kill him. The court finds that the entire village—men and women alike—are guilty. The sovereigns, who are none other than the Reyes Católicos, intervene and quash the conviction. In a study written at the end of the nineteenth century the distinguished scholar, Menéndez y Pelayo, became lyrical over the political implications of the play. 'There is', he wrote, 'no more democratic work in the Spanish theatre.' We can see that this view fits in with what Jouvet said about Junie. It has not gone unchallenged. A recent critic accused Menéndez y Pelayo of introducing irrelevant political considerations. 'It is impossible', he said, 'to explain Lope's play as a democratic work'. We should concentrate, he argued, on its dramatic force, its form and its beauty which are the result of another conflict that enables us to explain the work in terms of its own age.[17]

I must confess that long before reading what these writers have to say, I myself had been struck by what appeared to be a marked democratic element not simply in *Fuenteovejuna*, but also in other plays: Lope's *El mejor alcalde, el rey* and Calderón's *El alcalde de Zalamea*. *El mejor alcalde* is in some ways the most striking example of all. A great landowner agrees to attend the wedding of one of his peasants. The moment he catches sight of the bride he takes a fancy to her, calls off the wedding and abducts her. The bridegroom has an audience with the king and appeals to him for help, addressing him in the Spanish fashion in the second person singular. The king sits down, writes an order for the return of the bride and tells the bridegroom to hand it to the landowner. He does so. The landowner, who by this time has taken the girl by force, ignores the order. There is another appeal to the king. This time the king disguised as a mayor enters the scene in person. He calls for a priest and an executioner. He then reveals his identity and has the landowner married to the girl in order to repair the damage to her honour. The landowner is executed immediately the ceremony is over and the young couple are free to proceed with their marriage.

This leads to another interesting point. For thirty years adaptations and imitations of Spanish *comedias* were extremely popular in France. In 1656 the fashion came to an abrupt end. Thomas Corneille observed that French taste condemned 'ces entretiens de valets et de bouffons avec des princes et des souverains'. Antoine Adam carries the explanation a stage further. 'When the monarchical order was re-established after the defeat of the Fronde', he writes, 'and when French society learnt once again to respect the hierarchies, the public was shocked by the familiarity with which the valets in Spanish comedy treated their masters and ceased to find it amusing.'[18] We might add that this particular form of familiarity is exactly the reverse of the form used by the inhabitants of Racine's palaces which I described earlier.

The Spanish 'drama of honour' is a little more difficult. The ethics of those plays by Lope and Calderón in which wives are suspected, usually wrongly, of adultery and slaughtered by outraged husbands have been a considerable worry to critics, particularly as both dramatists ended up in Holy Orders. Menéndez Pidal has shown that though peculiar to medieval and Renaissance Spain, this sort of honour was very much a reality and part of the social code.[19] In Lope's *El castigo sin venganza*, which has been called the greatest Spanish tragedy, there is a situation similar to that in *Phèdre* except that the son returns the stepmother's love and the affair is consummated, making them both guilty. The husband, who like Thésée is by way of being a reformed rake, is alerted by an informer. He has the wife bound, gagged and covered with a rug. He then orders the son to kill the hidden person who is simply described as an 'enemy'. The son does so; the identity of the dead woman is revealed; the son himself is then killed on the spot on his father's instructions. Menéndez Pidal remarked, in the course of an impressive study, that in order to make it acceptable to modern audiences the final scene of the play would need to be entirely re-written.[20] I must confess to feeling some doubts about the argument. For one thing, the essay was originally written before the modern cult of violence and audiences are a good deal tougher today than they were at that time. The main point, however, is that the fundamental human impulses remain unchanged, but that circumstances are continually changing. What we see in a play like *El castigo sin venganza* is impulses which are familiar erupting in circumstances and in a setting which are not. It is the dramatist's insight into these impulses which counts, which gives them their actuality and their power.[21] In any case, except that it takes place on the stage, is the father's punishment of his guilty son in *El castigo* any more shocking or any more difficult to 'take' than the father's punishment of his innocent son in *Phèdre*?

The conclusion I reach is that in the case of the masters the claim to universal validity is justified and that it is precisely this which distinguishes the true master from the lesser figures: Shakespeare from a Webster or a Tourneur; Pierre Corneille and Racine from a Thomas Corneille or a Quinault.

The second criticism of Racine is a matter of pure artistic judgement. If one critic can only find an aggregate of twenty-seven lines of poetry in the whole of the plays; if another thinks that 99 per cent of the verse in *Bajazet* is rhetoric and only 1 per cent poetry, we are bound to suspect that they have failed signally to secure 'access'. But since these views have been expressed by sensitive and intelligent people, they cannot be dismissed out of hand. An attempt must be made to answer them briefly in general terms.

There is one factor which cannot be too strongly emphasized. Racine displays enormous skill in placing his characters in a virtually impossible situation which is a combination of temperament and circumstance. It is impossible in the sense that none of the characters can extricate themselves from it and live happy, peaceful lives without inflicting irreparable damage on other characters. The basic situation explains the immense impact of the greatest of the tragedies when properly presented to the right audience. It can only be communicated because the other qualities of the work match the dramatist's genius in devising the basic situation.

Although it is necessary for the purpose of analysis and appreciation to discuss versification, language, structure and psychology separately, the end-product naturally depends on a very close synthesis of all these elements. Versification and language are largely responsible for the formality which is characteristic of palace life. Together they have the effect of raising tragedy to the special plane which is proper to it. Structure, which is the method of presenting situations dramatically, is necessarily of the first importance: it makes or mars the play. Lytton Strachey once remarked that the technique of Elizabethan drama had been taken over by the novelists and that Racine's technique had been adopted by modern playwrights.[22] Comparisons between Racine and modern dramatists must not be pushed too far, particularly as Strachey's comment was made nearly sixty years ago, but in substance it is correct. Racine's genius enabled him to turn even the rule of the three unities to his advantage.[23] The essence of the tragedies is their intense concentration on emotional states. For this he relies on simplicity of action, tightness of structure—the way in which one scene leads to another, in which they fit into one another, contrast with or are parallel to one another, in which words and phrases from different scenes echo and answer one another—and above all the *speed* with which the drama unfolds, the couples come and go, which explains why Racine unlike Corneille is now always performed without an interval, as he should be. We are near boiling point at the start; we are carried along by the rising temperature and gathering momentum until we reach the tremendous ending.

It is hardly surprising in an age like our own that critics have tended to dwell on the psychology of his characters and to treat him primarily as a master psychologist. Their view has recently been attacked by Raymond Picard. 'The psychological depth which is commonly admired in Racine', he writes, 'is to a large extent an optical illusion.'[24] This does not or should not mean that Racine's psychology is shallow or that the findings of a psychoanalytical critic like Charles Mauron are necessarily wrong. It simply means that the form of classic tragedy inevitably precluded a minute and leisurely examination of the characters' psychology and that the dramatist was mainly confined to the basic human emotions. Although Baudelaire once spoke of 'the power of Racinian analysis' the truth is that, as I have said in other places, there is no such thing in Racine as analysis. His characters do not brood over their feelings, argue about them, take them to pieces. Their discoveries are the result of intuition, the sudden insights into their own and other people's minds. The expression of emotion is spontaneous and immediate. It is something like 'instant' emotion: the direct presentation of the basic impulses unencumbered by the kind of detail that we find in the psychological novel. What I want to stress is that the closeness of the synthesis mentioned above depends to a large degree on this psychological simplicity of presentation.

I have discussed the importance for the final synthesis of four different but closely connected elements. It remains to add that there is one other which is difficult to define, which is something more than a combination of versification and language, something that transcends them. It is the *poetry*. For it is the poetry which provides the unifying element and transforms the play into an experience which has an immediate impact on the audience and is ultimately responsible for transmitting the dramatist's vision to them.[25]

If there are grounds on which Racine is open to criticism, the main one is that though his insight into human nature often went deep the field is comparatively narrow and several tragedies are variations on the same theme. This takes us back to comparisons between Corneille and Racine. Corneille's supporters admired him because they found his plays uplifting. They criticized Racine's because they were not. 'Tendre' in its seventeenth-century sense was not a term of unqualified praise; it meant that Racine was sensitive, easily moved and that though his tragedies were moving, too, they were not exalting and did nothing to boost morale.

The answer is of course that their professional rivalry is a thing of the past, and that they are both 'constants' of the French genius who complete and possibly correct one another. They both give expression to something permanent in human nature. It is the sign of a master that he is irreplaceable. Corneille occupies a place that Racine could never have filled and the same is true of Racine. Their effect on us is entirely different. We love Racine because he speaks to us as man to man, exposes our weaknesses to our shocked and fascinated gaze. This should not prevent us from responding to the immense élan, the enormous 'lift', that comes from a good production or even a proper reading of Corneille. Speaking for myself, there are some moods in which I prefer Racine and others in which I prefer Corneille. But of one thing I am certain: they are both necessary to me.

NOTES

[1] *Journal*, III, 1940, p. 203.

[2] *Cahiers de la Compagnie Madeleine Renaud-Jean-Louis Barrault*, No. 8, 1955, pp. 2–6.

[3] Reprinted in *Sur Racine*, 1963, pp. 135, 143.

[4] Quoted in *Europe*, No. 453, January, 1967, p. 76.

[5] *Ibid.*, p. 90.

[6] *Europe*, No. 453, pp. 76–90.

[7] *Historia del teatro español*, 1956, p. 143.

[8] This is discussed in greater detail in the chapter on *Bérénice*. See pp. 130–31, 133–36 below.

[9] All statistics of word usage are taken from B. C. Freeman and A. Batson, *Concordauce du Théâtre et des Poésies de Jean Racine*, 1968.

[10] See A. Adam, *Le Théâtre classique*, 1970, p. 71.

[11] It is interesting to notice that while Racine uses the word 'aveugle' of love, Corneille uses it of obedience. Roxane and Achille both speak of 'mon aveugle amour', Pauline of 'cette aveugle et prompte obéissance', meaning her father's order to marry Polyeucte instead of Sévère.

I am aware that in view of what I have said about 'passion' and 'love', the quotation from *Phèdre*—it is Hippolyte who is speaking—looks a bit like cheating, but I shall explain when the time comes that Hippolyte is a special case.

[12] The best example is the first six lines of Phèdre's *aveu* in Act I, Sc. 3. They are discussed on pp. 250–51 below.

[13] See pp. 85 and 201 below.

[14] See S. Doubrovsky, *Corneille et la dialectique du héros*, 1963, pp. 474 et seq.

[15] In the introduction to her edition of *Andromaque*, 1961, p. 54.

[16] *Tragédie classique et théâtre du XIXᵉ siècle*, 1968, p. 18 (*italics in the text*).

[17] Joaquín Casalduero, *Estudios sobre el teatro español*, 2nd ed., 1967, pp. 13–15.

[18] *Le Théâtre classique*, p. 102.

[19] *De Cervantes y Lope de Vega* (Colección Austral), 5th ed., 1958, pp. 145–71.

[20] *El Padre Las Casas y Vitoria* (Colección Austral), 1958, p. 151.

[21] There are naturally occasions when classic plays acquire a special actuality because the circumstances of the play happen to match current events. Cervantes' stupendous tragedy, *La Numancia*, which treats of the siege of a Spanish city by Roman invaders, was revived at the time of the Napoleonic invasion of Spain and again at the time of the siege of Madrid during the Spanish civil war, when the Romans were treated as Italian fascists. (See Francisco Ruiz Ramón, *Historia del teatro español*, 1967, pp. 135–6.)

[22] *Landmarks in French Literature*, 1912, p. 94.

[23] It was propounded by Italian theorists, accepted by French and firmly rejected by English and Spanish dramatists. See R. Bray, *La Formation de la doctrine classique en France*, 1927, pp. 34–61.

[24] *Two Centuries of French Literature*, 1970, p. 102.

[25] It has been well described by Francisco Ruiz Ramón in terms which apply equally to English, French and Spanish drama (*Op. cit.*, pp. 158–9).

THE BEGINNINGS

I. 'LA THÉBAÏDE OU LES FRÈRES ENNEMIS'

1664

La catastrophe de ma pièce est peut-être un peu trop sanglante. . . L'amour, qui a d'ordinaire tant de part dans les tragédies, n'en a presque point ici. Et je doute que je lui en donnasse davantage si c'était à recommencer.

RACINE

CHAPTER 2

THE BEGINNINGS

I. 'LA THÉBAÏDE OU LES FRÈRES ENNEMIS'

1664

RACINE took the material for his first surviving play from one of the most celebrated of all Greek legends: the tragic story of Oedipus, his incestuous marriage to his mother and the consequences.

Although there are a number of different versions of the legend, it divides into three phases. In the first Oedipus unwittingly kills his father, marries his mother and when he discovers what has happened, blinds himself and abdicates the throne of Thebes. The second deals with the conflict between the sons of Oedipus. It is caused by the refusal of Eteocles to obey his father's decree that he is to take it in turns with his brother Polyneices to rule Thebes. It ends with the death of both brothers and the defeat of the army which Polyneices, who had married the daughter of an enemy king, brought to Thebes to enforce his rights against his brother who was the first of the pair to occupy the throne. In the last phase Antigone, one of Oedipus's daughters, commits suicide after being imprisoned by her uncle, Creon, because she gave a proper burial to Polyneices who was regarded as a traitor on account of his attempted invasion of his native city. It is followed by the suicide of Creon's son, Hemon, who was engaged to Antigone, and the destruction of Thebes as a punishment for Creon's failure to obey the order of the gods not to harm Antigone.

In his preface Racine pays tribute to Rotrou's *Antigone* and then goes on to criticize him for trying to combine two phases of the legend in a single play: the conflict between the brothers and what I am inclined to call the aftermath. Although we may question the validity of Racine's criticism of Rotrou—Euripides after all had done the same—it throws a revealing light on one of his most constant preoccupations throughout his career as a dramatist: structure. For it is important to observe that in this first play he adopts the method which was to become characteristic of the plays that followed. He selects a single phase of the legend, devotes the whole of his play to it and does not hesitate to telescope events in order to give it an effective ending. What we find is that in spite of the criticism of Rotrou he manages to combine the middle phase and a shortened aftermath in the same play. It is also important to notice that he is careful to give full weight to the events which preceded the tragedy and led up to it. The result is that whatever its shortcomings, *La Thébaïde* already possesses something of the economy, the compactness and the shapeliness of the mature tragedies, qualities which were enhanced by revisions that will be mentioned later.

La Thébaïde was long regarded as a youthful work which was of no particular interest and gave no hint of what was to come.[1] It is true that if Racine had written nothing more or nothing except *Alexandre le Grand*, it would have been relegated to the minor works of the age and forgotten. Looked at in the light of the later masterpieces, it assumes a different significance.

It not only demonstrates Racine's gift for dramatic construction; it contains in embryo several of the themes which will reappear in the later plays: the family feud, particularly the strife between brothers or half-brothers; thirst for power symbolized by crown and throne as well as the fear that surrounds it; the deadly effects of passion; incest or near incest. Nor should we overlook the fact that though the play is dominated by hatred, the *jeunes premiers* make a first shadowy appearance in the persons of Antigone and Hémon.

There are two other similarities. One is a special kind of pessimism which was the result, as I have suggested, of Racine's gloomy Jansenism and is reflected in the insistence on destiny which is stronger in this than in any other play. The other is that in the verse there are signs, fitful but unmistakable, of Racine's *griffe*.

In her prayer in the opening scene Jocaste says of her sons:

> Tu sais qu'ils sont sortis d'un sang incestueux,
> Et tu t'étonnerais s'ils étaient vertueux.

Her words are repeated by Étéocle in Act IV when he describes his relations with his brother as

> Triste et fatal effet d'un sang incestueux!

The tragedy stems from the unintentional crime of Oedipe and Jocaste. Their marriage generated a contaminated or 'incestuous' blood which is the cause of the fratricidal strife between Étéocle and Polynice that leads to the spilling of 'innocent' blood and the destruction of all the protagonists.

The brothers are predestined to disaster by their contaminated blood. Their rivalry or, to use Racine's word, the 'discord' over the throne brings matters to a head and is the pretext for open warfare. In *La Thébaïde* the throne exerts an hypnotic influence on the characters. Étéocle makes no bones about it. Oedipe may have decreed that his sons should take it in turn to rule and Étéocle may have promised to observe the decree, but he is on the throne and intends to stay there. His excuse is that he has been accepted by the Theban people and that his brother, who has married the daughter of the King of Argos and invaded the city, would be a tyrant and an oppressor. He can therefore pose as a liberal, 'democratic' monarch who is loved by his subjects:

> Thèbes m'a couronné pour éviter ses chaînes;
> Elle s'attend par moi de voir finir ses peines:
> Il la faut accuser si je manque de foi;
> Et je suis son captif, je ne suis pas son roi.

Polynice adopts a much less altruistic attitude. The throne, he declares, is his by right; it is not for the people to choose their ruler. The king owes his position to one thing only: 'blood':

> Est-ce au peuple, Madame, à se choisir un maître? . . .
> Le *sang* nous met au trône, et non pas son caprice:
> Ce que le *sang* lui donne, il le doit accepter;
> Et s'il n'aime pas son prince, il le doit respecter.

The drama of the classical age in France, as we know, is essentially aristocratic with kings and queens heading the cast lists. It is axiomatic that 'blood' determines 'rank'. The work is used 70 times in the play and on six occasions rhymes with 'rang':[2]

> Vous le savez, mon fils, la justice et le *sang*
> Lui donnent, comme à vous, sa part à ce haut *rang*.

Jocaste is pleading with Étéocle for the rights of Polynice who expresses himself to her in the same terms in Act II:

> J'espérais que du ciel la justice infinie
> Voudrait se déclarer contre la tyrannie,
> Et que lassé de voir répandre tant de *sang*,
> Il rendrait à chacun son légitime *rang*.

These pronouncements fit comfortably into contemporary political theory. 'Blood' and 'rank' go together; the ruler is an absolute monarch and his job is to govern whether the people like it or not. The throne itself is a source of danger and the ruler is entitled to use any means he chooses to make, or to try to make, his throne secure.[3] When the 'blood' that puts a man on the throne is contaminated, the danger becomes much greater and the means used by the ruler to safeguard his position or by his enemies to remove him is still more ruthless. That is why Jocaste regards the throne of Thebes with a mixture of horror and fascination:

> Ce trône fut toujours un dangereux abîme:
> La foudre l'environne aussi bien que le crime.
> Votre père et les rois qui vous ont devancés,
> Sitôt qu'ils y montaient, s'en sont vus renversés.

The dangers do nothing to diminish its hypnotic power. When Jocaste tries to persuade Étéocle to obey his father's decree and to give his brother his due, he makes no attempt to question Polynice's undoubted rights. He simply replies:

> il faut que je vous die
> Qu'un trône est plus pénible à quitter que la vie . . .

Créon puts it more forcibly or, rather, more recklessly still:

> Du plaisir de régner une âme possédée . . .
> Croit n'avoir point vécu tant il n'a point régné.

One of the merits of this first play, as I have suggested, is the skill with which the dramatist weaves his themes into a whole. The characters, as we have seen, are predestined to disaster by their contaminated 'blood'. The hatred of the two brothers crystallizes round the 'throne' which is at once the symbol and the source of power. Mother and daughter try in vain to bring about a reconciliation, but any hope of success they might have had is ruined by the machinations of Créon who is equally fascinated by the prospect of succeeding to the throne once he has engineered the destruction of the brothers.

The hatred of Étéocle and Polynice is something which will not be repeated in any of the later plays. It deserves special attention on account of the light that it throws on Racine's conception of passion. Its absolute nature is evident in a passage of Étéocle's from which I have already quoted:

> Ce n'est pas son orgueil, c'est lui seul que je hais.
> Nous avons l'un et l'autre une haine obstinée:
> Elle n'est pas, Créon, l'ouvrage d'une année;
> Elle est née avec nous; et sa noire fureur
> Aussitôt que la vie entra dans notre coeur.
> Nous étions ennemis dès la plus tendre enfance;
> Que dis-je? nous l'étions avant notre naissance.
> Triste et fatal effet d'un sang incestueux!
> Pendant qu'un même sein nous renfermait tous deux,
> Dans les flancs de ma mère une guerre intestine
> De nos divisions lui marqua l'origine.
> Elles ont, tu le sais, paru dans le berceau,
> Et nous suivront peut-être encor dans le tombeau.
> On dirait que le ciel, par un arrêt funeste,
> Voulut de nos parents punir ainsi l'inceste,
> Et que dans notre sang il voulut mettre au jour
> Tout ce qu'ont de plus noir et la haine et l'amour.[4]

The passage shows very clearly that the throne is a pretext rather than the cause of the brothers' strife, that the real source is heredity. The hatred which is described as beginning in the mother's womb is an absolute, unexplained and, in purely human terms, inexplicable antipathy. The brothers try to justify it or to get rid of any sense of guilt by their insistence that it is the result of their parents' incestuous union and that it reduces them to a state of helplessness. 'We are,' says Étéocle in effect, 'the children of a criminal marriage. The gods decided to punish us for our parents' crime by making us deadly enemies who are bound to fight one another to the death. Why try to resist? We're thirsting to get at one another. Let's give in and go to it. Besides, the winner stands to get a handsome prize.'

The last line is particularly striking:

> Tout ce qu'ont de plus noir et la haine et l'amour.

It enunciates one of the fundamental principles underlying all Racine's work which will be demonstrated in play after play. What he is saying is that *passion* as such is deadly, whether it is passionate love or passionate hatred. It is a powerful anonymous charge whose form is determined by environment and events. It takes the form of love or hate because in Racine, as we shall see later, there is no halfway house between those extremes.

In another place Créon remarks of the brothers:

> Tous deux feront gémir les peuples tour à tour:
> Pareil à ces torrents qui ne durent qu'un jour,
> Plus leur cours est borné, plus ils font de ravage,
> Et d'horribles dégâts signalent leur passage.

It is of the essence of Racinian passion that it carries all before it. The normal restraints of civilization merely serve to intensify the violence of the eruption when it comes. 'Obstacles' are swept aside, 'chains' smashed, 'knots' ripped apart. The 'torrent'—symbol of a powerful and entirely mindless force—demolishes everything, leaving in its wake only 'ravages' and 'ruin'.

Although the passion of the brothers reminds us of the 'aggressors' of other plays, there is one great and obvious difference. Their passion is purely negative and destructive. The 'throne', as I have indicated, is really a pretext: there is nothing comparable to the 'aggressor's' pursuit of his 'victim'.

The conflict of the play is twofold: the conflict between the inhuman brothers and the unequal conflict between the forces of humanity and inhumanity. Humanity is represented by mother and sister, assisted by Hémon. Hatred, particularly hatred between brother and brother, must always lead to conduct which by any standards is 'inhuman' and 'unnatural'. The conduct of the brothers is continually denounced for its inhumanity by Jocaste and Antigone:

Mais, hélas! leur fureur ne pouvait se contraindre:
Dans des ruisseaux de sang elle voulait s'éteindre.
Princes *dénaturés*, vous voilà satisfaits ...

La *nature* pour lui n'est plus qu'une chimère:
Il méconnaît sa soeur, il méprise sa mère ...

Ne renouvelez point vos discordes passées:
Vous n'êtes pas ici dans un champ *inhumain*.

In the first three acts there are meetings at which mother and daughter try to persuade first Étéocle, then Polynice, to stop the feud. Étéocle must obey the decree and let his brother have his turn on the throne; Polynice is entitled to claim his rights, but whatever happens there must be no bloodshed. Rather than that, let Polynice win fame by waging war against real enemies instead of invading his native city.

The turning point comes in Act IV: the meeting of the two brothers in the presence of their mother and sister. This is the direct conflict between the united forces of humanity and inhumanity in which the forces of humanity are completely defeated. In one sense it might be described as paradoxical. We recall that Jocaste was the first character to use the expression 'sang incestueux' and to suggest that the gods would be surprised if children born of it turned out to be 'virtuous'. At the meeting at which she tries to heal the 'discord' she says:

Surtout que le *sang* parle et fasse son office.

The use of 'sang' without any qualification can scarcely have been accidental. What she is doing in fact is to behave as though the 'sang incestueux', which is the source of the brothers' hatred, were ordinary blood which instead if dividing, unites members of the same family. Ironically, 'blood' will indeed 'speak' and 'perform its office', but not in the sense intended by Jocaste. Polynice's answer to his mother's attempt to reconcile the brothers is this:

Il suffit aujourd'hui de son sang ou du mien.

When she expresses horror at his desire to shed his brother's blood, he replies:

Oui, Madame, du sien.
Il faut finir ainsi cette guerre *inhumaine*.

This prompts Étéocle's

J'accepte ton dessein, et l'accepte avec joie.

Racine's *griffe* is nowhere more apparent than in the speeches of Jocaste which touch fresh heights in Act IV. These are her last words before committing suicide:

Surpassez, s'il se peut, les crimes de vos pères;
Montrez en vous tuant comme vous êtes frères:
Le plus grand des forfaits vous a donné le jour;
Il faut qu'un crime égal vous l'arrache à son tour.
Je ne condamne plus la fureur qui vous presse;
Je n'ai plus pour mon sang ni pitié ni tendresse.
Votre exemple m'apprend à ne le plus chérir;
Et moi, je vais, cruels, vous apprendre à mourir.

In this extraordinary last scene of Act IV her words simply do not register with her sons who are so obsessed by their hatred and the prospect of coming to grips that they are incapable of taking them in. In their impatience to slaughter one another, they dash from the scene like a couple of schoolboys on the spree with words to their sister that are the equivalent of 'So long, old girl!'

Créon is in some way the most interesting character in the play. He has been described by more than one writer as its 'producer'. Although all the protagonists seem predestined to disaster, Créon is the instrument of the gods and while pretending to be firmly on the side of Étéocle, he is sedulously fanning the flames of hatred in the hope that they will both lose their lives and that he will succeed to the throne. There is, indeed, a ritual element in the play. The arguments of Jocaste and Antigone carry no weight with the brothers: Créon's machinations steer them relentlessly towards the arena and the final combat. This means that the rest of the cast are turned into helpless spectators watching events from the ramparts overlooking the arena.

It has been argued that for practical purposes the play ends with Act IV. The last act is uneven, but it is clearly essential for Racine's handling of the legend and the development of Créon's curious role.[5] Although the villain of the piece, he bears a certain resemblance to two characters of Corneille's: Félix in *Polyeucte* and Prusias in *Nicomède*. There is an element of fatuity in his character which makes him at moments a figure of fun of a kind that we shall not meet again in Racine with the possible exception of Mathan in *Athalie*.

In the last act Olympe, the confidant of the dead Jocaste, gives Antigone an incomplete report of the combat between the brothers, leaving her with the impression that Étéocle is the only casualty. It is not until Créon appears that she learns the full extent of the disaster: that her fiancé is dead as well as both brothers.

The element of fatuity, which heightens the macabre effect of the closing scenes, first appears when, in spite of the shattering blow, Créon naïvely offers Antigone marriage and a crown. It provokes a very Racinian rejoinder:

Je la refuserais de la main des Dieux même . . .

CRÉON

Que faut-il faire enfin, Madame?

ANTIGONE

M'imiter.

CRÉON

Que ne ferais-je point pour une telle grâce
Ordonnez seulement ce qu'il faut que je fasse:
Je suis prêt . . .

ANTIGONE, *en s'en allant*

Nous verrons.

CRÉON

J'attends vos lois ici.

ANTIGONE, *en s'en allant*

Attendez.

Créon fails completely to detect the bitter irony in what Antigone has
said and gives full rein to his fatuity:

Oui, oui, mon cher Attale:
Il n'est point de fortune à mon bonheur égale,
Et tu vas voir en moi, dans ce jour fortuné,
L'ambitieux au trône, et l'amant couronné.
Je demandais au ciel la Princesse et le trône:
Il me donne le sceptre et m'accorde Antigone.

When the shocked Attale observes that he has after all lost both his
sons, Créon brushes his loss aside with an unfeeling 'Oui, leur perte
m'afflige'.[6]

The fatuous boasting becomes still more macabre when Créon reflects
that the death of his second son is really another blessing from heaven:

D'ailleurs tu sais qu'Hémon adorait la Princesse,
Et qu'elle eut pour ce prince une extrême tendresse.
S'il vivait, son amour au mien serait fatal:
En me privant d'un fils, le ciel m'ôte un rival.

He goes rattling on. Olympe appears. Attale notices that she is in tears.
The confidant has come to announce the suicide of Antigone, revealing
the bitter irony behind her 'M'imiter' and 'Attendez', and providing a
devastating comment on Créon's foolish, insensitive boasting.

The announcement produces another change of mood or, more exactly,
reveals another side of Créon's nature. His situation is not altogether unlike Oreste's in *Andromaque*. The scales fall from his eyes and he realizes
what he has done. His monstrous ambitions, his plotting, his trickery, or
as he rightly calls them, his 'crimes', are the immediate cause of all the
disasters and all the deaths. The others may have been in the last resort

the victims of the gods, but in human terms he is the culprit. The really terrible thing for Créon, as for Oreste, is the knowledge that his crimes have been in vain and have simply led to the loss of everything. In the last lines reason totters:

> La foudre va tomber, la terre est entr'ouverte;
> Je ressens à la fois mille tourments divers,
> Et je m'en vais chercher du repos aux enfers.

We infer that he has indeed 'imitated' Antigone.

Racine's first play underwent a good deal of revision for the editions of 1676, 1687 and 1697. It affected structure, language and to some extent characterization.[7] The most interesting of the changes in language are those which reveal a movement away from the early style to what is indubitably the Racinian *idiom*, as we can see from the two following examples:

> *1664–87*
> O toi, qui que tu sois, qui rends le jour au monde

> *1697*
> O roi, Soleil, ô roi qui rends le jour au monde

> *1664–87*
> Je leur criais d'attendre et d'arrêter leurs pas;
> Mais loin de s'arrêter ils ne m'entendaient pas;
> Ils ont couru tous deux vers le champ de bataille . . .

> *1697*
> Ils ne m'entendaient plus, et mes cris douloureux
> Vainement par leur nom les rappelaient tous deux.
> Ils ont tous deux volé vers le champ de bataille . . .

The important changes are clearly the substitution in the first example of 'Soleil' for 'qui que tu sois' and the introduction in the second of the words 'cris douloureux', 'vainement' and 'volé', as well as the tightening up of the syntax.

The result of the general changes is that the definitive edition of 1697 is considerably superior to the version performed by Molière's troupe in 1664. We know, however, from Boileau that Racine was decidedly desultory over the way in which he revised his plays for later editions—this is confirmed by the things he failed to put right—and we should be careful not to exaggerate what he actually did.[8] There was no question of rewriting; there was a good deal of tidying up, but in spite of the general improvement the version of 1697 is basically the same play. Although there has been a tendency to underrate *La Thébaïde*, there is no point in trying to make up for it by exaggerating its merits. The fact remains that there is nothing in it to suggest that in three years' time Racine would produce an indubitable masterpiece like *Andromaque*.

NOTES

[1] See, for example, D. Mornet, *Jean Racine*, 1943, pp. 134–5.

[2] The total number of times the word is used in the plays is 289. *Iphigénie* is the runner-up with 51 times; then *Phèdre* and *Athalie* with 36 each.

[3] This was in part the teaching of Machiavelli which was not without its influence on French as well as on English drama.

[4] It should be observed that lines 7 to 11 were added in the edition of 1697.

[5] This is what I had in mind when I spoke of 'telescoping' events.

[6] Ménécée, his other son, had committed suicide in the hope of appeasing the gods and leading to peace.

[7] They are discussed in detail by M. Edwards in *La Thébaïde de Racine*, 1965.

[8] *Bolaeana ou Bons mots de M. Boileau ou Entretiens de M. de Monchesnay avec l'auteur*, 1742, pp. 107–8.

THE BEGINNINGS

II. 'ALEXANDRE LE GRAND'
1 6 6 5

Depuis que j'ai lu *le Grand Alexandre*, la vieillesse de Corneille me donne moins d'alarmes, et je n'appréhende plus tant de voir finir avec lui la tragédie.

SAINT-ÉVREMOND

II. 'ALEXANDRE LE GRAND'

1665

ALEXANDRE has begun the invasion of India. He is opposed by two
Indian kings: Porus and Taxile. Porus is a genuine warrior who is engaged
in organizing resistance to the invader; Taxile is the weak, vacillating man.
They are both in love with an Indian queen. Axiane returns Porus's love;
she has no use for Taxile as a person, but tries to stiffen his resistance because his troops are indispensable if India is to have any chance of putting
a stop to the invasion. Taxile has a sister. Cléofile has been well described
by one critic as 'the fifth column'.[1] She has been Alexandre's prisoner. She
fell in love with him and he with her. The last thing she wants is to see her
brother waging war against her lover. She therefore tries to prevent his
alliance with Porus on the grounds that they are bound to meet with defeat
and that it would be wiser to give in and rely on Alexandre's famous magnanimity. She succeeds only too well. Porus is defeated. Taxile makes a
personal attack on him and is killed. Alexandre carries all before him,
which does not prevent the play from having something like a happy
ending.

Alexandre is a play of a very different stamp from *La Thébaïde*. No seventeenth-century dramatist was more sensitive than Racine to the mood of
the age or more astute in organizing his career. In *La Thébaïde* he had
written the sort of play he felt impelled to write. It had about twenty performances when mounted by Molière's company. This was regarded as
reasonably successful for a first play. It was not, however, the sort of
success at which the ambitious dramatist was aiming. He clearly made up
his mind that in his second play he would give the public what it wanted.
He was well rewarded for his pains. In spite of the trick he played on
Molière by arranging for the Hôtel de Bourgogne to stage a rival production, *Alexandre* was an outstanding box office success.

The theme of *Alexandre* is one that was familiar in the seventeenth
century. It is love-and-glory. In *Alexandre* 'gloire' means primarily success on the battlefield. We shall find, however, that the characters' reactions to it and their ways of interpreting it vary considerably. This brings
us to a contradiction which goes to the heart of the play. We are invited to
regard Alexandre, no doubt out of respect for Louis XIV, as the *preux
chevalier sans peur et sans reproche*. Yet it is evident from the outset that he
is open to 'reproach' on many grounds, that his wars are essentially

aggressive wars which are undertaken solely for personal aggrandisement. In her first speech, in which she is trying to persuade her brother not to join with his compatriot against the invader, Cléofile speaks in these terms of his successes:

> Mon frère, ouvrez les yeux pour connaître Alexandre:
> Voyez de toutes parts les trônes mis en cendre,
> Les peuples asservis, et les rois enchaînés;
> Et prévenez les maux qui les ont entraînés.

This is of course the voice of 'the fifth columnist'. The argument is devious. Her real reason for trying to keep her brother out of the war is purely personal. She is the first of the characters to put 'love' before 'glory' though we shall find that the rest of them follow her example. This does not alter the fact that her account of Alexandre's successes is perfectly accurate. The price of 'gloire' is shattered thrones, kings in chains and subjugated nations. It differs little from the view of the conqueror's enemies, as we can see from Porus's reaction to the proposal that India should make peace with Alexandre and accept his overlordship:

> La paix! Ah! de sa main pourriez-vous l'accepter?
> Hé quoi? nous l'aurons vu, par tant d'horribles guerres,
> Troubler le calme heureux dont jouissaient nos terres,
> Et le fer à la main entrer dans nos États
> Pour attaquer des rois qui ne l'offensaient pas;
> Nous l'aurons vu piller des provinces entières,
> Du sang de nos sujets faire enfler nos rivières,
> Et quand le ciel s'apprête à nous l'abandonner,
> J'attendrai qu'un tyran daigne nous pardonner?

In conversation with Alexandre's henchman, Éphestion, Porus declares somewhat sententiously:

> La gloire est le seul bien qui nous puisse tenter.

Éphestion fastens at once on the word:

> C'est ce qui l'arrachant du sein de ses États,
> Au trône de Cyrus lui fit porter ses pas,
> Et du plus ferme empire ébranlant les colonnes,
> Attaquer, conquérir, et donner les couronnes . . .

It is obvious that Porus and Éphestion are using the word 'gloire' in very different senses. For Porus 'gloire' means victory in a defensive war against an aggressor. Éphestion's criterion is a purely sporting one. 'Gloire' is no more than the pretext which draws Alexandre from his own country so that he can give what might almost be described as a series of 'exhibition matches' all over the world. The cost of his successes is immaterial.

A stable and peaceful empire, merely because it is stable and peaceful, is a temptation to the conqueror and must be smashed in order to add another laurel to his collection.

Éphestion's reference to Alexandre's practice of handing back his crown to a defeated enemy is intended to emphasize the conqueror's magnanimity. It unwittingly introduces a note of frivolity. We are reminded of the keen fisherman who throws his catch back into the water, but in this case the 'catch' has been preceded by appalling suffering by the inhabitants of the countries chosen by Alexandre as suitable for conquest.

Éphestion stigmatizes Porus's 'gloire' as 'orgueil': the only form of 'gloire' open to Alexandre's enemies is to surrender and meekly accept his pardon for some non-existent offence: in other words, a grovelling humility.

Porus's reply shows that he has an even poorer opinion of Alexandre's conception of 'gloire' which is equally dismissed as pride:

> Quelle étrange valeur, qui ne cherchant qu'à nuire,
> Embrase tout, sitôt qu'elle commence à luire;
> Qui n'a que son orgueil pour règle et pour raison;
> Qui veut que l'univers ne soit qu'une prison,
> Et que maître absolu de tous tant que nous sommes,
> Ses esclaves en nombre égalent tous les hommes!

Yet it is precisely this senseless destruction, the reduction of the world to a vast prison in which the distinction between men is obliterated, that provides Porus, or so he believes, with an opportunity of winning genuine fame:

> Dans son avide orgueil je sais qu'il nous dévore;
> De tant de souverains nous seuls régnons encore.
> Mais que dis-je, nous seuls? Il ne reste que moi
> Où l'on découvre encor les vestiges d'un roi.

There is undoubtedly a strong element of pride in this declaration, but it strikes the right note: two warriors ready to face one another and fight to the death.

It is hardly surprising to learn that at one time Racine considered calling his play *Porus*, as one of his predecessors had done. For at bottom it resolves itself into a conflict between Alexandre and Porus. Porus is there from the start. Alexandre himself does not make his first appearance until the middle of Act III. The ground, however, has been well prepared and a portrait built up of him as he strikes the other characters. The preliminary portrait stresses two qualities: his invincibility and his magnanimity. His prowess in war is compared to a force of nature. Cléofile speaks of a 'tempête', Éphestion of an 'orage', Taxile of 'la foudre' and 'un torrent'. It is Taxile, too, who describes the almost hypnotic impression made by the man:

> ... sa présence auguste appuyant ses projets,
> Ses yeux comme son bras font partout des sujets.

Although the second line describes a phenomenon which is by no means uncommon, it is of particular interest in view of the emphasis which some critics have placed on the references to 'eyes' in Racine. Taxile and Porus are opposites. Everything that Taxile says provokes dissenting judgements by Porus belittling the conqueror's achievements:

> Quelle gloire en effet d'accabler la faiblesse
> D'un roi déjà vaincu par sa propre mollesse ...

But we shall find in the end that it is Alexandre's 'presence' as much as anything that 'gets' Porus.

It must be confessed that when he does at last appear Alexandre is a considerable disappointment. He enters with a flourish and his first words reveal the famous magnanimity:

> Allez, Éphestion. Que l'on cherche Porus;
> Qu'on épargne sa vie, et le sang des vaincus.

Although Alexandre has been engaged in a demanding campaign, he is perfectly composed. Indeed, everything about him is perfect in its way. He is the perfect gentleman whose beautiful manners and absolute control over every gesture, every word he utters, belong to the drawing-room rather than the military camp. He is soon at odds with Axiane over Taxile whose suit he supports. She discharges some of her heaviest broadsides. Alexandre is completely unruffled; the control never falters for a moment:

> AXIANE
> Que le traître se flatte, avec quelque justice,
> Que vous n'avez vaincu que par son artifice;
> Et c'est à ma douleur un spectacle assez doux
> De le voir partager cette gloire avec vous.

> ALEXANDRE
> En vain votre douleur s'arme contre ma gloire:
> Jamais on ne m'a vu dérober la victoire,
> Et par ces lâches soins, qu'on ne peut m'imputer,
> Tromper mes ennemis, au lieu de les dompter.

She gets no change out of him. He treats her as a rather wayward child, explaining patiently that he knows that she is trying to make him lose his temper and say something disparaging about Porus, but he is not having it. Poor girl! Even if she had not succeeded in charming him, she has attacked a warrior who has laid his arms aside. He is really very sorry for her indeed. He understands only too well how she feels, how incapable her grief makes her of appreciating *his* charm and *his* virtues. If it were not for that, she would realize that his feats aren't all eyewash, that he really is quite a chap.

Axiane's 'virtue' to which he refers in slightly, very slightly patronizing terms, isn't all eyewash either. The truth is that she is, at any rate artistically, the better man. Alexandre is just a little too sure of himself: his gentleness and his gentility turn into something resembling complacency. Although he knows that she is in a bit of a state over Porus—now reported dead—it does not prevent him from pushing Taxile's suit in order to please his own girl. This produces a very understandable outburst from Axiane:

Quoi? le traître?

In another fourteen soothing lines Alexandre explains the political advantages of the union he is advocating. Then even he seems to realize that an amazon and a double-crosser don't mix well and beats a retreat:

Il vient. Je ne veux point contraindre ses soupirs . . .
L'entretien des amants cherche la solitude:
Je ne vous trouble point.

His marvellous tact, one cannot help feeling, deserts him at this point. Nothing could have been better calculated to exasperate Axiane than the assumption that she and Taxile are lovers in search of solitude. She at once turns her guns on the wretched Taxile and we hear the authentic Racinian ring in her contemptuous greeting:

Approche, puissant roi,
Grand monarque de l'Inde, on parle ici de toi.

Racine was of course to make very effective use in his later plays of the sudden switch from 'vous' to 'tu'. In this passage there is no switch, no sudden rise in temperature: the tone is one of cold contempt which is conveyed by the combination of the second person singular and the ironical mode of address in 'Approche, puissant roi'. Although the passage is effective in its context, it is precisely the absence of heat, whether the characters are declaring their love or their hatred of one another, or extolling 'gloire', that explains our dissatisfaction with the play as a whole and the feeling that it is somehow un-Racinian.

At her prickly meeting with Alexandre, Axiane declares:

Porus bornait ses voeux à conquérir un coeur.

It is a revealing line. We find that even in the plays of Racine's maturity 'gloire' is usually subordinated to 'love'. In *Alexandre* it is not merely subordinated, it is ousted by love. Yet the love we find in *Alexandre* has virtually nothing in common with the devouring passion of *Andromaque* or *Bajazet* or *Phèdre*. It is presented as a genteel, chivalrous love of the kind made fashionable by contemporary novelists and playwrights like Quinault. In spite of its genteel appearance, however, there is a decidedly sexual underside. For what the warriors on their own showing really want is a girl and a nice comfortable well-sprung bed. In the last resort victory in the field only interests them in so far as it opens the path to the girl and the bed.

The primacy of 'love' over 'glory', the recognition that ultimately 'glory' is simply the best way of getting the girl, is explicitly asserted by both Alexandre and Porus. When Cléofile says fretfully to Alexandre:

> Je crains que satisfait d'avoir conquis un coeur,
> Vous ne l'abandonniez à sa triste langueur ...
> Et peut-être, au moment que ce grand coeur soupire,
> La gloire de me vaincre est tout ce qu'il désire,

he very quickly disposes of the objections:

> Que vous connaissez mal les violents désirs
> D'un amour qui vers vous porte tous mes soupirs!
> J'avoûrai qu'autrefois, au milieu d'une armée,
> Mon coeur ne soupirait que pour la renommée ...
> Mais, hélas! que vos yeux, ces aimables tyrans,
> Ont produit sur mon coeur des effets différénts!
> Ce grand nom de vainqueur n'est plus ce qu'il souhaite;
> Il vient avec plaisir avouer sa défaite ...

The language is instructive. It is neither martial language nor the ferocious language of the lovers in the plays which were to follow. There is no punch behind the 'violents désirs'. Alexandre with his 'sighs', his emphasis on the 'heart' and his preciosity ('vos yeux, ces aimables tyrans') emerges as the Man of Feeling.

Porus is convinced that Axiane is reserved for the man who vanquishes Alexandre:

> Il faut vaincre, et j'y cours, bien moins pour éviter
> Le titre de captif que pour le mériter.
> Oui, Madame, je vais, dans l'ardeur qui m'entraîne,
> Victorieux ou mort, mériter votre chaîne;
> Et puisque mes soupirs s'expliquaient vainement
> A ce coeur que la gloire occupe seulement,
> Je m'en vais, par l'éclat qu'une victoire donne,
> Attacher de si près la gloire à ma personne ...

Porus is to some extent a Cornelian figure, but though there is an occasion on which he uses Cornelian expressions like 'mâle assurance' and 'grand coeur', we can see from this passage that the vigorous language of Corneille has been undermined by the same softness that is visible in Alexandre's and is particularly marked in the weakness of the adverbs in lines 5 and 6.

That is not all. From early times love and war had been linked in the mind and imagination of the people. It was natural therefore that military imagery should be used to describe prowess in love. Racine makes abundant use of the love-war imagery in this play. It is strongly tinged with preciosity and there is a change in the usual form. Instead of victory in battle being followed by 'victory' over the lady, the reward, as the man sees it, is 'defeat' by the lady and 'captivity' in her 'chains'. In short, the aim of victory in the field is to find yourself caught not in the lady's 'chains', but between her legs in the soft, well-sprung bed:

> je pourrai peut-être amener votre coeur
> De l'amour de la gloire à l'amour du vainqueur.

Axiane is still more explicit. When she believes that Porus has been killed she reproaches herself bitterly, in the soliloquy at the beginning of Act IV, for not putting first things first, for not declaring her love, and to hell with 'gloire'!

> J'expliquais mes soupirs en faveur de la gloire:
> Je croyais n'aimer qu'elle. Ah! pardonne, grand Roi,
> Je sens bien aujourd'hui que je n'aimais que toi.
> J'avoûrai que la gloire eut sur moi quelque empire:
> Je te l'ai dit cent fois; mais je devais te dire
> Que toi seul en effet m'engageas sous tes lois.

They all speak continually of 'soupirs'; they all imagined that they were in love with 'gloire' only to find that they were really sighing for something rather different. Porus wants to turn himself into the lady's 'captive'; she realizes that in her heart she never cared for anyone or anything except Porus. She puts it a little differently from the gentleman, reverts in fact to the traditional image: victory in the field will be followed not by captivity, but by 'victory' over her. 'Lois' of course is another euphemism: she wants to find herself underneath the 'grand Roi' in that delicious bed.

Alexandre, who has been happily described as the perfect *soupirant*, goes even further when he stigmatizes 'glory' without love as a 'stérile gloire'.

This mixture of martial and erotic language recalls the scene in which Éphestion, who is busy trying to convince Cléofile of Alexandre's devotion to her, draws what is evidently an unintentionally amusing distinction between the bold 'conqueror' on the battlefield and his much more modest demeanour when he is striving to become a different sort of 'conqueror' in a different sphere:

> Mais après tant d'exploits, ce *timide vainqueur*
> Craint qu'il ne soit encor bien loin de votre coeur.[2]

The play ends suitably with the victory of Alexandre's charm which is at the same time a victory for sentiment all round. The captured Porus is far from being daunted by Alexandre or his reputation:

> Alexandre, il est temps que tu sois satisfait.
> Tout vaincu que j'étais, tu vois ce que j'ai fait.
> Crains Porus; crains encor cette main désarmée
> Qui venge sa défaite au milieu d'une armée ...
> Aussi bien n'attends pas qu'un coeur comme le mien
> Reconnaisse un vainqueur, et te demande rien.
> Parle; et sans espérer que je blesse ma gloire,
> Voyons comme tu sais user de la victoire.

'There's really nothing one can do about your pride, Porus', replies the conqueror. 'How do you want me to treat you?' 'As a king', comes the answer. Alexandre could wish for nothing better:

> Hé bien! c'est donc en roi qu'il faut que je vous traite.

This is the point at which Porus's resistance collapses. He has addressed the victor in the second person singular though Alexandre has remained the perfect gentleman with his 'vous'. He does so no longer:

> Seigneur, jusqu'à ce jour l'univers en alarmes
> Me forçait d'admirer le bonheur de vos armes;
> Mais rien ne me forçait, en ce commun effroi,
> De reconnaître en vous plus de vertu qu'en moi:
> Je me rends; je vous cède une pleine victoire.
> Vos vertus, je l'avoue, égalent votre gloire.
> Allez, Seigneur: rangez l'univers sous vos lois;
> Il me verra moi-même appuyer vos exploits.
> Je vous suis; et je crois devoir tout entreprendre
> Pour lui donner un maître aussi grand qu'Alexandre.

We observe, with amusement, that there has been a complete change of attitude on the part of Porus. After denouncing the aggressor who invaded peaceful countries and peoples and the softness of their resistance, he simply gives in and undertakes to join Alexandre in his world-conquest.

There have been marked differences of opinion about *Alexandre le Grand*. Some critics regard it as an advance on *La Thébaïde*; others as a regression. One thinks that the characters look forward to those in the mature works; another, while admiring the play, argues that it is a kind of 'sport' which has nothing to do with the later plays.[3]

I do not share the view of those critics who think that *Alexandre* is superior to *La Thébaïde* nor do I agree that it is out on a limb with no bearing on anything that came after it. The truth of the matter is that the play is a brilliant *tour de force*. The gloom of the first play has vanished for the moment; the hatred of the *frères ennemis* has been replaced by what will turn out to be a very un-Racinian form of love. The change in subject matter is reflected in the change in language. There are some passages in which we can detect albeit faintly the authentic Racinian note, but in general it is lacking in the vigour that is frequently present in *La Thébaïde* and impresses us by its remarkable accomplishment, by its smoothness and its measure.

Its principal, its basic weakness is that it consists of heterogeneous material taken from various sources. It does not possess any real unity, but Racine displayed extraordinary virtuosity in giving it the appearance of unity or, better, a surface unity. In this purely technical sense it is more accomplished than the admittedly uneven *Thébaïde*. In some ways it looks forward to what is to come; in others it contains things which will not be seen again. The Racinian triangle makes a second appearance. Porus and Taxile are not related, but they are for a time partners and to this extent look back to the 'good' and 'bad' brothers in *Nicomède* and forward to a similar pair in *Mithridate*. Taxile is not without a certain resemblance to Oreste and a preliminary sketch of the Racinian weak man. Equally, Porus strikes me as a pale imitation of the Cornelian hero who will not be seen again in Racine because Porus cannot be regarded as a forerunner of either Xipharès or Achille. Axiane looks back to the Cornelian strong woman and forward to the Racinian amazons in *Britannicus*, *Bajazet* and *Iphigénie*.

The greatest failure of all is clearly the hero. Alexandre's appearance was due in part to the influence of contemporary dramatists and Racine's own anxiety on this occasion to give the public what it wanted. We must not, however, overlook the part played by the courtier who already enjoyed the royal favour and made up his mind to pay for it by the offer of what he regarded as a suitable tribute to the sovereign. While we may feel glad that Racine's shrewdness paid off, we must feel even gladder that nothing like this is to be found in any of the plays which came after *Alexandre*.

NOTES

[1] P. Guéguen in *Poésie de Racine*, published, as we should observe, in 1946. He calls the play 'the tragedy of the resistance' and Porus 'an Indian de Gaulle'! (pp. 119–20).

[2] It is interesting to observe that in this supposedly martial play the word 'vainqueur' is used 34 times. The grand total for all the plays put together is only 62.

[3] J. D. Hubert, *Essai d'exégèse racinienne*, 1956, pp. 53–4, 71–2; T. Maulnier, *Langages*, 1946, p. 114.

'ANDROMAQUE'

1667

Did I understand the play at that first reading? Oh,
certainly not. Haven't I put the gathered experience
of years into my recollection of it? No doubt. What
is certain is that it gave me my first conception of
tragedy, of the terror and complication and pity of
human lives. Strange that for an English child that
revelation should have come through Racine instead
of through Shakespeare. But it did.

Olivia by Olivia

CHAPTER 3

'ANDROMAQUE'

1667

I

THE Trojan War is over, Troy a heap of ruins, its leaders dead. King Pyrrhus, the son of Achilles, is back in his capital city of Epirus. He has brought with him, as his captives, Andromache, the widow of Hector who was barbarously slain by his father, and her son Astyanax. Pyrrhus is betrothed to Hermione, the daughter of Menelaus and Helen, but he has lost interest in her and fallen in love with his captive whose only thoughts are for her dead husband and her living son. The Greeks are beginning to murmur. They are alarmed at the prospect of one of their leaders becoming the protector of Hector's son who may live to start a second Trojan war which might not end as happily for them as the first. Orestes, the son of Agamemnon and a scion of the disastrous House of Atreus, has obtained for himself the appointment of ambassador extraordinary to Pyrrhus. His public mission is to put a stop to the troubles which are brewing in the aftermath of war: to ensure that Pyrrhus hands over Astyanax to the Greeks for execution with the expectation that he will abandon the idea of marriage to Andromaque and marry Hermione. His private mission is very different. He himself is madly in love with Hermione who in the past has repeatedly rebuffed him in the harshest manner.

We see at once that there is a direct conflict between Oreste's public and his private mission. The success of the private depends on the failure of the public mission. He is desperately anxious that Pyrrhus shall persist in his intention to marry Andromaque and that he himself will be able to carry off Hermione. The conflict between public and private interests is one of the principal themes of the play and affects all the characters in one way or another.[1]

2

We never cease to marvel at the gulf which separates *Andromaque* from the first two plays, the distance that Racine seems to have travelled in the space of two years. It is plain that a major change had taken place in the man and the writer. *La Thébaïde* and *Alexandre* are not merely apprentice works; they are essentially literary exercises by a talented young man of letters. They are literary exercises in the sense that they are little more than a very ingenious rehash of material taken from books and contain no evidence of personal experience. This means that they belong to the same category as the works of minor playwrights like Thomas Corneille and Quinault. Racine's awakening may have been the result of his liaison with Marquise du Parc. Whether it was or not, we are aware that some experience provided the dramatist with a new understanding of human nature, gave him fresh insights into its workings which are the fruit of inspiration and not of books. In short, the man of letters has become a creative writer.

Although *Britannicus*, *Phèdre* and *Athalie* possess greater weight and range than *Andromaque*, it is undoubtedly the best introduction to Racine: his poetry, his dramatic power, his skill in construction and the psychology of his characters. The situation is brilliantly conceived. Andromaque faces the choice between marriage to Pyrrhus and the death of her son; Pyrrhus between marriage to Hermione and marriage to Andromaque; Oreste between the loss of Hermione and the murder of Pyrrhus; Hermione between resigning herself to the loss of Pyrrhus and having him murdered.

Andromaque's dilemma is different from those of the other three. It is not a conflict between public and private interest: it is a matter of conscience. Is she justified in marrying the destroyer of her country and the son of the man who killed her husband in order to save her son's life? Can she bring herself to sacrifice her son, and would she be right in doing so, in order to preserve her own integrity?

With the other three it is a straight choice between public and private interest. Pyrrhus is under an obligation to fulfil his pledge to Hermione and to avoid the risk of civil war which might follow marriage to Andromaque and a refusal to hand over Astyanax. Equally, Oreste is under an obligation to give up the woman who is betrothed to another and nothing can excuse the murder of the sovereign to whom he is accredited.[2] Hermione's is in some respects the worst case of all. Instead of resigning herself to Pyrrhus's defection, she goads a weak and unstable man into murder by false promises.

There is one marked difference between *Andromaque* and the other tragedies. Although they are not of the same moral stature, all the main characters rank as protagonists and play equally important parts in the development of the drama; there are no intermediate figures like Antiochus in *Bérénice*, Acomat in *Bajazet* or Abner in *Athalie*. There are, strictly speaking, five of them. Andromaque's devotion to her dead husband is so strong, they remain so united even after death, that we are conscious of Hector's presence at every stage of the play. The tie is strengthened by the feeling that though we do not see him, Astyanax is the living representative of Hector and by the association of both with the tragedy of the Trojan War.

It is impossible to extract any precise information from legend about the ages of the characters, but it seems clear that Andromaque is rather older than the other three. Her age, the loss of her husband, her fears for her son and ten years of a disastrous war have given her a maturity, a sense of responsibility, a wisdom to which none of the others can pretend. She is, indeed, the moral pivot of the play and creates a standard by which they are measured. This calls for some qualification. Andromaque does not possess the moral perfectionism of the Cornelian heroine. She makes the only conceivable choice in deciding to marry Pyrrhus, but her decision is not free from Racinian 'artifice'. She has already sacrificed another woman's son to save her own and tricked the Greeks for a time into believing that they had executed Astyanax. She is only saved from what she is pleased to call an 'innocent stratagem'—suicide immediately after the wedding ceremony in the rather naïve belief that Pyrrhus would carry out his side of the bargain—by the crime of Oreste and Hermione. This prepares the way for her ultimate triumph and whatever our reservations, it is only fair to say that in Racine's particular world the triumph is not undeserved.

Although Racine is one of the writers who is credited with 'the demolition of the hero', it would be more accurate to describe his contribution as cutting the Cornelian hero down to somewhere near life size.[3] In his first preface he said that he had taken the liberty of toning down or 'softening' the 'ferocity' of Pyrrhus which had been pushed too far by Seneca and Virgil. There is of course a streak of ruthlessness in most of Racine's protagonists. In spite of their plotting Pyrrhus gives the impression of being a good deal tougher than either Oreste or Hermione, but though he was notorious for his brutality during the Trojan War it must be remembered, as he himself will explain and as many of us know from experience, that in wartime the whole of man's talents are concentrated on the destruction of the enemy and ordinary civilized standards go by the board, which applies equally to people engaged in a just or an unjust war. It must also be remembered that in Racine the ruthlessness of the protagonists is very much a product of human frailty. Andromaque puts it well when she describes Pyrrhus as 'violent, mais sincère'. 'Violent' is a sign of weakness, of helplessness in the throes of passion. Pyrrhus breaks all his pledges to Hermione and excuses himself on the grounds that they were imposed on him, but he is meticulous in carrying out his promises to Andromaque which are of his own making, and so careful to ensure that Astyanax is properly protected during the wedding ceremony that he leaves himself without defences and an easy target for the assassin.

Hermione is not exactly a sympathetic character, but she is perhaps the most brilliantly original creation in the play, an extraordinary example of feminine unbalance. What impresses us is her vitality, the way in which she comes to life, the convincingness of her changes of mood and the variety of tone of her principal speeches.

The character of Oreste has come in for some severe criticism on artistic grounds. One critic has observed that he is not the Orestes of legend and that 'nowhere else does Racine go quite so far in betraying the ancient world to please modern taste'.[4] I am not myself convinced by these criticisms. The inconsistencies, if they exist, do not impair the dramatic effectiveness of the role and seem to me to be a matter for the 'study' rather than the 'stalls'. Whatever concessions he may have made to contemporary taste, we know from *La Thébaïde* that Racine regarded heredity as 'destiny'. I do not think that there can be any doubt that he associated Oreste's 'melancholy' with the House of Atreus. In any case, whether hereditary or not, his 'melancholy' makes him unique among Racine's male characters. He is, as we shall see, in a technical sense a 'case' with his suicidal tendencies and his switches from a manic depressiveness to something like exaltation.

3

We have seen that the Racinian triangle made its appearance in the first two plays. In *Andromaque* the sequence is much longer and more complex. Oreste is in love with Hermione who is in love with Pyrrhus who is in love with Andromaque who is still in love with the dead Hector. What distinguishes it from all the other secular tragedies is that there is not a single example in it of requited love. That is not all. The triangle becomes a chain. A change on the part of any one of the characters has an immediate effect on all the others, but though Oreste's ambassadorship has a decisive effect on the turn of events, the outcome depends on Andromaque.

One of the reasons for the popularity of *Andromaque* on the stage and in the examination syllabus is that it may have created and certainly corresponds to the popular idea of Racine as a dramatist: the dramatist in whose work passion carries all before it and whose characters break every one of the Cornelian 'rules of love'.[5] With the exception of Andromaque, the characters' actions are not governed by moral considerations. I use the word 'governed' intentionally. We have seen that they are not people who are unaware of the differences between right and wrong, but are entirely at the mercy of their emotions. They admit in their more lucid moments that their conduct falls a good deal short of 'honour' and 'reputation'. The moral virtues only count when they happen to fit in with a character's emotional urge or when they can be used as a weapon against a recalcitrant lover. Hermione is prompt to invoke her 'duty' to her father in order to resist Oreste's advances which she certainly would never have done if she had been in love with him, and her 'gloire' in order to attack Pyrrhus's faithlessness. What the play really presents—once again Andromaque is the exception—is the spectacle of complete emotional instability. It is expressed with great clarity in the glimpse of Hermione trying to make up her mind to leave Epirus and return to her father:

> Toujours / prête à partir, // et demeurant / toujours,

where the balancing of 'toujours' at the beginning and end of the line and the *coupes* or pauses convey the impression of helpless and hopeless 'dithering'.

It is strikingly confirmed by Hermione herself when she is planning the assassination of Pyrrhus and says to the hesitating Oreste:

> S'il ne meurt aujourd'hui, je puis l'aimer demain.

She is simply applying to herself something that Pylade had already said of Pyrrhus in the opening scene of the play:

> Il peut, Seigneur, il peut, dans ce désordre extrême,
> Épouser ce qu'il hait, et punir ce qu'il aime.

It is as much a play about vacillation as *Iphigénie*. In her final encounter with Pyrrhus in Act IV, Sc. 5, Hermione summarizes almost the entire action in four lines:

> Me quitter, me reprendre, et retourner encor
> De la fille d'Hélène à la veuve d'Hector?
> Couronner tour à tour l'esclave et la princesse;
> Immoler Troie aux Grecs, au fils d'Hector la Grèce?

The nature of the urge is described in a celebrated speech of Pyrrhus to Andromaque:

> Oui, mes voeux ont trop loin poussé leur violence
> Pour ne plus s'arrêter que dans l'indifférence.
> Songez-y bien: il faut désormais que mon coeur,
> S'il n'aime avec transport, haïsse avec fureur.

In this world, as I said in discussing the first play, there is no middle course, no state like 'indifference' between the two extremes. We must, however, be clear about the real meaning of 'haïr' in this context. The truth is that the protagonists never cease to love passionately, that in *Andromaque* as surely as in *Bajazet*, the choice lies between love and death. The lover is determined to get his 'prey' or failing that to kill it.

When Hermione says to her confidant:

> Je n'ai pour lui parler consulté que mon coeur,

she speaks for everybody except Andromaque. The 'heart', mentioned 60 times in the play, is in a constant state of eruption and provides it with its

driving force. It is these eruptions which are responsible for the emotional
'disorder' mentioned by Pylade which blinds the characters to every consideration except their personal pursuit of the 'prey'.

The violence of the eruptions and the painfulness of the situation are
greatly intensified by two characteristics which belong to all the protagonists and to Hermione in particular: a remarkable insight into their
own and other peoples' feelings, a 'touchiness' which seems peculiarly
acute in *Andromaque*. When Cléone tries to persuade her mistress at the
beginning of Act II that Pyrrhus's behaviour should make her hate him,
Hermione replies:

> Pourquoi veux-tu, cruelle, irriter mes ennuis?
> Je crains de me connaître en l'état où je suis.

Her one wish is to be free of this painful insight because it brings home
to her the dangers of the 'disorder' in which she is involved. Nor can one
help wondering whether or not the idea of assassination has already
entered her head.

At his first meeting with Hermione Oreste says:

> Déjà même je crois entendre la réponse
> Qu'en secret contre moi votre haine prononce.

He has come too near to divining her feelings and is suitably snubbed.

The protagonists are only too well aware of their dilemma. The movements of the 'heart' reduce them to a state of complete helplessness, but
they are violent in their rejection of the one faculty which could save them.
'Reason', as I have shown, is a word of provocation whose very mention
produces hysterical outbursts from women like Hermione and Roxane or
a man like Oreste.

4

Racine's opening scenes deserve to be studied with special care because
they are the key to an understanding of the tragedy as a whole. The cause
of most of the tragedies is something that happened several months before
the start of the play. There has been a steady deterioration in the situation
and by the time the play begins it has become critical. It follows that there
will be constant references to the past. It is important to grasp that though
the speakers necessarily use past tenses, the *récits* and the great *tirades* are
not descriptions or reports: they are essentially a *re-enactment* of past
events—the equivalent in fact of the cinematic 'flashback'. In this way the
events are completely integrated into the tragedy and transformed into
live issues which play a dynamic role in the unfolding of the drama.

The task that faced Racine in *Andromaque* was to introduce the main
themes in the first scene and to put the audience in the picture without one

character giving the impression that he is telling another something already known to him. Six months ago Oreste and his friend Pylade were on their way to Greece by sea.[6] Their vessels were separated by a storm. They have had no news of one another until they suddenly and unexpectedly come face to face in a room in Pyrrhus's palace as Oreste arrives with his ambassadorial suite. The result is that each of them is in possession of part of the available information about the situation created by Pyrrhus's offer of marriage to Andromaque and his refusal to surrender her son to the Greeks. The exchange between them provides the audience with the essentials:

> Oui, puisque je retrouve un ami si fidèle,
> Ma fortune va prendre une face nouvelle;
> Et déjà son courroux semble s'être adouci,
> Depuis qu'elle a pris soin de nous rejoindre ici.

It is the first of three of Racine's tragedies which begin with the word 'Yes'. Oreste is evidently responding to Pylade's greeting or answering some question put to him a moment before the curtain went up. Dramatically, it is a highly effective way of beginning a play.[7] The affirmation behind the 'Yes' is important too. The play opens on a note of high hope which will be horribly disappointed.

There is a touch of irony in the next two lines:

> Qui l'eût dit, qu'un rivage à mes yeux si funeste
> Présenterait d'abord Pylade aux yeux d'Oreste?

This is the first of eight occasions on which 'Oreste' rhymes with 'funeste'. Whether or not it was intentional on Racine's part, there is no gainsaying the significance of those eight rhymes. 'Funeste' rhyming with 'Oreste' stamps him, unmistakably, as the Man of Destiny whose impact on the community will be decisive.

Knowing his friend's difficult temperament, Pylade has been very worried by the separation and the absence of any news of him. He is naturally delighted that the storm was followed by a calm which has brought them together again and declares enthusiastically:

> J'en rends grâces au ciel, qui m'arrêtant sans cesse
> Semblait m'avoir fermé le chemin de la Grèce,
> Depuis le jour fatal que la fureur des eaux
> Presque aux yeux de l'Épire écarta nos vaisseaux.

I shall have something to say presently about Racine's marine imagery. For the moment it is sufficient to observe that the storm at sea is the prelude to very different storms and that the calm which brought the two friends together will turn out to be illusory.

Pylade goes on:

Surtout je redoutais cette mélancolie
Où j'ai vu si longtemps votre âme ensevelie.
Je craignais que le ciel, par un cruel secours,
Ne vous offrît la mort que vous cherchiez toujours.

Pylade's greeting might almost be described as 'diagnosis'. He is describing Oreste's main symptoms objectively: the 'melancholy', the fits of depression, the suicidal tendencies. He suffers, however, from a serious illusion: he believes that Oreste is cured and proceeds to congratulate him:

Le pompeux appareil qui suit ici vos pas
N'est point d'un malheureux qui cherche le trépas.

Oreste promptly disabuses him with the words

L'amour me fait ici chercher une inhumaine.

In view of what will happen, it is not without significance that Oreste's repetition of the word 'chercher' establishes a link between 'trépas' and 'inhumaine'.

Pylade is distressed to learn that there has been no recovery. 'Vous me trompiez, Seigneur', he says reproachfully. 'Je me trompais moi-même', answers Oreste.

In order to explain the position, Oreste goes on to give his own account of his symptoms. When he arrived in Greece, he found trouble brewing and her princes assembled in order to deal with a 'serious difficulty'. He decided to try a new method of overcoming his passion. This produces some of Racine's most powerfully evocative lines:

Je pensai que la guerre et la gloire
De soins plus importants rempliraient ma mémoire;
Que mes sens reprenant leur première vigueur,
L'amour achèverait de sortir de mon coeur.
Mais admire avec moi le sort dont la poursuite
Me fait courir alors au piège que j'évite.

It sounds at first as though Oreste is advocating martial activities as a cure for love in much the same way that one might advise a person who is feeling liverish to have a game of golf or go for a brisk walk. This should not blind us to the importance of the issue. It is plain that for Oreste love is a *disease*. It supports my description of him as a 'case'. It is characteristic of mental illness that it has physical repercussions. That is the significance of the reference to 'mes sens'. Oreste leaves us in no doubt about the complete failure of the kind of therapy he adopted. There is a certain élan in the references to 'guerre', 'gloire' and 'reprenant leur première vigueur'. It is promptly stifled by the muffled sounds of 'sortir' and 'sort' as well as the *ou*-s of 'poursuite' and 'courir', while the sharp sounds of 'piège' and 'évite' give the impression of something snapping and the victim falling into a trap.

He proceeds in fact to announce his surrender:

> Puisqu'après tant d'efforts ma résistance est vaine,
> Je me livre en aveugle au destin qui m'entraîne.

It is normal practice for anybody writing about *Andromaque* to remind the reader that until 1697 the second of these lines read

> Je me livre en aveugle au *transport* qui m'entraîne.

The change reinforces other uses of the word 'destin'. For Oreste 'destin' means the disease of love. But 'destin' is hereditary. Therefore Oreste is suffering from an incurable hereditary disease.

I have mentioned the link between 'trépas' and 'inhumaine'. We shall find that it is the conduct of the 'inhumaine' coupled with Oreste's disease that leads directly to 'trépas': first the murder of Pyrrhus, then the suicide of the 'inhumaine' herself, and finally the conversion of Oreste's mental illness into raving insanity.

The exposition divides into three parts. The first amounting to rather more than a third of the whole scene is taken up with Oreste's passion for Hermione. Her rejection of him before the beginning of the play is what I have called the source of the tragedy. Without it he would not be in Epirus and Pyrrhus would not be assassinated. With the help of Pylade's comments Oreste's re-enactment of his love affair gives us in little over sixty lines a clear picture of his personality.

The second part begins when he says:

> J'entends de tous côtés qu'on menace Pyrrhus;
> Toute la Grèce éclate en murmures confus . . .

Up to the present Oreste's passion for Hermione has been a purely private and personal matter. Pyrrhus is in a different position. His passion for Andromaque and the refusal to hand over Astyanax is already a cause of public concern. The rest of Oreste's speech is an account of the reports which have reached him of the situation in Epirus. Although he naturally interprets everything in terms of his own interests, the second part links private and public interests as well as explaining the reasons for his appearance as Greek ambassador.

In the third part Pylade completes the picture by giving a first hand account of the relations between Pyrrhus, Andromaque and Hermione which in addition to factual information provides a preliminary sketch of their personalities and prepares the way for the audience's first meeting with them.

There are three statements in the last part of the scene which invite consideration.

Oreste says:

> je viens chercher Hermione en ces lieux,
> La *fléchir*, l'enlever, ou mourir à ses yeux.

Pylade says of Pyrrhus and Andromaque:

> chaque jour encore on lui voit tout tenter
> Pour *fléchir* sa captive, ou pour l'épouvanter.

It is followed by his comment on Pyrrhus and Hermione:

> Hermione, Seigneur, au moins en apparence,
> Semble de son amant dédaigner l'inconstance,
> Et croit que trop heureux de *fléchir* sa rigueur
> Il la viendra presser de reprendre son coeur.

I have called *Andromaque* a play of unrequited love. We have before us the triple spectacle of the unloved or *mal-aimés* all desperately anxious to make the beloved or *bien-aimés* 'yield'.[8] 'Fléchir' describes the aim and to some extent the methods of all three lovers. It is the first objective in the attack on the beloved. If the attack succeeds 'fléchir' will be followed by 'enlever' or 'épouser'. Oreste is much the worst off of the three; he is the one person whom nobody loves. In his heart he knows that this is so and sees the situation in terms of the alternatives 'fléchir/mourir', success in love or death with the premonition, which turns out to be right, that death will prevail. Pyrrhus's ruthlessness is apparent in one of the most striking couplets in the play with the antithesis 'fléchir/épouvanter' which describes exactly the technique, or rather the form of 'blackmail', that he will employ at his meetings with Andromaque in Act II, Sc. 4 and Act III, Scs. 6 and 7. Hermione is deluding herself into the belief that the present position will be reversed and that Pyrrhus will reappear in the role of suppliant, which looks forward ironically to his change of mind—it can scarcely be called a 'change of heart'—in Act II which does not even bring them face to face until there has been another change.

Pylade remarks unwisely of Hermione:

> Quelquefois elle appelle Oreste à son secours.

Oreste's reaction is instantaneous and obviously unbalanced:

> Ah! si je le croyais, j'irais bientôt, Pylade,
> Me jeter ...

Pylade interrupts by saying gravely:

> Achevez, Seigneur, votre ambassade.

Not that he has any illusions about the outcome:

> Pressez, demandez tout, pour ne rien obtenir.

Oreste will see the king, but he is determined to see Hermione as well.

He tells Pylade to arrange the meeting with her in words that confirm his
real objective:

> va donc disposer la cruelle
> A revoir un amant qui ne vient que pour elle.

So much for his 'ambassade'!

I want to return now to the marine imagery.

Although it is virtually certain that, as a naval critic remarked some
years ago, Racine never saw the sea even when he was only a few miles
away from it at Uzès, *Andromaque* is one of the tragedies in which marine
imagery plays a prominent part.[9] When Oreste says

> En ce calme trompeur j'arrivai dans la Grèce,

the word 'calme' has a double meaning. It stands for the illusory mental
calm in which he arrived in Greece and the physical calm of the sea which
got him there. It is an interesting example of the way in which Racine's
imagery frequently has both a physical and a psychological connotation.
The physical storm which separated the friends looks forward to the
psychological storms which will rage through most of the play. Calm is
nearly always 'deceptive' in Racine's world. What in fact happens is that
the calm at sea lets into Epirus the intruder whose arrival will unleash the
psychological storms that bring disaster.

Oreste is not sailing into a serene climate. The protagonists have been
thrown together in a palace standing on a storm-swept promontory. They
are isolated physically and psychologically from the rest of the world with
nothing to control their feelings or their actions. It is the perfect setting
for the psychological storms which reach their climax in a different form
of 'physical' storm—the murder of Pyrrhus by massed Greeks in the
temple and the rising that follows.

In the second scene of the play Pyrrhus refuses categorically to hand
Astyanax over to the Greeks which means that he is determined to keep
Andromaque and would be glad to see the last of Hermione whose devotion is an embarrassment to him. Speaking of Oreste and Hermione in the
brief transitional scene that follows, he says to his confidant:

> Qu'elle parte.
> Que charmés l'un de l'autre, ils retournent à Sparte:
> Tous nos ports sont ouverts et pour elle et pour lui.

He makes it sound as though Oreste is going to bring off his private
mission without striking a blow, and that for once two lovers will be free
to make their escape from the palace without being separated, exiled or
banished.

There could be no greater illusion. On the face of it, Pyrrhus's announcement in Act II that he has decided to marry Hermione after all means that

the palace will become her home, that Astyanax will be surrendered, and that Oreste will depart from Epirus alone in order to inform the Greeks of the success of his public mission. Oreste naturally has no intention of accepting the position. Whatever the cost, he is determined to break out and take Hermione with him. In the first scene of Act III, to which I shall return later, Pylade reluctantly agrees to become his accomplice and proceeds to tell him, in four very impressive lines, how he can bring off his *coup*:

> Je sais de ce palais tous les détours obscurs;
> Vous voyez que la mer en vient battre les murs;
> Et cette nuit, sans peine, une secrète voie
> Jusqu'en votre vaisseau conduira votre proie.

The sea beating against the walls of the palace is a symbol of the psychological storms and of the unloved flinging themselves against the beloved in a desperate attempt to make them 'yield'. It is at the same time a tantalizing symbol of freedom and for Oreste the success of his private mission. The 'secrète voie' will of course never be used, or only when it is too late: when Hermione is dead and Oreste himself a broken man on the run from people who are outraged by the murder of Pyrrhus. The palace is a labyrinth of dark and devious passages corresponding to the devious methods —'détours' is another word with psychological and physical implications— that the characters use against one another.

The storms are the reality; the moments of calm no more than brief and deceptive pauses which are the prelude to even more violent outbursts. They occur when the characters think that things are going better for them personally. Hermione is calm when she hears that Pyrrhus is going to marry her and more violent than ever when he rejects her again. She is surprised at the apparent calm with which Oreste receives the news. He is outwardly calm because he is convinced that, come what may, his plan to carry off Hermione is bound to succeed. There is a more striking example in Act IV. Hermione has just learnt of her final rejection by Pyrrhus and has sent for Oreste. This time it is her confidant who is surprised, or rather alarmed, by her calm:

> CLÉONE
> Ah! que je crains, Madame, un calme si funeste!
> Et qu'il vaudrait bien mieux . . .
> HERMIONE
> Fais-tu venir Oreste?
> CLÉONE
> Il vient, Madame, il vient . . .

Cléone's fears are only too well founded. Hermione's calm is 'funeste' because she has hit on the idea of murdering Pyrrhus and is waiting for the Man of Destiny to put her plan to him. It is in some ways the most striking use of the rhyme 'Oreste/funeste'. It stands for the conversion of a disastrous idea into action and will lead to the greatest storms, physical and psychological, of all.

5

The Trojan War is over, but it has branded itself on the minds and imaginations of all the protagonists. The play is filled with images of the blazing city, the ferocious Greeks in the midst of flame and smoke savagely slaughtering every Trojan in sight regardless of age or sex, the streams of human blood, the charred ruins, the wilderness of rubble and ashes which mark the transition from war to peace.

The image of the capture and destruction of Troy not only dominates the imagination of the protagonists. Their attitude towards it defines their moral stature. Nor is that all. They may be living in the aftermath of war and struggling with the problems that inevitably follow, but the real theme is somewhat different. What happens is that the Trojan War is refought in miniature on the psychological plane and ends in a Trojan victory.

The revelations begin in Scene 2. There is a cinematic 'cut' from a very intimate, a confidential talk between friends to a formal meeting between the king and the ambassador who has come to present his credentials and inform the sovereign of the Greek demand:

> Avant que tous les Grecs vous parlent par ma voix,
> Souffrez que j'ose ici me flatter de leur choix,
> Et qu'à vos yeux, Seigneur, je montre quelque joie
> De voir le fils d'Achille et le vainqueur de Troie.
> Oui, comme ses exploits nous admirons vos coups:
> Hector tomba sous lui, Troie expira sous vous;
> Et vous avez montré, par une heureuse audace,
> Que le fils d'Achille a pu remplir sa place.

Oreste's first speech is an excellent example of what is known as 'pattern rhetoric'.[10] He pays handsome tribute in the introductory lines to father and son who are carefully balanced in 'fils d'Achille'—'vainqueur de Troie', 'ses exploits'—'vos coups', and best of all, 'tomba sous lui'—'expira sous vous' in line 6. The tribute ends with the flattering declaration that Pyrrhus alone could have replaced his dead father. Then, very neatly and ingeniously, Oreste passes on to criticism:

> Mais ce qu'*il* n'eût point fait, la Grèce avec douleur
> *Vous* voit du sang troyen relever le malheur.

He goes on to ask

> Ne vous souvient-il plus, Seigneur, quel fut Hector?

It sounds like a rhetorical question. In fact, it is a perfectly logical move designed, in view of Oreste's mission, to concentrate attention on Hector and his family. The triumphant 'conqueror of Troy' may no longer bother his head about the dead Hector, but the unfortunate Greek people who have lost husbands, fathers and boy friends feel very differently:

> dans toute la Grèce il n'est point de familles
> Qui ne demandent compte à ce malheureux fils
> D'un père ou d'un époux qu'Hector leur a ravis.

He has reintroduced the father-and-son theme—dead fathers and living sons—but this time he is opposing the Greek and Trojan couples. It is for the Greek son to deal with the Trojan son. Pyrrhus has emulated his father's feats. May not the same thing happen with the Trojan son?

> Et qui sait ce qu'un jour ce fils peut entreprendre?
> Peut-être dans nos ports nous le verrons descendre,
> Tel qu'on a vu son père embraser nos vaisseaux,
> Et, la flamme à la main, les suivre sur les eaux.

This is followed by a more personal approach:

> Oserai-je, Seigneur, dire ce que je pense?

He does so:

> Vous-même de vos soins craignez la récompense,
> Et que dans votre sein ce serpent élevé
> Ne vous punisse un jour de l'avoir conservé.

We observe that the 'malheureux fils' has now become a 'serpent' brought up in Pyrrhus's 'bosom'.

Finally, there is an appeal to Pyrrhus to satisfy the wishes of the Greeks by ensuring their vengeance and his own safety:

> Perdez un ennemi d'autant plus dangereux
> Qu'il s'essaîra sur vous à combattre contre eux.

Our immediate impression is that whatever his personal views, Oreste is 'doing his stuff', 'going through the motions'. All the arguments for handing over Astyanax are carefully and logically presented. They are supported by the skilful use of various rhetorical devices: the alternation of fulsome tributes and discreet criticism; the antitheses between fathers and sons; the suggestion that Astyanax is a danger to the Greek people because he may turn out to be just as much his father's son as Pyrrhus himself, rubbed in by the change from 'malheureux fils' to 'serpent'; the emotional appeal contained in the picture of unhappy Greek families who have all suffered heartbreaking bereavements; finally, the attempt to show that the son will prove a personal threat to Pyrrhus as well as to the ordinary people.

Oreste appears to be 'doing his stuff', but when we look more closely at what he has been saying we seem to detect a slightly sardonic note, begin to wonder whether the nicely turned speech was not perhaps intended to get under Pyrrhus's skin. Pyrrhus may have had the same impression. This would explain the ironical tone of the first part of his reply:

> La Grèce en ma faveur est trop inquiétée.
> De soins plus importants je l'ai crue agitée,
> Seigneur; et sur le nom de son ambassadeur,
> J'avais dans ses projets conçu plus de grandeur.
> Qui croirait en effet qu'une telle entreprise
> Du fils d'Agamemnon méritât l'entremise;
> Qu'un peuple tout entier, tant de fois triomphant,
> N'eût daigné conspirer que la mort d'un enfant?

Pyrrhus is using a two-edged weapon. It is directed against Greek policy and against Oreste personally. Oreste had felt 'flattered' at being chosen by the Greeks as their ambassador. He had gone out of his way to compliment Pyrrhus on being such a worthy successor of his father. Pyrrhus deliberately reverses the process; he is surprised to find Oreste engaged in a procedure which in his opinion is unworthy of the son of Agamemnon.

There follows what is intended to be a point by point refutation of the reasons for the Greek demand. He grows more and more scornful of the Greek fears and says of the supposed danger of harbouring Astyanax:

> Seigneur, tant de prudence entraîne trop de soin . . .

The tone changes when he looks back on the fall of Troy:

> Je ne vois que des tours que la cendre a couvertes,
> Un fleuve teint de sang, des campagnes désertes,
> Un enfant dans les fers; et je ne puis songer
> Que Troie en cet état aspire à se venger.

It is a vivid glimpse of post-war Troy. It is also a moving one, particularly the reference to 'un enfant dans les fers' compared with Oreste's 'serpent', or the adult warrior 'la flamme à la main', which suggests that Pyrrhus has undergone a change of heart. It is confirmed by what follows:

> Tout était juste alors: la vieillesse et l'enfance
> En vain sur leur faiblesse appuyaient leur défense;
> La victoire et la nuit, plus cruelles que nous,
> Nous excitaient au meurtre, et confondaient nos coups.
> Mon courroux aux vaincus ne fut que trop sévère.
> Mais que ma cruauté survive à ma colère?
> Que malgré la pitié dont je me sens saisir,
> Dans le sang d'un enfant je me baigne à loisir?
> Non, Seigneur.

When the ambassador in his reply hints at reprisals by the Greeks, Pyrrhus is unmoved:

> J'y consens avec joie:
> Qu'ils cherchent dans l'Épire une seconde Troie . . .

Pyrrhus's attitude is much less straightforward than he wishes it to appear. There is no reason to doubt the genuineness of his regrets or the correctness of the view that, as I have already suggested, people do things in the fury of war that they would not dream of doing at other times. It is clear, however, that his conduct is governed by his determination to have Andromaque for his wife and that nothing else really counts for him. The reference to Epirus becoming a 'second Troy' betrays a complete indifference to the public interest and is not diminished by his assertions that there is no real danger in saving Astyanax's life. He speaks sympathetically of Astyanax, but in reality he is no more than a pawn in Pyrrhus's game. He derides the Greeks' fear of him growing up to be the avenger of Troy, but will contradict himself flatly, or rather go back on his word, when at the first meeting with Andromaque, he declares

> Je l'instruirai moi-même à venger les Troyens;
> J'irai punir les Grecs de vos maux et des miens

Andromaque's attitude is naturally completely different. She remembers the fall of Troy as a time of national disaster and bitter personal tragedy: a continuing tragedy because her son is still in danger. It inspires some of the most moving poetry in the play:

> Dois-je les oublier, s'il ne s'en souvient plus?
> Dois-je oublier Hector privé de funérailles,
> Et traîné sans honneur autour de nos murailles?
> Dois-je oublier son père à mes pieds renversé,
> Ensanglantant l'autel qu'il tenait embrassé?
> Songe, songe, Céphise, à cette nuit cruelle
> Qui fut pour tout un peuple une nuit éternelle.

This was her first sight of the man whom she is now being pressed to marry:

> Figure-toi Pyrrhus, les yeux étincelants,
> Entrant à la lueur de nos palais brûlants,
> Sur tous mes frères morts se faisant un passage,
> Et de sang tout couvert échauffant le carnage.
> Songe aux cris des vainqueurs, songe aux cris des mourants,
> Dans la flamme étouffés, sous le fer expirants.
> Peins-toi dans ces horreurs Andromaque éperdue:
> Voilà comme Pyrrhus vint s'offrir à ma vue;
> Voilà par quels exploits il sut se couronner;
> Enfin voilà l'époux que tu me veux donner.

When we compare the accounts of Pyrrhus and Andromaque, we observe that Pyrrhus's liveliest recollection is of the ruined city, the city that he had helped to conquer and destroy. He only speaks in the most general terms of the fighting which seems to have been blotted out by the dark. We see no individuals; we merely hear of 'enfance', 'vieillesse', 'nous excitaient au meurtre', 'confondaient nos coups'. It is the actual details of the fighting which have fixed themselves in Andromaque's memory: the death and ignoble treatment of Hector; Priam at her feet clinging to an altar and covering it with his blood; the sight of Pyrrhus with flashing eyes and smothered in Trojan blood storming through the burning city. We hear the combatants choking in 'étouffés' and the clash of steel in 'mourants', 'expirants' and 'peins'. The intensity of feeling, the emotional appeal depend to a considerable extent on the use of the simplest poetical devices: the repeated 'Dois-je oublier' alternating with the repeated 'Songe' which turn her account into lamentation in an almost technical sense.

The difference of outlook, the gulf which separates Andromaque and Pyrrhus, are strikingly illustrated by a celebrated passage from their meeting in Act I. Pyrrhus is trying simultaneously to excuse his brutality in the war and to upbraid Andromaque for her supposed cruelty to him:

> Je souffre tous les maux que j'ai faits devant Troie.
> Vaincu, chargé de fers, de regrets consumé,
> Brûlé de plus de feux que je n'en allumé,
> Tant de soins, tant de pleurs, tant d'ardeurs inquiètes . . .
> Hélas! fus-je jamais si cruel que vous l'êtes!

It has been suggested, understandably enough, that Pyrrhus's comparison between his own sufferings and those of the unfortunate Trojans is simply an example of the preciosity which turns up not infrequently in this first play of Racine's maturity. It seems to me that the correct answer is rather different. Is not the truth of the matter that Pyrrhus's passion for Andromaque has so completely disrupted all rational values that he really does believe that his personal sufferings as a rejected lover are comparable to those he inflicted on others? And does not this demonstrate more clearly than almost anything the blinding effect of Racinian passion?

There is one other point which deserves notice. When Pyrrhus renews his offer of a crown and promises to bring up her son to avenge Troy, Andromaque replies:

> Seigneur, tant de grandeurs ne nous touchent plus guère.

She no longer sees the situation in terms of Greeks versus Trojans. Her one desire—it is probably a reflection of Racine's own horror of war—is to get away from it all, to live alone with her son and memories of her husband:

> c'est un exil que mes pleurs vous demandent.
> Souffrez que loin des Grecs, et même loin de vous,
> J'aille cacher mon fils et pleurer mon époux.

We only see Andromaque when she is on the way to or from a visit to her son or Hector's cenotaph.[11] We assume that owing to the unity of place or some architectural oddity in Pyrrhus's palace she is obliged to pass through the same room every time she pays one of these visits. The result is interesting. For her the room is no more than a *lieu de passage* which leads, or promises to lead, to something outside the present conflicts and becomes a symbol of Andromaque's passionate desire to dissociate herself from the quarrels, to seek refuge in a better world.

The attitudes of Andromaque, Pyrrhus and Oreste towards the war, in so far as Oreste can be said to have an attitude, are consistent and unchanging. The interest of Hermione's lies primarily in the way in which it does change, the way in which it is determined by her relations with Pyrrhus at a given moment.

When Pyrrhus announces that he has decided to marry her after all, her joy knows no bounds; she speaks to her confidant about his exploits in a tone of girlish rapture for all the world like a child listening to a bedtime story:

> Hè bien! chère Cléone,
> Conçois-tu les transports de l'heureuse Hermione?
> Sais-tu quel est Pyrrhus? T'es-tu fait raconter
> Le nombre des exploits . . . Mais qui les peut compter?
> Intrépide, et partout suivi de la victoire,
> Charmant, fidèle enfin, rien ne manque à sa gloire.

When Pyrrhus finally rejects her she speaks of his exploits in far more violent terms than Andromaque:

> sans chercher ailleurs des titres empruntés,
> Ne vous suffit-il pas de ceux que vous portez?
> Du vieux père d'Hector la valeur abattue
> Aux pieds de sa famille expirante à sa vue,
> Tandis que dans son sein votre bras enfoncé
> Cherche un reste de sang que l'âge avait glacé;
> Dans des ruisseaux de sang Troie ardente plongée;
> De votre propre main Polyxène égorgée
> Aux yeux de tous les Grecs indignés contre vous:
> Que peut-on refuser à ces généreux coups?

Hermione is denouncing precisely the same sort of ruthlessness that she herself displayed a few moments earlier in plotting Pyrrhus's death with Oreste. Her 'ruisseaux de sang' recalls her order to him:

> Revenez tout couvert du sang de l'infidèle . . .

Finally, she displays the same irresponsible attitude to the public interest as Pyrrhus himself. His reference to the Greeks turning Epirus into a 'second Troy' is matched by her words to Oreste at their first meeting when she urges him to rouse the Greeks against Pyrrhus:

> Qu'on fasse de l'Épire un second Ilion.

6

In *Andromaque* Racine adopts a pattern which will become familiar, almost standard, in the plays which follow. The greater part of the scenes take place between pursuer and pursued, or in this particular play, between *mal-aimés* and *bien-aimés*, preceded by exchanges with their confidants and interspersed with one or two scenes between 'rivals' or apparent rivals.

The opening scene, in which Pylade tries to discourage Oreste's pursuit of Hermione, prepares the way for his first meeting with her. In the brief transitional scene which follows Oreste's presentation of his credentials, Pyrrhus's confidant tries to steer his master away from Andromaque and back to Hermione. Andromaque is sighted on her way to visit her son. Pyrrhus hastily dismisses Phoenix and cries rapturously:

> Andromaque paraît.

It is our first sight of her. These two words and the tone in which they are spoken are sufficient to invest her with a special aura which is peculiarly her own.

In spite of the vigorous use of the 'fléchir/épouvanter' technique, the meeting appears to end inconclusively with Pyrrhus telling Andromaque to see her son in the hope that it will make her change her mind, and then meet him again. I said that the meeting 'appears' to end inconclusively because without any warning or further meeting Pyrrhus undergoes his temporary change of mind.

Oreste's meeting with Pylade is matched in a minor key by Pyrrhus's brief exchange with Phoenix and much more closely by Hermione's discussion with her confidant in the scene following the meeting between Pyrrhus and Andromaque. It is interesting at this stage to compare the different approaches of the three confidants. Pylade tried to steer Oreste away from Hermione, but had no alternative to offer. Phoenix, as we have just seen, tried to steer Pyrrhus away from Andromaque and back to Hermione while Pyrrhus himself expressed the wish that Oreste and Hermione would depart together and leave him in peace to concentrate on his suit for Andromaque. Cléone does her best to discourage Hermione's infatuation for Pyrrhus and persuade her to respond to Oreste's overtures.

She is therefore at odds with the other two confidants and in agreement with Pyrrhus.

Like the meeting between Oreste and Pylade, Hermione's talk with Cléone is another example of stocktaking and it tells us a good deal about her. She agrees to see Oreste with considerable reluctance. She is reluctant because after rebuffing him she finds herself rebuffed by Pyrrhus and is afraid that Oreste will have the laugh on her. The meeting begins on a conciliatory note. Hermione is in no sense in love with Oreste, but feels that he may be useful to her and in spite of her irritation deploys her wiles to keep him sweet. She greets him coquettishly with the words

> Le croirai-je, Seigneur, qu'un reste de tendresse
> Vous fasse ici chercher une triste princesse?

We catch the wheedling tone in the sighing *s*-s, which are heightened by the rhyme, as well as the *c*-s and *ch*-s of 'ici', 'chercher' and 'princesse'.

What is really upsetting Oreste, for all his plans to carry her off, is the knowledge that Hermione will never love him. Although the meeting is not going too well she suddenly says, coquettishly again:

> Vous que mille vertus me forçaient d'estimer;
> Vous que j'ai plaint, enfin que je voudrais aimer.

Oreste replies bitterly:

> Je vous entends. Tel est mon partage funeste:
> Le coeur est pour Pyrrhus, et les voeux pour Oreste.

It is another of those damaging insights that the characters have into their own and other peoples' feelings and is emphasized by the reappearance of the 'Oreste/funeste' rhyme. It reveals the deep divisions in the personalities of the protagonists. They recognize the line they ought to take—the line that might lead to happiness—but are powerless to take it. 'Voeux' stands for reason and will power, but neither has any chance against 'coeur'.

Hermione tries to cover up by declaring:

> Ah! ne souhaitez pas le destin de Pyrrhus:
> Je vous haïrais trop.

A few moments later Oreste remarks, admittedly not very tactfully, of Pyrrhus:

> Car enfin il vous hait; son âme ailleurs éprise
> N'a plus . . .

Although Hermione has just implied that she 'hates' Pyrrhus, the suggestion that he hates her produces a flare-up. She at once becomes the shrew with her lightning retort:

> Qui vous l'a dit, Seigneur, qu'il me méprise?

Oreste proceeds to challenge Hermione's pretence—for pretence it is—that she 'hates' Pyrrhus. This produces one of Racine's superbly evocative single lines. Love, he says, is not something which can be hidden away inside us:

Tout nous trahit, la voix, le silence, les yeux ...

Clearly, they cannot hit it off. Equally clearly, Hermione is determined to make every possible use of the man for her own purposes. Oreste is to tell Pyrrhus that he must either send her home or surrender the Trojan child:

Adieu: s'il y consent, je suis prête à vous suivre.

It is a highly ambiguous promise—a promise to marry Oreste on the rebound if Pyrrhus finally rejects her—which looks forward to the disastrous promise in Act IV. If the meeting seems less inconclusive than the one between Pyrrhus and Andromaque, it is another illusion.

Then comes the bombshell. Oreste has just had one of his rare moments of exaltation. In an excited soliloquy he has told himself that Pyrrhus is bound to agree and that all will end happily for everybody:

Quelle joie
D'enlever à l'Épire une si belle proie!
Sauve tout ce qui reste et de Troie et d'Hector ...

His excitement reaches its peak when he suddenly sees Pyrrhus coming towards him:

Mais un heureux destin le conduit en ces lieux.
Parlons. A tant d'attraits, Amour, ferme ses yeux!

Pyrrhus makes his announcement in the most painful way possible for Oreste. The change is due to Oreste's own arguments:

J'en ai senti la force et connu l'équité.

Worse is to come. We had the impression at their first meeting that Pyrrhus feels a certain antipathy for Oreste. We know from his own words that he is aware of Oreste's passion for Hermione whom he himself is proposing to marry out of duty or on the rebound from Andromaque. These two factors are no doubt responsible for the extreme brutality of his

Je l'épouse. Il semblait qu'un spectacle si doux
N'attendît en ces lieux qu'un témoin tel que vous.

Oreste is to break the glad tidings to Hermione and to give her away at the wedding which will take place next day.

Pyrrhus's temporary change of mind is the most tragic of all the illusions in this play of illusions. It is Hermione's rage over the false hopes created by the temporary change which really provokes the assassination.

This is the stage at which the confidants begin to play a still more prominent part. We have noted the differences in their attitudes at the start. Phoenix will stick to his guns; Cléone will retain her sympathy for Oreste; Pylade, as we know, will become Oreste's accomplice. With the exception of Céphise, who so far has been seen but not heard, they all meet with defeat.

We know that there are two scenes between Pyrrhus and his confidant in Acts II and III in which Racine uses the methods of the comic dramatist. According to the Abbé Dubos eighteenth-century audiences laughed loudly during the last scene of Act II.[12] Philip Butler endorses their attitude and describes the scene as 'high comedy' which provides a few moments of relaxation.[13] I said earlier that in *Andromaque* the characters form a chain. Harald Weinrich goes further than this. In an interesting study of the two scenes, he argues that the basic structure of the play is a technique borrowed from comedy and known in Germany as the *Liebeskette*. Tragic and comic elements are combined in a way that ensures that the comic elements do not disturb the tragic atmosphere, but rather enhance it.[14]

This seems to me to be the right view. I cannot help suspecting that the eighteenth-century productions which aroused loud laughter were misconceived. The scenes can hardly be described as 'comic relief' in the Shakespearean manner in *Macbeth* or *Hamlet*. They are equally without the robust and at the same time macabre humour which distinguished the Royal Shakespeare Theatre Company's 1970 production of *Richard III* and did indeed move the audience to loud laughter. Nor do I feel that there is anything in them which can be described as 'relief' or 'relaxation' for the simple reason that Pyrrhus is wrestling all the time with a major problem, trying to convince himself that he has found a way of resolving it and continually betraying the fact that he has not. Although there is an element of fatuity in some of his remarks, there is no question of turning his problem into a joke or laughing it off. Far from providing relief or relaxation, the technique of comedy adds a new element of grimness to the situation. Perhaps after all the right term is a dash of 'black comedy'.

After announcing his intention to marry Hermione, Pyrrhus turns to his confidant and remarks smugly:

> Hé bien, Phoenix, l'amour est-il le maître?
> Tes yeux refusent-ils encor de me connaître?

This is plainly an unconvincing attempt to convince himself and his confidant.

Phoenix congratulates him in suitably fulsome terms:

> C'est Pyrrhus, c'est le fils et le rival d'Achille,
> Que la gloire à la fin ramène sous ses lois,
> Qui triomphe de Troie une seconde fois.

The first line looks back to Oreste's sardonic tribute when presenting his credentials. The irony of the last line goes a good deal deeper. Far from triumphing over Troy a second time, Pyrrhus is heading for disaster. This was the sort of thing I had in mind when I suggested that a touch of 'black comedy' was the right description of the scene rather than 'comic relief' or 'high comedy'.

Phoenix soon begins to realise that he has spoken too soon. Pyrrhus says:

> Tous les Grecs conjurés fondaient sur un rebelle.
> Je trouvais du plaisir à me perdre pour elle.

Phoenix replies a little nervously:

> Oui, je bénis, Seigneur, l'heureuse cruauté
> Qui vous rend . . .

Pyrrhus cuts him short with

> Tu l'as vu, comme elle m'a traité.

He is launched into a series of reflections on Andromaque's attitude— musings addressed to himself rather than to the confidant whose very presence is momentarily forgotten. Phoenix is now feeling distinctly worried and says hurriedly:

> Sans doute. C'est le prix que vous gardait l'ingrate.
> Mais laissez–la, Seigneur.

But Pyrrhus cannot 'leave her alone':

> Elle est veuve d'Hector, et je suis fils d'Achille:
> Trop de haine sépare Andromaque et Pyrrhus.

He is evidently trying to bolster up his decision to marry Hermione. He has no illusions about Andromaque's attitude, but it will not prevent him from switching back to her.

Phoenix does his best to strengthen his resolve to marry Hermione:

> Commencez donc, Seigneur, à ne m'en parler plus.
> Allez voir Hermione . . .

It is no use. His words simply haven't registered. Pyrrhus puts to him the sort of question he has been asking himself:

> Crois-tu, si je l'épouse,
> Qu'Andromaque en son coeur n'en sera pas jalouse?

It sounds absurd, but the words are a clear indication of his state of mind. A moment ago he appeared to have no illusions about Andromaque's attitude. Now he is starting to harbour them again. This suggests that the sudden decision to marry Hermione may have been due to an unconscious desire to put Andromaque to the test or to increase the pressure on her.

The impression becomes stronger when he hits on the pretext for going to
see Andromaque instead of Hermione. He claims, very unjustly, that he
has let her off too lightly and must go and tell her a few home truths.

Phoenix is growing desperate. He sees the way things are going and
says:

> Allez, Seigneur, vous jeter à ses pieds.

Then, still more bluntly:

> Vous aimez: c'est assez.

Pyrrhus is nettled and replies indignantly: 'Moi, l'aimer? une in-
grate . . .'

He appears to come round to Phoenix's view and goes off ostensibly to
see Hermione with the words: 'Faisons tout ce que j'ai promis'. We are
not deceived. His exchanges with Phoenix support the distinction I drew
between 'change of mind' and 'change of heart'. Pyrrhus is a divided personality. He has decided mentally to do 'the right thing', but emotionally
there has been no change. The spectacle of Pyrrhus hesitating between a
personal visit to Andromaque or Hermione and his subsequent failure to
locate Hermione are typical of the vacillations which give the play its
particular atmosphere. Unity of personality will only be restored when he
goes back on his word and decides to do 'the wrong thing'. It will be the
equivalent of the first nail in his coffin.

We have seen the effect of his change of mind on Pyrrhus himself. We are
now shown the effect on the rest of the characters. At the opening of the
third act we find Pylade having a very bad time with Oreste. He is shattered by Pyrrhus's change of mind. He speaks in the same reckless tone
that he used at moments in the first scene of the play:

> Il épouse, dit-il, Hermione demain;
> Il veut, pour m'honorer, la tenir de ma main.
> Ah! plutôt cette main dans le sang du barbare . . .

The last line is of course prophetic.

In spite of his words to Hermione about 'the heart being for Pyrrhus',
Oreste is even less able than Pyrrhus to grasp, or at any rate to accept, the
fact that he is a *mal-aimé*:

> Ses yeux s'ouvraient, Pylade; elle écoutait Oreste,
> Lui parlait, le plaignait. Un mot eût fait le reste.

Pylade counters with one of those insights which belong to the good
confidant. He says of Pyrrhus:

> Jamais il ne fut plus aimé.

It is as completely lost on Oreste as some of Phoenix's comments to

Pyrrhus. He is deaf to 'reason'. Pylade's shocked 'Oreste ravisseur!' simply makes the unbalanced man worse if that is possible.

One of the signs that Oreste is a 'case' is that there is no real justification for his complaints. He has not been betrayed or tricked or jilted; he has simply fallen violently in love with his cousin Hermione who made it plain from the start that she did not respond. He is now planning to kidnap her in order to prevent Pyrrhus from doing what is obviously 'the right thing' —marrying the princess to whom he is betrothed. Oreste is equally indifferent to the fact that his plot could lead to a grave political crisis.

Nobody is more conscious of the issues than Pylade. We can only assume that his surrender is the result of his fear of Oreste's suicidal tendencies. Whatever the reasons, he tries to make the best of it:

> Allons, Seigneur, enlevons Hermione.
> Au travers des périls un grand coeur se fait jour.

There is a marked element of brittleness in Hermione's make-up. When things go wrong she cracks; when they appear to be going well for her she is so delighted that she has neither thought nor feeling for anybody else's troubles. The good news about Pyrrhus's change of mind seems to have reached her between Acts II and III before she had seen either Oreste or, rather oddly, Pyrrhus whose apparent failure to locate her looks like a Freudian error. When Oreste arrives to make his belated announcement, she receives him coolly and tells him that she already knows. There is nothing she can do for him. Her troth has been plighted for her—it is an example of the way in which 'duty' is invoked when it happens to suit her —she must marry Pyrrhus. She is surprised that Oreste takes the news so calmly. It is of course the scene of false 'calm' because Oreste is convinced that with the help of Pylade he is going to win.

In the scene with Cléone which follows she becomes lyrical about Pyrrhus and his wartime feats. She is interrupted by Cléone who has caught sight of Andromaque.

Hermione wanted to avoid Andromaque, but it is too late. Andromaque, who also appears to have heard the news, appeals to her to intervene with Pyrrhus on behalf of her son. The reply is freezing:

> Je conçois vos douleurs. Mais un devoir austère,
> Quand mon père a parlé, m'ordonne de me taire.
> C'est lui qui de Pyrrhus fait agir le courroux.

It is because she feels sure for the moment that she has won back Pyrrhus that she can speak complacently once again of her 'duty' to her father. She is singularly lacking in generosity; she cannot even now forgive Andromaque for unintentionally luring Pyrrhus away from her or recognize that it is her refusal to marry him which has in fact brought him back to her. 'Fléchir' turns up ominously when she remarks sarcastically:

> S'il faut fléchir Pyrrhus, qui le peut mieux que vous?

She rubs it in when she goes on sarcastically:

> Vos yeux assez longtemps ont régné sur son âme.
> Faites-le prononcer: j'y souscrirai, Madame.

In Racine the third act is usually a turning point. Although the effects may not begin to make themselves felt until the next act—this is what happens in *Andromaque*—something takes place which decides the issue and brings about the downfall of the victims in the last two acts.

That is the significance of Andromaque's encounter with Hermione in the present scene and her meeting with Pyrrhus which follows immediately afterwards. Technically, it is Andromaque who 'yields' by overcoming her scruples and agreeing to marry Pyrrhus. But Hermione's hardness of heart and her tactlessness play an important part by reducing her to a state of despair in which she decides to 'yield' and by making her formidable confidant tougher and more determined than ever.

The spiteful Hermione departs. Pyrrhus turns up unexpectedly. Racine uses a different borrowing from comedy this time: the appearance of two couples on the stage talking to one another and ensuring that what they say is overheard by the other couple. Andromaque automatically begins to use the technique of the coquette. She says audibly:

> Hélas! tout m'abandonne.

Pyrrhus is piqued. He says to Phoenix:

> Daigne-t-elle sur nous tourner au moins la vue?

Then he resorts to the technique of 'fléchir/épouvanter' again:

> Allons aux Grecs livrer le fils d'Hector.

This is more effective than the promptings of Céphise. Andromaque bursts out with

> Ah! Seigneur, arrêtez!

The dialogue is engaged. Phoenix is dismissed. Pyrrhus is ready to throw Hermione overboard and marry Andromaque, but this is her last chance. He delivers what in fact is an ultimatum:

> Mais ce n'est plus, Madame, une offre à dédaigner:
> Je vous le dis, il faut ou périr ou régner.
> Mon coeur, désespéré d'un an d'ingratitude,
> Ne peut plus de son sort souffrir l'incertitude.

This is the stuff of tragedy. The human being, however misguided his views, is at the end of his tether and is determined to settle the business one way or the other. He leaves Andromaque to decide on her reply to the ultimatum.

Céphise still has her role to play. When she sees that Andromaque is hesitating again she adopts Pyrrhus's technique:

> Hé bien! allons donc voir expirer votre fils:
> On n'attend plus que vous.[15]

Andromaque goes to meditate at her husband's cenotaph in the hope that a solution will be suggested to her.

From the first line of Act IV we know that the die is cast, that there is going to be trouble. The news comes to us in the delighted words of Céphise:

> Ah! je n'en doute point: c'est votre époux, Madame,
> C'est Hector qui produit ce miracle en votre âme.

Andromaque's decision to marry Pyrrhus looks like a 'miracle' to Céphise until she hears about the 'innocent stratagem'. Raymond Picard compares the scene which led to the 'miracle' to a particular kind of comic scene, 'la réconciliation après une scène de dépit amoureux'.[16] It seems to support my theory of 'black comedy'. In comedy reconciliation usually leads to happiness all round with reconciliation between servants matching the reconciliation of masters and mistresses. In *Andromaque* 'reconciliation' is the death sentence for Pyrrhus and Hermione, and the equivalent of certification for Oreste.

7

The immense effectiveness of the last two acts lies largely in the variations in the speed with which events succeed one another, in the contrast between the formal style and open violence, in the spectacle of the complete disintegration of personality within the walls of the alexandrine. The word 'menace', heard earlier in the play, reappears and is reinforced by the word 'coup(s)' which is used 16 times in the last two acts. The threats are now being fulfilled. The blows, whether they are the smashing verbal blows of an outraged mistress or the blows of daggers plunged into human flesh, reverberate all through these acts as they land with dull, muffled thuds.

Hermione has learnt of her final rejection by Pyrrhus. She sends for Oreste. He at once begins to speak in the fatuous tones of a lovesick swain —tones which are almost a caricature of the language of gallantry:

> Ah! Madame, est-il vrai qu'une fois
> Oreste en vous cherchant obéisse à vos lois?

She cuts him short with the stern

> Je veux savoir, Seigneur, si vous m'aimez.

This produces another gushing speech by Oreste. When he hears what is expected of him, he begins to hesitate, to argue. The temperature rises at once. Hermione gives a display of something which could be described in a literal sense as 'rhetoric':

> Ne vous suffit-il pas que je l'ai condamné?
> Ne vous suffit-il pas que ma gloire offensée
> Demande une victime à moi seule adressée ... ?

Then the threat:

> S'il ne meurt aujourd'hui, je puis l'aimer demain.

He asks for time and is met by the astonished reply:

> Mais cependant ce jour il épouse Andromaque.

Her language is already full of images of blood and slaughter:

> Revenez tout couvert du sang de l'infidèle;
> Allez: en cet état soyez sûr de mon coeur

There is a grim irony about the last line, particularly when contrasted with Hermione's 'S'il ne meurt aujourd'hui . . .' The idea that murder could produce a change of 'heart' is incredible in itself and Oreste will learn belatedly and in the most painful manner imaginable that in this world the one thing of which one can never be certain are the vagaries of the human heart.

Hermione uses plenty of imperatives in this scene. 'Parlez', she says to him near the end of her speech. When he begins with the words 'Mais, Madame, songez . . .' she interrupts violently with the attack on 'reason' which shows that the emotions are now completely out of control, that reason itself is breaking loose from its moorings. A furious denunciation of Oreste's 'cowardice' ends with a particularly vicious swipe:

> Et tout ingrat qu'il est, il me sera plus doux
> De mourir avec lui que de vivre avec vous.

These prophetic lines are delivered in a low voice seething with rage. The *ou*-s and *v*-s in 'doux', 'vivre' and 'vous' sound once again like the muffled thud of blows raining down on the victim.

Oreste gives in and departs with the most specious of all promises:

> Allez. De votre sort laissez-moi la conduite,
> Et que tous vos vaisseaux soient prêts pour notre fuite.

This reappearance of marine imagery points to the kind of outward journey which never materializes in Racine.

The most tragic thing of all is that Pyrrhus is doing exactly what Oreste was hoping from the start that he would do, but instead of leading to the success of the private mission it produces total disaster.

'Vous vous perdez, Madame', cries the horrified Cléone. Hermione doesn't care. There is still more blood in the exchange with the confidant. Ought she to have trusted another person? Ought she not to do the deed herself? She displays the sadistic streak that she shares with a number of Racine's protagonists and what she says actually looks forward to what Roxane will say about her plans to kill Bajazet and Atalide:

> Quel plaisir de venger moi-même mon injure,
> De retirer mon bras teint du sang du parjure . . .

She even goes to the length of telling Cléone to run after Oreste and give him a last reminder that Pyrrhus must know that she is the real assassin. Then, as Pyrrhus is suddenly sighted, she characteristically changes her order: Cléone is to tell Oreste not to do anything without seeing her again.

Pyrrhus, we remember, is 'violent, mais sincère'. He is not afraid of facing Hermione. She must hear from his own lips what he has decided to do and why. He delivers a nicely turned speech:

> Je ne viens point, armé d'un indigne artifice,
> D'un voile d'équité couvrir mon injustice . . .

'Indigne artifice' reminds us of the 'innocent stratagème' which Andromaque is planning and from which she will only be saved by what is really Hermione's crime. 'Équité' looks back to Pyrrhus's previous use of the word when telling Oreste that he recognized the 'équité' or fairness of his arguments and had decided to marry Hermione.

In spite of his smoothness Pyrrhus contrives, as usual, to say some very wounding things. He is, in fact, making the sort of speech that he was talking of making to Andromaque in the first of the scenes of 'black comedy', but one suspects that it is inspired by his sense of guilt towards her. The choice of Hermione, he says, was forced on him.[17] He had hoped to make a go of it, but unfortunately he met Andromaque:

> Mais cet amour l'emporte, et par un coup funeste
> Andromaque m'arrache un coeur qu'elle déteste.

Whatever illusions he may have had about her attitude in the past, he has none now. There is, indeed, a sort of tragic lucidity about the pronouncement. He is convinced that Andromaque hates him, but is completely in her thrall. The technique of 'fléchir/épouvanter' has worked, but 'fléchir' is no guarantee of requited love.

We know that temperamentally Pyrrhus and Hermione are not unlike. Pyrrhus speaks of Andromaque's effect on him as 'un coup funeste'. His

defection is a smashing blow for Hermione and will provoke a terrible re-
taliation. Her reply begins in a tone of icy calm:

> Seigneur, dans cet aveu dépouillé d'artifice,
> J'aime à voir que du moins vous vous rendiez justice . . .

Except for the plot which Hermione is trying to delay, the characters
are coming clean with one another. Hermione continues with the bitterest
sarcasm:

> Est-il juste, après tout, qu'un conquérant s'abaisse
> Sous la servile loi de garder sa promesse?

She goes on to attack his fickleness in lines already quoted:

> Me quitter, me reprendre et retourner encor. . .

She is so divorced by now from reality that Pyrrhus's words about the
hatred of Andromaque have not registered:

> Vous veniez de mon front observer la pâleur,
> Pour aller dans ses bras rire de ma douleur.

The lurid imagination is conjuring up the preliminaries of sexual intercourse: Pyrrhus happily whipping off his pants, Andromaque letting down
her knickers or whatever she wore, and the two lovers falling on top of one
another, roaring with laughter at the thought of the jealous rival who has
been successfully ditched. The lines are delivered in the same low tone of
suppressed rage that she had used a few minutes earlier with Oreste, but
her voice rises to a shriek when she suddenly plunges into the denunciation of Pyrrhus's exploits in Troy.[18]

The smoothness of Pyrrhus's reply and the suggestion that at bottom
Hermione is 'indifferent' to him—the very same word he had rejected
categorically in his pursuit of Andromaque—produces the switch from
the 'Seigneur' of the protocol to the second person singular:

> Je ne t'ai point aimé, cruel? Qu'ai-je donc fait?
> J'ai dédaigné pour toi les voeux de tous nos princes . . .
> Je t'aimais inconstant, qu'aurais-je fait fidèle?
> Et même en ce moment où ta bouche cruelle
> Vient si tranquillement m'annoncer le trépas,
> Ingrat, je doute encor si je ne t'aime pas.

It is an intensely moving speech whose effectiveness is heightened by
the sarcasms which preceded it and by the coolness of Pyrrhus's replies as
well as by the brilliant linguistic compression of the third line.

The voice rises to a scream again as she dismisses Pyrrhus with the
warning that though she wishes to be excused attendance at the wedding
Pyrrhus may nevertheless find her at the altar.

* * *

We have seen several Hermiones: the coquette using her wiles on Oreste;
the touchy shrew replying testily to anything which gets her on the raw;
the aloof aristocrat crushing in turn Oreste, Andromaque and Pyrrhus; the
abandoned mistress casting aside the protocol and using the language of
the fishwife. At the beginning of Act V we come face to face with the soli-
tary figure of the abandoned mistress who is reduced to a truly pitiable
state:

> Où suis-je? / Qu'ai-je fait? // Que dois-je faire encore?
> Quel transport / me saisit? // Quel chagrin / me dévore?
> Errante, / et sans dessein, // je cours / dans ce palais.
> Ah! ne puis-je savoir // si j'aime, / ou si je hais?

The pauses, the way in which Racine bends the alexandrine to his purposes, the accumulation of the short staccato questions, reflect the total
disarray of a woman who is really beside herself, whose fear of 'knowing
myself in the state in which I am' was only too well founded. The effect of
the lines is considerably increased by the concrete image in line 3 of a
woman physically lost in the palace, not knowing which way to turn or in
which direction she wants to go.

Cléone returns. The interrogation is turned on to her. She has failed to
communicate with Oreste, but she has seen the wedding procession on its
way to the temple. She mentions Pyrrhus 'au comble de ses voeux'.
Hermione fastens on it.

> Et l'ingrat? . . .
> Goûte-t-il des plaisirs tranquilles et parfaits?
> N'a-t-il point détourné ses yeux vers le palais?
> Dis-moi, ne t'es-tu point présentée à sa vue?
> L'ingrat a-t-il rougi lorsqu'il t'a reconnue?

Ironically, she is echoing Pyrrhus's question about Andromaque after
the announcement of his return to Hermione in Act III, Sc. 6. The
answer is that Pyrrhus is oblivious of everyone and everything except
Andromaque. Oreste is hesitating. This produces another extraordinary
change. A moment ago Hermione was wondering whether she still loved
Pyrrhus and was filled with doubts about the plot. Now, when there is a
possibility of Oreste falling down on the job, she thinks again of going and
doing it herself to make sure.

Then Oreste arrives with the news of the assassination.

Racine's tragedies usually end with a rapid series of violent actions
taking place off stage and reported by confidants and others. *Andromaque*
is no exception. What we should observe, however, is the skill of the planning. Once Oreste has departed on his mission, we know that an appalling
disaster lies ahead. It did not matter to Racine whether his audiences knew
the story or not: the meeting, first with Pyrrhus, then with Cléone, are

designed to heighten the suspense by delaying the *dénouement*. Nor is knowledge of the 'plot' really material. The production of a play of Racine's, as we know, is essentially an *experience*: what we are all waiting to see by the time we get to Act V is how the performers will bring off that terrific ending.

Oreste, then, reappears and proudly announces what he regards as the success of his mission:

> Madame, c'en est fait, et vous êtes servie:
> Pyrrhus rend à l'autel son infidèle vie.

Hermione greets the news with a gasp of horror:

> Il est mort?

Oreste replies:

> Il expire . . .

He uses the present tense and by his choice of adjective delivers, as it were, a final blow: 'rend . . . son infidèle vie'. When Hermione asks: 'Il est mort?' he corrects her with another present indicative: 'Il expire'. The reply places the tragedy vividly before us. Pyrrhus is done for, but he is still writhing in a stream of blood.

Hermione listens in stunned silence as he describes in detail the wedding ceremony, the crowning of Andromaque, the recognition by Pyrrhus of her son as King of Troy, the Greeks swooping on their victim and the devastating effect on the people. There is another horrified gasp:

> Qu'ont-ils fait!

Oreste continues his account. When she hears the words, 'Vous seule avez poussé les coups', which are intended to show how carefully her instructions have been carried out, Hermione suddenly grasps the full horror of what has happened, seems to come to herself, realizes that whatever she had said and whatever Pyrrhus had done, she is still madly in love with him. She turns on the unhappy Oreste in the middle of a sentence and screams at him:

> Tais-toi, perfide,
> Et n'impute qu'à toi ton lâche parricide . . .

The voice sinks to an agonizing moan with the words

> Barbare, qu'as-tu fait? Avec quelle furie
> As-tu tranché le cours d'une si belle vie?

It rises to a shriek again when she says:

> Mais parle. De son sort qui t'a rendu l'arbitre?
> Pourquoi l'assassiner? Qu'a-t-il fait? A quel titre?
> Qui te l'a dit?

It is another impressive example of Racine's use of a succession of short, sharp sentences which give the speech its drive and offset the formality of the alexandrine. The fact that she had bludgeoned him into murder is brushed aside. He should never have listened to anyone in her state; he should have made her repeat the order a hundred times before lifting a finger. Although it comes too late this time, she again exhibits that insight into the workings of her own mind which belongs to the Racinian character:

> Ah! fallait-il en croire une amante insensée?
> Ne devais-tu pas lire au fond de ma pensée?
> Et ne voyais-tu pas, dans mes emportements,
> Que mon coeur démentait ma bouche à tous moments?

It is fascinating in these closing scenes to watch the different threads drawing together to complete Racine's chosen pattern. Hermione goes on to 'place' Oreste and the voice rises once more to a scream:

> Voilà de ton amour le détestable fruit:
> Tu m'apportais, cruel, le malheur qui te suit.
> C'est toi dont l'ambassade, à tous les deux fatale,
> L'a fait pour son malheur pencher vers ma rivale.

This is the last word on Oreste's role as the Man of Destiny whose arrival in Épirus has brought nothing but disaster to everyone who has come into contact with him.

Then the furious and at the same time bitingly contemptuous dismissal:

> Adieu. Tu peux partir. Je demeure en Épire:
> Je renonce à la Grèce, à Sparte, à son empire,
> A toute ma famille; et c'est assez pour moi,
> Traître, qu'elle ait produit un monstre comme toi.

When we remember Hermione's monstrous promise, we can hardly avoid feeling some sympathy for Oreste in spite of all his *méfaits*.

Hermione's denunciation of Oreste's role is echoed by him with a terrible lucidity in the soliloquy which follows Hermione's exit:

> Est-ce Pyrrhus qui meurt? et suis-je Oreste enfin?' . . .
> J'assassine à regret un roi que je révère;
> Je viole en un jour les droits des souverains,
> Ceux des ambassadeurs, et tous ceux des humains,
> Ceux même des autels où ma fureur l'assiège:
> Je deviens parricide, assassin, sacrilège.

These four lines illustrate once again how much the closing scenes depend for their effect on conciseness; on the rapid succession of short

staccato sentences, anguished questions, and the accumulation of substantives and adjectives such as we find in the last four lines.

Pyrrhus's end is horrible, but one cannot help feeling that there is a sort
of poetic justice about it. He may have felt some regret over his conduct in
the Trojan War, but he was a decidedly ruthless character, as we have seen
from his treatment of Andromaque. He had slaughtered Priam while the
old man was clutching an altar covered in his blood. Now he himself has
just been struck down at the altar by people on his own side. He had told
Andromaque that there was no middle way between love and hate:
Hermione has demonstrated the truth of the observation by having him
murdered after he had abandoned her.

Pylade had agreed to become Oreste's accomplice in carrying off Hermione
and escaping from the palace by a 'secret way'. Now he arrives on the
scene and tells Oreste that there is no time to lose, that they must get out
at once or resign themselves to never leaving it alive. The situation has
undergone a radical change. It is no longer a question of the 'grand coeur'
dashing off triumphantly with his beloved. The 'grand coeur' has been
reduced to an assassin—the assassin, it must be repeated, of the monarch
to whom he was accredited—and is in danger of meeting with rough
justice at the hands of the mob. Hermione has killed herself at the altar,
bending over the body of Pyrrhus as though trying to achieve in death the
union which had eluded her in life.

The announcement of Hermione's suicide by Pylade is the final blow
for Oreste. His collapse into insanity is a realization of the worst fears of a
friend who has always been worried by his 'mélancolie' and his suicidal
tendencies. It is the only occasion in Racine when a character goes mad:

> Quoi! Pyrrhus, je te rencontre encore?
> Trouverai-je partout un rival que j'abhorre?
> Percé de tant de coups, comment t'es-tu sauvé?
> Tiens, tiens, voilà le coup que je t'ai réservé.
> Mais que vois-je? A mes yeux Hermione l'embrasse?
> Elle vient l'arracher au coup qui le menace?
> Dieux! quels affreux regards elle jette sur moi!
> Quels démons, quels serpents traîne-t-elle après soi?
> Hé bien! filles d'enfer, vos mains sont-elles prêtes?
>   Pour qui sont ces serpents qui sifflent sur vos têtes?

It is a scene of tragic farce with a raving madman brandishing his dagger
and swiping wildly at the phantoms of his disordered mind. The word
'coup' is used three times and the vain thrusts are reflected in the construction of the sentences and the pauses. The hallucinatory spectacle of
Hermione embracing Pyrrhus, snatching him out of reach of the dagger
and then giving Oreste a savage look shows the distorting effect of madness on what has happened and what has been said. Pyrrhus and Hermione

are replaced by other and more frightening phantoms: the Furies whose hair is a mass of hissing serpents. The last line shows the remarkable effects that Racine could achieve by simple alliteration.

This is the last and the greatest of the psychological 'storms': it looks back to the storm at sea and completes the drama.

8

In the original version of the play Andromaque made a final appearance when Oreste came to announce the assassination of Pyrrhus. In a speech of twenty-five lines she declared:

> Pyrrhus de mon Hector semble avoir pris la place.

The appearance was a mistake from every point of view. It delayed Oreste's account of the tragedy and gave the impression that instead of marrying Pyrrhus to save her son Andromaque had fallen in love with him, which was quite out of character and reduced her to the same level as the other protagonists, destroyed her special position as the one protagonist who stands for moral values. The present ending avoids all these faults and is in fact perfect. Pylade announces Andromaqué's triumph in these words:

> Aux ordres d'Andromaque ici tout est soumis;
> Ils la traitent en reine, et nous comme ennemis.
> Andromaque, elle-même, à Pyrrhus si rebelle,
> Lui rend tous les devoirs d'une veuve fidèle,
> Commande qu'on le venge, et peut-être sur nous
> Veut venger Troie encore et son premier époux.

Pyrrhus may have been unfaithful to Hermione whom he had never loved, but we know that he had been exemplary in fulfilling his promises to Andromaque. She behaves exactly as she would have expected him to behave if she and not he had died at the altar.

The wheel has come full circle. The Trojan War was been refought on the psychological plane. It has ended in a Trojan victory which has been transferred from the psychological plane to the plane of action. The widow of Hector is Queen of Epirus and her son King of Troy.

NOTES

[1] Racine made three changes in the legend which were essential to the play. In the best known versions the Greeks killed Astyanax before leaving Troy. Andromache was Pyrrhus's reluctant mistress for ten years. He then abandoned her and married Hermione. Orestes turned up and murdered Pyrrhus out of jealousy, but his ambassadorship like Pyrrhus's courtship of Andromache is an invention of Racine's.

[2] The ambassadorship clearly makes his murder of Pyrrhus more heinous than the murder by the Orestes of legend.

[3] See P. Bénichou, *Morales du grand siècle*, 1948, *passim*.

[4] R. C. Knight in *Racine et la Grèce*, 1950, pp. 279–80 and *Racine, Convention and Classicism*, 1952, p. 16.

[5] See p. 14 above.

[6] Pylade is described in the *dramatis personae* as 'ami d'Oreste' which is in keeping with legend. In the play he performs the role of confidant, using the 'standard form of address' when speaking to Oreste who always calls him by his name and uses the second person singular.

[7] It was not an invention of Racine's. Corneille had done it fifteen years earlier in *Pertharite*.

[8] The *mal-aimé* is a recurrent figure at different periods in different literatures. Among modern examples are François Mauriac's *Les Mal-aimés* and Apollinaire's 'La Chanson du mal-aimé'.

[9] Commandant Jules Rouch, 'Le Thème de la Mer dans Racine', in *Comité des Travaux Historiques et Scientifiques: Bulletin de la Section Géographique*, Tome LXIII, 1949 and 1950, p. 29.

[10] P. France, *Racine's Rhetoric*, 1965, pp. 114–63.

[11] Racine uses the word 'tomb', but Hector's body was not brought to Epirus.

[12] *Réflexions critiques sur la poésie et la peinture*, I, 1719, pp. 125–6.

[13] *Classicisme et baroque dans l'oeuvre de Racine*, 1959, p. 135.

[14] *Tragische und komische Elemente in Racines 'Andromaque'*, 1958, pp. 17–18.

[15] This is her reply to the splendid speech discussed on pp. 68–9 above!

[16] *O.C.* I, p. 1108.

[17] An argument used, incidentally, by Hermione when rejecting Oreste!

[18] See p. 70 above.

'BRITANNICUS'

1669

Le combat de la mère et du fils dans *Britannicus* est comme un des ces enchevêtrements monstrueux de reptiles qui ne se défont que lorsque l'un a dévoré l'autre.

THIERRY MAULNIER

CHAPTER 4

'BRITANNICUS'

1669

I

IT is two years since Néron became emperor. He owes his position entirely to his mother. Agrippine stopped at nothing to get her son on to the throne. She induced her husband, the Emperor Claudius, to disinherit his own son and to nominate hers as his successor. His reward was a poor one. Agrippine no doubt felt that she would have a better chance of managing the empire, or managing it in her own way, with a teen-age son instead of a weak and ailing husband on the throne. She therefore persuaded the doctor who was attending the emperor in what might have been his last illness to hurry things up by giving him a dose of poison.

Néron's role seems to have been a passive one. Although he presumably wanted the job, there is no evidence that he took any part in the plotting. He was the obedient youth who simply did as he was told. He even married a girl for whom he felt no attraction because his mother thought that it would improve his prospects of becoming emperor. For the first two years of his reign he has been the docile son.[1] He has enjoyed his position as emperor, but has been content to let his mother do the work and run the empire.

When the play opens there are unmistakable signs that this happy state of affairs is a thing of the past. The trouble began when foreign ambassadors flocked to Rome to pay tribute to the new emperor in the names of their own rulers. It went to Néron's head. He suddenly felt tired of being nagged and lectured by his mother, tired of being treated as a little boy who in spite of his great office was still expected to do as he was told. He made up his mind to be independent, to run the show himself. He has the support of his tutors as well as of the Roman people who are equally tired of being pushed around by an autocratic, interfering woman. Néron is also heartily sick of his demure wife and intends to get rid of her. The turning point came when he caught sight of Junie, the girl who is betrothed to Britannicus, the discarded heir to the throne, and was completely bowled over by her.

There is a radical difference between *Britannicus* and the rest of the secular plays. After the success of *Andromaque* the word went round, or was put round by his enemies, that Racine was only capable of writing about love. His reaction was characteristically vigorous. He at once made up his mind to show people that they were wrong. *Britannicus* is essentially a political drama. The main conflict is not sexual, or sexual with political implications. It is a conflict between mother and son: a mother who is determined to preserve her political power at all costs; a son who is equally determined to break his mother's hold over him, to become emperor in fact as well as in name—and who holds all the trump cards. Although Néron's passion for Junie is as violent as the passions of other protagonists, she is primarily an instrument in the struggle for power between mother and son.

It is commonly assumed that, whatever its political implications, *Britannicus* is a play about good and evil, that Néron's counsellors are almost the equivalent of good and bad 'angels'.[2] This view has recently been challenged by Philip Butler who regards it as a drastic simplification.[3] Although references, or possible references, to religion are reduced to a minimum in *Britannicus*, I remain convinced that Racine presents and intended to present an evil world, that in view of the corruption which is inherent in power, politics was the best way of doing it. We must, however, take into account a number of neglected factors if we are to appreciate the complexity of the play to the full. Nobody defends the murder of Britannicus, but we can see that Néron's own position is one of great danger. Britannicus is a political as well as a sexual rival. In spite of his mother's indignant denials, Néron knows perfectly well that if he does not capitulate she will throw in her lot with Britannicus which could lead to his dethronement and probably to his death. He also knows that as long as Britannicus is alive he will be a threat to his position. It follows that for Néron there is only one solution: the death of Britannicus. It will remove his sole rival for the throne and at the same time deprive his mother of her only real weapon. Néron also believes, mistakenly, that it will automatically deliver Junie to him.

The argument against good and bad counsellors seems to be based to some extent on the view that Burrhus does not possess the complete integrity that we expect of a good counsellor, that he is fully aware of the crimes committed by Agrippine and simply turns a blind eye, relying on the fact that whatever the claims of the discarded heir Néron has been legally recognized as emperor. No one defends Narcisse on moral grounds, but it is clear that he is much shrewder politically than Burrhus and therefore much better equipped to protect the life and throne of his master.

Now we are bound to recognize that in this evil world some compromise on the part of Burrhus is inevitable. He does his best in an impossible situation. He urges Néron to assert himself as emperor, but to remain friendly with his dangerous mother and to drop his plan for divorcing Octavie and marrying Junie. Narcisse successfully counters this sound advice. Néron eliminates his rival, breaks the power of his mother, keeps his throne and loses Junie. Burrhus fails because in this world a decent man stands no chance of succeeding, or could only hope to succeed by discarding his principles and using the same methods against Néron, who is after all his emperor, and Narcisse that they use against Britannicus and Agrippine. Nor can we reasonably overlook the categorical assertion in Racine's second preface. 'J'ai choisi Burrhus', he wrote, 'pour opposer un honnête homme à cette peste de cour.'

2

The scene is a room in the imperial palace. It is the small hours and still pitch dark. Agrippine's confidant is shocked to find her mistress standing alone outside the emperor's bedroom door:

> errant dans le palais sans suite et sans escorte.

Agrippine is waiting for her son to wake so that she can deliver a vigorous protest against the arrest of Junie. The solid common sense of the people is heard in the confidant's firm but respectful

> Madame, retournez dans votre appartement.

The reply is instantaneous:

> Albine, il ne faut pas s'éloigner un moment.

The tension behind the line is a sign that serious trouble is brewing, that Agrippine dare not keep away from her son for a moment if she can avoid it.

It is one of Racine's most impressive openings. We can almost see the entire play in embryo in it. The darkness of the room is the darkness of Racine's world. We shall be reminded continually that it is a physical, moral and psychological darkness. It is plain that Agrippine has already begun to lose her bearings psychologically. It is symbolized by her wandering fumblingly in the dark in the vain hope of establishing contact with her son and eventually recovering her hold over him. But from this moment every step she takes will turn out to be a wrong one.

Racine displays the same mastery in the rest of the scene. He said in his second preface that the tragedy is as much the fall of Agrippine as the death of Britannicus. Agrippine is the source of all the trouble. It is right that she should not only be the first protagonist to make an appearance, but that she should dominate the first act.[4] In the opening scene Racine shows us the various stages which have brought her and everybody else to the present pass and introduces the principal themes. Finally, we should observe that Agrippine's behaviour is identical in one respect with that of all

the other characters: they are all wandering in the dark, trying to find a
way out of an impossible situation.

The protagonists are wandering in the dark. Their immediate aims are in
strong conflict; their ultimate goal is the same. It is described by Agrippine in some lines which show unmistakably that she is already preparing
to take sides with Britannicus and Junie against her son:

> Néron jouit de tout; et moi, pour récompense,
> Il faut qu'entre eux et lui je tienne la balance,
> Afin que quelque jour, par une même loi,
> Britannicus la tienne entre mon fils et moi.

The operative word is 'balance'. The characters are all seeking 'balance'
or a state of equilibrium, meaning the safety of their skins, the security of
their positions, peace of mind. In this world one party can only achieve
equilibrium at heavy cost to the others. There are two ways of doing it:
reconciliation or elimination. Agrippine works for reconciliation; Néron
chooses elimination or liquidation.

Agrippine may favour reconciliation now, but in the past she was the
great exponent of elimination. Albine is startled when she announces
support for Britannicus and Junie. This is the reply:

> Arrête, chère Albine.
> Je sais que j'ai moi seule avancé leur ruine;
> Que du trône, où le sang l'a dû faire monter,
> Britannicus par moi s'est vu précipiter.
> Par moi seule éloigné de l'hymen d'Octavie,
> Le frère de Junie abandonna la vie,
> Silanus, sur qui Claude avait jeté les yeux,
> Et qui comptait Auguste au rang de ses aïeux.

'Ruine' is perhaps the most vital single word in the play. All the characters are doomed, and even though it does not happen in some cases until
after the end of the play, 'ruine' will overtake the lot of them. 'Précipiter'
and 'chute' describe the way it comes about. Someone is 'flung' from the
throne and 'falls' dead after drinking the poison cup.

In the fourth and last scene of Act I Britannicus himself will speak of
Agrippine's activities and will use the same language:

> N'est-ce pas cette même Agrippine
> Que mon père épousa jadis pour sa ruine?[5]

This is one of five occasions on which 'Agrippine' rhymes with 'ruine'.
It is used twice by Britannicus, twice by Agrippine herself, and once by
Néron. Whatever Racine's intention, it seems to me to be as significant as
the rhyme 'Oreste/funeste' in *Andromaque*. It stamps Agrippine as the
instrument of the 'ruine' of everybody with whom she comes into contact:

the Emperor Claudius, Britannicus, Junie, her own ruin, and ultimately that of her son.

Britannicus has no illusions about Agrippine's motives. He will tell Junie in the first scene of Act V that she has changed sides purely in the hope of staving off her own 'ruin':

> Cet ouvrage, Madame, est un coup d'Agrippine:
> Elle a cru que ma perte entraînait sa ruine.

It is a prophetic utterance. If Britannicus has no illusions about Agrippine's motives, he has fatal illusions about Néron's. He fondly imagines that reconciliation is about to take place with his half-brother. He has no idea that a few minutes earlier Néron had told the horrified Burrhus:

> C'en est trop: il faut que sa ruine
> Me délivre à jamais des fureurs d'Agrippine.

Agrippine has changed her tactics; her son has decided to adopt her earlier practices. She was responsible for the first stage in Britannicus's 'ruine'; he will finish the job.

Agrippine has been complaining of the poorness of her 'recompense' or reward for the great services that she has rendered to her son. When her confidant counters by praising Néron's excellent start as emperor, describes him as governing his people like a 'father' and declares that he is beginning where the benevolent Augustus finished, she gets a very dusty answer from Agrippine:

> Que m'importe, après tout, que Néron, plus fidèle,
> D'une longue vertu laisse un jour le modèle?
> Ai-je mis dans sa main le timon de l'État
> Pour le conduire au gré du peuple et du sénat?
> Ah! que de la patrie il soit, s'il veut, le père;
> Mais qu'il songe un peu plus qu'Agrippine est sa mère.

I shall have something more to say later about the word 'conduire'. Its use in this context is particularly revealing. Agrippine is actually denouncing right government—the proper deference to the views of the senate and 'the people'—and demanding instead complete control by herself over the emperor and his policies, or dictatorship instead of democratic rule.

We can see from these exchanges between mistress and confidant that Agrippine is concerned exclusively with her personal interests and that Albine is a good deal more public spirited.

Agrippine is not alone in this. The first impression that the family makes on us is that of a tiny élite isolated from the world in their palace where they are engaged in private quarrels. That, at any rate, is how it strikes Albine. She is not convinced that Agrippine has been badly treated by a son who in the eyes of the people has made such an excellent start as emperor:

> Une injuste frayeur vous alarme peut-être.

She goes on to make a very pertinent comment:

> Mais si Néron pour vous n'est plus ce qu'il doit être,
> Du moins son changement ne vient pas jusqu'à nous,
> Et ce sont des secrets entre César et vous.

Albine speaks with the authoritative voice of 'the people'. 'Nous', in this context, stands for 'us', the public, the Roman people, as distinct from 'you', the royal family engaged in incomprehensible private squabbles. She is convinced, or more probably is trying to convince herself, that these private squabbles will not go any further, will not develop into public scandals and upset 'us', the people.

That of course is where she is wrong. It is precisely because they are the royal family that, as I suggested earlier, their private feuds will spread outwards and become events: that 'the people' will kill the infamous Narcisse and escort Junie to the temple of the Vestals, making sure in that way that their emperor does not get the girl he wants.

Agrippine's imagination is dominated by the past. In the passage in the first scene recounting the stages which have landed her in her present unhappy position, she looks back nostalgically to the days when the youthful Néron did indeed remember that Agrippine was his mother and left her virtually in control of the empire.

The recital is preceded by a remarkable line which shows the way things are moving:

> Je vois mes honneurs croître, et tomber mon crédit.

The gutteral 'croître' suggests the brittleness of her position and her 'honours'; the heavy thud of 'tomber' a fall which somehow demolishes the fragile 'crédit' with its thin, shrill sound. The antithesis between 'croître' and 'tomber' is emphasized by the firm caesura at the hemistich.

Agrippine goes on:

> Non, non, le temps n'est plus que Néron, jeune encore,
> Me renvoyait les voeux d'une cour qui l'adore,
> Lorsqu'il se reposait sur moi de tout l'État,
> Que mon ordre au palais assemblait le sénat,
> Et que derrière un voile, invisible et présente,
> J'étais de ce grand corps l'âme toute-puissante.
> Des volontés de Rome alors mal assuré,
> Néron de sa grandeur n'était point enivré.

The spectacle of Agrippine hidden from sight yet dominating the proceedings—'invisible, et présente' and the last word rhyming with 'toute-puissante'—is remarkable in itself. It also looks forward both to Néron standing in the shadow watching the arrival of Junie after her arrest and to the cruel game he plays with her at her first meeting with Britannicus.

We should observe Racine's use of tenses in Agrippine's recital of her misfortunes. She begins with the present tense:

> Non, non, le temps n'est plus . . .

She changes to the imperfect to describe what once appeared to be a stable situation. Caesar used to send her greetings from an adoring court; he used to rely on her in all matters of State; she used to convene the senate, was indeed the moving spirit in everything:

> J'étais de ce grand corps l'âme toute-puissante.

She recalls the first hitch: the day when the sight of the foreign ambassadors suddenly made Néron aware of his grandeur, went to his head—this is the meaning of 'enivré' in the final line of the last passage reinforced by 'ébloui' in the next—and prompted him to administer a crushing rebuff to his mother in public:

> Ce jour, ce triste jour frappe encor ma mémoire,
> Où Néron fut lui-même ébloui de sa gloire,
> Quand les ambassadeurs de tant de rois divers
> Vinrent le reconnaître au nom de l'univers.
> Sur son trône avec lui j'allais prendre ma place.
> J'ignore quel conseil prépara ma disgrâce:
> Quoi qu'il en soit, Néron, d'aussi loin qu'il me vit,
> Laissa sur son visage éclater son dépit.
> Mon coeur même en conçut un malheureux augure.
> L'ingrat, d'un faux respect colorant son injure,
> Se leva par avance, et courant m'embrasser,
> M'écarta du trône où je m'allais placer.
> Depuis ce coup fatal, le pouvoir d'Agrippine
> Vers sa chute, à grands pas, chaque jour s'achemine.

There is a tragic reverberation about the line which introduces the second part of the recital:

> Ce jour, ce triste jour frappe encor ma mémoire . . .

She is not simply looking back from a troubled and insecure present to the days when she was triumphant; the present tense shows that she is still suffering from the painful shock of her public rebuff. Past definites are used to describe the disastrous occasion. They are made more effective, more telling by being interspersed with imperfects describing unfinished movements in the direction of the throne when the blow fell: 'Sur son trône avec lui j'*allais* prendre ma place . . . Néron, d'aussi loin qu'il me

vit, Laissa sur son visage . . . Se *leva* par avance . . . M'*écarta* du trône où je
m'*allais* placer . . .'

It is an example of the way in which words seem to do what they say by
interrupting Agrippine's actions. She was moving, no doubt in a slow and
dignified manner, in the direction of the throne. Néron suddenly caught
sight of her, showed his displeasure by the expression on his face, jumped
to his feet, ran towards her, embraced her and at the same time brutally
shoved her in a different direction, cutting her off from the throne which
is underlined by the sharp 'M'écarta'. The past definites have the additional effect of cancelling, as it were, the imperfect indicatives used in the
first part of the recital where they describe not unfinished movements, but
what I called an apparently continuing and stable situation.

The recital closes with a return to the present tense which emphasizes
the lasting pain of the rebuff and enlarges on its consequences:

> Depuis ce coup fatal, // le pouvoir d'Agrippine
> Vers sa chute, / à grands pas, // chaque jour / s'achemine.

The couplet is a good illustration of Racine's skill in placing his verbs and
the striking effects that he achieves by it. The distance between subject
and verb and the pushing of the verb to the end of the second line make us
feel the slow, inescapable disintegration of Agrippine's power, convey the
impression of a relentless movement towards some doom which is hidden
in the future. Nor should we miss the connection between 'se leva par
avance' and Agrippine's 'avancé leur ruine' a few lines earlier. Agrippine
thrust Britannicus on to a path leading to disaster; she will be dragged to
disaster in his wake.

The effect of the passage is enhanced by the versification, particularly
the regular pauses in the last line after the third, sixth and ninth syllables
with the equivalent of a second caesura after the twelfth which heightens
the grim sense of slow, inexorable movement towards the abyss. In short,
the process of disintegration, which began in the first line I quoted, concludes with the prospect of something even worse to come.

Although Agrippine takes a pessimistic view of the situation, she has no
intention of abandoning the struggle. This brings her into conflict not only
with her son, but with both his counsellors. She remarks of her switch to
Britannicus's side:

> Je m'assure un port dans la tempête.
> Néron m'échappera, si ce frein ne l'arrête.

She is working for reconciliation, but it is clear from the word 'frein'
that it is a decidedly tough form of reconciliation. 'Frein' is one of five
words which describe the nature of the antagonisms it sets up. The other
four are 'affranchir' or 'affranchissement', 'conduire', 'contrainte' and

'joug'. Agrippine simply wants to put the clock back. For her 'affranchir', which means the end of 'brakes', 'restraints' and 'yokes', is simply a dirty word. In spite of her unorthodox moral views, she is highly indignant at the idea of the break-up of Néron's marriage:

> A son épouse on donne une rivale;
> On *affranchit* Néron de la foi conjugale.

It was a *mariage de raison* which no longer affects Néron's position as emperor. Agrippine's only objection is that divorce would be the undoing of something that she had done.

When Britannicus is dead she will say to Néron:

> Dans le fond de ton coeur je sais que tu me hais;
> Tu voudras t'*affranchir du joug de mes bienfaits.*

It is an unintentionally neat description of the way in which her 'bien-faits' have become for him a burden or a 'yoke'. The use of the future tense suggests a reluctance on the part of Agrippine to admit that by the murder of Britannicus he has in fact removed or broken the 'yoke'.

Burrhus and Narcisse, as we know, are both in favour of two very different forms of 'affranchissement'. When Burrhus says to Agrippine:

> Mais, Madame, Néron suffit pour se *conduire.*
> J'obéis, sans prétendre à l'honneur de l'instruire,

it is clear that he is using the word 'conduire' in a different sense—a posi-tive sense—from Agrippine when she spoke of Néron 'running' the State in the manner desired by the people and the senate.

We can see that these words not only have a different meaning for different speakers, but that they can be spoken with a different intonation by the same speaker. When Burrhus realizes that control has been irre-mediably lost and that Néron has decided on the kind of 'affranchisse-ment' advocated by Narcisse, he reproaches himself in these terms:

> Cette férocité que tu croyais fléchir
> De tes faibles liens est prête à s'*affranchir.*

We shall see presently that the most striking use of the word will be made by Néron himself.

3

Racine's description of Néron as *un monstre naissant* is revealing. Since the war there have been two outstanding interpretations of the role, one by Daniel Ivernel at the Vieux Colombier, the other by Robert Hirsch. Ivernel with his large figure and powerful voice interpreted the part as that of a violent teen-ager. Hirsch, an immensely versatile actor who has greatly distinguished himself in comic roles in the plays of Georges Feydeau, presented him with plenty of force but rather more subtlety as a juvenile delinquent. The sight of him sidling down the wide staircase in the Marie Bell production in London in 1960 was the only occasion on which I have heard *legitimate* laughter at a performance of any of Racine's tragedies.[6]

It seems to me that this is probably what Racine intended. It is because of his fear of his mother that Néron finally rejects the respectable form of 'affranchissement' proposed by Burrhus and follows the advice of the ruthlessly clearsighted Narcisse. What is important is that this character is not so much a developing as an evolving one. He is potentially bad, but his immaturity is evident in his perpetual vacillations and it is not until the end of the play that the juvenile delinquent turns into the adult criminal. For most of the time he is caught between the cross-fire of Burrhus and Narcisse. He reacts violently against his mother's domination, but until the meeting with Narcisse in the last scene of Act IV it is uncertain, or appears uncertain, which direction he will take.

We know that Junie's arrest has brought the palace troubles to a head. The hostility between the occupants is coming into the open. They are moving towards what is known as 'confrontation' or a showdown, beginning with Agrippine's unsuccessful attempts to see her son and give him a rating for his treatment of Junie. This leads naturally and very effectively to Néron's entry at the beginning of Act II and to his eye-witness account of the incident which will prove decisive in the lives of all the characters.

It can hardly have been an accident that when we first meet Néron both Burrhus and Narcisse are present or that he quickly gets rid of Burrhus so that he can be alone with Narcisse who is theoretically Britannicus's confidant. He announces that he is in love with Junie and goes on to describe her arrival at the palace in a speech which contains some of the finest poetry that Racine ever wrote:

> Excité d'un désir curieux,
> Cette nuit je l'ai vue arriver en ces lieux,
> Triste, levant au ciel ses yeux mouillés de larmes,
> Qui brillaient au travers des flambeaux et des armes:
> Belle, sans ornements, dans le simple appareil
> D'une beauté qu'on vient d'arracher au sommeil.
> Que veux-tu? Je ne sais si cette négligence,
> Les ombres, les flambeaux, les cris et le silence,
> Et le farouche aspect de ses fiers ravisseurs
> Relevaient de ses yeux les timides douceurs.
> Quoi qu'il en soit, ravi d'une si belle vue,
> J'ai voulu lui parler, et ma voix s'est perdue:
> Immobile, saisi d'un long étonnement,
> Je l'ai laissé passer dans son appartement.

J'ai passé dans le mien. C'est là que solitaire,
Trop présente à mes yeux, je croyais lui parler;
J'aimais jusqu'à ses pleurs que je faisais couler.
Quelquefois, mais trop tard, je lui demandais grâce;
J'employais les soupirs, et même la menace.
Voilà comme, occupé de mon nouvel amour,
Mes yeux, sans se fermer ont attendu le jour.

The arrest took place shortly before the opening of the play. It was
therefore the dead of night. We see and hear the procession of soldiers
tramping through the palace with their captive. There is a vivid contrast
between the timid, weeping prisoner, who has been dragged out of bed
and is still presumably wearing her nightdress, and the rough, tough
soldiery with their clanking weapons. The most important thing is the
torches which the soldiers are carrying. They are the only form of light in
the huge dark room. They have the effect of spotlighting the victim. What
we are watching in fact is Innocence being brought into a dark and evil
world and her white dress standing out against the surrounding darkness.
She does not see Néron. He is like his mother on a different occasion,
'invisible and present'. He is also all-powerful: the hidden figure who gave
the order for the arrest and who dominates the proceedings.

That is the general impression created by the scene. What is even more
important is the personal effect on Néron:

> Excité d'un désir curieux,
> Cette nuit je l'ai vue arriver en ces lieux.

In the first two lines the sharp vowel sounds, the *c*-s and *s*-s convey perfectly the young man's sensual excitement at the sight of the gentle captive
being hustled along by the soldiers.

> Triste, / levant au ciel // ses yeux / mouillés de larmes,
> Qui brillaient au travers // des flambeaux / et des armes:
> Belle, / sans ornements, // dans le simple appareil
> D'une beauté / qu'on vient // d'arracher au sommeil.

There is a rapturous lyrical note in these lines with the liquid *l*-s and
the pauses. Néron suddenly becomes almost engagingly boyish as he
dilates on the sight of the girl among the soldiers and the harsh 'arracher'
sounds the discordant note. We observe, too, the shapeliness of the presentation, 'Triste, levant au ciel' matching the 'Belle, sans ornements'.

Néron begins to speculate on the reasons for his own rapture:

> Je ne sais // si cette négligence,
> Les ombres, / les flambeaux, // les cris / et le silence
> Et le farouche aspect // de ses fiers ravisseurs
> Relevaient de ses yeux // les timides douceurs.

Once again the words do what they say. The effect depends on a series of contrasts: the liquid *l*-s, the swish of the *s*-s and *c*-s, the shrill *i*-s, the grating *r*-s in 'farouche', 'fiers' and 'ravisseurs' coupled with the heavy sound of 'ombres' and 'flambeaux'. They emphasize the way in which the sight of the rough guards and their gentle prisoner titilates the desires of the onlooker. He, too, would like to find himself in possession, to become a 'ravisseur' in a somewhat different sense.

One of the most interesting things about the passage, indeed, is the way in which the movement of the procession is reflected in the movement of his feelings. The rapid march of the soldiers produces a rapid rise in his excitement. A limit is reached and feeling, so to speak, comes to a halt:

> J'ai voulu lui parler, // et ma voix // s'est perdue:
> Immobile, / saisi // d'un long étonnement,
> Je l'ai laissé passer // dans son appartement . . .

The lines give the impression of something like a switch to slow motion in film. We are conscious of the effort in 'voulu'. It is brought to a stop at the firm caesura. The voice drops. It is emphasized in performance by another strong pause after the ninth syllable and the fading of the voice in 's'est perdue'. The effect on Néron becomes hypnotic. In the heavy four-syllable 'immobile', balanced by the equally heavy four-syllable 'étonnement', we feel him clamped to the ground. The two words together evoke the image of the lovesick young man gazing, motionless, unable to speak, as the prisoner and her savage escort pass on and vanish from the scene.

In his own room he comes to life again, grows positively histrionic. We see him marching up and down, composing speeches like the traditional lover in the throes of a violent passion:

> Trop présente à mes yeux, je croyais lui parler;
> J'aimais jusqu'à ses pleurs que je faisais couler.
> Quelquefois, mais trop tard, je lui demandais grâce;
> J'employais les soupirs, et même la menace.

It is an extraordinary picture of a *coup de foudre*: the young man wandering out of curiosity to watch his men bring in the prisoner; carried away by the sight of her beauty which engraves itself on his mind and by the contrast between captors and captive; rooted to the ground, spell-bound by the enormous impact the girl makes on him; then like an amorous swain creeping away to his room where in a sort of trance he almost imagines that the girl is there and rehearses speeches which will be rather different when he comes to deliver them.

There is a contrast, too, between 'soupirs' and 'menace'. It hints at a dualism in Néron's make-up. 'Soupirs' belongs to the amorous swain, 'menace' to the potential aggressor.

Néron is young and unsure of himself. He looks to Narcisse for re-assurance:

> Mais je m'en fais peut-être une trop belle image;
> Elle m'est apparue avec trop d'avantage:
> Narcisse, qu'en dis-tu?

Narcisse, always ready with the subversive remark, expresses surprise that Junie should have been kept hidden from Caesar for so long. Néron fixes on it:

> soit que sa colère
> M'imputât le malheur qui lui ravit son frère;
> Soit que son coeur, jaloux d'une austère fierté,
> Enviât à nos yeux sa naissante beauté;
> Fidèle à sa douleur, et dans l'ombre enfermée,
> Elle se dérobait même à sa renommée.
> Et c'est cette vertu, si nouvelle à la cour,
> Dont la persévérance irrite mon amour.

It is going too far to suggest, as I myself once did, that Néron has undergone a change, has moved in front of our eyes from a position inside the moral code to one outside it. It is clear, however, from the element of perversity in these last lines that he has begun to change and we can see the direction he will take. When he saw Junie arrive in the palace his first reactions were spontaneous. Without realizing it, he was moved by the spectacle of injured innocence. A sleepless night spent brooding over what he had seen and contact with Narcisse have started the change. 'Timides douceurs' was a young man's tribute to innocence; 'austère fierté' and 'cette vertu, si nouvelle à la cour' are criticisms. They 'irritate' not only his love, but his pride. At the slightest encouragement Roman women fall over themselves to try to please Caesar. Only Junie is aloof:

> Seule dans son palais la modeste Junie
> Regarde leurs honneurs comme une ignominie,
> Fuit, et ne daigne pas peut-être s'informer
> Si César est aimable, ou bien s'il sait aimer.

Narcisse is quick to see that Néron's passion for Junie could be a very effective weapon for resolving his problems. He urges him to repudiate Octavie and marry Junie. He cites precedents for imperial divorce. Néron is afraid of the opposition: Octavie herself, Agrippine, Burrhus, Sénèque, the Roman people and what he describes, in a reference to his own good behaviour, as 'trois ans de vertus.'[7] It soon becomes apparent, however, that what is really worrying him is the opposition of 'l'implacable Agrippine', and this produces another remarkable piece of self-revelation:

> Éloigné de ses yeux, j'ordonne, je menace,
> J'écoute vos conseils, j'ose les approuver;
> Je m'excite contre elle, et tâche à la braver.
> Mais (je t'expose ici mon âme toute nue)
> Sitôt que mon malheur me ramène à sa vue,
> Soit que je n'ose encor démentir le pouvoir
> De ces yeux où j'ai lu si longtemps mon devoir;

Soit qu'à tant de bienfaits ma mémoire fidèle
Lui soumette en secret tout ce que je tiens d'elle,
Mais enfin mes efforts ne me servent de rien;
Mon génie étonné tremble devant le sien.
Et c'est pour m'affranchir de cette dépendance,
Que je la fuis partout, que même je l'offense,
Et que de temps en temps j'irrite ses ennuis
Afin qu'elle m'évite autant que le la fuis.

Since the first appearance over forty years ago of Leo Spitzer's famous essay on Racine's style, it has become almost a commonplace of Racine criticism that the plays are full of references to 'eyes'.[8] They are specially important in *Britannicus*. There are eyes turned towards Junie who seems to offer hope of some kind of salvation in an evil world; there are the eyes of people watching in concealed positions like Néron himself and the anguish of the victims knowing that hostile eyes are following every movement, every change of expression on their faces. Finally, there is Néron's own anguish at the recollection of his mother's terrifying look.[9]

It is interesting to compare Néron's account of Junie's arrival at the palace with the present passage. The first passage contains four references to eyes, the second three. We have seen that the appearance of Junie had an hypnotic effect on Néron who stood rooted to the ground as she passed, unable to utter a word. The effect of his mother's eyes is quite different. It is not so much hypnotic as paralysing. Néron and Agrippine are engaged in a psychological struggle for power. *Legally*, the power is in Néron's hands; *psychologically* he is still the underdog who is unable to wield it because of his mother's hold over him. This passage shows us why. Néron is a divided personality. It would scarcely be an exaggeration to say that there are two Nérons: the emperor and the 'little boy'. When his mother is out of the way he is the master, commanding, threatening. He is terrified of a direct confrontation with her. He knows that the usual tricks, subterfuges, pretences will not work, that he will be reduced by her gaze to a state of complete helplessness, that he will become once again the 'little boy' who remembers all she has done for him and will be sternly rebuked for some deviation from the path of duty or what his mother, with her somewhat unusual system, regards as her son's duty. Worst of all, he knows that he will be quite incapable of refusing any of her demands which are always in conflict with his own plans.

The paralysing effect of the long appraising look is apparent in

Mon génie étonné tremble devant le sien.

It is an example of the way in which we have to adapt ourselves to Racine's idiom. 'Étonné' was a far stronger word in the seventeenth century than it is today and is roughly the equivalent of the modern 'foudroyé'. The look leaves Néron speechless. It penetrates his innermost being and creates an intense sense of guilt combined with very real fear. It is responsible for the feeling that he must break her hold at all costs. He is not yet, as we know, either an adult or an integrated person. In his mind 'affranchissement'—this is what I called earlier the lost striking use of the word—is synonymous with growing up. It has a positive and a negative meaning. Néron must somehow get rid of or, better, 'eliminate' the frightened 'little boy' from his make-up and assert himself, must become the master who 'commands, threatens' on all occasions. That is exactly what his mother is trying to prevent. She is determined that so long as she is alive he shall never be allowed to grow up, that behind the imperial façade he shall remain the 'little boy' while she wields the real power. That is the cause of the disaster. Underlying the entire passage is a deeper sense: the sense that it is a struggle to the death.

Narcisse advises Néron to banish Britannicus so that he can repudiate Octavie and marry Junie. Néron suddenly catches sight of Junie who is on her way to visit Octavie. This suggests a more ruthless plan. Narcisse is sent to fetch Britannicus: Néron intercepts Junie.

It is a highly effective piece of stagecraft. We have seen the re-enactment of the *coup de foudre* and heard Néron rehearsing the speeches he intended to make when he met Junie. Then, before he is fully prepared for it, he finds himself face to face with his prospective 'victim'.

Néron begins in a tone of conventional gallantry:

> Vous vous troublez, Madame, et changez de visage.
> Lisez-vous dans mes yeux quelque triste présage?

There is an underlying irony. Junie is badly upset when she unexpectedly finds herself in Néron's presence while she is on her way to visit another gentle soul. She may well read some 'triste présage' in his eyes. The irony lies in the fact that those eyes will be watching her from a concealed position when she meets Britannicus.

Néron continues in the same vein:

> Quoi, Madame! Est-ce donc une légère offense
> De m'avoir si longtemps caché votre présence? . . .
> Pourquoi, de cette gloire exclus jusqu'à ce jour,
> M'avez-vous, sans pitié, relégué dans ma cour?

The irony of the reference to 'eyes' in the first passage is heightened by the 'caché votre présence' in the second.

Junie makes no secret of her love for Britannicus. She remarks that Claudius and Agrippine both intended her to marry him. The reference to Agrippine gets Néron on the raw:

> Ma mère a ses desseins, Madame, et j'ai les miens.
> Ne parlons plus ici de Claude et d'Agrippine.

She is appalled when he goes on to announce that he intends to repudiate Britannicus's unfortunate sister and marry her. Yet she remains courteous, dignified, logical—and firm. She cannot understand why she has been brought to the palace like a 'criminal' and then offered Octavie's place. It is very well put:

> J'ose dire pourtant que je n'ai mérité
> Ni cet excès d'honneur, ni cette indignité.

There is a moving picture of her unhappy childhood which is at the same time a condemnation of the world in which she finds herself:

> Et pouvez-vous, Seigneur, souhaiter qu'une fille
> Qui vit presque en naissant éteindre sa famille,
> Qui dans l'obscurité nourrissant sa douleur,
> S'est fait une vertu conforme à son malheur,
> Passe subitement de cette nuit profonde
> Dans un rang qui l'expose aux yeux de tout le monde,
> Dont je n'ai pu de loin soutenir la clarté,
> Et dont une autre enfin remplit la majesté?

Although Junie does not know it, this is an answer to Néron's own speculations in the previous scene. There is no 'colère'; there is perhaps a touch of 'austère fierté'; there is certainly a 'vertu' which is new at Néron's court, and her 'conforme à son malheur' confirms his 'Fidèle à sa douleur, et dans l'ombre enfermée'. Her references to 'darkness', to 'night' and to 'light' are different from most of the others in the play. There is nothing sinister about them. Her start in life was so terrible that all she wants is to hide from the 'glare'—this is the real meaning of 'clarté'—of publicity, to marry Britannicus and comfort someone who has been even more unfortunate than herself or, as she puts it:

> Ses honneurs abolis, son palais déserté,
> La fuite d'une cour que sa chute a bannie . . .

It is a striking example of Racinian concision. In two lines we have a vivid glimpse of the completely abandoned heir to the throne. It is the third and last appearance of the word 'chute' which has now been used by Agrippine, Britannicus and Junie who will all suffer 'falls'.

Néron is unmoved. The blackmailer gets to work. There is first the threat of the danger of refusing the 'solide gloire' offered by Caesar, then the announcement of the cruel game he intends to play:

> Caché près de ces lieux, je vous verrai, Madame.
> Renfermez votre amour dans le fond de votre âme.
> Vous n'aurez point pour moi de langages secrets:
> J'entendrai des regards que vous croirez muets;
> Et sa perte sera l'infaillible salaire
> D'un geste ou d'un soupir échappé pour lui plaire.

It is cruelty of the most wanton kind. If Junie had denied her attachment to Britannicus, it might have been a way of putting her to the test. Instead, she is to be tortured as a reward for her frankness. She makes a desperate effort to escape. It is too late. The rapturous Britannicus is already there and she has to go through with the anguished meeting. She has, however courteously, rebuffed the impassioned emperor: she must therefore be made to rebuff his rival, knowing that if she fails Britannicus will pay for the failure with his life. She tries, in some powerfully evocative lines, to warn him, to make him understand that she is playing a part:

> Vous êtes en des lieux tout pleins de sa puissance.
> Ces murs même, Seigneur, peuvent avoir des yeux;
> Et jamais l'Empereur n'est absent de ces lieux.

The attempt is a failure. Néron has won the round. In fact, he has done better than he expected: Britannicus leaves in a huff.

In *Britannicus* the *jeunes premiers* come into their own for the first time. It is a nice point to decide whether Junie or Monime is the most attractive of Racine's heroines. It is a matter of personal choice, but we can see that they have a good deal in common. They are both people of absolute integrity and show great courage in standing up to the aggressors who try to force marriage on them. Junie is visibly much more mature than Britannicus. He has suffered greater wrongs than any of the other characters. It has made him into a sad, abandoned and rather sulky youth. He turns impetuously against Junie after the monstrous trick Néron plays on them. The next time they meet she explains what happened. He is still not satisfied. Surely she should have found a way of warning him by the expression on her face. This attitude is one of the clearest signs of his immaturity. Junie very properly puts him in his place in lines which show how much more mature she is than he:

> Dans un temps plus heureux ma juste impatience
> Vous ferait repentir de votre défiance.

This does not affect their role in the play. Junie's comments on the world in which they find themselves in Act V, Sc. 1, place everything in the right perspective:

> hélas! dans cette cour
> Combien tout ce qu'on dit est loin de ce qu'on pense!
> Que la bouche et le coeur sont peu d'intelligence!
> Avec combien de joie on y trahit sa foi!
> Quel séjour étranger et pour vous et pour moi!

The last line is of particular importance. It is an outright condemnation of the conduct of the people on the other side, an assertion that in such an atmosphere of moral corruption the *jeunes premiers* are completely out of

place, are 'outsiders' in a world which is totally alien to them. She has
stated her own positive principles at the first meeting with Néron; they
are the opposite of what she is condemning here:

> Mais toujours de mon coeur ma bouche est l'interprète.
> Absente de la cour, je n'ai pas dû penser,
> Seigneur, qu'en l'art de feindre il fallût m'exercer.

They are matched by the forthrightness with which Burrhus addresses
Agrippine:

> Je répondrai, Madame, avec la liberté
> D'un soldat qui sait mal farder la vérité.

It is part of the irony of the situation that not even Junie and Britannicus can avoid some manoeuvring. Junie's pretended indifference at the
meeting with Britannicus was mild in all conscience. Britannicus's is more
serious. In the first act he complained to Narcisse that his supposed
friends had betrayed his 'secrets'. He made it clear that he had no intention of abandoning his claim to the throne and sent Narcisse to pry into
Néron's 'secrets'. Narcisse went straight to Néron and gave him away.

Their manoeuvres may be justified; their effect on their fortunes is
fatal. Junie's simulated indifference produces a temporary breach with
Britannicus. At their next meeting there is an equally impetuous reconciliation by Britannicus. But Narcisse has warned Néron of the meeting.
He arrives to find Britannicus at Junie's feet:

> Prince, continuez des transports si charmants.

It leads to a slanging match, to the most violent scene in the tragedy and
undoubtedly plays a large part in Néron's ultimate decision to have
Britannicus murdered. For there can be no possible doubt that he is
Néron's rival in politics and in love, and a danger to him.

This does not alter the fact that it is the *jeunes premiers*, together with
Burrhus, who provide a positive standard, place everything in the right
perspective. They stand for Innocence trapped in the world of the wicked
whose sins are in a very real sense visited on the children.

4

When we look back at the first three acts we see how effectively they are
conceived. The first scene of all introduces the main themes and places
the audience completely in the picture. At the same time it reveals Agrippine's state of mind and her dangerous intentions. In the second she is
surprised to see Burrhus emerge from Néron's room which shows that he
was engaged in business with her son and that she had been deliberately

kept out. He has come to announce a new order by the emperor. There is
so much friction between them that we do not learn until the first scene of
Act II that it was an order for the banishment of Agrippine's ally Pallas.
It is the first of a series of refusals by Agrippine to listen to Burrhus's
advice: refusals that she will come to regret bitterly and will admit were
mistakes when she learns of the murder of Britannicus. In the third scene
Britannicus comes running on to the stage in a state over Junie's arrest.
Agrippine has no idea of Narcisse's sinister role and though he is present
she hints at the help she is prepared to give Britannicus. We know that in
the final scene Britannicus gives himself away to the man whom he believes to be his trusty servant and who will be mainly responsible for his
death.

In the second act there is the same kind of parallelism that we found in
Andromaque. We have been given Agrippine's view of the situation; we
now have Néron's. Although Narcisse is officially Britannicus's confidant,
his talk with Néron in Scene 2 corresponds to Agrippine's talk with Albine
in the opening scene of the play. The same is true of the next scene.
Néron's meeting with Junie matches Agrippine's with Britannicus. She
was dealing with a past victim whom she is now prepared to help purely
in her own interests; Néron deals with his future victims. His cat-and-
mouse game is the first step in their downfall which will nullify Agrippine's intentions towards them.

It is almost entirely on account of Néron's jealousy that in Act III hostilities become open and avowed and there are more clashes. Those who
are trying to restrain or to put the 'brake' on Néron begin to realize what
is in store for them. In the first scene Néron, who expresses himself with
youthful arrogance, tells Burrhus that though he accepts his advice on
military questions, 'love is a different matter' on which he is not qualified
to speak and that whatever his views Néron is determined to have Junie.
This leads to Burrhus's changed attitude to 'affranchissement' in Scene 2.
It is followed by another tiff with Agrippine, a further attempt by Albine
to reason with her mistress and a second meeting between Agrippine and
Britannicus which like the earlier one takes place in the presence of
Narcisse. Britannicus chides Agrippine petulantly for having done her
work too well is dispossessing him of the throne. She behaves with her
usual haughtiness, but is rather more forthcoming about help. He is to
trust her and all will be well. Given the presence of Narcisse, nothing
could be more dangerously indiscreet than the words she uses:

> J'ai promis, il suffit . . .
> Le coupable Néron fuit en vain ma colère . . .

Narcisse does his best to foster Britannicus's bad feeling towards Junie
and engineers the disastrous clash in Scene 8 which leads to Britannicus's

arrest. The act closes with another protest by Burrhus who gets very short shrift from Néron.

Act IV is decisive. The short opening scene, in which Burrhus tells Agrippine that her son has agreed to see her and sternly urges reconciliation, is followed by Néron's meetings with Agrippine, Burrhus and Narcisse.

Agrippine's speech in Scene 2 is rightly regarded as one of the highlights of the play and of Racine's work. It is a superb piece of dialectic in which every imaginable device is used to restore the mother's hold over the son and is combined with an impressive range of tone.

It begins with the voice of a tired and long-suffering mother addressing a naughty, wayward child:

> Approchez-vous, Néron, et prenez votre place.
> On veut sur vos soupçons que je vous satisfasse.
> J'ignore de quel crime on a pu me noircir:
> De tous ceux que j'ai faits je vais vous éclaircir.

The alliteration, the *p*-s, *s*-s and *c*-s, give the impression of a discourse punctuated by weary sighs.

She describes calmly and yet with complete cynicism the steps she took to secure the throne for her son:

> Quand de Britannicus la mère condamnée
> Laissa de Claudius disputer l'hymenée,
> Parmi tant de beautés qui briguèrent son choix,
> Qui de ses affranchis mendièrent les voix,
> Je souhaitai son lit, dans la seule pensée
> De vous laisser au trône où je serais placée.
> Je fléchis mon orgueil, j'allai prier Pallas.
> Son maître, chaque jour caressé dans mes bras,
> Prit insensiblement dans les yeux de sa nièce
> L'amour où je voulais amener sa tendresse.
> Mais ce lien du sang qui nous joignait tous deux
> Écartait Claudius d'un lit incestueux.
> Il n'osait épouser la fille de son frère.
> Le sénat fut séduit: une loi moins sévère
> Mit Claude dans mon lit, et Rome à mes genoux.

A great deal has been written about the smallness of Racine's vocabulary. This is one of the passages which demonstrate how greatly the simple colourless words and the resulting understatement heighten the effect. When she says

> Je fléchis mon orgueil, j'allai prier Pallas,

we know that 'prier' means: 'I gave myself to him in return for a promise to help me into the emperor's bed and on to his throne'.

In spite of the euphemisms and the understatement, Agrippine's brazenness comes out in the repeated 'throne', 'bed' and power. The ageing emperor is seen as an old goat, delighted to jump into bed with his well-favoured niece, but hesitating to commit himself to a union which was officially 'incestuous'. Her own lack of enthusiasm for the game is apparent in the tired reference to her 'sole aim':

> Je souhaitai son lit, dans la seule pensée
> De vous laisser au trône où je serais placée.

At this point she emerges plainly as the strumpet, ready to barter her body for power and to use the strumpet's wiles to achieve her end:

> Son maître, chaque jour caressé dans mes bras,
> Prit insensiblement dans les yeux de sa nièce
> L'amour où je voulais amener sa tendresse.

The s-s and the slow movement of the lines suggest once again the strumpet engaged in her sexual games, skilfully goading the old man on until he becomes frenzied, determined to have her for good. 'Tendresse' is a euphemism for lecherousness: 'l'amour' is the trap in which he becomes a prisoner. It is underlined by the last two verses:

> Le sénat fut séduit: une loi moins sévère
> Mit Claude dans mon lit, et Rome à mes genoux.

In the use of the active verb 'mit', rhyming internally with 'lit', we hear the snap of the trap closing. A moment ago she was saying, 'Je souhaitai *son* lit': now, a changed law 'Mit Claude dans *mon* lit'. Nor should we miss the striking way in which the single verb governs the emperor and Rome, the bed and the people. The order of the words, the strong caesuras in both lines and the absence of any other pauses give the couplet its extraordinary conciseness which invests the process described with a sort of relentless logic: seduction of senate; change in the law; emperor in 'my' bed; Rome at 'my' knees.

In the next line Agrippine reverts to the weary, patient tone:

> C'était beaucoup pour moi, ce n'était rien pour vous.

Five lines later it is repeated:

> Ce n'était rien encore.

She takes Néron remorselessly through the list of crimes by which she ensured that Claudius disinherited his own son in favour of hers, turning the usurper into the legal heir:

> L'exil me délivra des plus séditieux . . .

This is another euphemism. Anyone who opposed her outrageous plans was branded as 'seditious' and quietly removed from the centre of political

intrigue by banishment or murder. Britannicus was systematically isolated. With her usual cynicism she describes the way in which she prevented the repentant emperor from doing tardy justice to his son:

> Il connut son erreur . . .
> Et voulut, mais trop tard, assembler ses amis.
> Ses gardes, son palais, son lit m'étaient soumis.

We see the old man twisting and turning in his efforts to break out of
the trap. It is too late. Guards, palace, bed—she controlled the lot. The
pauses after 'gardes', 'palais' and 'lit' distinguish the different forms of
control, or rather the different ruses she used: the accumulation of substantives gives a feeling of complete finality to 'm'étaient soumis' which is
emphasized in performance by placing the main pause after 'lit'.

The lines that follow are even more brutal:

> Je lui laissai sans fruit consumer sa tendresse;
> De ses derniers soupirs je me rendis maîtresse.
> Mes soins, en apparence épargnant ses douleurs,
> De son fils, en mourant, lui cachèrent les pleurs.
> Il mourut. Mille bruits en courent à ma honte.

The last line, with the staccato 'Il mourut', looks like a veiled reference
to the way in which she 'finished him off'. The impression is strengthened
by the switch from past definites to the present tense, suggesting that the
emperor's death is still a subject of gossip.

Her plotting did not end there:

> J'arrêtai de sa mort la nouvelle trop prompte . . .

In view of the controversial nature of the succession she sent Burrhus
to make sure that Néron had the support of the army before she released
the news of the emperor's death. It produces a moment of macabre
comedy:

> tandis que Burrhus allait secrètement
> De l'armée en vos mains exiger le serment,
> Que vous marchiez au camp, conduit sous mes auspices,
> Dans Rome les autels fumaient de sacrifices;
> Par mes ordres trompeurs tout le peuple excité
> Du prince déjà mort demandait la santé.

When she hears that the army has been won over, she puts an end to the
spectacle of the people praying for the recovery of the dead emperor by
exhibiting the corpse:

> On vit Claude; et le peuple, étonné de sont sort,
> Apprit / en même temps / votre règne // et sa mort.
> C'est le sincère aveu que je voulais vous faire . . .

The cynicism of the story of the emperor's death is heightened by the presence of the word 'sincère' and the antithesis of 'règne' and 'mort' in a single hemistich which again in performance is emphasized by placing the main pause after 'règne'.

It is the prelude to a frontal attack on Néron for his 'ingratitude':

> Voilà tous mes forfaits. // En voici // le salaire.
> Du fruit de tant de soins à peine jouissant
> En avez-vous six mois paru reconnaissant. . .

The caesura at the hemistich and another strong pause after 'voici' in performance bring out the sharp antithesis between 'forfaits' and 'salaire' or reward. Agrippine is guilty of a string of 'crimes', but the crimes were also services of which her son is now enjoying the fruits without having made the least effort to reach his position and without properly rewarding her for doing the job for him. The use of the word 'forfaits' is a deliberate attempt to implicate him, to show that mother and son are inescapably linked by crime in order to strengthen her hold over him. The *s*-s in 'soins', 'six', 'jouissant' and 'reconnaissant' show that the temperature is rising rapidly. Agrippine does, indeed, plunge into a stream of violent denunciation in which *s*-s and *c*-s alternate with heavy nasals:

> Et lorsque vos mépris ex*cita*nt mes murmures,
> Je vous ai *demandé* raison de *tant* d'*inju*res
> (Seul recours d'un *in*grat qui se voit *confondu*),
> Par de nouveaux affronts vous m'avez répondu.

At the end of the diatribe the *s*-s and *c*-s are joined by guttural *r*-s and cuttingly shrill *i*-s, *é*-s, *er*-s:

> Je vois de votre cœur Octavie *effacée*,
> Prête à sortir du *lit* où je l'avais *placée*;
> Je vois Pallas ban*ni*, votre frère *arrêté*;
> Vous attentez enfin jusqu'à ma liber*té*:
> Bur*r*hus ose su*r* moi po*r*ter ses mains ha*r*dies.
> Et lorsque, conva*in*cu de tant de per*fi*dies,
> Vous deviez ne me vo*ir* que pou*r* les ex*pi*er,
> C'est vous qu*i* m'ordonnez de me just*ifi*er.

She is a woman hissing, spitting and spluttering with rage, but a woman who retains all her lucidity.

Agrippine's *tirade* is one of the longest in any of the plays and lasts for 108 lines. Néron begins by replying calmly and scores some palpable hits, particularly the first:

> Vous n'aviez, sous mon nom, travaillé que pour vous.
>
> *
>
> Mais Rome veut un maître, et non une maîtresse.
>
> *
>
> Vous avez vu cent fois nos soldats en courroux
> Porter en mumurant leurs aigles devant vous . . .

Finally, he accuses her of plotting to put Britannicus on the throne. This produces a fresh outburst:

> Moi, le faire empereur, ingrat? L'avez-vous cru?
> Quel serait mon dessein? Qu'aurais-je pu prétendre?

The falsity of the denial does not diminish its force in any way, or the roughness of the language.

Then, cunningly, she switches to lamentation, playing on the word 'importune' which is always calculated to arouse pity:

> Que je suis malheureuse! Et par quelle infortune
> Faut-il que tous mes soins me rendent importune?
> Je n'ai qu'un fils.

In the last line the voice rises to a wail—she is now in tears—and it does the trick. It is the point at which the emperor collapses and the 'little boy' re-emerges. He invites his mother to state her terms.

She does it very succinctly in seven lines. Her detractors or 'accusers' must be punished; there is to be a reconciliation with Britannicus who must be allowed to marry Junie; Pallas's banishment is to be cancelled, and Agrippine is to have access to the emperor whenever she chooses without interference from Burrhus. Néron agrees to everything:

> Oui, Madame, je veux que ma reconnaissance
> Désormais dans les coeurs grave votre puissance;
> Et je bénis déjà cette heureuse froideur,
> Qui de notre amitié va rallumer l'ardeur.
> Quoi que Pallas ait fait, il suffit, je l'oublie;
> Avec Britannicus je me réconcilie;
> Et quant à cet amour qui nous a séparés,
> Je vous fais notre arbitre, et vous nous jugerez.
> Allez donc, et portez cette joie à mon frère.
> Gardes, qu'on obéisse aux ordres de ma mère.

The only way of describing the final passage of the scene is 'unconditional surrender'. We notice in particular the phrases, 'je veux que ma reconnaissance . . . dans les coeurs grave votre *puissance* . . . Je vous fais notre arbitre . . . portez cette joie à mon frère', and the neatness with which the matter is clinched by the last line.

I have quoted the passage in full because of the violent gulf between what Néron is saying now and the events which will follow.

Burrhus comes bustling in to express his delight and to congratulate his master on the double reconciliation with mother and brother. He is promptly disillusioned:

> Elle se hâte trop, Burrhus, de triompher.
> J'embrasse mon rival, mais c'est pour l'étouffer.

We can hear the swish of garments in 'embrasse' and the gurgle followed by a choking sound in 'étouffer'. There will be more to say presently about 'embrasser'. We need only observe here that the combination of 'embrasser' and 'étouffer' and the reappearance in the next couplet of the rhyme 'ruine/Agrippine' shows that Racine's pattern is nearing completion.

Burrhus is appalled and ends up on his knees. On the face of it, it looks as though Néron has been guilty of a particularly ugly piece of treachery at the meeting with his mother. I have no doubt myself that the answer is to be found in the passage in Act II describing the paralysing effect of his mother's eyes on Néron. It seems to me that the 'unconditional surrender' was due to the psychological effect of his mother's presence and that by the time Burrhus arrives the effect has worn, or is beginning to wear off. The meeting with Burrhus raises a similar problem. It is no doubt a sign of Néron's immaturity that he always gives in, at least temporarily, to the latest person to speak to him. So it is here when he says of Britannicus:

> Dans mon appartement qu'il m'attende avec vous.

That Burrhus not only appeared to succeed, but has achieved a temporary success, seems evident from the next scene: the crucial meeting with Narcisse.

Burrhus came bustling in: Narcisse comes in stealthily to tell Néron that the poison cup is ready:

> Seigneur, j'ai tout prévu pour une mort si juste.
> Le poison est tout prêt. La fameuse Locuste
> A redoublé pour moi ses soins officieux:
> Elle a fait expirer un esclave à mes yeux;
> Et le fer est moins prompt pour trancher une vie
> Que le nouveau poison que sa main me confie.[10]

This is the audience's first news of the plan to poison Britannicus. The manner of the announcement shows that Narcisse is referring to something that has already been discussed by Néron and himself. It looks back to his sinister pronouncement when he found himself alone at the end of Act II which was when we last saw him:

> La fortune t'appelle une seconde fois,
> Narcisse: voudrais-tu résister à sa voix?
> Suivons jusques au bout ses ordres favorables;
> Et pour nous rendre heureux, perdons les misérables.

With these two passages in front of us there can no longer be any serious doubt that Narcisse is evil. We know that politically he is much shrewder than Burrhus and much more competent to defend his master's interests. In Act II he urged the banishment of Britannicus. It can certainly be argued that in the circumstances the step was necessary to ensure

Néron's safety. Narcisse is now going beyond what is necessary and is determined to see Britannicus murdered. He is displaying the same attitude as Shakespeare's Iago and advocating evil for evil's sake. It is apparent from the relish with which he says 'perdons les misérables', the way in which he describes the wanton murder of Britannicus as 'une mort si juste' which is the exact opposite of the truth, and the coldblooded account of the death of the slave.

Néron starts by trying to carry out his promises to his mother:

> Narcisse, c'est assez; je reconnais ce soin,
> Et ne souhaite pas que vous alliez plus loin.

One assumes that Néron's reply comes as something of a shock to Narcisse, but the way he sets about reconverting Néron to his own views is masterly. He does not blow up like Burrhus. He is very glad, he says, to hear of the reconciliation:

> Je me garderai bien de vous en détourner,
> Seigneur; mais . . .

Everything is in that 'but'. Néron is unmoved by Narcisse's talk about the danger of Britannicus or even the need to give up Junie. It is very different when Narcisse mentions the behaviour of his mother:

> Agrippine, Seigneur, se l'était bien promis:
> Elle a repris sur vous son souverain empire.

The shot goes home:

> NERON
> Quoi donc? Qu'a-t-elle dit? Et que voulez-vous dire?
>
> NARCISSE
> Elle s'en est vantée assez publiquement.
>
> NERON
> De quoi?
>
> NARCISSE
> Qu'elle n'avait qu'à vous voir un moment:
> Qu'à tout ce grand éclat, à ce courroux funeste
> On verrait succéder un silence modeste;
> Que vous-même à la paix souscririez le premier,
> Heureux que sa bonté daignât tout oublier.

He touches on all Néron's most vulnerable feelings: pride, guilt, the meek behaviour of the 'little boy'. What is more, the news of his mother's boasting, which Néron himself later describes as her 'triomphe indiscret', is the thing most calculated to get Néron on the raw, to undermine his good intentions in so far as they exist. The next line shows that Néron is beginning to waver again:

> Mais, Narcisse, dis-moi, que veux-tu que je fasse?

It is a repetition in almost identical words of the question he asked his mother when he capitulated in Scene 2. It suggests that Narcisse, too, only has to state his terms. His reply is as prompt as Agrippine's. The emperor doesn't know his subjects. The Romans don't want a meek, indulgent ruler. They are used to being pushed around; they worship the hand that keeps them in chains:

> D'un empoisonnement vous craignez la noiceur?
> Faites périr le frère, abandonnez la soeur:
> Rome, sur ses autels prodiguant les victimes,
> Fussent-ils innocents, leur trouvera des crimes.

Agrippine had complained that for reasons she could not understand people 'blackened' her character. Narcisse makes light of the idea that this could happen to Néron. We are conscious of the presence of the ex-slave in his description of a people in a state of complete moral confusion—an accusation which they will refute by his death—who are incapable of distinguishing between right and wrong, who are ready after a blatant murder to find excuses for the murderer by imputing improbable crimes to the murdered.

Néron replies by referring weakly to his promise to Burrhus. Narcisse is never at a loss for an answer. He at once throws doubts on Burrhus's good faith:

> Burrhus ne pense pas, Seigneur, tout ce qu'il dit:
> Son adroite vertu ménage son crédit . . .

The final blow is his story that people are saying that Néron wasn't born to be emperor, that he is being managed by Burrhus and Seneca and simply doing what they tell him. Néron brings the scene to a close with the words:

> Viens, Narcisse. Allons voir ce que nous devons faire.

'Devons' is ambiguous. It could mean 'what we must do because it is the right thing' or 'what we must do in our own interests'. We are not misled. We know that Néron is lost.

We can see what has happened. Néron, who seems bereft of any genuine moral standards, has been exposed in lightning succession to three powerful attacks. All the arguments and all the criticisms used in the past by Agrippine, Burrhus and Narcisse have been restated in concentrated form in consecutive scenes. Although there is a difference between the ultimate objectives of Agrippine and Burrhus, there has been a shifting of the focus since the arrest of Britannicus. His fate is now the immediate issue. In this Agrippine and Burrhus are on the same side and though like the audience they were ignorant of the plot to poison him, they have been striving together to rescue Néron from Narcisse's clutches. Néron's immaturity is such that he gives in to all three in turn. He takes the path he does partly because the last attack is the most effective of all and partly because it is the last attack and goads the impetuous youth into action.

5

With the outbreak of hostilities in Act III Néron's opponents appeared to be on the verge of collapse. The fourth act, as sometimes happens in tragedy, creates the illusion that owing to a sudden change all may yet be well and the tragedy averted. That is part of the irony of tragedy. It is precisely because the hopes turn out to be an illusion that the tragedy, when it does take place, is the more horrifying. We also find that the fourth act of *Britannicus* like the fourth act of *Andromaque* heightens the suspense by delaying the *dénouement*. This means that in *Britannicus* the illusory hopes started in Act IV are maintained until the last moment.

It may sound a trifle odd, but the contrast between Racine's fourth and fifth acts reminds me of the saying about 'reculer pour mieux sauter'. The slowing down of the tempo in the fourth act, which is occupied by important debates between the leading characters, adds considerably to the impact of the fifth act where events move with greater speed than in any other part of the play.

Act V opens with the final meeting between Britannicus and Junie. Britannicus is on his way to meet Néron for what he believes is the great reconciliation. Although Junie is deeply worried about the possible outcome, Britannicus is filled with a boyish confidence and is convinced that Néron really will welcome him with open arms:

> Oui, Madame, Néron (qui l'aurait pu penser?)
> Dans son appartement m'attend pour m'*embrasser*.
> Il y fait de sa cour inviter la jeunesse;
> Il veut que d'un festin la pompe et l'allégresse
> Confirment à leurs yeux la foi de nos serments,
> Et réchauffent l'ardeur de nos *embrassements* . . .

The words 'embrasser/embrassements' look back to Néron's words to Burrhus,

> J'embrasse mon rival, mais c'est pour l'étouffer,

—and forward to what is to come.

The image of one man embracing another in order to crush him conveys the very essence of the play with its stifling atmosphere, its intrigues, above all its treachery. The horror is increased by assembling the youth for what they believe is a party, but will turn out to be murder.

Agrippine arrives on the scene filled with the same confidence as Britannicus and chides him for dawdling while Néron is waiting impatiently to give him what will turn out to be the kiss of death. When he hurries away she upbraids Junie for her fears and for her lack of confidence in her power over her son:

> Il suffit. J'ai parlé, tout a changé de face . . .
> Ah! si vous aviez vu par combien de caresses
> Il m'a renouvelé la foi de ses promesses!
> Par quels embrassements il vient de m'arrêter!
> Ses bras, dans nos adieux, ne pouvaient me quitter . . .

The tone of this speech deserves special attention. *Britannicus* is one of the most violent of the tragedies. A large proportion of the speeches are delivered in a loud, harsh, angry tone. In stage productions this throws into relief the remarkably youthful voices of Britannicus and Junie and the low, insinuating tone of Narcisse who never raises his voice. Agrippine's present speech is in strong contrast to most of her other speeches. Her voice is smooth, calm, urbane. She is convinced that she has regained her old position, that Néron will fulfil his promises and that all will be well, recalling her words to Britannicus in Act III, 'J'ai promis, il suffit'. The satisfaction with which she dwells on 'embrassements' shows that for the time being she has forgotten the 'embrassement' which steered her away from the throne and started all the trouble.

Junie's innocence—the innocence of the 'outsider' who is uncontaminated by the corruption of the world of Néron and Agrippine—gives her an insight into motives to which Agrippine with her blunted moral sense cannot pretend. She continues what is part homily on Junie's fears and part tribute to her son:

> Non, il le faut ici confesser à sa gloire,
> Son coeur n'enferme point une malice noire . . .

The frequency with which the rhyme 'gloire/victoire' turns up in Racine makes 'gloire/noire' particularly arresting—and particularly ominous.

The bitterest stroke of irony is still to come. Agrippine has just said:

> Passons chez Octavie, et donnons-lui le reste
> D'un jour autant heureux que je l'ai cru funeste.

There is a sudden tumult. In a moment Burrhus is there with the tragic news:

> A peine l'Empereur a vu venir son frère,
> Il se lève, il *l'embrasse*, on se tait, et soudain
> César prend le premier une coupe à la main . . .

Narcisse hands Britannicus the poison cup:

> Mais ses lèvres à peine en ont touché les bords . . .
> Il tombe sur son lit sans chaleur et sans vie.

The story had begun with Agrippine's intrusion into Claudius's 'bed' which had cost his son the throne: it ends with the son's dropping dead on another 'bed' in the banqueting room, murdered by Agrippine's son. The continual use of the words 'embrasse/embrassement' and the reappearance of 'lit' complete the pattern with the customary neatness.

There is a final clash between Agrippine and the murderers:

> Et ton nom paraîtra, dans la race future,
> Aux plus cruels tyrans une cruelle injure.
> Voilà ce que mon coeur se présage de toi.
> Adieu: tu peux sortir.

Néron had struck a note of defiance when first accused of the murder. His collapse is immediate. In a moment he is the 'little boy' again who is unable to face his mother. When he hears the supremely contemptuous dismissal of the final line, he slinks guiltily away, muttering to his accomplice: 'Narcisse, suivez-moi'.

Agrippine has just admitted her 'injustice' in 'condemning' Burrhus and listening to Narcisse when Albine arrives with the news of Narcisse's death and Junie's escape to the Vestal Virgins:

> Elle a feint de passer chez la triste Octavie;
> Mais bientôt elle a pris des chemins écartés,
> Où mes yeux ont suivi ses pas précipités.
> Des portes du palais elle sort éperdue.

A very mild 'feinte' has succeeded this time. Junie is one of the few characters to find her way out of a palace which at times seems to be without an exit.

Then Néron:

> Il rentre. Chacun fuit son silence farouche.
> Le seul nom de Junie échappe de sa bouche.
> Il marche sans dessein; ses yeux mal assurés
> N'osent lever au ciel leurs regards égarés.

A glance back at the first scene of Act I and the second scene of Act II brings home to us the perfection of the completed pattern. It is night again. This time it is Néron who is wandering 'sans dessein' as Agrippine was found wandering alone, 'errant dans le palais sans suite et sans escorte'. She was trying without success to contact Néron and protest against the arrest of Junie. It is now Néron who is calling in vain for Junie. In Act II we saw him watching, spellbound, as she was escorted by the soldiery into a room which was the equivalent of a prison cell. This time she has been escorted by the people to the temple of the Vestals from which there is no return. While she was in the palace she was the target of everybody's eyes. The target has gone; Néron dare not even look up. His confusion is reflected in his 'yeux mal assurés' and his 'regards égarés'. Instead of the 'désir curieux' and irritation at the idea that Junie has been hiding from him, he is overcome by a 'despair' at her final disappearance which makes Albine fear that he may be harbouring suicidal tendencies. In short, the characters end where they began: wandering helplessly in the dark, lost souls only too likely to continue as they began.

6

Britannicus is one of the most powerful plays in the canon. We can see that the dramatist has made considerable progress since *Andromaque*, that there has been a deepening of his vision of the human condition which is much more sombre and may have been due to events in his private life. It still remains to disentangle the meaning of the tragedy which has given rise to differences of opinion.

The suggestion has been made that at the end of the play 'moral order is restored'. The signs are the killing of Narcisse by the people and the offer of 'permanent protection' to Junie by the House of the Vestals.[11] I find this view surprising and suspect that the truth is somewhat different.

We must remember that Néron is a young man and that the character will not bear the symbolism which is sometimes attached to it. He finds himself in a position for which he does not possess any of the right qualifications. In this evil world he is surrounded by bad examples and exposed to pressures which are continually forcing him in the wrong direction. He is not a strong man; he is another example of human frailty and succumbs. The magnitude of the disaster is caused by the fact that he is not an ordinary citizen, but occupies the highest position in the State. He is a threat not simply to members of his immediate entourage, but to innumerable people in the empire who will follow his example and make wrong choices. His mother's last words to him are prophetic. Although he still behaves like the 'little boy' the last time we see him, the murder of Britannicus is a turning point: the point at which the *monstre naissant* is transformed, morally and psychologically, into the adult criminal.

There can be no question of 'moral order' being restored. The last vestiges of any moral order are destroyed by the rejection of Burrhus's advice and the murder of Britannicus. What happens is that an evil order is maintained and gains in strength by changing hands: the change from Agrippine's hands to Néron's which is the result of 'affranchissement'. Narcisse is punished, but except for the loss of Junie, Néron, who bears the final responsibility for the crime, goes unpunished, at any rate for the time being. Junie's departure to the Vestal Virgins is the equivalent of 'taking the veil' in a Christian society. It marks her escape from an evil world and does indeed offer 'permanent protection'. This does not alter the fact that in purely human terms it is a sign of defeat, or rather that following the murder it completes the defeat of Innocence by the evil forces at work. With the murder of Britannicus she has lost everything and her life is to all intents and purposes finished. The move is not a matter of 'vocation' or even of free choice. It is forced on her and she is simply left to play out time in the temple.

NOTES

[1] There is some confusion about the period. Racine originally said three years. In the edition of 1676 he changed it to two years in line 27, but apparently forgot to make the change in line 25, which reads 'depuis trois ans entiers', or in line 462 where Néron speaks of 'trois ans de vertus'.

[2] See J. D. Hubert, *Essai d'exégèse racinienne*, p. 101; R. Jasinski, *Vers le vrai Racine*, I, 1958, pp. 302 *et seq.*

[3] In the introduction to his edition of *Britannicus*, 1967, pp. 42 *et seq.*

[4] Her role and the way attention is focused on her at the start invites comparisons with Oreste in *Andromaque*.

[5] In some versions, including one of the acting versions, Britannicus speaks of '*ma ruine*'. It matters little. Agrippine's marriage to Claudius was responsible for the ruin of father and son.

The word is used 7 times in the sense of personal disaster in the play: the total number of times for all the plays is only 10.

[6] Shortly after this production Hirsch returned to the Comédie Française and played Néron in their production of *Britannicus*. I was amused to observe that it was a much more restrained performance than the one I had seen in London and that there was no laughter at the Comédie Française.

[7] Historically, Seneca was the emperor's other tutor and the partner of Burrus. He does not appear in Britannicus because he was absent from Rome on business. For 'trois ans de vertus', see Note 1 above.

[2] 'Die klassische Dämpfung in Racines Stil' was first published in *Archivum Romanicum* in 1928 and republished in *Romanische Stil- und Literaturstudien*, I, 1931.

[9] The total number of uses for the twelve plays is 413. *Britannicus* holds the record for a single play with 70. *Andromaque* and *Phèdre* are runners-up with 54 and 51.

[10] Professor Butler points out that the murder of the slave, which he calls a 'trait of particular ferocity', is not found in Tacitus, but is an invention of Racine's (*Britannicus*, p. 173). It seems to confirm everything that is said here about the nature of Racine's Narcisse.

[11] O. de Mourgues, *Racine or The Triumph of Relevance*, 1967, p. 127.

'BÉRÉNICE'

1670

Oui, elle est la plus racinienne des tragédies de Racine, cette chère *Bérénice*, parce qu'elle est la plus simple, la plus simple et aussi la plus tendre.

BÉATRIX DUSSANE

Non, mille fois non, *Bérénice* n'est pas le chef-d'oeuvre des harmonies raciniennes . . . l'*invitus invitam* en cinq acts reste une oeuvre de petite zone, un jeu de cour, une prouesse de salon.

PIERRE BRISSON

Mais le plus gros de la tâche était pour nous de travailler les vers. Essayer de dire les alexandrins . . .

JEAN-LOUIS BARRAULT

CHAPTER 5

'BÉRÉNICE'

1670

I

Bérénice is the most controversial and the most problematical of all Racine's plays. For three hundred years critics and scholars have vigorously debated its genesis, its meaning, its artistic merits. Was there really a competition between Corneille and Racine engineered by Henriette d'Angleterre? Or did one of the dramatists get wind of his rival's plans and enter the lists of his own free-will: Corneille with the idea of staging a resounding comeback and meeting with honourable defeat; Racine with the intention of delivering a knock-out blow and ending with something less than total victory? Or was it sheer chance that both dramatists hit independently on the same theme, which was by no means an unknown situation in the seventeenth century when possible subjects were limited and different dramatists frequently treated the same one? Did Racine intend to portray Louis XIV's romantic attachment to his sister-in-law or his affair with Marie Mancini, or both? Or did he simply choose a subject from history which was popular in his time without giving a thought to contemporary events?

There is no certain answer to any of these questions. In the eighteenth and nineteenth centuries it was taken for granted that Henriette did prompt each of the dramatists to write a play about Titus and Berenice without either knowing that the other had been 'got at'. Michaut's monograph was once supposed to have demolished the theory, but owing to lack of satisfactory documentary evidence his view is no longer accepted without considerable qualifications.[1]

It is not my intention to examine the different theories. Antoine Adam's strikes me as by far the most convincing of the various explanations that have been put forward. In 1719 the Abbé Dubos said that Racine chose his subject 'sur les instances d'une grande princesse'. His source is believed to have been Boileau. The story of a competition planned by Henriette d'Angleterre was related for the first time in 1728 by Fontenelle, a nephew of Corneille's, in a life of his uncle. He offered no proof of the authenticity of his version and as he admitted his uncle's defeat, one has the impression that he may have been embroidering on the Abbé Dubos's version in order to excuse the defeat and perhaps to conceal the facts. Professor Adam accepts the Abbé Dubos's version. He thinks that

Henriette invited Racine, who was her favourite dramatist, to write a play about Titus and Berenice, that there was a leakage of information about the composition of *Bérénice* and that as it was to be produced at the Hôtel de Bourgogne, members of the Palais-Royal company obtained a copy of Racine's text and persuaded Corneille to write his *Tite et Bérénice*.

If this view is correct, the intervention of Henriette, her death shortly before the plays were produced and the knowledge that Corneille was the challenger would together have been sufficient to account for the absence of controversy at the time of production, which has appeared puzzling to later generations.[2]

While critics are sometimes too prone to discover topical allusions in the work of writers of the past where none was intended, or to identify the supposed originals of their characters, I do not think myself that there can be any serious doubt that *Bérénice* does contain deliberate references to Louis XIV's compulsory abandonment of Marie Mancini, Mazarin's niece, for the purest *raison d'État*. Professor Adam suggests that Henriette put the idea into Racine's head. She may well have done so and been prompted by memories of her romantic friendship for her brother-in-law. We might add that her intervention and its implications would explain why Racine wrote a play which is so different from the pattern of the rest of his work.

Racine's treatment of Roman history in *Bérénice* is not without interest. The historical Titus and Berenice met for the first time in A.D. 67 when Berenice was nearly forty and Titus thirteen years younger. He had already been married twice and she three times. She was regarded by contemporaries as a thoroughly dissolute character who was reputed to have had an incestuous relationship with her brother Agrippa. Titus was not much better. Suetonius tells us that he was considered 'morally unprincipled' because he owned a 'troop of inverts and eunuchs'.[3]

Suetonius speaks of Berenice as 'Regina Berenice'. It is a curious fact that though the entire action of Racine's play depends on Bérénice's position as queen, historically it was no more than a courtesy title. Berenice was a Jewess who tried to mediate in the Roman-Jewish war, but was never queen of Palestine. Racine refers several times to the association lasting five years. It is significant that this was the length of Louis XIV's affair with Marie Mancini. The liaison of the historical Titus and Berenice was spread over twelve years and there was a long break in the middle. When her attempts at mediation failed, she sought refuge in Rome where she arrived in A.D. 75. The liaison was re-started and went on until Titus succeeded his father as emperor in A.D. 79. Although Suetonius says, in a passage quoted in Racine's preface, that 'he sent Queen Berenice away from Rome which was painful to both of them', the suggestion has been made that as she was now over fifty the new emperor was not really sorry to be rid of her.[4]

Titus had not abandoned the practices he had learnt in his youth at the court of Nero. He did not in fact mend his morals until the final break with Berenice. The sentence in which Suetonius describes it ends with the words 'and broke off relations with some of his favourite boys'.[5] For sexually Titus seems to have been as versatile as other Roman emperors.

Such are the scabrous materials out of which Racine wove his chaste play.

2

I said in my first chapter that *Bérénice* is one of Racine's most effective openings because we are invited to identify ourselves with Arsace who is introduced by his master into a new world. We are in the palace of the Caesars 'dans un cabinet qui est entre l'appartement de Titus et celui de Bérénice'. It is to the 'cabinet' that our attention is specially directed in the first lines addressed by Antiochus to his confidant:

> Arrêtons un moment. La pompe de ces lieux,
> Je le vois bien, Arsace, est nouvelle à tes yeux.
> Souvent ce cabinet superbe et solitaire
> Des secrets de Titus est le dépositaire.
> C'est ici quelquefois qu'il se cache à sa cour,
> Lorsqu'il vient à la Reine expliquer son amour.
> De son appartement cette porte est prochaine,
> Et cette autre conduit dans celui de la Reine.

It would not be altogether an exaggeration to suggest that practically every word of these first eight lines counts because it illuminates the main theme. The two men pause for a moment to gaze at the décor of the 'cabinet'. In the same way life in Rome, which had moved smoothly to the deification of the dead emperor and which seemed to be moving with the same smoothness towards the marriage of the new emperor and Bérénice, will suddenly come to a stop. The protagonists will take stock, review their plans in the light of a new attitude and change direction. 'Direction' means psychology which will lead to physical moves: the withdrawal of Antiochus to the East.

'Pompe', 'superbe' and 'solitaire' are descriptions of the protagonists' physical environment; they also have strong moral and psychological associations. 'Pompe' and 'superbe' reflect the proud, lofty, intransigent attitude of Rome towards foreign monarchs which will end by breaking the protagonists. 'Solitaire' is equally important. Although the protagonists are in continual contact with one another, they are at the same time isolated, struggling in private and 'in solitude' with their personal problems which have become problems of State on account of the Roman attitude.

Although it is used 15 times, 'secret' has a more limited meaning than in other plays. There is no plotting and no trickery in *Bérénice*. The word refers in the main to 'private feelings', 'private meetings' and 'private places': the private feelings which create in the protagonists a sense of 'solitude'; the helpless struggle against alien and hostile forces; the need to come to terms with oneself without being able to look to anybody for help. It will be used later to point the contrast between 'private' and 'public' life, between the claims of the individual and the claims of State. The 'cabinet' is, indeed, a 'private place': the room where Titus can withdraw temporarily from the cares of public life and meet Bérénice. For this reason its situation is important. It stands somewhere, perhaps midway, between their living quarters where they are both 'on show', where they can be and are visited by unwelcome officials and importunate courtiers. Although it is a private place it is also the place where 'private' decisions will be taken that resolve the 'public' controversy.

This brings us to the palace itself. It does not suffer from the same frightening atmosphere as Néron's palace in *Britannicus*, but like all Racine's palaces it is in a special way a prison: a prison from which one of the characters is already contemplating flight. In the third scene we hear Arsace telling his master about

> Des vaisseaux dans Ostie armés en diligence,
> Prêts à quitter le port de moments en moments . . .

In Act III Antiochus, speaking to Bérénice, will remark:

> Peut-être en ce moment je serais dans Ostie,
> S'il ne m'eût de sa cour défendu la sortie.

Ostia is the port of Rome. Its particular significance in *Bérénice* is that it is also a sort of junction: the place between Rome and the 'Orient'—there will be a good deal to say later about the contrast between the two—where anyone escaping from 'prison' or being removed from Rome will board ship for the East. In one sense—a delusory sense—it stands for freedom; in another—the real sense—it stands for separation and banishment. There is a certain parallel between Ostia and the 'cabinet'. They are both neutral zones between two worlds. Ostia is the place of *final* escape or departure; the 'cabinet' the place of *temporary* refuge inside the prison. Titus will turn out to be the real prisoner for whom there is no escape. The temporary refuge inevitably looks forward to the final separation of the protagonists and what is in fact the exile of Bérénice.

There is something more. The 'cabinet' is a 'love nest' where you can let your pants as well as your hair down though naturally in their five long years of courtship Racine's Titus and Bérénice never dreamed of doing such a thing.

A number of writers have spoken disparagingly of Antiochus. Whatever they may say, he is in no sense a superfluous or even a minor character. He plays an essential part in the action. Although there is no real jealousy in *Bérénice*, the Racinian triangle is there. In the last act Antiochus will describe himself as Titus's 'rival'. His love for Bérénice, indeed, and the possibility of taking Titus's place when the marriage is called off, turn into something resembling a sub-plot. He also shares some of Titus's characteristics which emphasize the weaknesses and the innate defeatism of Titus himself.

Antiochus's first meeting with Bérénice in the fourth scene is a good illustration of the importance of his role. In spite of the fact that she appears to be on the verge of marriage to Titus, he is determined to make a final declaration of love before he leaves Rome. He tells his confidant to arrange a private audience, or what he calls 'un entretien secret'. We can see what he is doing. He is inveigling Bérénice away from her apartment into the 'love nest' so that he can imitate Titus and make a declaration which could not be made, psychologically at any rate, in any other place. This much is evident from the way that Bérénice greets him:

> Enfin je me dérobe à la joie importune
> De tant d'amis nouveaux que me fait la fortune;
> Je fuis de leurs respects l'inutile longueur,
> Pour chercher un ami qui me parle du coeur.
> Il ne faut point mentir: ma juste impatience
> Vous accusait déjà de quelque négligence.

Bérénice is delighted to make her escape from public life and seek refuge in the 'cabinet'. The people who wait on her are bores; they never 'speak from the heart' and though she does not know it will be the first to drop her when they hear that her marriage to Titus is off. She is having great difficulty, as she will tell us in a moment, in seeing Titus because of the protracted mourning for his father which 'even in private has suspended his love'. She is therefore particularly pleased to see Antiochus. He is the one person with whom she can discuss her love for Titus, the friend who speaks to her 'from the heart', which looks forward ironically to her fury when he does indeed speak from his heart.

Although she knows perfectly well that he was a suitor for her hand before she met Titus, it never occurs to her for a moment that chatting about Titus may not be much fun for the ex-lover. She scolds him gently for not waiting on her. Her complete preoccupation with her own feelings and her imperviousness to other peoples' appears again in a striking pronouncement:

> Cent fois je me suis fait une douceur extrême
> D'entretenir Titus dans *un autre lui-même*.

'Poor Antiochus!' one cannot help saying. His job is simply to deputize for Titus, to understudy him for the pleasure of Bérénice when he himself is not available.

What emerges from these observations is that Bérénice's love is entirely self-centred. She does not care a rap for anyone or anything except Titus and herself.[6] Antiochus puts it splendidly when he explains the reasons for his departure:

> Je fuis des yeux distraits,
> Qui me voyant toujours, ne me voyaient jamais.

Antiochus's announcement of his departure in line 10 of the opening scene introduced a major theme. For this is a play about separations and departures caused by love or the conflict between love and duty. It is used as the excuse for the private audience and is reintroduced by Antiochus as a prelude to his declaration of love. Bérénice is shocked by the news that he is proposing to leave immediately instead of staying on—it is another sign of her self-centredness—to witness her triumph: marriage to Titus and crowning as empress. He gets very short shrift indeed when he makes the declaration. The angry Bérénice goes into reverse, tells him that he is never to see her again and had better leave Rome at once. This brings out one of the underlying ironies of the play: she has no idea that they will both leave at the same time in a mood of the deepest distress.

Bérénice's confidant is clearly upset by her mistress's harsh treatment of Antiochus:

> Que je le plains! Tant de fidélité,
> Madame, méritait plus de prospérité.
> Ne le plaignez-vous pas?

We notice in passing that Phénice uses the homely language of the confidant which is markedly different from the more refined and sophisticated language of the protagonists.

Bérénice is rather shaken herself:

> Cette prompte retraite
> Me laisse, je l'avoue, une douleur *secrète*.

There is, perhaps, a premonition of the much more serious encounters between Titus and Bérénice. When Bérénice learns Titus's 'secret'—the calling off of the marriage—she will feel that she has been very hardly done by and hers will be anything but a 'douleur secrète'. This, however, is not the most important function of the meeting. Phénice goes on to remark 'Je l'aurais retenu'. Bérénice is highly indignant:

> Qui ? moi ? le retenir ?
> J'en dois perdre plutôt jusques au souvenir.
> Tu veux donc que je flatte une ardeur insensée ?

I suggested earlier that Racine's handling of the confidants is particularly impressive in *Bérénice*. Paulin and Phénice are outstanding examples of the 'good' confidants who try their hardest to keep master and mistress on the right path, or what seems to them the right path, while Arsace is the weak confidant who encourages false hopes and increases the bitterness of his master's defeat. There is nothing sentimental or provocative about Phénice's 'Je l'aurais retenu'. Her next words show that she had a sound reason for saying what she did:

> Titus n'a point encore expliqué sa pensée.
> Rome vous voit, Madame, avec des yeux jaloux;
> La rigueur de ses lois m'épouvante pour vous.
> L'hymen chez les Romains n'admet qu'une Romaine;
> Rome hait tous les rois, et Bérénice est reine.

The passage demonstrates the importance of the meeting between Antiochus and Bérénice and the skill with which Racine used it. It leads in the most natural way to the first direct statement of the problem which faces the protagonists. For reasons which will turn out to be entirely valid, Racine puts it into the mouth of a confidant and will do exactly the same when the time comes for Titus to hear the bad news.

Phénice's momentous statement was intended to bring her mistress down to earth. It simply doesn't register. Bérénice pushes it on one side with the words,

> Le temps n'est plus, Phénice, où je pouvais trembler.
> Titus m'aime, il peut tout, il n'a plus qu'à parler.

Her confidence is in the tone and in the three brief phrases of the second line. Far from coming down to earth, she is moving in the opposite direction:

> Il verra le sénat m'apporter ses hommages,
> Et le peuple, de fleurs couronner ses images.
>   De cette nuit, Phénice, as-tu vu la splendeur ?
> Tes yeux ne sont-ils pas tout pleins de sa grandeur ?
> Ces flambeaux, ce bûcher, cette nuit enflammée,
> Ces aigles, ces faisceaux, ce peuple, cette armée,
> Cette foule de rois, ces consuls, ce sénat,
> Qui tous, de mon amant empruntaient leur éclat;
> Cette pourpre, cet or, que rehaussait sa gloire,
> Et ce lauriers encor témoins de sa victoire;
> Tous ces yeux qu'on voyait venir de toutes parts
> Confondre sur lui seul leurs avides regards;
> Ce port majestueux, cette douce présence.
> Ciel! avec quel respect et quelle complaisance

Tous les coeurs en secret l'assuraient de leur foi!
Parle: peut-on le voir sans penser comme moi
Qu'en quelque obscurité que le sort l'eût fait naître,
Le monde, en le voyant, eût reconnu son maître?
Mais, Phénice, où m'emporte un souvenir charmant?
    Cependant Rome entière, en ce même moment,
Fait des voeux pour Titus, et par des sacrifices
De son règne naissant célèbre les prémices.
Que tardons-nous? Allons, pour son empire heureux,
Au ciel, qui le protège, offrir aussi nos voeux.
Aussitôt, sans l'attendre, et sans être attendue,
Je reviens le chercher, et dans cette entrevue
Dire tout ce qu'aux coeurs l'un et l'autre contents
Inspirent des transports retenus si longtemps.

The richness, the colour, the variety of the spectacle, the harmony and the music of the verse make this one of the most splendid passages in a play which is rightly admired for its poetry. It is a rapturous account by a young woman, who is as different as she could well be from the middle-aged mistress of history, of the magnificence of Rome which she sees as a tribute to the emperor and her future husband. The first two lines prepare the way for a procession. She begins with the setting, described by a brilliant accumulation of substantives in lines 5–6, and passes on in lines 6–7 to the people, the army, the crowd of kings, consuls and the senate. They are all seen to be converging on the emperor. The return to the setting with the 'purple', 'gold' and 'laurels' in lines 9–10 and the suggestion that the splendour is somehow a 'borrowing' from Titus's personal 'gloire' creates a sort of apotheosis. We become identified with the crowd, craning our necks, gazing 'avidly' and in our 'hearts' privately pledging our faith to this superman:

Ce port majestueux, cette douce présence.

Now in spite of the vividness of the spectacle and the richness of the colours, we are aware of a certain unreality on the part of Bérénice. It is conveyed with great subtlety and its nature indicated by the word 'images'. What Bérénice has actually seen is a tribute to the emperor, to the public figure, which takes no account of the human being, the private person with whom she is in love. The celebrations have the effect of transforming him into an 'image' or a monument and eliminating the human qualities altogether. It shows what is to come. Titus the Man will be sacrificed to Titus the Emperor and his human qualities will to all intents and purposes be eliminated, leaving nothing but the public figure.

Bérénice's illusion is twofold. She believes that she is witnessing a tribute to somebody whose public position could only have been achieved by his personal qualities:

peut-on le voir sans penser comme moi
Qu'en quelque obscurité que le sort l'eût fait naître,
Le monde, en le voyant, eût reconnu son maître?

The answer is that unless he had been born or accepted as Vespasian's heir, they would have done nothing of the sort.

The other illusion lies in uniting in her imagination two conflicting forces: an emperor who *appears* to be all-powerful and a State which for practical purposes *is* all-powerful. It is a critical moment in the play because from now onwards everything will be directed to dissipating, in the cruellest way, Bérénice's illusions and revealing what really lies behind the imaginative picture she has drawn of Rome's splendour or, for that matter, of Titus himself.

For these reasons I feel inclined to describe the scene as a *gloire figée*.

3

In *Bérénice* we see three principal characters and their followers. There is a fourth who is compellingly present all through the play, but whom we never actually *see*. It is 'the people' and their official representatives, the senate, who are referred to collectively as 'Rome'. The 'cabinet', as we know, serves several purposes. It is a 'love nest', a temporary escape from the cares of public life, a refuge from the court bores. It also has the effect of insulating the protagonists from everyday life, preventing direct contact with 'the people'. 'Private feelings' have now become a matter of public concern. Although Titus already recognizes in his heart that he can never marry Bérénice, he is determined to leave nothing to chance. He needs a confidential report on Rome's attitude: a 'private eye' who will tell him the truth—what the public voice is saying about the projected marriage, what is going on in 'the hearts of the people'. At the end of the brief opening scene of Act II, in which he makes his first appearance, he dismisses his retinue so that he can be alone with his confidant:

Hé bien! de mes desseins Rome encore incertaine
Attend que deviendra le destin de la Reine,
Paulin; et les secrets de son coeur et du mien
Sont de tout l'univers devenus l'entretien.
Voici le temps enfin qu'il faut que je m'explique.
De la Reine et de moi que dit la voix publique?
Parlez: qu'entendez-vous?

We feel at once that there is an element of false confidence in the tone and in the references in lines 3–4 to his 'private' feelings—the meaning of 'secrets' here—becoming the subject of public discussion.

The 'private eye' makes an inauspicious start:

> J'entends de tous côtés
> Publier vos vertus, Seigneur, et ses beautés . . .
> Vous pouvez tout: aimez, cessez d'être amoureux,
> La cour sera toujours du parti de vos voeux.

This is pure flattery. It is also an evasion of the question which was put to him. Titus is not interested in what 'the court' thinks; he wants to discover the attitude of 'the people'. Nor is he taken in by what he has been told. He presses for a straight answer and brings out very clearly in lines 7–8 of the passage which follows the way in which the palace 'insulates' the protagonists from everyday life:

> je l'ai vue aussi cette cour peu sincère,
> A ses maîtres toujours trop soigneuse de plaire . . .
> Je ne prends point pour juge une cour idolâtre,
> Paulin: je me propose un plus noble théâtre;
> Et sans prêter l'oreille à la voix des flatteurs,
> Je veux par votre bouche entendre tous les coeurs.
> Vous me l'avez promis. Le respect et la crainte
> Ferment autour de moi le passage à la plainte . . .
> Parlez donc. Que faut-il que Bérénice espère?
> Rome lui sera-t-elle indulgente ou sévère?

We observe that *enjambement* twice carries Paulin's name to the beginning of a new line. In spite of brave words, it already contains a hint of weakness, a sense that Titus is appealing for support rather than interrogating his confidant.

This time the 'private eye', who has been behaving in the manner attributed to members of a 'cour peu sincère', responds to the request and comes clean:

> N'en doutez point, Seigneur. Soit raison, soit caprice,
> Rome ne l'attend point pour son impératrice.

Although much more detailed, this scene clearly matches the earlier one between Bérénice and Phénice. Paulin's answer is identical with hers. The truth is that though we never see 'the people' we do see two very typical representatives: Paulin and Phénice. Indeed, later in the same speech we shall find Paulin going on to identify himself explicitly with 'the people's' point of view. In these scenes they dispose between them of the double illusion of Titus and Bérénice that 'the people' are on their side, pinning their hopes on them.

One very striking feature of the play is the recurrence and the reverberation of the word 'Rome'. When a character is enquiring about the attitude of Rome, the word either appears in the middle of a line or is qualified by a mark of interrogation:

> Hé bien! de mes desseins Rome encore incertaine . . .
> Rome lui sera-t-elle indulgente ou sévère?

Now when Paulin or Phénice is making a statement about Rome's attitude to the marriage it frequently appears at the beginning of the line, is followed by an active, usually a transitive verb, and turns into a ruthless declaration of principle which echoes and re-echoes throughout the play like the knell of doom. We remember Phénice's

> *Rome* vous *voit*, Madame, avec des yeux jaloux . . .
> *Rome hait* tous les rois, et Bérénice est reine.

There are four examples altogether in Paulin's speech:

> *Rome*, par une loi qui ne se peut changer,
> *N'admet* avec son sang aucun sang étranger.

> en bannissant ses rois,
> *Rome* à ce nom si noble et si saint autrefois,
> *Attacha* pour jamais une haine puissante . . .

What I want to stress is the dynamic use of language. 'Rome' is the first word in lines which though placed in the mouths of servants are the instruments of crashing blows delivered in the name of 'the people' against the wishes, hopes or ambitions of the two royal protagonists.

The word occurs 52 times in the play. That is the measure of its domination: a domination which imposes itself dramatically and gradually crushes the protagonists. 'Orient' appears only 10 times, but the balancing of 'Rome' and 'Orient' plays a very important part in the lives of the principal characters and the contrast between the two is the pivot of Paulin's speech.

Paulin, whose great speech is remarkable for its firmness and skill, begins with a general statement on Rome's policy towards the marriages of her emperors. He goes on to give concrete examples of right and wrong behaviour:

> Jules, qui le premier la soumit à ses armes,
> Qui fit taire les lois dans le bruit des alarmes,
> Brûla pour Cléopâtre, et, sans se déclarer,
> Seule dans l'Orient la laissa soupirer.
> Antoine, qui l'aima jusqu'à l'idolâtrie,
> Oublia dans son sein sa gloire et sa patrie,
> Sans oser toutefois se nommer son époux.
> Rome l'alla chercher jusques à ses genoux,
> Et ne désarma point sa fureur vengeresse,
> Qu'elle n'eût accablé l'amant et la maîtresse.

For Julius Caesar the 'Orient' was a place of temptation. He was in love with Cleopatra, but remembered his duty to Rome and did the right thing. The story of Mark Antony is much less creditable in Paulin's eyes and is intended as a warning to Titus. Antony's failure is not argued; it is placed brilliantly before us in an image of undutiful voluptuousness:

> Oublia dans son sein sa gloire et sa patrie . . .

In the next line,

> Rome l'alla chercher jusques à ses genoux,

we see the punitive expedition setting out from Rome, the angry warriors bursting into another 'love nest'—the parallel with the 'cabinet', purity apart, seems obvious—where they find the erring emperor slumped ig-nominiously at the feet of the Eastern Queen.[7]

A few lines later he describes a different situation. Rome had snatched her emperor from the feet of the Eastern Queen. The 'Orient' replied by snapping up a mere ex-slave only recently released from the rigours of Rome's 'chains' and providing him with a couple of oriental queens for his wives.

This is the point at which Paulin emerges as a vigorous and open champion of 'the people'. The speech turns into a homily and a reproach:

> Et vous croiriez pouvoir, sans blesser *nos* regards,
> Faire entrer une reine au lit de *nos* Césars,
> Tandis que l'Orient dans le lit de ses reines
> Voit passer un esclave au sortir de *nos* chaînes?

For Paulin the contrast between 'Rome' and 'Orient' is a contrast be-tween splendour and ignominy. These sordid queens belonged to the same race as Bérénice. The 'Orient' is the 'love nest' again: an image of voluptuousness contained in the repeated 'lits' and the spectacle of the ex-slave slipping, with a shiver of anticipation, between the sheets of the eastern queens. The implication is that if he married Bérénice, Titus would cut the same sort of figure. 'Do you really believe that *we*, the people, will put up with this sort of thing, that we will allow a foreign queen like Bérénice into the bed of *our* emperors?'

Finally:

> C'est ce que les Romains pensent de votre amour;
> Et je ne réponds pas, avant la fin du jour,
> Que le sénat, chargé des voeux de tout l'Émpire,
> Ne vous redise ici ce que je viens de dire;
> Et que Rome avec lui tombant à vos genoux,
> Ne vous demande un choix digne d'elle et de vous.

Then, coldly:

> Vous pouvez préparer, Seigneur, votre réponse.

Rome and the Orient are opposites. Rome stands, or rather is supposed to stand—I emphasize this for reasons which will become apparent later—for strength, principle, dignity, a community which gets its values right. The Orient represents weakness, cowardice, temptation, indulgence. Rome is the centre of power; the Orient a 'desert', a place of banishment or exile, a refuge for disappointed lovers from problems they cannot face: a place where they brood listlessly over their misfortunes.

At the meeting with Antiochus in Act I, Bérénice speaks of 'cet Antiochus'

> dont les soins
> Ont eu tout l'Orient et Rome pour témoins . . .

Antiochus replies:

> Rome vous vit, Madame, arriver avec lui.
> Dans l'Orient désert quel devint mon ennui!

In the first couplet there is a certain balance between 'Rome' and 'Orient'. The Orient is here the place where the warriors made their name on the battlefield and returned to Rome in triumph. In Antiochus's reply the picture changes. Bérénice was intoxicated by the splendour of Rome and left the lovesick Antiochus to languish in the 'desert'. It is a mistake to suggest, as some writers have done, that too much attention has been paid to 'l'Orient désert'. We are enormously and rightly impressed by the spectacle of huge vistas of desolation unfolding in front of our eyes. The line, however, is a good deal more than that. The juxtaposition Rome/Orient is closely interwoven with the main theme. They are the alternatives which present themselves to the protagonists, the symbols of success and failure. For Titus success in the eyes of the world means acceptance of Rome's marriage laws, and failure a bolt to the East.

If Rome for Titus is a grim reality, for Bérénice it begins as a mirage. Success means marriage to Titus and a seat by his side on the throne; failure, not a bolt but banishment to the Orient. The mirage dissolves. Antiochus has followed her to Rome. They will leave, as we know, at the same time, moving down in the scale to finish their lives buried in the boring desolate East.

4

Act I has been called 'the illusion of Bérénice'. Act II might be called 'the disillusion of Titus' whose worst fears are confirmed by Paulin, and Act III 'the disillusion of Bérénice' who learns that in spite of her immense optimism in Act I Titus, incredibly, is going to break off the engagement and send her back to the Orient.

Act IV is the act in which Titus explains, or rather endeavours to explain, his decision. When we examine his reasons or, more accurately, his excuses, we find that there is something decidedly enigmatic about his motives.

We should begin by looking at his soliloquy in Scene 4. It is by way of being a rehearsal for his meeting with Bérénice in Scene 5. He asks himself

some of the questions that she will put to him and tries to answer
them:

> Je viens percer un coeur que j'adore, qui m'aime.
> Et pourquoi le percer? Qui l'ordonne? Moi-même.
> Car enfin Rome a-t-elle expliqué ses souhaits?
> L'entendons-nous crier autour de ce palais?
> Vois-je l'État penchant au bord du précipice?
> Ne le puis-je sauver que par ce sacrifice?...
> Non, non, encore un coup, ne précipitons rien.
> Rome sera pour nous.

Then the answer:

>   Titus, ouvre les yeux!
> Quel air respires-tu? N'es-tu pas dans ces lieux
> Où la haine des rois, avec le lait sucée,
> Par crainte ou par amour ne peut être effacée?
> Rome jugea ta Reine en condamnant ses rois.
> N'as-tu pas en naissant entendu cette voix?...
> Ah lâche! fais l'amour, et renonce à l'Empire.
> Au bout de l'univers va, cours te confiner,
> Et fais place à des coeurs plus dignes de régner.
> Sont-ce là ces projets de grandeur et de gloire
> Qui devaient dans les coeurs consacrer ma mémoire?

The tone is highly emotional with its two references to 'percer un
coeur', its self-questioning, its staccato phrasing. Although he sucked it in
with his mother's milk, he is extremely sceptical about Rome's antipathy
to kings and queens. He resorts to a curious form of rhetoric in order to
bolster up his decision: 'Titus, ouvre les yeux!... Ah lâche! fais l'amour
...Au bout de l'univers va... te confiner... fais place à des coeurs plus
dignes de régner...'

In Scene 5 Bérénice, speaking of her response to Titus's original declaration of love, puts the 64,000 dollar question:

>   Ignoriez-vous vos lois,
> Quand je vous l'avouai pour la première fois?
> A quel excès d'amour m'avez-vous amenée!
> Que ne me disiez-vous: 'Princesse infortunée,
> Où vas-tu t'engager, et quel est ton espoir?
> Ne donne point un coeur qu'on ne peut recevoir.'

Titus's reply could hardly be weaker or less convincing:

> Mon coeur se gardait bien d'aller dans l'avenir
> Chercher ce qui pouvait un jour nous désunir.
> Je voulais qu'à mes voeux rien ne fût invincible,
> Je n'examinais rien, j'espérais l'impossible.
> Que sais-je? j'espérais de mourir à vos yeux,
> Avant que d'en venir à ces cruels adieux.
> Les obstacles semblaient renouveler ma flamme.

> Tout l'Empire parlait; mais la gloire, Madame,
> Ne s'était pas encor fait entendre à mon cœur
> Du ton dont elle parle au cœur d'un Empereur.

The courtship has lasted five years. Titus always intended to marry Bérénice, but it appears that there were difficulties during Vespasian's lifetime. Bérénice reproaches Titus for not telling her about the 'laws', but she goes on to say:

> Tout l'Empire a vingt fois conspiré contre nous.

It seems to be the reason why Titus postponed the marriage until his father died and he was free to decide for himself. His answer amounts to this: 'Yes, I knew about the law, but I simply couldn't do without you. I tried not to think about the future. I simply hoped that something would turn up, that things would work out. It wasn't until I became Emperor that I suddenly realised to the full my obligations and knew that we couldn't go on with it.'

Bérénice suggests a compromise:

> pourquoi nous séparer?
> Je ne vous parle point d'un heureux hyménée:
> Rome à ne vous plus voir m'a-t-elle condamnée?
> Pourquoi m'enviez-vous l'air que vous respirez?

Titus wavers:

> Hélas! vous pouvez tout, Madame. Demeurez:
> Je n'y résiste point. Mais je sens ma faiblesse:
> Il faudra vous combattre et vous craindre sans cesse,
> Et sans cesse veiller à retenir mes pas
> Que vers vous à toute heure entraînent vos appas.

In spite of the *bienséances* this is a possible solution. They have lived chastely in Rome for five years. They could continue to do so if Titus were willing. He is not, but his reasons are no more convincing than those he gave for the break: if she were around he wouldn't be able to concentrate on his job as Emperor; he would always be slipping off to the 'love nest'!

It is a strange situation. Titus has decided against marriage. There has been no official pressure. He has made no attempt to have the law changed which is what happens in Corneille's *Tite et Bérénice* or what happened, as we are told in *Britannicus*, when the Emperor Claudius wanted to marry his niece. He has not even discussed the position with the senate. All he has done is to consult Paulin about public opinion. Paulin's report confirmed his worst fears. He accepted it without argument and made up his mind to stand by the decision he had already taken provisionally. There is nothing to prevent him, as Emperor, from changing the law by decree. He refuses to do so on the ground that it might provoke immediate violence or trouble in the future. This view is understandable; his refusal to engage in consultation is not. If he had tried to negotiate, found that he could not marry Bérénice without creating a dangerous situation and then decided against marriage, we should clearly have taken a different view of his character from the one we do now.

It becomes plain that Titus is determined that there shall be no marriage, that Bérénice shall not be allowed to remain unmarried in Rome, that he is bent on separation. We might go on to say that he seems determined to create the maximum unhappiness for the pair of them. In spite of the statement that he did not fully appreciate his obligations to the State until he was actually on the throne, which is difficult to reconcile with his remark that he avoided thinking about the future, he had long known that the marriage would meet with opposition and was unlikely to take place. The truth is that far from being carried away by passion like the characters in other plays, he walked with his eyes open into one of those impossible Racinian dilemmas. In most cases they end in death: in the present instance the outcome is possibly even more painful.

Death of course is by no means ruled out, but it can take more than one form. Andromaque and Bajazet face a choice between the throne and death. For Titus the two go together. The throne without Bérénice is a living death:

> Mais il ne s'agit plus de *vivre*, il faut *régner*.

He is not at all sure that he can go through with it. He tells Paulin that he does not know whether he will be able to survive his decision to send Bérénice away which points to suicide. There is another hint at the meeting with Bérénice in Act IV. When he learns from her letter in Act V that she intends to kill herself, he announces that if she does he will do the same. The double suicide is only prevented by a pact that they will both live it out and Bérénice's declaration:

> Je vivrai, je suivrai vos ordres absolus.

Two conflicting interpretations of Titus's motives have been advanced by Raymond Picard and Philip Butler. Professor Picard takes Titus's statement that he did not appreciate his obligations to the full until he became Emperor literally. He sees it as the influx of a kind of secular grace leading to 'conversion'.[8] Professor Butler attaches the utmost importance to the first line of Titus's reply to a speech of Bérénice's ending with the words, 'je n'ai plus à redouter que vous':

> Et c'est moi seul aussi qui pouvais me détruire.[9]

'This line', he writes, 'illumines the whole tragedy like a flash of lightning'. It does so because it is a revelation of the *Todesmotiv*. For Professor Butler a 'kind of strange and terrible death-wish' is the explanation of Titus's 'fever to trample on all he holds most dear'.[10]

I find this view a good deal more convincing than Professor Picard's theory of 'conversion'. It brings Titus into line with a number of Racine's other characters. Death, or rather a hankering after death and self-destruction, is seldom far from the minds of even the most robust of them like Xipharès and Monime.

There are other factors which throw further light on Titus's attitude. Although Bérénice does not suffer from the violent passion of an Hermione, a Roxane or a Phèdre, there is no reason to think that she is in any way under-sexed. Strong sexual feeling would appear to explain her concentration on her 'man', her apparent indifference to the position of empress and her readiness to stay on in Rome unmarried. It is a fair inference that by comparison Titus is decidedly under-sexed. If he were not he would surely have been a good deal less eager to 'trample on all he holds most dear', less disposed to take the ban on marriage to a queen lying down.

Nor is that all. Something which is usually described as self-esteem, but which I am tempted to call vainglory, plays a considerable part in his decision. That much is apparent from the soliloquy. It is seen again when he says to Bérénice:

> Mais, Madame, après tout, me croyez vous indigne
> De laisser un exemple à la postérité,
> Qui sans de grands efforts ne puisse être imité?

It reappears in the picture he draws in Act V of the emperor who prefers love to 'gloire':

> et je dois moins encore vous dire
> Que je suis prêt pour vous d'abandonner l'Empire,
> De vous suivre, et d'aller trop content de mes fers,
> Soupirer avec vous au bout de l'univers.
> Vous-même rougiriez de ma lâche conduite:
> Vous verriez à regret marcher à votre suite
> Un indigne empereur, sans empire, sans cour,
> Vil spectacle aux humains des faiblesses d'amour.

The first passage is a positive, the second a negative approach. Titus is anxious to seize the opportunity of setting an example to the world and seems oblivious of the fact that the banishment of Bérénice will be taken for granted by the Roman people and is unlikely to bring him the celebrity he expects. He is even more anxious to avoid turning himself into a humiliating spectacle which might well have a more lasting impact on peoples' memories than what they regard as correct behaviour. There is an element of cruelty in the statement in the second passage that he is not prepared to give up the Empire 'for you'. The idea that she would be ashamed of such a man is used to play down the real reason: his own horror at the idea of being reduced to a 'vil spectacle . . . des faiblesses d'amour'. One suspects that Paulin's account of the bad example of Mark Antony in Act II has registered with Titus. The last lines are an echo of words used by Titus in the soliloquy. 'Au bout de l'univers' is almost certainly another reference to the 'Orient'.[11]

I want to stress particularly the vividness of the final couplet with its accumulation of sordid images—they inevitably recall by way of contrast Bérénice's description of the splendour of the celebrations in Act I—and the acuteness of the feeling behind it:

> Un indigne empereur, sans empire, sans cour,
> Vil spectacle aux humains des faiblesses d'amour.

For Titus this represents another form of the 'living death' that I have already mentioned. We may conclude that the choice before him is three-fold: 'living death' on the throne; 'living death' wandering, humiliated, at the other end of the earth; or suicide. Only a Racinian protagonist could fail to see that the last alternative is the most inimical of all to 'gloire'.

5

I must confess to taking a less sympathetic view of Titus than either Professor Picard or Professor Butler or, for that matter, a good many other people who have written about *Bérénice*. For me it is as much a study of human frailty as any other play of Racine's. In the final scene, addressing himself to Antiochus, Titus says:

> Soyez ici témoin de toute ma faiblesse.

Titus's verdict on himself echoes Arsace's verdict on his master which brings out the resemblances between them that I have already mentioned:

> Jamais dans un grand coeur vit-on plus de faiblesse?

Titus and Antiochus are both distinguished soldiers. There are plenty of references to their feats in the Roman-Jewish war. What strikes us, however, is the gap between their martial and their moral qualities. They are as bold as brass on the battlefield, but their physical courage is not matched, as we should expect it to be, by a corresponding moral courage. That is why 'gloire', which stood for victory in the field, takes on a different meaning in the later scenes and will be stigmatized as 'cruel' and oppressive. It is also the reason why the emphasis falls on a different word.

'Faiblesse' is more than a key-word. It is almost a shorthand statement of the different forms of weakness which inhabit the 'grand coeur'. Titus

is struggling to do what he believes to be his duty, but there is no grandeur, nothing glorious about the way it is done. Bérénice is the unfortunate victim of his various weaknesses. She is the passionate Racinian
woman who has been led on, then cruelly abandoned amid a chorus of the
highest sounding and most abject pronouncements. Antiochus is the defeated lover who is both a mirror and a warning to the others. While he is
hardly a character who commands admiration, his unfeeling treatment by
Bérénice inevitably qualifies the sympathy we feel for her when it comes to
her turn to be rejected.

Although he is bent on sacrificing his happiness without putting up a
fight, Titus goes through the same vacillations as a Pyrrhus, an Hermione
or an Agamemnon. There is a dramatic illustration in Act IV, Sc. 8. He
learns at the same moment that Bérénice is threatening suicide and that
the assembled tribunes, consuls and senate are asking for him 'au nom de
l'État'. He is faced with the *physical* choice between the door leading to
Bérénice's apartment and the door leading to the room where the officials
of the State await him. Antiochus cries imploringly 'Courez chez la
Reine', while the horrified Paulin only just carries the day with his

> Quoi? vous pourriez, Seigneur, par cette indignité,
> De l'Empire à vos pieds fouler la majesté?

Titus's departure in the direction of the senate is a sign of the part
played by authority in the final struggle and of his defeat.

After speaking with girlish enthusiasm of the people decorating Titus's
statues with laurels in Act I, Bérénice has come to recognize the insincerity of the people who have been obsequiously and boringly waiting on
her in her apartment and of whom she speaks so disparagingly at her first
meeting with Antiochus. She is haunted by the fear of being exposed to
the derisive laughter of the crowd if she stays long enough in Rome and is
driven out at the behest of the senate:

> Qui? moi? j'aurais voulu, honteuse et méprisée,
> D'un peuple qui me hait soutenir la risée?

She is anxious to leave at once. For Paulin the attitude of the people is
seen as a positive inducement to get rid of her:

> Rome, qui gémissait, triomphe avec raison;
> Tous les temples ouverts fument en votre nom;
> Et le peuple, élevant vos vertus jusqu'aux nues,
> Va partout de lauriers couronner vos statues.

It is exactly the opposite of the situation dreamed of by Titus who spoke
of himself as being

> Dans l'espoir d'élever Bérénice à l'Empire,
> De reconnaître un jour son amour et sa foi,
> Et de voir à ses pieds tout le monde avec moi.

It is the reappearance of the double illusion. Arsace, who is vainly hoping that his master will take Titus's place in the affections of the rejected Bérénice, looks at things from a different point of view and is perhaps closer than Paulin to a correct reading of Titus's character. Titus, he says, has not seen Bérénice:

> Le peuple avec transport l'arrête et l'environne,
> Applaudissant aux noms que le sénat lui donne;
> Et ces noms, ces respects, ces applaudissements,
> Deviennent pour Titus autant d'engagements,
> Qui le liant, Seigneur, d'une honorable chaîne,
> Malgré tous ses soupirs et les pleurs de la Reine,
> Fixent dans son devoir ses voeux irrésolus.

'Arrête', 'environne', 'engagements', 'liant', 'chaîne', 'fixent', 'voeux irrésolus'—the use of a succession of words in ascending order, all suggesting some form of bond, followed by the downward plunge to 'voeux irrésolus', provide a striking picture of the weak man caught in a trap which is slowly but inexorably closing in on him. The long, heavy words, 'applaudissant', 'applaudissements', 'engagements', then the sharp, cutting 'chaîne' convey the impression of Titus's own inclinations being completely smothered. He is the bewildered individual surrounded by the cheering crowd, swamped by the people with no will to resist them. The final line summarizes the process:

> Fixent / dans son devoir // ses voeux irrésolus.

The sharp 'fixent', sounding almost like the click of handcuffs, the pause and the strong caesura at the hemistich, coupled with the ethical associations of 'devoir', somehow pin him down.

The picture is completed by Titus's own account to Bérénice of the meeting with the senate:

> Je croyais ma vertu moins prête à succomber
> Et j'ai honte du trouble où je la vois tomber.
> J'ai vu devant mes yeux Rome entière assemblée;
> Le sénat m'a parlé; mais mon âme accablée
> Écoutait sans entendre, et ne leur a laissé
> Pour prix de leurs transports qu'un silence glacé.

It would clearly be absurd to speak of the 'triumph' of 'duty' over 'inclination'. What we see is a man who is doing the right thing technically, but so far from producing any moral satisfaction, it leaves him standing speechless and unable to take in or find any reply to the eulogy and applause of the august assembly. What we also observe is the vast gap between Titus's public image and the man he really is. He is reduced to an uncomprehending cipher by the din and excitement going on around him, demolished by the boom of 'succomber/tomber', but the people are so

anxious that the affair shall be settled in the way they want that wishful
thinking prevents them from seeing the sort of man they have got for their
emperor—a dummy.

Titus and Bérénice have lived together for five years—the period recurs
obsessively—and are now being torn apart. The law which tears them
apart is felt to be an empty, meaningless, repugnant imperative. Caligula
and Nero were 'monsters'—'monsters whose names I mention with regret', says Paulin a trifle primly—but as they were careful not to infringe
this one law no objection was taken to their excesses, which is a damaging
comment on the values at stake and the sycophantic attitude of the court,
already mentioned disparagingly, as we remember, by Titus in his discussion with Paulin in Act II. For at bottom the law is a fraud:

> Ces festons, où nos noms enlacés l'un dans l'autre . . .
> Sont autant d'imposteurs . . .

Bérénice's criticism is justified. It is bitterly ironical. The 'festons' are
tantalizingly interwoven like the intertwined limbs of lovers: the real
people will be wrenched apart before they ever achieve this kind of union.

This is also the moment when the illusions so eloquently described by
Bérénice in the closing speech of Act I are seen for what they are. Nor
should we miss the link with Paulin's

> Et le peuple, élevant vos vertus jusqu'aux nues,
> Va partout de lauriers couronner vos statues.

There are no 'noms enlacés' here. The people are decorating Titus's
statues, knowing that he will do what they expect of him. Paulin's
'statues' match Bérénice's 'images' and her own reference to 'lauriers' in
the first act. Titus has now in fact been reduced to something which in its
lifelessness resembles a statue. He has become the frozen, inhuman
figure of the 'Ruler' which conceals the speechless dummy whose 'âme
accablée'

> ne leur a laissé
> Pour prix de leurs transports qu'un *silence glacé*.

'It is not necessary', said Racine in his preface, 'that there should be blood
and corpses in a tragedy: it is sufficient that its action should be great and
its actors heroic, that passions should be aroused by it, and that everything should breathe the majestic sadness which is the source of all the
pleasure that comes from tragedy.'

The fact that he has given us the portrait not of a hero, but of a weakling
does not detract from his particular achievement in *Bérénice* or affect what
he chose to describe as 'tristesse majestueuse'. It explains, indeed, the
peculiar flavour of the play and its poetry which is apparent in its tone
and vocabulary or, more precisely, the contrast between them. In this, as

in other plays, the ordinary mortal is transposed into a world which is a
poetic creation and in which all his actions take on a heightened significance—the feeling that this is larger, more intense than life—which is
proper to poetry. The poetry is not the poetry of disastrous and destructive passion, but of jangling nerves, resignation, separations and departures which give it a softness, a languor, a strange autumnal flavour
emphasized by the references to 'la dernière fois'.[12] A number of words
are continually recurring and reinforce one another: 'faiblesse', 'cruel',
'larmes', 'sacrifice'. The characters are not pursuers; they are pursued and
never left for a moment in peace:

> Ma gloire inexorable à toute heure me suit.

Titus and Antiochus are passive; their nerves register the least tremor.
Antiochus says of himself:

> Tous mes moments ne sont qu'un éternel passage
> De la crainte à l'espoir, de l'espoir à la rage.
> Et je respire encor?

The word 'cruel' echoes and re-echoes all through the play, registering
the impact of inhuman demands on the weak, fallible human being:

> Résolu d'accomplir ce cruel sacrifice . . .

> Ah! que sous de beaux noms cette gloire est cruelle!

> plus j'y pense,
> Plus je sens chanceler ma cruelle constance.

Racine's 'tristesse majestueuse' is something of a paradox, a combination of opposites. The manner is lofty and dignified, but is qualified by the
inner softness and languor. The grand manner is used to expose the
hollowness of grandeur:

> Plaignez ma grandeur importune.
> Maître de l'univers, je règle sa fortune;
> Je puis faire les rois, je puis les déposer:
> Cependant de mon coeur je ne puis disposer . . .

One of the clearest signs of Titus's weakness is his self-pity which is
even more strikingly expressed by 'grandeur importune' than the recurrence of the word 'cruel'. The passage brings out admirably the contrast
between the public figure and the private individual, between the grandeur of the palace—we remember 'la pompe de ces lieux'—and the sorry
state of its inhabitants. Finally, it invites a comparison with Auguste's 'Je
suis maître de moi comme de l'univers' which describes the perfect unity
of the public figure and the private person which is precisely what is
lacking in Titus—a lack reflected in the contrast between 'tristesse' and
'majestueuse'.

Nothing that I have said is intended as criticism of the poetry. I merely wish to illustrate the effectiveness of the remarkable Racinian formula. It operates all through the play and is felt especially in individual lines of lamentation:

> Exemple infortuné d'une longue constance . . .
>
> Et je viens donc vous dire un éternel adieu.
>
> J'aimais, Seigneur, j'aimais: je voulais être aimée.

It offers one of the great moments of French poetry:

> Pour jamais! Ah! Seigneur, songez-vous en vous-même
> Combien ce mot cruel est affreux quand on aime?
> Dans un mois, dans un an, comment souffrirons-nous,
> Seigneur, que tant de mers me séparent de vous?
> Que le jour recommence et que le jour finisse,
> Sans que jamais Titus puisse voir Bérénice,
> Sans que de tout le jour je puisse voir Titus!

The anguish is marvellously expressed in the slow, dragging subjunctives of the last three lines, the internal rhymes with their sighing *s*-s and *c*-s, their sharp *i*-s and the pauses beautifully balancing the beginning and ending of 'the day' in the fifth line as well as Titus and Bérénice in the last two lines.

6

What we discover at the heart of *Bérénice* is something totally unexpected. It is a new kind of 'secret' which is never described as such: the secret of Titus's motives. Racinian characters are placed in a Cornelian situation. Their reactions to it turn *Bérénice* into what one writer has called the least Cornelian of Racine's plays. On the face of it, Rome stands for right, the Orient for wrong values. The protagonists appear to do the right thing in submitting to the Roman 'law'. It is clear, however, that in one respect at least there is something badly wrong with Rome's values and that Titus's repugnance for a thoroughly unreasonable law is justified. This means that everybody is wrong which produces the tragedy. M. Picard's theory of 'secular grace' is an excellent account of what happens in Corneille. His characters do, indeed, emerge strengthened from the conflict; they really are 'new men'. This is precisely the reverse of what happens in *Bérénice*. The protagonists are without a semblance of the moral buoyancy of Corneille's characters; they are completely broken by the conflict, and are left to play out time in the most agonizing circumstances: Titus on a throne which is equated with living death; Bérénice and Antiochus in the desolate Orient which becomes something like a secular hell. Bérénice's final pronouncement is a splendid example of the 'tristesse majestueuse', a sort of requiem following an overwhelming defeat:

Adieu: servons tous trois d'exemple à l'univers
De l'amour la plus tendre et la plus malheureuse
Dont il puisse garder l'histoire douloureuse.

'*Bérénice*', said Sainte-Beuve in one of his memorable overstatements, 'est une charmante et mélodieuse faiblesse dans l'oeuvre de Racine comme la Champmeslé le fut dans sa vie'.[13] The point of view was not new though the manner of expressing it was. Already in his own lifetime critics were saying that this, Racine's favourite secular tragedy, was not up to his usual standard, and some of them have continued to say it ever since. There are broadly speaking two views. The first is that in making duty triumph over inclination Racine was betraying his own genius and was only saved from disaster by his own virtuosity. The other view is that far from being a failure, *Bérénice* is his masterpiece because it really shows us the 'tender' Racine—using the word 'tender' in the modern and not the seventeenth-century sense. These are extreme views. If neither is convincing, if the truth lies somewhere between the two, it is because neither takes sufficient account of the variety of Racine's output or his virtuosity. The virtuosity, the desire to do something that nobody else had attempted, to write a tragedy which was still a genuine tragedy in spite of the absence of blood and corpses, is obvious from Racine's preface. He succeeded in that he produced something exceptional, something which stands alone among his plays. This does not alter the fact that for me it represents what I am inclined to call the soft centre of his work. And that is its principal weakness. While therefore I put it below *Andromaque*, *Britannicus*, *Phèdre* and *Athalie*, it nevertheless remains a unique work which offers an experience that is not to be found in any of his other plays.

NOTES

[1] G. Michaut, *La Bérénice de Racine*, 1907.

[2] *Histoire de la littérature française au XVIIᵉ siècle*, IV, 1954, pp. 333–5; *Littérature française: l'Age Classique*, I, 1624–1660, 1968, p. 301; *Le Théâtre classique*, 1970, pp. 79–80.

[3] Gaius Suetonius Tranquillus, *The Twelve Caesars*, Tr. Robert Graves, 1962, p. 266.

[4] and [5] *Ibid., loc. cit.*

[6] Exactly the same is true of Titus, as we can see from his meeting with Antiochus in Act III, Sc. 1, though he is presumably unaware that Antiochus was once a suitor. He is anxious for Antiochus's help and Antiochus's description of himself as 'un prince malheureux' simply does not register. Titus almost echoes Bérénice when he says:

Elle ne voit dans Rome et n'écoute que vous;
Vous ne faites qu'un coeur et qu'une âme avec nous.

[7] Paulin's account is hardly in keeping with the historical facts. Caesar certainly avoided marriage with Cleopatra, but after winning a war on her behalf in 47 B.C., he took her back to Rome with him where she lived openly as his mistress until his assassination. She realized that she was *mal vue* in Rome and returned to Egypt.

Although it was not legally valid, Antony went through a marriage ceremony with her in 37 B.C.

[8] *O.C.* I, pp. 475–6.

[9] This appears to echo a line from the soliloquy in Act IV, Sc. 4:

    Et pourquoi le percer? qui l'ordonne? Moi-même.

[10] In *Racine* (Modern Judgements), Ed. R. C. Knight, 1969, pp. 212 *et seq.* See also *Classicisme et baroque dans l'oeuvre de Racine*, pp. 232–44.

[11] I find it a little odd that this passage with its 'je dois encore moins voux dire' prompted André Stegmann to declare that Corneille's Tite is 'much less Cornelian than Racine's because he is ready to renounce the Empire' (*L'Héroisme cornélien*, II, 1968, p. 640).

[12] This evidently prompted Antoine Adam's somewhat surprising comparison with Lamartine (*Le Théâtre classique*, p. 81).

[13] *Oeuvres*, I, (Pléiade), 1949, p. 760.

'BAJAZET'

1672

Avec *Bajazet*, il atteint les bas-fonds.
            JEAN-LOUIS BARRAULT
    .l'admirable *Bajazet*.
                ANTOINE ADAM

CHAPTER 6

'BAJAZET'

1672

I

ALTHOUGH the Palace of the Sultans in Istanbul has long been a museum and suffers from the coldness and hollowness that invariably afflict buildings which were once inhabited and have been turned into national monuments, it has a particular interest for admirers of Racine. It is generally assumed that the setting of *Bajazet* is a room near the entrance to the women's quarters. When I was there some years ago they were disappointingly closed for repairs. I could therefore only speculate from a distance on the precise location of the tragedy. There was, however, no difficulty in discovering the place 'at the foot of the walls lapped by the sea' from which Racine's vizir and his fellow conspirators made their escape after the collapse of the palace revolution: reminding us, incidentally, that the history of the Turkish sultans ended with a reversal of the role and the rescue of the last sultan from the victorious revolutionaries by a British gunboat.

Not the least interesting of the many exhibits are the life size models of past sultans clothed in their royal apparel. They include Amurat IV whose sinister expression reminds us forcibly of Racine's description of him as 'le cruel Amurat'.

Amurat or Mourad IV became sultan in 1623 at the age of thirteen. He owed his early rise to the formidable janissaries. We hear a good deal about their power in the first act of *Bajazet*. In 1622 they killed Osman, the reigning sultan, who is said to have been a brother or half-brother of Amurat's. The following year they deposed Mustapha, another brother, and put Amurat on the throne. Amurat took part in campaigns against the Persians in 1635 and 1638. The sultans were particularly afraid of the rivalry of brothers. Amurat had two brothers or half-brothers, Bayezid and Suleiman, murdered in 1635. The murders were reported in an official dispatch by the Comte de Césy who was French ambassador to the Ottoman Empire from 1618 to 1642 and who was Racine's original source of inspiration for *Bajazet*.[1] It is true that Amurat appointed as sultana a favourite member of his harem, who was renowned for her beauty and whose name may have been Roxana, before she had borne him a son. In spite of Racine's insistence that this part of the story had come to him

from the Comte de Césy, there is no evidence that she made advances to
Bayezid.

In Segrais' version of the story, which is thought to be closer to history
than Racine's, Amurat's mother, who is called Roxane and who is
Bajazet's stepmother, develops a passion for her stepson. He responds to
her advances, then cools off. She discovers that he is in love with a seven-
teen-year-old slave named Floridon. There is a pact. Roxane has Bajazet
for six nights a week and Floridon for one, which says a good deal for his
sexual capacity. Roxane becomes afraid that she is losing her looks. She
feigns illness and spies on Bajazet to see how he is reacting. She discovers
that he is exceeding his quota with Floridon. A first messenger from
Amurat ordering the death of Bajazet had been executed, but moved by
her jealousy Roxane obeys a second order and has Bajazet strangled by the
mutes.[2]

Amurat died in 1640. According to some accounts his death was the
result of the excessive demands made by the favourite on a man whose
health had been seriously undermined by the orgies of an oriental court.
He was succeeded by his brother Ibrahim, a sickly character who is mentioned disparagingly by the vizir in *Bajazet* and by Racine himself in his
second preface. The janissaries deposed Ibrahim in 1648 and in 1651 they
killed the sultan-mother who was reputed to have been her stepson's
mistress.

2

In his first preface it appeared sufficient to Racine to tell his readers that
his play was a true account of an affair which had taken place 'not more
than thirty years ago'. When he came to write the second preface in 1676
he seems to have felt that he must offer some justification for drawing on
recent history. There was nothing against it in 'the rules', but it would be
a mistake for a dramatist to present people and events from the recent
history of his own country. He should choose another people and another country as Aeschylus had done with his Persians. 'The distance of
the country', he said, 'makes up for the closeness in time.' Turkey, he
added disarmingly, was so far away that her people gave the impression
of belonging to a different century and for that reason possessed the dignity
necessary to tragedy.

If Racine had been the first dramatist to take his material from recent
history his arguments would have sounded more convincing, but at least
two other dramatists had written plays about the same period and the
same country.[3] We therefore have the feeling that he is indulging in the
sort of 'artifice' practised by a number of his own protagonists. A hint of
his real reasons appears in the final paragraph. In that paragraph he insists

that his play is a faithful picture of Turkish life and that those people are mistaken who have suggested that his heroines are 'too knowing in love and too delicate for women born among people who are regarded here as barbarians.'[4]

The truth of the matter is that Racine fastened on the Césy story because it offered opportunities which were not to be found in Greek myth or Roman history. It provided an outlet for some of the most ruthless impulses in his own make-up. *Bajazet* is the toughest play in the entire canon. That is why there have always been people, as Racine had come to realize, who find it difficult to 'take'.

It does not matter whether *Bajazet* is an exact picture of Turkish life or not. It is essentially a creation which is why I used the word 'inspiration' in discussing the sources. We know that the basic human instincts are unchanging and that the particular form they take is determined by circumstance and environment. That is what happens in *Bajazet*. It conforms to the general pattern of Racine's plays. What distinguishes it from them is its atmosphere: that extraordinary suffocating atmosphere of violence, savagery and sex.

The savagery is in no sense confined to the slaughter at the close: it is woven into the very fibres of the play and projected overwhelmingly in the figure of Roxane. For Roxane is unique among Racine's characters. She is the only one of his princesses who is not of royal blood and has risen from the ranks. She owes her rise not to her beauty or intelligence though she possesses both: she owes it to her dexterity in bed. Osmin puts it well. Many countries had sent the flower of their young womanhood to fill Amurat's harem, but Roxane had come out top:

> Car on dit qu'elle seule a fixé son amour.

'Amour' is a euphemism; the operative word is 'fixé'. The owner of a harem is hardly likely to fall in love in any acceptable sense. He is looking not for a permanent union with a single woman, but for variety. It was because she was better at satisfying his needs than any other member of the harem that Roxane managed to introduce something like a temporary stability into the sultan's sexual life.

A puritanical critic has spoken of Roxane as an adept of 'the rank sort of love to be expected of the inmate of a harem'. The suggestion that she is a professional, a 'top' courtesan, is warranted; the deprecatory attitude is not. What makes her for all her savagery a moving and at times a pathetic figure is her enormous vitality and her very genuine desire to become an 'honest woman', to quit the ranks of the court strumpets by ridding herself of the odious Amurat and marrying the amiable, normal and slightly 'wet' Bajazet. That is why the play itself is a moving as well as a horrifying experience.

If my description of Bajazet seems a trifle uncharitable, it is because comparisons between Roxane and her victims make us feel that they are somehow unsatisfactory both artistically and as people. Although they have been promoted to the rank of protagonist, they are clearly modelled on the *jeunes premiers* of earlier plays. Jean Dutourd went much too far in describing them as 'impossible', but there can be no doubt that the weakness is there and that it lies in the fact that though they possess some of the virtues of the *jeunes premiers* they represent an intermediate stage; they lack the charm and spontaneity of their predecessors and the maturity of their successors.

Bajazet is one of the plays in which statistics are illuminating. Roxane's role, as we should expect, is the longest in the play with 461 lines. Atalide's is only a little shorter with 443 lines. There is a large gap between the length of their roles and Bajazet's which has a mere 262 lines. It is not only far shorter than those of the other protagonists; it is appreciably shorter than Acomat's which contains 372 lines. The truth is that though he is the protagonist who gives his name to the tragedy there is remarkably little for him to do or say. Racine must have been conscious of the weakness. The need to improve Bajazet's standing artificially and give him more weight explains why Acomat speaks of the reputation he had acquired by his martial exploits before the play opens for which there is no historical evidence. Nor were his efforts to boost Bajazet confined to the play. In his second preface he remarks that men probably do not love with the same delicacy as women and goes on:

> Aussi ai-je pris soin de mettre une grande différence entre la passion de Bajazet et les tendresses de ses amantes. Il garde au milieu de son amour la férocité de la nation.

It would be difficult to imagine a less convincing description of Bajazet. We shall find, indeed, that he is singularly lacking in 'passion' and in the 'ferocity' which might have enabled him to save the situation. For in spite of what Racine says, 'passion' and 'ferocity' belong exclusively to Roxane.[5]

3

The stage direction tells us that 'La scène est à Constantinople, autrement dite Byzance, dans le Sérail du Grand Seigneur'. Racine took a special interest in the characters' environment in *Bajazet* as we can see from details like the use of archaic place names—'Byzance' for 'Constantinople' and 'Babylone' for 'Baghdad'—and the ambivalent 'Sérail'. The result is that the Palace of the Sultans makes an even greater contribution to the prevailing tension than the palace of the Caesars in *Britannicus*. Whatever Corneille and Mme de Sévigné may have had to say about his handling of Turkish manners, he is immensely successful in conveying the atmosphere of an oriental palace with its corruption and intrigues, its subterfuges and deceptions, its dark winding passages, its grotesque inhabitants: the flitting shadows, the silent cowering slaves, the horrifying 'mutes' clutching their knotted cords, the spies passing furtively in both directions.

There are vivid glimpses of the degenerate offspring of the sultans:

> L'imbécile Ibrahim, sans craindre sa naissance,
> Traîne, exempt de péril, une éternelle enfance.
> Indigne également de vivre et de mourir,
> On l'abandonne aux mains qui daignent le nourrir.

Bajazet is commended by Acomat precisely because of his superiority over the sultans' children:

> Car enfin Bajazet dédaigna de tout temps
> La molle oisiveté des enfants des sultans.

One group of interrelated images plays a major part in building up the sense of unrelieved tension which is characteristic of life in the sultan's palace and of the tragedy: 'slaves', 'mutes', 'walls', 'passages' and 'doors'.

This is how Roxane describes the inhabitants and their setting:

> je tiens sous ma puissance
> Cette foule de chefs, d'esclaves, de muets,
> Peuple que dans ses murs renferme ce palais,
> Et dont à ma faveur les âmes asservies
> M'ont vendu dès longtemps leur silence et leurs vies.

It is a striking glimpse of oriental corruption: everybody has his price; nobody has any pride; they are not merely 'slaves'; they are 'âmes asservies'. Acomat, the soldier, speaks with biting contempt of people like that who spend their lives skulking inside the walls of the palace:

> esclaves obscurs,
> Nourris loin de la guerre à l'ombre de ses murs.

'Doors' open and shut. There are occasions when they open to admit a vizir to a secret meeting or a slave sent by the sultan on an errand of death:

> La porte du Sérail à ma voix s'est ouverte;
> Et d'abord une esclave à mes yeux s'est offerte,
> Qui m'a conduit sans bruit dans un appartement
> Où Roxane attentive écoutait son amant.
>
> *
>
> Et quoique sur la mer la porte fût fermée,
> Les gardes sans tarder l'ont ouverte à genoux
> Aux ordres du Sultan qui s'adressent à vous.

This is not the commonest function of doors. Usually we hear them slamming in the face of a conspirator who is trying to make his way into the palace or behind the back of a prisoner shutting him even more tightly inside the frightening walls:

> Sortez. Que le Sérail soit désormais fermé . . .
>
> *
>
> Songez-vous que je tiens les portes du Palais,
> Que je puis vous l'ouvrir ou fermer pour jamais . . .

Bajazet laments 'l'indigne prison où je suis renfermé' and pleads with the vizir:

> Du Sérail, s'il le faut, venez forcer la porte.

In the end Acomat and his men do force the door of the palace, but it is too late. Another door has already opened for a different purpose. It has opened on to death, on to the spectacle of the 'mutes' with their cords waiting, impatiently, for their victim.

In one place Acomat recalls his upbringing in the palace:

> Nourri dans le Sérail, j'en connais les détours . . .

We find the usual link between physical and verbal 'détours'. Bajazet reproaches Atalide for what he calls 'cet indigne détour', meaning the spurious declarations of love that she has made to Roxane on his behalf. Roxane flings the word back at Bajazet himself in the last act when she denounces his 'détours si bas'.

There are 'détours' of still another kind which prevent spies and messengers from completing their mission and returning to base. Amurat has sent a first messenger with an order to Roxane to have Bajazet executed. Acomat tells his confidant that the sultan's order was ignored and that another order disposed of the unfortunate messenger:

> Cet esclave n'est plus. Un ordre, cher Osmin,
> L'a fait précipiter dans le fond de l'Euxin.

In 'précipiter' we detect the sound of a scuffle in some dark corner of the palace, catch a glimpse of a body hurtling through the air. In the faint reverberation of 'le fond de l'Euxin' we hear the distant thud of the body hitting the surface of the water followed by the splash as it closes over the vanished slave.

4

Amurat has been away from his capital city for six months laying siege to Babylon. Acomat is planning a palace revolution which will remove him from the throne and make Bajazet sultan in his place. The success of the palace revolution depends primarily on two things: the failure of Amurat's campaign and Bajazet's agreeing to marry Roxane. She has developed a violent passion for him to which he does not respond. There will be plenty to say later about the conflicts at work in the play. For the moment it is sufficient to observe that there are three inter-related conflicts: military, political, psychological.

Acomat's confidant has just returned from a secret mission. Its aim was to discover two things: the state of the siege and the sultan's standing with the ferocious janissaries. When he hurries him into the palace so that he can hear his report before the arrival of Roxane for whom he is waiting in order to discuss plans for the palace revolution, the startled confidant says:

> Jadis une mort prompte eût suivi cette audace.

Bajazet is a play about love and death and despotism. What I want to emphasize is that the entire play takes place under the shadow of death, that all the characters face a threat of sudden violent death which will be realized with a vengeance in the last act. Although we never see him, 'le cruel Amurat' is more compellingly there than the dead Hector in *Andromaque* or Calchas in *Iphigénie*. He dominates the play because all the threats of death, and eventually the actual murders, either come from him or are the result of his position. That is the significance of 'une mort prompte' in the fifth line of the play.

After listening to the confidant's report on the present state of the campaign, Acomat puts a leading question:

> Amurat jouit-il d'un pouvoir absolu?

This is the reply:

> Amurat est content, si nous le voulons croire,
> Et semblait se promettre une heureuse victoire.
> Mais en vain par ce calme il croit nous éblouir:
> Il affecte un repos dont il ne peut jouir.
> C'est en vain que forçant ses soupçons ordinaires,
> Il se rend accessible à tous les janissaires:
> Il se souvient toujours que son inimitié
> Voulut de ce grand corps retrancher la moitié,
> Lorsque pour affermir sa puissance nouvelle,
> Il voulait, disait-il, sortir de leur tutelle.
> Moi-même j'ai souvent entendu leurs discours;
> Comme il les craint sans cesse, ils le craignent toujours.

Amurat is a despot, but an uneasy despot. He is uncertain of the loyalty of his army in the field, his mistress, his vizir, his half-brother and everybody else at the palace. He affects a 'calm' and a 'repose' which like most Racinian protagonists he ardently desires, but does not really enjoy because he is racked by suspicion. He has tried to break the hold or 'tutelle' that the janissaries have over him—nearly everybody in this play is haunted by the sensation of being under somebody's thumb—by halving their strength in order to assert his 'new power'. He has failed to do so. 'Affermir' describes an aim which is thwarted by the repeated 'en vain'. The geometrical division of the last line expresses with remarkable succinctness the profound fear and distrust which prevail on both sides in spite of the sultan's hobnobbing with his men. In the frightening world of *Bajazet* nothing is what it appears to be on the surface; there is a precarious balance based on fear which may collapse at any moment and let loose the horrors.

In this passage the sultan's uneasiness is described in negative terms. We are told of the absence of 'calm' and 'repose'. In other passages it is described in positive terms:

> Le superbe Amurat est toujours *inquiet* . . .
>
> Il n'en faut point douter, le Sultan *inquiet*
> Une seconde fois condamne Bajazet.

Amurat is not alone. All the characters suffer from an acute sense of uneasiness. Roxane speaks of the uneasiness felt by the sultan's mistresses who clearly include herself.

> Mais toujours *inquiète* avec tous ses appas . . .

The uneasiness is accompanied by a pervasive sense of frustration expressed by the words 'inutile' and 'impuissant'. In his report on the military situation Osmin remarks:

> Lui-même, fatigué d'un long siège *inutile*
> Semblait vouloir laisser Babylone tranquille,
> Et sans renouveler ses assauts impuissants,
> Résolu de combattre, attendait les Persans.

The siege is 'useless' in what appears to be an indecisive campaign; the sultan is disposed to give up his 'ineffectual' attacks and abandon the city to the 'tranquillity' which eludes him in his public and his private life. Acomat shares his master's frustration:

> et moi, dans une ville,
> Il me laisse exercer un pouvoir *inutile*.

In a later scene he refers even more pointedly and more desperately to a vizir's position under a despot as his 'fortune flottante'.

In the course of his report Osmin uses another important word, 'combat':

> Le succès du combat réglera leur conduite:
> Il faut voir du Sultan la victoire ou la fuite.

The word occurs on two more occasions in the same speech. Osmin is telling Acomat that the attitude of the janissaries towards their ruler will depend on the outcome of the battle. Amurat is suspended precariously between 'victory' and 'flight'—alternatives which are compressed into a single hemistich. If he wins, their attitude will be one of 'blind and base obedience'; if he loses, one of 'hatred' and hostility, probably leading to deposition and death.

The word 'combat' takes us to what I have already suggested is the central theme. In the brief exchange between Roxane and Acomat which follows the first breach between herself and Bajazet, she says:

> Acomat, c'en est fait.
> Vous pouvez retourner, je n'ai rien à vous dire.
> Du sultan Amurat je reconnais l'empire.
> Sortez. Que le Sérail soit désormais fermé,
> Et que tout rentre ici dans l'ordre accoutumé.

The last line is one of the most important, perhaps the most important of all, for an understanding of the play. Roxane purports to withdraw her support of the conspiracy against the sultan and to revert to the official legal position. What transpires is that all the different conflicts—military, political, psychological—form part of a larger conflict which contains them and at the same time introduces the moral element. It is a conflict between 'l'ordre accoutumé', or the 'old order', and the 'new order' which is expected to emerge from the palace revolution.

It is of the essence of the play that 'l'ordre accoutumé' is an evil order. What is of special importance is that the evil of the 'old order' is contagious. It infects even those who are trying to overthrow it and replace it by something better. This is the source of the moral devaluation which is characteristic of the world of *Bajazet*. Ironically, Bajazet's own attempt to reverse the trend will play a major part in the disaster.

We have seen, in some of the passages quoted earlier, the persistent, the almost obsessive references to 'slaves'.[6] It is in the nature of despotism that it reduces all the inhabitants of the palace to a condition of slavery. It is not confined to those who are technically slaves—Zatime and Zaïre are described not as 'confidants', but as the 'slaves' of Roxane and Atalide— all the protagonists except Atalide refer to themselves as 'slaves' or the victims of 'slavery'. I know, says Acomat of his relations with the sultan, that

> une mort sanglante est l'unique traité
> Qui reste entre *l'esclave* et le maître irrité.

There is Roxane's bitter comment on bed with Amurat:

> *Esclave*, elle reçoit son maître dans ses bras ...

It is matched by Bajazet's comment on marriage to Roxane:

> J'épouserais, et qui ...?
> Une *esclave* attachée à ses seuls intérêts ...

His observation on the offer by her of a crown is different:

> Je chéris, j'acceptai, sans tarder davantage,
> L'heureuse occasion de sortir d'*esclavage* ...

The inference is plain. All the characters, including the unseen Amurat, are engaged in their different, contradictory and conflicting ways in a struggle for freedom. It is the first and most important step towards that stability for which they all yearn. For Amurat it means the maintenance of the 'old order'; for the protagonists the overthrow of the 'old order' and the creation of a 'new order'.

In spite of the vital importance of the issues at stake, both parties are divided by internal conflicts. Amurat can only achieve his goal by victory in the field which will secure the loyalty of the janissaries and release him from their 'tutelle' which is his particular brand of 'slavery'. We shall see from what follows that he succeeds in consolidating his dissatisfied troops and that this does in fact bring him victory in the field.

Although Acomat has a personal interest in the fall of Amurat who is a threat to his life, he is single-minded. His primary aim is the removal of a ruthless tyrant and his replacement by a humane sultan. His intention of marrying Atalide is simply an additional safety measure and a minor matter, as he himself will demonstrate when he learns belatedly that she is in love with Bajazet. If his palace revolution seems doomed to failure from the start, it is because unlike Amurat he is incapable of overcoming the internal conflicts which would enable him to go into action with a united force behind him. In spite of internal dissensions, there is no conflict between the aims of the sultan and his men. They have a common aim: victory in the field. With the protagonists there are far-reaching conflicts between private and public interests. There are times, indeed, when they give the impression of being almost oblivious of the public interest and only caring about a 'new order' because it would enable them to achieve their personal goals.

Roxane's goal is marriage to Bajazet which would satisfy her passion, free her from the 'slavery' of Amurat's bed and legalize her position as sultana of which she is inordinately proud. Bajazet's goal is marriage to Atalide as hers is marriage to him, but he also wants the throne, as the last quotation showed, because it would free him from the 'slavery' of Amurat's palace.

We know that the dramatic power of the plays depends to a large extent on Racine's skill in placing the characters in a virtually impossible situation. Their position in *Bajazet* is probably the most desperate in any of the tragedies. If there is no palace revolution the odds are that, whether victorious or not, Amurat will find a way of murdering Bajazet, Roxane and Acomat. If the palace revolution fails, their doom is even more certain. It can only succeed, if at all, at the cost of enormous sacrifices by one or other of the protagonists. If it succeeds without the marriage of Bajazet and Roxane, she will lose her position as sultana as well as her man. She is not prepared to surrender either of them. Life with its tensions and its terrors has become so intolerable that if she cannot get her man and keep her throne, she will kill him and then commit suicide. Bajazet is therefore faced with three alternatives: marrying Roxane and abandoning Atalide; marrying Roxane and then getting rid of her as soon as he is safely on the throne; or death. Although Bajazet and Atalide are both ready to sacrifice their lives in order to save one another, nothing will induce him to marry Roxane, which would be a continuation of 'slavery', or to go on deceiving her.

There are three ways of mounting a palace revolution or, better, three requirements: violence, trickery and negotiation. Violence is inevitable. All the leading characters are guilty of trickery and deception. Acomat deceives the sultan. Roxane does the same. Bajazet and Atalide go far beyond their predecessors in *Britannicus* and for all their repugnance practise the most blatant deception on the unhappy Roxane. For we can hardly help sympathizing with her when she says bitterly to her slave:

> Avec quelle insolence et quelle cruauté
> Ils se jouaient tous deux de ma crédulité!

There remains negotiation. Peter France has remarked that 'metaphors of bargaining are common in *Bajazet*'.[7] Orientals have long had the reputation in the west of being ardent bargainers. The words 'prix', 'payé' and 'vendu' occur with some frequency, particularly in the later acts. Morally, the negotiations take place on different levels. Some involve sacrifices, others terrorization and blackmail. In Act V Atalide, who has already offered to sacrifice Bajazet to Roxane, raises her bid: if Roxane will spare his life, she will commit suicide forthwith and remove the 'rival' once for all. It is a cruel stroke of irony: at the time she makes the offer she does not know that Bajazet is already dead.

We shall find that the meetings between Bajazet and Roxane are largely taken up with bargaining and that this is reflected in the changes of tone. The bargaining is on a lower level morally than that between Roxane and Atalide, at any rate on Roxane's side. Her method is a reversal of the usual process which will be repeated in *Phèdre*. Instead of the man trying to 'buy' the woman, it is the woman who is trying to buy her way into the man's bed by the offer of the throne and merely insisting on marriage to secure her political position and become respectable. When Bajazet tries to tell her in his ambiguous manner what he is prepared to do in exchange for the throne, she cuts him short. These are not the sort of terms to satisfy the predatory female. 'Marry me', she says:

> Ta grâce est à ce *prix*, si tu veux l'obtenir.

This is the point at which negotiations finally break down.

It is a sign of their natural integrity that both Bajazet and Atalide are shocked by the way in which they deceived Roxane into believing that Bajazet returned her love and their feeling that they were driven into doing so by a situation that was not of their making. Bajazet says to Atalide:

> Le ciel punit ma feinte, et confond votre adresse . . .
> Je meurs plus tard: voilà tout le fruit de ma feinte . . .

This is Act II, Sc. 5. He is a good deal more downright in speaking to her in Act III, Sc. 4:

> Je me trouvais barbare, injuste, criminel.

Their deceptions were practised during the period immediately preceding the opening of the play. It is one of the clearest indications of the inherent evil of the 'old order' that their repentance followed by the change from 'trickery' to straight-forward 'negotiation' is a major factor in the collapse of the plans for the creation of a moral 'new order'. The real reason, indeed, for the failure of the negotiations is Bajazet's strong moral revulsion against what he has already done and his utter refusal to accept the advice of Acomat:

> ACOMAT
> Ne rougissez point. Le sang des Ottomans
> Ne doit point en esclave obéir aux serments.
> Consultez ces héros que le droit de la guerre
> Mena victorieux jusqu'au bout de la terre:
> Libres dans leur victoire, et maîtres de leur foi,
> L'intérêt de l'État fut leur unique loi;
> Et d'un trône si saint la moitié n'est fondée
> Que sur la foi promise et rarement gardée.
> Je m'emporte, Seigneur . . .

> BAJAZET
> Oui, je sais, Acomat,
> Jusqu'où les a portés l'intérêt de l'État;
> Mais ces mêmes héros, prodigues de leur vie,
> Ne la rachetaient point par une perfidie.

Although Acomat emerges as the one really sane and well-balanced character in the play, we cannot shut our eyes to the fact that he is, as perhaps one has to be in this world, the complete opportunist, almost a Machiavellian figure. He uses words with a strong moral connotation, 'saint' and 'foi' (twice) in an effort to persuade Bajazet to adopt a course which is anything but moral. The throne is described as 'sacred'. It follows that since the throne is a symbol of the State, 'the interest of the State' must be equally sacred. In that case it must take precedence over any private obligation ('foi'). In short, he twists the meaning of words in order to give the appearance of moral conduct to sheer opportunism: the subordination of all private vows or promises to 'the interest of the State', of 'foi' to 'loi'. What he wants Bajazet to do is to marry Roxane, be proclaimed sultan, then, if he chooses, to ditch the unhappy woman. Bajazet is not taken in. He has refused marriage as another form of servitude, but he realizes that in arguing that one need not honour vows 'en esclave' Acomat is in fact trying to reduce him to the moral slavery of the 'old order'.

His reply reflects the positive moral outlook of the play. He is really the classics' equivalent of the athlete of our own time. His moral code can be summed up in the words honesty, uprightness, decency, 'playing the game'. There is, indeed, a sort of athlete's 'heartiness' in his reply to Acomat which is the equivalent of 'Yes, I know, old boy, but the chaps didn't really behave like that, and you can't expect me to either'. We can't, but in the crooked world of *Bajazet* his 'decency' can only end in personal disaster.

5

I felt inclined to say that there are three different kinds of love in *Bajazet*. It would perhaps be more accurate, for reasons which will become apparent, to speak of three different attitudes to love.

There is first and foremost the devouring passion of Roxane. She is the professional who gives the impression of a woman itching to rip open Bajazet's flies, tear off his pants and drag him into bed. The puritans may talk primly of 'the rank sort of love to be expected of the inmate of a harem', but in spite of the grimness of the context the rest of us can only marvel at the magnificent vitality of a line like this:

> Viens m'engager ta foi: le temps fera le reste.

A woman who speaks in these terms is convinced that she is ultimately irresistible, that once she has 'made' her man he will be hers for ever. Although Roxane's is the most sexual passion of any in the plays except *Phèdre* and her methods the most brutal, we must never forget that she is trying to free herself from the sexual slavery of the harem and replace it by something better.

There is naturally a strong contrast between Roxane's passion and the love of Bajazet and Atalide. Theirs is basically the balanced and reasonable love of the *jeunes premiers* which places Roxane's passion in perspective. It has been tarnished by using the methods of the 'old order', but its reasonableness and moderation explain Bajazet's physical revulsion for the predatory Roxane.

Although the love of Bajazet and Atalide appears moderate and reasonable compared with the passion of Roxane, I shall anticipate by suggesting that Roxane is to some extent a 'case' and that like Titus Bajazet is undersexed, which plays its part in his downfall. We shall also find that in one respect there is an unexpected similarity between the attitudes of Atalide and Roxane.

There remains Acomat and his intended 'political' match with Atalide. It was of Acomat that I was thinking when I spoke of 'attitudes to love' rather than love. He is really an example of non-love. When he announces his intention to Osmin who asks whether he loves her, Acomat replies:

> Voudrais-tu qu'à mon âge
> Je fisse de l'amour le vil apprentissage?

This is the attitude that he adopts in the third act when he makes what one is tempted to describe as the eunuch's proposal of marriage to Atalide. His indifference to love is not without effect on his planning of the palace revolution. It explains his failure to discover that Bajazet and Atalide are in love until Roxane tells him near the end of the fourth act and his inability to understand Bajazet's refusal to marry Roxane.

The highlights of the play are the encounters between Roxane and Bajazet. There are four of them, but the audience only sees three: the first in Act II, Sc. 1, the second in Act III, Sc. 5, and the third in Act V, Sc. 4.

We saw that in the opening scene Osmin made his report on the military situation. It leads very neatly to the next scene in which Roxane makes her first appearance in the company of Atalide. Acomat gives a balanced and very fair account of the military situation without making any attempt to conceal the risks involved. On the strength of it Roxane agrees that they shall proceed with the palace revolution. In the next scene, in which she is alone with Atalide and their confidants, she tells her that instead of continuing to use her as an intermediary she has decided to see Bajazet herself so that she can be certain that he loves her, as Atalide has always assured her that he does.

It is characteristic of the extraordinary atmosphere of the play that she remarks to Atalide, as though it were the most natural thing in the world, that the choice for Bajazet lies between love and death:

> Voilà sur quoi je veux que Bajazet prononce.
> Sa perte ou son salut dépend de sa réponse.

Although there are times when we cannot help sympathizing with Roxane and even admiring her, there is one fact to which we cannot shut our eyes. Hers is not only the most sexual love in any of the plays except

Phèdre; she is equally the most sadistic of any of Racine's characters, which is why I suggested that she is to some extent a 'case'. Her sadism goes much deeper than the streak we find in Pyrrhus or in the youthful Néron. There are moments when we have the impression that the death of the beloved would bring almost as much satisfaction as bedding him, that she is oscillating between the bedchamber and the mutes' chamber of horrors, between two forms of orgasm. This determines the nature of the meetings between the couple. Roxane naturally uses the blackmailing tactics of the 'aggressor', but she does a good deal more than that. Julien Gracq puts it well. 'All Roxane's moves from beginning to end', he writes, 'proceed from the technique of strangulation: pressure, then relaxation, then renewed and stronger pressure'.[8]

The meeting opens in a solemn, almost a stilted tone:

> Prince, l'heure fatale est enfin arrivée
> Qu'à votre liberté le ciel a réservée.

The first part of the speech resembles a diplomatic survey. Roxane passes on the information that she has just received about the military and the political situation. She explains that she is not offering him a sinecure; there are serious dangers:

> C'est à vous de courir
> Dans le champ glorieux que j'ai su vous ouvrir.

The price is naturally marriage to her:

> par le noeud sacré d'un heureux hyménée
> Justifiez la foi que je vous ai donnée.

They soon become involved in a debate on what she calls the 'odieuse loi' which is the sultans' practice of not marrying their mistresses. Roxane cites the glorious example of Soliman which supports her case and comes out with the splendid line:

> Mais l'amour ne suit point ces lois imaginaires.

The explosion comes halfway through the scene. Bajazet concedes that there have been exceptions to the law, but suggests modestly that he is not of the calibre of the sultans who married their favourites:

> Il est vrai. Mais aussi voyez ce que je puis,
> Ce qu'était Soliman, et le peu que je suis.

In spite of his remorse over the deceptions he has practised, Bajazet is still deceiving Roxane by using the 'law' as an excuse for not marrying her and as a means of concealing the real reasons. What is most interesting about the lines is the way in which the choice of words and the sound, particularly the rhyme, 'puis/suis', betray his peculiar weaknesses.

He ends with a plea for moderation and caution:

> Ne précipitons rien, et daignez commencer
> A me mettre en état de vous récompenser.

Nothing could have been better calculated to get Roxane on the raw than this: 'Put me in a position to reward you; give me the throne, then we'll see'. She replies in a tone of studied politeness and we feel the immense effort she is making to control herself:

> Je vous entends, Seigneur. Je vois mon imprudence;
> Je vois que rien n'échappe à votre prévoyance.
> Vous avez pressenti jusqu'au moindre danger
> Où mon amour trop prompt vous allait engager.

We are conscious of the suppressed rage in the ironical reference to her 'imprudence', to his 'prévoyance', in the deprecating allusion to her 'amour trop prompt' which was to carry everything before it. She goes on in the same tone:

> Pour vous, pour votre honneur, vous en craignez les suites,
> Et je le crois, Seigneur, puisque vous me le dites.

She has ironically commended his foresight, but surely he has overlooked one rather important thing:

> Mais avez-vous prévu, si vous ne m'épousez,
> Les périls plus certains où vous vous exposez?
> Songez-vous que sans moi tout vous devient contraire,
> Que c'est à moi surtout qu'il importe de plaire?

The tone is still one of studied politeness, but at a stroke the irony reduces all the accepted values—'honour', 'foresight', 'prudence'—to nothing. Only one thing counts in this violent world: it is the obligation to 'please' Roxane. Then she suddenly lets fly:

> Songez-vous que je tiens les portes du Palais,
> Que je puis vous l'ouvrir ou fermer pour jamais,
> Que j'ai sur votre vie un empire suprême,
> Que vous ne respirez qu'autant que je vous aime?
> Et sans ce même amour, qu'offensent vos refus,
> Songez-vous, en un mot, que vous ne seriez plus?

The words burst out of her in a torrent. The points are rammed home by the repeated 'Songez-vous', the phrases in apposition: 'Songez-vous que je tiens . . . que je puis . . . que j'ai . . . que vous ne respirez . . . Songez-vous . . . que vous ne seriez plus'. The effect is intensified by the spluttering *p*-s in 'portes', 'Palais', 'puis', 'pour', 'empire', 'suprême'; by the alternation of the *ou* sounds and the nasals; by the seething *s*-s, the rugged *r*-s, the *m*-s and the *f*-s in the last three lines.

Nothing counts except Roxane. Nothing counts for Roxane at this moment except love. Bajazet is reduced, at any rate in her imagination, to a cipher. He only exists in virtue of her devouring love which blows life into this puppet, as she expresses it in one remarkable line:

vous ne respirez qu'autant que je vous aime ...

Although love is treated as a positive force, the use of the negative with the verb indicates the alternative: ceasing to 'breathe' through strangulation.

The reply is characteristically clumsy:

Oui, je tiens tout de vous; et j'avais lieu de croire
Que c'était pour vous-même une assez grande gloire,
En voyant devant moi tout l'Empire à genoux,
De m'entendre avouer que je tiens tout de vous.
Je ne m'en défends point, ma bouche le confesse,
Et mon respect saura le confirmer sans cesse:
Je vous dois tout mon sang. Ma vie est votre bien.
Mais enfin voulez-vous ...

The clumsiness, which looks forward to Hippolyte's dealings with Phèdre, is equally apparent in what he says and the way he says it: the repeated 'je tiens tout de vous' and 'je vous dois tout mon sang'. She is panting for love and all he has to offer is 'respect'. She has told him that without her he doesn't exist, that she is prepared to give him everything. The blundering answer to this is that it should be quite enough for her to see the empire at his feet and listen to some complimentary remarks about her contribution without trying to rush him into marriage and cash in on her handiwork! The reply produces one of those highly effective switches to the second person singular:

Non, je ne veux plus rien.
Ne m'importune plus de tes raisons forcées.
Je vois combien tes voeux sont loin de mes pensées.
Je ne te presse plus, ingrat, d'y consentir.
Rentre dans le néant dont je t'ai fait sortir.
Car enfin qui m'arrête? et quelle autre assurance
Demanderais-je encor de son indifférence?
L'ingrat est-il touché de mes empressements?
L'amour même entre-t-il dans ses raisonnements?
Ah! je vois tes desseins. Tu crois, quoi que je fasse,
Que mes propres périls t'assurent de ta grâce ...

There is a splendid swagger about the first five lines in which Roxane denounces the reluctant lover and compares her position with his:

Rentre dans le néant dont je t'ai fait sortir.

In the sixth things begin to get out of hand. Roxane speaks to herself, as Racine's characters commonly do when tension reaches a certain height, and refers to Bajazet in the third person as though he were some nonentity who couldn't hear or couldn't understand what she is saying:

> L'ingrat est-il touché de mes empressements?
> L'amour même entre-t-il dans ses raisonnements?

She turns to him with a series of hisses:

> Ah! je vois tes desseins. Tu crois, quoi que je fasse,
> Que mes propres périls t'assurent de ta grâce . . .

Then she plays the brothers off against one another:

> Il m'aime, tu le sais; et malgré sa colère,
> Dans ton perfide sang je puis tout expier,
> Et ta mort suffira pour me justifier.
> N'en doute point, j'y cours, et dès ce moment même.

We are conscious of a weakening in the last line. In the next there is another change, this time to a warm pleading tone:

> Bajazet, écoutez, je sens que je vous aime.
> Vous vous perdez. Gardez de me laisser sortir.
> Le chemin est encore ouvert au repentir.
> Ne désespérez point une amante en furie:
> S'il m'échappait un mot, c'est fait de votre vie.

The contemptuous second person singular is abandoned, but so is the formal 'Seigneur' of the opening speech. They are now on equal terms and she addresses him by name: 'Bajazet, écoutez . . .' We can also see the destructive, subterranean impulses emerging: the antithesis love-death. For Roxane realizes by one of those insights which are common to Racine's protagonists that she is only too likely to be swept away by uncontrollable emotions if she once leaves the room. We should notice, too, the way in which words with strong moral connotations recur in the different speeches and are distorted: 'expier', 'justifier', 'repentir' and 'perfide'. Their use is rhetorical. Right conduct is equated with pleasing Roxane or placating Amurat. Failure to please by doing what she wants is stigmatized as 'perfide'. Roxane is trying to convince herself that she is doing 'the right thing' and the moral overtones for all the element of distortion enable her to give an extra drive to what she says.

Threats and pleading simply prompt another clumsy reply from Bajazet. He is equally 'indifferent'—the word is Roxane's—to calls to 're-pentance' and threats to take his life:

> Vous pouvez me l'ôter: elle est entre vos mains.
> Peut-être que ma mort, utile à vos desseins,
> De l'heureux Amurat obtenant votre grâce,
> Vous rendra dans son coeur votre première place.

These lines seem to support my contention that Bajazet is slightly 'wet'. There is no irony in his reference to Roxane's using his death to reinstate herself with Amurat. The truth of the matter is that in spite of his decency, his uprightness and his horror at the tricks that he and Atalide have played on Roxane, the long years of oppression and virtual imprisonment in the palace have broken Bajazet's spirit, deprived him of any true zest for life. He is fond of Atalide; he tries chivalrously to save her life, irrespective of the fact that for her life without him would be as meaningless as for Roxane, but he is not prepared to take a tough line, muzzle Roxane and proceed with the palace revolution without her support. The only conclusion that we can draw is that his personal standards of decency and uprightness hide a profound moral defeatism. This seems to be the answer to Racine's remarks quoted earlier on his 'passion' and his 'ferocity'. It was this kind of defeatism that I had in mind when I suggested that like Titus he is undersexed.

Roxane is cut to the quick and makes one of her most moving rejoinders which is also one of the finest passages of poetry in the play:

> Dans son coeur? Ah! crois-tu, quand il le voudrait bien,
> Que je perds l'espoir de régner dans le tien,
> D'une si douce erreur si longtemps possédée,
> Je puisse désormais souffrir une autre idée,
> Ni que je vive enfin, si je ne vis pour toi?
> Je te donne, cruel, des armes contre moi,
> Sans doute, et je devrais retenir ma faiblesse:
> Tu vas en triompher. Oui, je te le confesse,
> J'affectais à tes yeux une fausse fierté.
> De toi dépend ma joie et ma félicité.
> De ma sanglante mort ta mort sera suivie.
> Quel fruit de tant de soins que j'ai pris pour ta vie!

There is no contempt behind the second person singular this time. Bajazet has unwittingly called her bluff and the shot has gone home.

It is precisely Roxane's weakness, her very human 'faiblesse', which makes her in spite of everything at moments almost an endearing figure. The swagger and the threats, the cruelty and the insolence have vanished: we hear only the voice of the suffering human being. It applies particularly to lines 3–5 with their 'si douce erreur' and the multitude of s-s in 'possédée', 'puisse', 'faiblesse' and 'confesse' which this time express not venom, but extreme anguish. In these lines she has run through the whole gamut of contradictory human feelings. Her pride was a 'false pride'; all she wants is her man. Yet none of this prevents the contrast between 'ma félicité' and 'ma sanglante mort' which will follow Bajazet's own death, and confirms everything that has been said about her psychological make-up.

Roxane does not give up hope. She suddenly feels, wrongly, that she has made an impression:

> Tu soupires enfin, et sembles te troubler.
> Achève, parle.

He does, but merely repeats in different words what he has been saying all the time:

> Daignez m'ouvrir au trône un chemin légitime,
> Ou bien, me voilà prêt, prenez votre victime.

Clearly, Bajazet is not one of the most skilful negotiators. Not surprisingly this is the moment when Roxane has him arrested and announces the return to 'l'ordre accoutumé'.

The breach causes consternation. Acomat and Atalide set to work to repair it. The result is a fresh series of misunderstandings and some of the least satisfactory scenes in the play. Acomat is present at the meeting between Roxane and Bajazet which the audience does not see. He is too far away to hear what is said and, incredibly, jumps to the conclusion that all is well. He upsets Atalide badly by telling her that Bajazet has made his peace by agreeing to do what Atalide herself after all had advised him to do: marry Roxane. Bajazet's opening words to Atalide increase the confusion:

> C'en est fait, j'ai parlé: vous êtes obéie.

He later explains that there has been no promise; there was such an outpouring from Roxane that he could hardly get a word in. But he frightens Atalide by saying that the time has come to put an end to the tricks they have been playing on Roxane and paying an unexpected tribute to what he calls 'un amour si tendre et si peu mérité'.

Roxane arrives in a state of rapture to call on Bajazet to fulfil his supposed promise. There is a typical love-and-death aside to Atalide:

> L'auriez-vous cru, Madame, et qu'un si prompt retour
> Fît à tant de fureur succéder tant d'amour?
> Tantôt, à me venger fixe et déterminée,
> Je jurais qu'il voyait sa dernière journée.

'Un si prompt retour', which is sheer illusion, is matched ironically with her 'amour trop prompt' at the first meeting.

Her suspicion about the relations between Bajazet and Atalide are aroused by his hurried exit and ambiguous words. The act ends, ominously, with the announcement that another and a particularly frightening messenger has arrived from Amurat.

* * *

Racine's fourth acts sometimes contain a faint and illusory hope that tragedy may be avoided. There is nothing of the sort in *Bajazet*. We simply see Roxane busily confirming her suspicions of Bajazet and Atalide. She puts Atalide to the test by telling her that she has been ordered by Amurat to have Bajazet executed and intends to carry out the order. Atalide faints. The slaves take charge of her, find the love letter from Bajazet which she received in the first scene of the act and bring it to Roxane.

Atalide is arrested at the beginning of Act V. Bajazet has been summoned to another meeting with Roxane. In a transitional scene which precedes his appearance Roxane says to her slave:

> Oui, tout est prêt, Zatime:
> Orcan et les muets attendent leur victime.
> Je suis pourtant toujours maîtresse de son sort.
> Je puis le retenir. Mais s'il sort, il est mort.

They are not among Racine's most elegant lines, but the rhyming of 'sort' and 'mort' and the triple use of words ending in *ort* give us the sensation of the victim choking as the cords tighten round his neck.

The final meeting opens on a sombre, disillusioned note:

> Je ne vous ferai point des reproches frivoles:
> Les moments sont trop chers pour les perdre en paroles.

Roxane goes on:

> Malgré tout mon amour, si je n'ai pu vous plaire,
> Je n'en murmure point. Quoiqu'à ne vous rien taire,
> Ce même amour peut-être et ces mêmes bienfaits
> Auraient dû suppléer à mes faibles attraits.
> Mais je m'étonne enfin que pour reconnaissance,
> Pour prix de tant d'amour, de tant de confiance,
> Vous ayez si longtemps, par des détours si bas
> Feint un amour pour moi que vous ne sentiez pas.

There is no irony in the 'faibles attraits': she has failed to attract him. There is a profound sadness in the reproaches which follow and which we can only regard as fully justified. Bajazet's surprised 'Qui? moi, Madame?', which in spite of his guilty feeling over the tricks he has played on her can only be described as another 'feinte', produces still another change of tone. Roxane is jealous and switches to the second person singular:

> Oui, toi. Voudrais-tu point encore
> Me nier un mépris que tu crois que j'ignore?

She shows him the letter which has been found in Atalide's possession. Bajazet comes clean. He has loved Atalide since childhood; he does not love Roxane, but is prepared to 'pay' for her goodness in giving him the throne in other ways. He seems blunderingly unaware of her immense pride in her position which comes out in her reply:

> Quels seraient de tes voeux les inutiles fruits?
> Ne te souvient-il plus de tout ce que je suis?
> Maîtresse du Sérail, arbitre de ta vie,
> Et même de l'État, qu'Amurat me confie,
> Sultane . . .
> A quel indigne honneur m'avais-tu réservée?
> Traînerais-je en ces lieux un sort infortuné,
> Vil rebut d'un ingrat que j'aurais couronné,
> De mon rang descendue, à mille autres égale,
> Ou la première esclave enfin de ma rivale?

Roxane's reply exposes the complete hopelessness of the position. They both use the obsessive words, 'esclavage' and 'esclave'. A moment ago Bajazet told her that he welcomed the offer of the crown as

> L'heureuse occasion de sortir d'esclavage.

She has to spell out to him that to make him sultan without marriage to her would mean a reversal of their roles, would lead to the loss of her great position, would turn her into an insignificant person in a vast crowd or, as she bitterly puts it, 'la première *esclave* . . . de ma rivale'—the 'rival' who would of course have taken over the position of sultana.

When Bajazet asks what he is to do, he gets a truly appalling answer:

> Ma rivale est ici. Suis-moi sans différer.
> Dans les mains des muets viens la voir expirer.

These two lines have been well described by Paul Guth as 'les plus vicieux de toute notre littérature érotico-sadique . . . qui font de l'allitération l'instrument des plus atroces jouissances'.[9]

For once Bajazet is really moved to anger:

> Je ne l'accepterais que pour vous en punir . . .

He realizes that he is lost and makes a final plea for Atalide:

> Ajoutez cette grâce à tant d'autres bontés,
> Madame. Et si jamais je vous fus cher . . .

This is the point at which she cuts him short with the celebrated 'Sortez'.

There has been a vast accumulation of emotion. It is obliterated by a single word which is made even more dramatic by the fact that it did cut short a genuine plea with its reference to Roxane's love for Bajazet. It is the first stage in the collapse of everything and that is what gives it an overwhelming force.

Bajazet's is the first of a series of 'exits' from life which explains the repeated use of 'sortir' in these last scenes. It had been foreshadowed in the

scene between Roxane and her confidant. There is an epilogue in the next
scene when Roxane uses the same inelegant rhyme scheme in an order to
her confidant:

> et toi, suis Bajazet qui sort,
> Et quand il sera temps, viens m'apprendre son sort.

She has a special reason for wishing to know when the mutes have done
their work. She must have realized that Bajazet would never dream of
going with her to see Atalide murdered. The alternative, described in an
earlier scene with her confidant, was to take Atalide to view the corpse of
her murdered lover:

> Quel surcroît de vengeance et de douceur nouvelle
> De le montrer bientôt pâle et mort devant elle,
> De voir sur cet objet ses regards arrêtés
> Me payer les plaisirs que je leur ai prêtés!

For the sadist the spectacle of a woman contemplating her murdered
lover, reduced to an 'object', in the presence of a 'rival' looks like another
substitute for sexual intercourse. We almost hear Roxane licking her lips
in the *l*-s, *s*-s and *ce*, heightened by the rasping *r*-s and *p*-s in the last two
lines. The gloating over 'douceur nouvelle' is in some respects even more
savage than her invitation to Bajazet to see Atalide strangled.

Racine boasted in the preface to *Bérénice* that blood and corpses were not
necessary for tragedy. He makes up for it in *Bajazet*. Roxane's imagination
is haunted not only by images of blood and death, but by the instruments
of death:

> Dans ton perfide *sang* je puis tout expier . . .
>
> De ma *sanglante* mort ta mort sera suivie.

The imagery is contagious. Bajazet says to Acomat:

> J'aime mieux en sortir *sanglant*, couvert de coups,
> Que chargé, malgré moi, du nom de son époux.[10]

Atalide, revealing the same contagion as Bajazet, says to him:

> Roxane, malgré vous, nous joindra l'un et l'autre.
> Elle aura plus de soif de mon *sang* que du vôtre.

That, literally, is what Roxane has in mind:

> *d'un même poignard les unissant tous deux*,
> Les percer l'un et l'autre, et moi-même après eux.

The image this evokes is of the two lovers pinned together by a dagger
going through both their hearts.

Roxane's imagination veers wildly between the dagger and the cord.

'Knot(s)' is another obsessive word meaning unity in love or in death. At
their first meeting Roxane says to Bajazet:

> par le *noeud sacré* d'un heureux hymenée
> Justifiez la foi que je vous ai donnée.

She says at a later stage to Atalide:

> Loin de vous séparer, je prétends aujourd'hui
> Par des *noeuds éternels* vous unir avec lui.

What is most striking in these couplets is the sadist's use of a similar
adjective for two very different kinds of 'knot'.

In another place she chooses a more realistic adjective:

> Qu'on le saisisse.
> Que la main des muets s'arme pour son supplice.
> Qu'ils viennent préparer ces *noeuds infortunés*
> Par qui de ses pareils les jours sont terminés.

The usual relish is heard in the *s*-s and *ce* of 'saisisse', 'supplice' and
's'arme' and the tug of the cords in the *m*-s of 'mains', 'muets' and 'arme'.
Yet all this conflicts with 'noeuds *infortunés*' which signifies the end of
everything for both Bajazet and Roxane.

These are not the only connections between love and death. I said earlier
that I intended to examine a pronouncement of Atalide's. She is telling
Bajazet that she intends to commit suicide and leave him to Roxane:

> Roxane s'estimait assez récompensée,
> Et j'aurais en mourant cette douce pensée
> Que vous ayant moi-même imposé cette loi,
> Je vous ai vers Roxane envoyé plein de moi;
> Qu'emportant chez les morts toute votre tendresse,
> Ce n'est point un amant en vous que je lui laisse.

On the face of it she appears to be saying that by insisting on sacrificing
herself to save Bajazet, he will be so full of memories of her that he will
never be able to love or enjoy Roxane. In reality she is saying something
a good deal more profound than she herself realizes or is generally understood. She is saying that love is the very marrow of the human being and
that if it is removed through the failure of the lovers to be united, there is
nothing left. It creates a new kind of impotence. The lover is in a literal
sense drained as though he had been reduced to impotence by castration
and the drying up of his spermatazoa. The man is no longer a man; he is
nothing, which echoes Roxane's

> vous ne respirez qu'autant que je vous aime.[11]

That is what might be called the 'message' of the play. The dynamic
power of man lies in his sexuality. It leads either to fulfilment or death

according to circumstances. Once it is removed without fulfilment the man is to all intents and purposes dead—a mere puppet who can do nothing, whose vitality has vanished. That is the impulse behind Roxane's demand for marriage or a double death—the execution of Bajazet followed by her own suicide. If she cannot get her man she, too, is to all intents and purposes 'finished'.

6

The play, as I have said, is dominated by the figure of 'le cruel Amurat' whom we never see. He holds all these people captive. The words they use build up a series of complicated interweaving patterns: love and death; power and impotence; tricks and secrecy; despotism and slavery. The palace is a seething cauldron with bloody images continually flashed on the screen. The characters who all began by trying to outwit somebody else in their frenzied efforts to escape from the slavery of 'l'ordre accoutumé' become enmeshed in their own contrivances and flounder more and more deeply. The images of silent slaves, executioners armed with knives and cords become more insistent, more obsessive. Then everything collapses; everything falls to pieces. The wheel has come full circle. Trickery has failed; bargaining has broken down completely; violence has triumphed. The plots and conspiracies end in the final 'combat' which destroys all the protagonists. The irony has grown ferocious. There are times during the play when we feel that if only the characters bargaining over life and death had played their cards better, if Atalide hadn't advised Bajazet to marry Roxane and then upset everything by growing jealous, the situation could have been saved. This is a complete illusion. All the negotiations, moral and immoral alike, take place in an atmosphere of doom. From the start we know that the protagonists are lost, that the sacrifices demanded of them are impossible, that the outcome is inescapable. In the opening scene we were shown Amurat suspended between 'victory' and 'flight' with everything depending on the result of the campaign. It is totally unaffected by the palace intrigues. We learn in Act IV that he has won, that after the capture of Babylon he is on his way back to Byzantium by forced marches. We feel him nearing the city, ready to pounce. We know that by the time he reaches it, it will be to discover that the job has been done for him, to find the palace littered with corpses and the sails of the surviving conspirators growing smaller and smaller in the distance. The siege of Babylon ended with the destruction of the enemy; Roxane's 'siege' of Bajazet in the deaths of the beloved and herself. 'L'ordre accoutumé' has been preserved: flight is not the lot of the hated tyrant, but of the exponents of the 'new order'.

We should not overlook the significance of Amurat's victory in the field. It means that even if Bajazet had married Roxane and occupied the throne, the rebellion would almost certainly have been crushed by the sultan and his janissaries and that the 'mutes' would have done their work just the same.

The play is a comment on the human condition. Not the simple one of violent passions bringing violent endings that we find in the lesser Elizabethan and Jacobean dramatists. Racine possessed precisely the maturity and the vision which are lacking in their work. Amurat comes to stand for something essentially evil and the architect of an evil order. It is clearly demonstrated by the arrival of the sinister messenger with his black skin and frightening name: Orcan. Although he is a minor character whom we do not see, his arrival at a moment when the play is moving towards its climax strikes dismay into all hearts, Roxane's as well as Atalide's. He is a projection of Amurat. He stands for naked evil stalking through the palace and bringing death and disaster in his wake, finishing off the 'new order' which had already been disrupted from within, restoring the 'old' in spite of his death. 'Orcan', cries the horrified Roxane. And her slave replies:

> Oui, de tous ceux que le Sultan emploie,
> Orcan, le plus fidèle à servir ses desseins,
> Né sous le ciel brûlant des plus noirs Africains.

Nothing could be simpler than the last line. Yet its vividness and its power are quite fantastic.

The slave tries in vain to keep him at bay while she warns her mistress. But it is too late. Roxane knows that she is lost, whatever she says to the contrary, and that this is the beginning of the end:

> Quel malheur imprévu vient encor me confondre?

The word 'confondre', looking forward to the massacre and total collapse of the 'new order', is singularly apt. Roxane sees that evil is about to carry everything before it. The essence of this form of evil is its corrosive power. What makes the experience tragic is the loss of the splendid human qualities of which we are aware in Roxane to a greater extent than in any of the other characters; qualities which though constantly thwarted struggle against the sense of hopelessness, the sense of irresistible doom, against an evil which at the least touch withers, blights, destroys.

7

Bajazet is one of the least popular of Racine's mature tragedies and compared with *Britannicus* and *Bérénice* is far too seldom performed. Its unpopularity, as we have seen, is due to a variety of reasons, most of them bad: the subject, the weakness of two of the protagonists, a certain puritanism which is not confined to the critic who spoke slightingly of Roxane's profession, and to a failure to appreciate what seem to me to be its special merits. Criticism has not been confined to the subject or the characters. It has been suggested that the style is inferior to that of other plays, that like the subject it is rougher. There is clearly a sense in which *Bajazet* is less 'poetical' or, better, less 'lyrical' than a number of the plays. There is nothing in it which has the immediate appeal of Néron's account of Junie's arrival at the palace, Phèdre's *aveux* or Athalie's dream. What is more striking still is that the 'roughness' of style is emphasized by the contrast with the 'softness' of the style of *Bérénice*. It is a rough, tough play; its particular attractions are evident in the encounters between Roxane and Bajazet and in the way in which the atmosphere of the oriental palace is conveyed. In short, the style is at one with the play. It reflects its peculiar tension and its peculiar rawness. For me it is by no means the least of the mature tragedies.

NOTES

[1] The dispatch has never been published, but is quoted at length by R. Jasinski in *Vers le vrai Racine*, II, pp. 10–11. Suleiman is called Orcan in some accounts including Racine's second preface. For obvious reasons Racine used this name for Amurat's second messenger.

[2] 'Floridon ou L'amour imprudent' was one of six *nouvelles* contained in *Les Nouvelles françoises ou Les Divertissements de la princesse Aurélie* which was published in 1656 and must have been known to Racine though he does not mention it as one of his sources. In this version, Amurat is so devoted to his half-brother that he can hardly bear to let him out of his sight. His attitude changes dramatically when he hears the janissaries, who are dissatisfied with his conduct of one of the campaigns, shouting that they want Bajazet as sultan. It is for this reason alone that Amurat gives the order for his murder (ed. of 1722, pp. 381, 445).

[3] They are Mairet's *La Mort de Mustapha*, 1637–8, and Tristan l'Hermite's *Osman* which was produced in 1646, but not published until 1656.

[4] He retained the paragraph in the edition of 1687, but omitted it from that of 1697 which was the last collected edition to be published in his lifetime.

[5] There are some amusing comments by Pierre Guéguen:
'Atalide, c'est Oreste en jupons . . . Atalide est une héroïne de Racine qui a lu Corneille, mais ne l'a pas digéré . . . Bajazet, c'est le Britannicus plus mûr de la pièce' (*Poésie de Racine*, pp. 204, 205, 210).

[6] The word and its variations occur 28 times in *Bajazet*. The total for all the plays is 73.

[7] In *Racine's Rhetoric*, p. 104.

[8] *Préférences*, new ed., 1961, p. 195.

[9] *Histoire de la littérature française*, I, 1967, pp. 372–3.

[10] With two exceptions, Roxane's use of the verb 'sortir' is associated with death or disaster. For Bajazet it means escape from slavery ('sortir d'esclavage'), but the first of these two lines from Act II, Sc. 4 is clearly prophetic.

11 The line is of course ambivalent. It means that Bajazet would already be dead if it were not for Roxane's protection. It also seems to me to have the second and more profound meaning that I attribute to it.

'MITHRIDATE'
1673

Mithridate est une pièce charmante; on y pleure; on y est dans une continuelle admiration; on la voit trente fois, on la trouve plus belle la trentième que la première.

MME DE SÉVIGNÉ

CHAPTER 7

'MITHRIDATE'

1673

I

ALTHOUGH it would be a mistake to try to discover in Racine's drama a formal pattern in which each play has a particular place, it is possible to distinguish different phases in his work. The move from secular to religious drama is the most obvious, but by no means the only change. Those critics are surely right who consider that *Mithridate* marks the beginning of a new phase. Jean-Louis Barrault puts it well. He argues that in *Andromaque* and *Britannicus* Racine takes a downward plunge into an evil world. The extreme limit, or the greatest depth, is reached in *Bajazet*. Then comes a sharp change of direction. Instead of the downward plunge 'the swimmer', as he calls Racine, moves upwards and slowly makes his way back to the surface.[1]

Andromaque is not altogether easy to classify and in this particular essay Barrault does not mention *Bérénice*, but in *Britannicus* and *Bajazet*, as we have seen, the forces of evil prevail and the innocent victims perish. In *Mithridate* and *Iphigénie* the process is reversed. It would no doubt be an exaggeration to speak of 'debunking', but in each of these plays Racine chooses as the model for his principal protagonist a man who has reached one of the highest positions in his own world and devotes a large part of the play to an exposure of his weaknesses and his vices. Whether he loses his life like Mithridate or manages to survive like Agamemnon, the tyrant is defeated and the *jeunes premiers*, or rather their successors, reap a just reward for their courage and integrity.[2]

This brings me to the influence of Corneille. Professional rivalry does not necessarily exclude influence. With Corneille and Racine the influence was mutual, but we need to be clear about its nature. In *Mithridate* Racine drew on *Attila*, first performed in 1664, for some of the material for the character of Mithridate himself and to a still greater extent on *Nicomède* which had originally been produced as long ago as 1651. I said earlier that owing to a change in the spirit of the age Corneille's last plays reveal a movement in the direction of Racine. On the face of it, it may seem strange that Corneille's influence should be most pronounced in a play produced only one year before *Suréna*. It is not really so. In both *Mithridate* and *Iphigénie* Racine's ingrained pessimism gives way for a time—the process will be strikingly reversed again in *Phèdre*—to a more optimistic view of life. Xipharès and Monime find themselves in a Cornelian situation and behave accordingly. Honour is upheld against personal inclination in the figures of the model son and the equally admirable Monime, perhaps the most attractive of all Racine's heroines. It should be emphasized, however, that though there are certainly Cornelian elements in the play, the characters remain Racinian and are in no sense copies or imitations of Corneille's own characters. It simply means that they follow the example of their virtuous predecessors and that this time circumstances favour them.

2

The play, as we know, opens with Xipharès's report of the night battle:

> On nous faisait, Arbate, un fidèle rapport:
> Rome en effet triomphe, et Mithridate est mort.
> Les Romains, vers l'Euphrate, ont attaqué mon père,
> Et trompé dans la nuit sa prudence ordinaire.
> Après un long combat, tout son camp dispersé
> Dans la foule des morts en fuyant l'a laissé,
> Et j'ai su qu'un soldat dans les mains de Pompée
> Avec son diadème a remis son épée.
> Ainsi ce roi qui seul a durant quarante ans
> Lassé tout ce que Rome eut de chefs importants,
> Et qui dans l'Orient balançant la fortune,
> Vengeait de tous les rois la querelle commune,
> Meurt, et laisse après lui, pour venger son trépas,
> Deux fils infortunés qui ne s'accordent pas.

The ground covered and the amount of work done by these fourteen lines are impressive even by Racinian standards. The 'fidèle rapport' is of course a false report which like the false report of Thésée's death in *Phèdre* will have a decisive effect on the minds and actions of the characters. The speech introduces some of the most important themes of the play: the night battle, the military reputation of Mithridate, his son's respect for him and the conflict between the brothers which prepares the way for related themes.

The speech is also important stylistically. Although Xipharès's account of the night battle is highly circumstantial, the strength of the affirmation behind 'fidèle rapport', the speed with which he moves on to the differences between the brothers and the events which follow suggest, at any rate to a modern audience, wishful thinking and the working of the un-unconscious. The impression is strengthened by the shocked exclamations which greet the confidant's announcement of Mithridate's return, particularly Xipharès's 'Qu'avons-nous fait!'

The third sentence is revealing. It begins with the words 'Ainsi ce roi' in line 9, but the main verb, which is significantly 'meurt' and heavily stressed by *enjambement*, is not reached until four lines later. The whole of Mithridate's military career is compressed into two subordinate clauses. In a curious way the sentence reflects the pattern of the play. Mithridate makes his first appearance early in Act II. There are continual references to his fortunes and misfortunes in war in the three middle acts. He makes his final appearance in the last scene of all where he dies in front of our eyes.

We have observed the reference to the differences between the two brothers at the end of the speech. We learn a few lines later that Xipharès's hostility to Rome and Pharnace's policy of appeasement are 'les moindres sujets de nos divisions'. What is really worrying Xipharès is their rivalry in love, their rivalry for the hand of their 'dead' father's fiancée. It introduces the central theme of the play. It is the dual theme of love and war with the implication that in the last resort love counts for more than war.

The false report of Mithridate's death removes at a stroke the characters' inhibitions and leads to declarations of love which would not otherwise have been made. What is equally important dramatically, it encourages them to speak their minds about Mithridate. Xipharès is the loyal son; he admires his father's military feats and we shall find that whatever Mithridate's failings, he regards his duty to him as absolute. This does not prevent him from taking a realistic view of his ruthlessness.

The criticism is twofold. There was an unworthy attempt to bribe Monime into becoming his mistress without marriage:

> Il la vit. Mais au lieu d'offrir à ses beautés
> Un hymen, et des voeux dignes d'être écoutés,
> Il crut que sans prétendre une plus haute gloire,
> Elle lui céderait une indigne victoire.

Then there were the fears for her life:

> . . . en ce malheur je tremblai pour ses jours;
> Je redoutai du Roi les cruelles amours.
> Tu sais combien de fois ses jalouses tendresses
> Ont pris soin d'assurer la mort de ses maîtresses.

We might observe in passing that the sentiments expressed in the first of these passages are clearly those of a well-behaved seventeenth-century prince rather than those of the son of an oriental despot.

There are similar criticisms by Pharnace in the scene which follows their joint meeting with Monime:

> Rarement l'amitié désarme sa colère;
> Ses propres fils n'ont point de juge plus sévère;
> Et nous l'avons vu même à ses cruels soupçons
> Sacrifier deux fils pour de moindres raisons.

> Craignons pour vous, pour moi, pour la Reine elle-même:
> Je la plains, d'autant plus que Mithridate l'aime.
> Amant avec transport, mais jaloux san retour,
> Sa haine va toujours plus loin que son amour.

We can see that the testimony of the devoted son is, if anything, more damaging than that of the traitor.

The criticisms of both sons are supported in much more discreet terms by Monime in the scene in which she seeks Xipharès's help against Pharnace and in the scene in which all three are present.

She describes her position to Xipharès movingly as

> Sans parents, sans amis, désolée et craintive,
> Reine longtemps de nom, mais en effet captive . . .

Then to the two half-brothers together:

> Il daigna m'envoyer ce gage de sa foi.
> Ce fut pour ma famille une suprême loi:
> Il fallut obéir. Esclave couronnée,
> Je partis pour l'hymen où j'étais destinée.

In the first passage the regular pauses coming after third syllables in line 1 and the careful arrangement of commonplace words create the impression of a succession of misfortunes. The absence of 'relatives' and 'friends' leads logically to a state of 'desolation' and 'fear'.[3] In the second line the balancing of 'Reine' and 'captive' is very effective in bringing out the contrast between the appearance and reality of Monime's position. The 'reality' is of course Mithridate's unwelcome passion.

In a very natural and very convincing manner the five passages provide us with a preliminary sketch of the central figure and prepare the way for his first appearance. Mithridate is cruel—the word is used by both Xipharès and Pharnace—jealous, lecherous, the exponent of a tyrannical love which reduces the object of his affections to the condition of slavery as we can see from Monime's memorable phrase, 'Esclave couronnée', which has the effect of blending the earlier antithesis, 'Reine/captive'. We also see that in spite of her deep feeling, Monime like Xipharès puts duty first; there is a finality about 'Il fallut obéir' which shows what is to come.

3

Although the brief meeting between Mithridate and his sons, when he makes his first appearance in Act II, Sc. 2, is no more than a transitional scene, it illustrates the tightness of Racine's construction. His reprimand because they are not at their posts, or what he regards as their posts, which leaves no room for an answer, is our first glimpse of the tyrant. There is also a veiled reference to his plans for a comeback which plays a major part in the development.

It is followed by a heart to heart talk with Arbate in which Mithridate describes the night battle at first hand and explains the origin of the false report of his death:

> Je suis vaincu. Pompée a saisi l'avantage
> D'une nuit qui laissait peu de place au courage.
> Mes soldats presque nus, dans l'ombre intimidés,
> Les rangs de toutes parts mal pris et mal gardés
> Le désordre partout redoublant les alarmes,
> Nous-mêmes contre nous tournant nos propres armes,
> Les cris que les rochers renvoyaient plus affreux,
> Enfin toute l'horreur d'un combat ténébreux:
> Que pouvait la valeur dans ce trouble funeste?
> Les uns sont morts, la fuite a sauvé tout le reste;
> Et je ne dois la vie, en ce commun effroi,
> Qu'au bruit de mon trépas que je laisse après moi.

Mithridate's account of the battle—the eye-witness's account—is naturally much more vivid than his son's hearsay report. We see the ragged, almost naked soldiers attacking their comrades in error, watch the ranks crumbling, hear the shouts echoing among the rocks and feel the peculiar horror and confusion of the night battle, all admirably brought out by the consonants and the nasals. In view of what is to come, we should note the use of the word 'vaincu' in the short, crisp opening sentence, and the later appearance of 'désordre' which looks forward to the disorder in which the characters will become more and more deeply involved.

The simple difference between a hearsay report and an eye-witness account of the battle is not of course the main point. It is clearly right and dramatically effective that the hearsay report should precede and prepare the way for the eye-witness account. What really counts, however, is the difference of emphasis. It shows for reasons that I have already indicated that the battle has a different significance for the two speakers: that Xipharès's feelings are a mixture of regret and relief while for Mithridate it is a matter of sheer disaster.

Although the second account of the battle corrects the first, it also reinforces it. We begin to see its importance for the structure of the play. There is evidently a very close parallel between this and the opening scene with the same confidant listening to both accounts of the battle and its implications. We know that Xipharès moved straight from the report of the battle to his love for Monime and his suspicions of his half-brother. Mithridate does precisely the same. He describes his escape briefly and goes on:

> Toujours du même amour tu me vois enflammé:
> Ce coeur nourri de sang, et de guerre affamé,

> Malgré le faix des ans et du sort qui m'opprime,
> Traîne partout l'amour qui l'attache à Monime,
> Et n'a point d'ennemis qui lui soient odieux
> Plus que deux fils ingrats que je trouve en ces lieux.

It is worth comparing this passage with the opening lines of Xipharès's *aveu* to Arbate:

> Cet amour s'est longtemps accru dans le silence.
> Que n'en puis-je à tes yeux marquer la violence,
> Et mes premiers soupirs, et mes derniers ennuis?

Xipharès's tone is youthful, gentle, lyrical—that lovely opening line—and for all its sadness not without hope. What strikes us at once about Mithridate's declaration, what makes him unique among Racine's lovers, is the feeling that we are listening to the voice not simply of a tyrannical, but of a *senile* lover. It is the slightly hysterical tone of an old man who is violently in love notwithstanding 'the weight of the years' and who knows in his heart, in spite of the disclaimer in the last two lines, that his love is not and cannot be returned. The hysterical element emerges not only in the tone, but in the melodramatic phrases which link love and war. The love which binds him to Monime is rooted in 'ce coeur nourri de sang, et de guerre affamé'. There is a sense of helpless frustration in 'traîne' and 'attaché'. The image of the warrior advancing on the enemy, thirsting for blood and war, is replaced by the figure of the elderly lover trailing along in spite of himself in the wake of a person who would be only too glad to be quit of him. The effect is heightened by the rhyming of 'affamé' and 'enflammé', 'opprime' and 'Monime'.

Xipharès's 'deux fils infortunés' is answered by Mithridate's 'deux fils ingrats'. Arbate goes to the rescue of Xipharès with his 'Deux fils, Seigneur?' but is clearly relieved when the appearance of Monime puts an end to the grilling to which he is being subjected by his master.

I shall anticipate by describing Mithridate's first encounter with Monime as a skirmish which becomes a prelude to the main battle between them in Act IV.

Mithridate's unexpected return places all the characters in an extremely difficult and uncomfortable position. It reproduces in their minds and their actions something of the confusion of the night battle, divides them into factions which leads to head-on collisions.

Politically, Mithridate, Xipharès and Monime are on the same side; they are united in their hostility to Rome and their opposition to Pharnace's policy of appeasement. When we turn from politics to love the picture is a different one. There are no longer two parties, but three. Instead of a single rival Mithridate has two, which is equally true of both his sons.

Mithridate plans a campaign which is designed to avenge his defeat in battle and to make sure of Monime. Pharnace organizes an uprising which is intended to defeat his father in battle, capture his fiancée and remove the other rival.

We can see from this that the military battle has its counterpart in the 'battles' which rage in the minds of the protagonists, that they are involved in war and in psychological warfare. I spoke of the dual theme of love and war because both forms of warfare are inextricably interwoven and remain live issues from the beginning of the play to the end, which gives it its unity and its complexity.

At this first encounter with Monime Mithridate begins by addressing her courteously. He is sorry to have kept her waiting so long, but they must plight their troth at once because in a matter of hours he will be leaving again. The answer is not exactly the one for which he was waiting, or at least hoping:

> Seigneur, vous pouvez tout. Ceux par qui je respire
> Vous ont cédé sur moi leur souverain empire;
> Et quand vous userez de ce droit tout-puissant,
> Je ne vous répondrai qu'en vous obéissant.

It is a good example of Valbuena Prat's 'sober, elevated palace style'. Monime's answer is simple, almost prosaic in content. The parents who gave birth to her have a right to dispose of her in marriage; they have done so; she will obey. The 'elevation' is apparent in 'Ceux par qui je respire', but still more in 'leur souverain empire' and 'ce droit tout-puissant'.

There is one inevitable difference between Mithridate and the younger tyrants of earlier plays. Pyrrhus is certain that Andromaque hates him and Roxane is well aware of Bajazet's reluctance, but they are both convinced that if only they can get their victims to the altar their charm will do its work—we remember Roxane's 'le temps fera le reste'. The senile lover knows that he cannot count on time or his non-existent attraction and demands far more. Mithridate's reply—it is really a counter-attack—is violent:

> Ainsi, prête à subir un joug qui vous opprime,
> Vous n'allez à l'autel que comme une victime;
> Et moi, tyran d'un coeur qui se refuse au mien,
> Même en vous possédant je ne vous devrai rien.

The violence is apparent in 'opprime', 'victime' and 'tyran'. It is of course unintentionally an exact description of Mithridate's despotic attitude and his methods. Monime's toughness begins to show. She stands firm. Mithridate believes, or affects to believe, that she is in love with Pharnace, the 'fils perfide', and decides to put her in charge of Xipharès in order to prevent contact with the supposed rival.

The opening of the next scene is slightly precious. Xipharès appears for a moment to share his father's suspicions and is rightly reproached by Monime. It pays off. Monime confesses her love for him, but displays precisely the same toughness that she had shown to Mithridate:

> Oui, Prince, il n'est plus temps de le dissimuler.
> Ma douleur pour se taire a trop de violence.
> Un rigoureux devoir me condamne au silence;
> Mais il faut bien enfin, malgré ses dures lois,
> Parler pour la première et la dernière fois.
> Vous m'aimez dès longtemps. Une égale tendresse
> Pour vous depuis longtemps m'afflige et m'intéresse.

Duty may be 'rigorous' and the rules 'hard'; the outcome is inescapable. Monime has already said to her confidant

> s'il m'aime il en jouira peu;
> Je lui vendrai si cher ce bonheur qu'il ignore,
> Qu'il vaudrait mieux pour lui qu'il l'ignorât encore.

She is even more forthright with Xipharès himself:

> quel que soit vers vous le penchant qui m'attire,
> Je vous le dis, Seigneur, pour ne plus vous le dire,
> Ma gloire me rappelle et m'entraîne à l'autel
> Où je vais vous jurer un silence éternel.

We should notice the way in which the placing of the words in the first line—'vers vous' preceding 'penchant' and the verb pushed to the end of the line—reflect the struggle going on in Monime's mind. It is reinforced, in the third line, by 'm'entraîne', a word which usually suggests someone being forced in the wrong direction, and the internal rhyming of 'rappelle/autel'. Nor should we overlook the way in which Monime's 'silence' looks back to Xipharès's 'Cet amour s'est longtemps accru dans le silence'. For Xipharès 'silence' had once been the fertile element: it now appears as the destructive element which will extinguish love altogether.

It is an ironical situation. Monime has appealed to Xipharès, with whom she is secretly in love, to protect her against Pharnace. Mithridate puts her in charge of the man she loves in order to prevent contact with the man she detests and unwittingly creates a situation which the courts describe as 'inclination and opportunity'. The virtuous couple naturally set their faces against 'opportunity'. For what we are witnessing is the Racinian treatment of a Cornelian situation: the traditional conflict between 'duty' and 'inclination'. When Xipharès first met Monime his love was 'légitime'. The moment his father entered the lists and though he never dreamed of contesting Mithridate's supposed 'rights', it became in his own eyes 'criminel'. And nothing could be more categorical than Monime's

> Ma gloire me rappelle et m'entraîne à l'autel
> Où je vais vous jurer un silence éternel,

where the point is rammed home by the strong caesuras.

Xipharès and Monime share the innocence and integrity of the young lovers in other plays, but they are clearly much more mature and decidedly tougher. Their behaviour is a good illustration of Corneille's dictum in the dedication to *La Place Royale*, but if they possess a Cornelian determination and are without the weaknesses from which some of Racine's young lovers suffer or the defeatism of Titus, they are equally without the moral buoyancy which is peculiar to Corneille. They see themselves as the 'slaves' of a 'duty' which is not merely 'rigoureux', but 'barbare' and 'funeste'. They remain, as we shall see, 'unbreakable', but in place of moral exaltation there is something which at times comes close to moral disarray, signalled in the present scene by the word 'égarer' with Monime leaving precipitately and Xipharès talking of suicide.

4

The night battle and its consequences dominate the play in a very striking manner. Although Mithridate's fortunes have undergone many fluctuations during the long wars against Rome, his crushing defeat by Pompey is an appalling shock for the ageing warrior. It has deprived him of hard won territories, done incalculable damage to his great reputation, and reduced him to ignominious flight.

Yet in spite of his age Mithridate is resilient. We know from the moment he appears that he is determined to stage a comeback, to avenge his defeat by turning the tables on the Romans. He gives an elaborate account of his plan in Act III. I shall examine it in some detail, but before doing so I want to look at a number of images which throw a revealing light on his state of mind. The images are of three kinds: defeat, recovery, and a blend of the two.

Up to the present Mithridate's wars against the Romans have been waged in other peoples' countries. His answer to the night battle is to be a frontal assault on Rome itself, presumably by daylight in order to avoid any repetition of the confusion which led, or so he believes, to his defeat by Pompey. His goal, however, is a double one: conquest of Rome and conquest of Monime symbolized by the 'Capitol' and the 'altar'. In Act IV, Sc. 4, he says to Monime:

> Tandis que mes soldats, prêts à suivre leur roi,
> Rentrent dans mes vaisseaux pour partir avec moi,
> Venez, et qu'à l'autel ma promesse accomplie
> Par des noeuds éternels l'un et l'autre nous lie.

It is another illustration of the interweaving of the dual theme of love and war. It is also an example of the image of recovery. Mithridate's eyes are fixed simultaneously on both his goals. His soldiers are actually embarking for the first stage in the invasion of Rome, but before setting sail himself he means to get Monime to the altar. His 'noeuds *éternels*' echo her own words to Xipharès: 'vous jurer un silence *éternel*'.

I have already referred to the importance of the sentence introducing his account of the night battle:

> Je suis vaincu.

The word 'vaincu' is constantly on his lips. Its first use sounds a note of doom which reverberates throughout the play, pointing to his death in Act V. It is linked with the words 'fuir' and 'persécuter' which in his fanciful plan for the invasion of Rome will be replaced by the word 'marcher'. The night battle was a personal disaster. It has turned him into a sombre figure on the run, moving in the shadow, surrounded by an aura of darkness. Unlike Phèdre, he does not shun the light and seek refuge in the dark; he is always trying to extricate himself from the shadow and to restore his public image as the great warrior. It is one of the signs of his failure that the image of the defeated king—the image that he is trying desperately to obliterate—never ceases to haunt his imagination:

> Quand le sort ennemi m'aurait jeté plus bas,
> Vaincu, persécuté, sans secours, sans États,
> Errant de mers en mers, et moins roi que pirate,
> Conservant pour tous biens le nom de Mithridate . . .

Although the use of the past conditional is intended to suggest that things might have been worse, it seems clear that his words apply partly to disasters which have already taken place and partly to the fear that instead of the triumphant come back at which he is aiming, they might turn out even worse in the future. The pauses in the second line mark the stages in the downfall of a ruler which leave him defeated, pursued, without allies, stripped of his many kingdoms. In the next line we have an image of complete confusion with the spectacle of a defeated monarch careering wildly across the seas—this is the sense of 'errant'—without any tangible goal. The conjunction of 'roi' and 'pirate' is specially striking. It reflects Mithridate's lurking fear for the future. It also contains a hint that there is and always has been something of the 'pirate' about the man and his martial exploits.

He clings to his name, in spite of the fact that it is badly tarnished, as a symbol of past triumphs and the only thing that is left to him. He is continually trying to boost his own morale and goes on to argue, in strangely boastful terms, that even if the worst happened the defeated Mithridate would still be a more glorious figure than other kings sitting cosily on their thrones:

> Apprenez que suivi d'un nom si glorieux,
> Partout de l'univers j'attacherais les yeux,
> Et qu'il n'est point de rois, s'ils sont dignes de l'être,
> Qui, sur le trône assis, n'enviassent peut-être
> Au-dessus de leur gloire un naufrage élevé,
> Que Rome et quarante ans ont à peine achevé.

'Naufrage élevé' is another striking image—the image of a grandiose wreck towering above and somehow dwarfing smaller vessels which are still intact. It should be compared with an earlier use of the word in Mithridate's first mention to his sons of his plan of revenge against Rome:

> Tout vaincu que je suis, et voisin du naufrage,
> Je médite un dessein digne de mon courage.

When we place 'voisin du naufrage' beside 'naufrage élevé', we can see that there has been something like convergence on the psychological plane, that a vessel which was on the verge of shipwreck has in fact been wrecked. It is confirmed by the last word in the first of the two quotations —'achevé'.

'Vaincu, persécuté' turn up again, obsessively, in the final appeal to Monime in Act IV to forget the inglorious present and turn her eyes towards an imaginary, an impossible future:

> Ne me regardez point vaincu, persécuté:
> Revoyez-moi vainqueur, et partout redouté.

It is an example of the mixed image or the image of defeat-and-recovery with the contrast between 'vaincu' and 'vainqueur', but though Mithridate is trying to convince Monime that the position described in the line,

> Vaincu, persécuté, sans secours, sans États,

at their first meeting, is in the process of being reversed, it is obvious from the 'revoyez-moi' that it is mere wishful thinking.

I must glance briefly at the images of recovery. The operative word is usually 'vaisseaux'. Mithridate sees himself either on the point of re-embarking after the disastrous disembarkation or already far from Nymphaeum which means that the comeback has started:

> Sortant de mes vaisseaux, il faut que j'y remonte.
>
> *   *   *
>
> Demain, sans différer, je prétends que l'Aurore
> Découvre mes vaisseaux déjà loin du Bosphore.

We can see that the images of defeat with their contrast between past splendour and present wretchedness, which is most apparent in the references to 'shipwreck' and 'flight', are vivid, concrete and convincing while the images of recovery or, for that matter, the mixed images, which look forward to an uncertain future, are vague and unconvincing.

It is evident from these passages with their continual use of words like 'mers', 'vaisseaux', 'naufrage' and 'pirate' that *Mithridate* is one of the plays in which Racine makes the greatest use of marine imagery. It is due in part, as I have already suggested, to the proximity of the sea and the royal palace. Nymphaeum is a port where most of the campaigns begin and end. We see a victorious, or potentially victorious, Mithridate charging across the sea in pursuit of the enemy, and a defeated Mithridate who has just scraped back to Nymphaeum by sea. It remains to add that the marine imagery is remarkably effective in conveying the atmosphere of the play and in reflecting the psychological vicissitudes of the principal character.

5

Mithridate's plan of campaign at the beginning of Act III is not one of my favourite *tirades*, but the scene is an impressive example of dramatic organization and in a sense the centre of the play. The opening speech, which runs to 108 lines, is divided into five paragraphs or sections preceded by a four-line introduction.[4] Mithridate begins on a note of great enthusiasm:

> Approchez, mes enfants. Enfin l'heure est venue
> Qu'il faut que mon secret éclate à votre vue.
> A mes nobles projets je vois tout conspirer;
> Il ne me reste plus qu'à vous les déclarer.

Each of the five sections begins with a statement which serves as a text that is carefully expanded and developed. The first starts with the words

> Je fuis, ainsi le veut la fortune ennemie.
> Mais vous savez trop bien l'histoire de ma vie
> Pour croire que longtemps soigneux de me cacher,
> J'attends en ces déserts qu'on me vienne chercher.

This is the announcement of the comeback with Mithridate about to emerge from the shadow of the 'deserts'. He goes on to give a survey of his military career. We can see that it is an expansion of Xipharès's brief summary in the first scene of the play and that it is intended to serve as a corrective to his own gloomy references to his defeat by concentrating on victory. He suffered defeats in the past, but they were followed by startling recoveries:

> Le Bosphore m'a vu . . .
> Renverser en un *j*our l'ouvrage d'une année.

He treats it, so to speak, as a precedent. He goes on to consider the actual situation, saying of the Romans

> Le bruit de nos trésors les a tous attirés:
> Ils y courent en foule, et jaloux l'un de l'autre
> Désertent leur pays pour inonder le nôtre.

The invading Romans are aggressors who have swamped Europe:

> Moi seul je leur résiste.

Everything depends on him. The grandiose plan emerges, a truc turning of the tables:

> C'est à Rome, mes fils, que je prétends marcher.
> Ce dessein vous surprend; et vous croyez peut-être
> Que le seul désespoir aujourd'hui le fait naître.
> J'excuse votre erreur . . .

This provides the cue for the second section. His sons may be surprised by the boldness of the plan, but he is convinced that he is the experienced warrior who knows his job. He began, as we saw, with the word 'fuis' in the second passage, went on to 'résiste', representing an intermediate stage, and now puts the emphasis on 'marcher' which converts 'flight' into 'advance'. He proceeds to explain how it will be carried out and takes as his text the vulnerability of Rome:

> Ne vous figurez point que de cette contrée
> Par d'éternels remparts Rome soit séparée.
> Je sais tous les chemins par où je dois passer;
> Et si la mort bientôt ne me vient traverser . . .
> Je vous rends dans trois mois au pied du Capitole.
> Doutez-vous que l'Euxin ne me porte en deux jours
> Aux lieux où le Danube y vient finir son cours?[5]

The reference to his death is of course ironical. He expects that he will reach Rome in three months and that the armies will have increased enormously in strength by recruiting on the way people who are united by their hatred of Rome. His allies have reproached him in the past for his laziness. They know that if he goes down, they all will. At this point there is a reference back to the Romans swamping all Europe which appeared in the first section:

> Ils savent que sur eux prêt à se déborder,
> Ce torrent, s'il m'entraîne, ira tout inonder.

'Torrent', as we know, is a favourite word in martial contexts of this nature; the reappearance of 'm'entraîne', with its sense of being dragged or pushed in the wrong direction, looks back to the earlier uses by Mithridate and Monime. It links two kinds of wrong direction: defeat in battle and defeat by somebody being forced to the altar—or refusing to go there, which is what will happen.

Fear of being forced back and defeated by the Romans is the reason why many different peoples will be ready to join Mithridate's growing army and follow him into Italy. This marks the transition to the next section:

> C'est là qu'en arrivant, plus qu'en tout le chemin,
> Vous trouverez partout l'horreur du nom romain . . .

There is a cry of triumph:

> Tes plus grands ennemis, Rome, sont à tes portes.

Mithridate has now arrived in imagination—we notice the use of the present tense—in Roman territory.

The Romans themselves are so busy invading and pillaging other countries that there will be nobody to defend the city:

> Vide de légions qui la puissent défendre . . .

The short fourth section is largely exhortation, beginning with a second use of the verb 'marcher':

> Marchons, et dans son sein rejetons cette guerre . . .

Mithridate uses a declaration of Hannibal's in support of his own plan for the invasion of Rome:

> Jamais on ne vaincra les Romains que dans Rome.

There follows a spate of images of destruction: an imaginary battle in which defeat in the night battle will be avenged by the expedition against Rome:

> Noyons-la dans son sang justement répandu.
> Brûlons ce Capitole où j'étais attendu.
> Détruisons ses honneurs, et faisons disparaître
> La honte de cent rois, et la mienne peut-être;
> Et la flamme à la main effaçons tous ces noms
> Que Rome y consacrait à d'éternels affronts.

The fifth section opens with the words

> Voilà l'ambition dont mon âme est saisie.

It is a sign that the statement of his plan is completed. The time has come for action. The commander-in-chief gives his first orders. He has confined himself so far to Europe. It must not be thought that he intends to leave the Romans a free hand in Asia. Pharnace is to depart at once and marry the daughter of the King of Parthia in order to cement the alliance. Mithridate himself will set out tomorrow. Pharnace's job is to show Asia 'un autre Mithridate'.

Stylistically, the speech is designed in the best classic manner, progressing logically from one stage to another. There is a short survey of Mithridate's military career, a panoramic view of all the countries engaged in the struggle against the Romans, a return to Mithridate as the only person capable of organizing the attack on Rome and saving the other countries from its depredations. These preliminaries, which are intended ostensibly to convince his sons but in reality Mithridate himself, are followed by the practical account of the plan of campaign and a forecast of the result. Each section brings Mithridate and his armies, in imagination, a step nearer Rome. The speech gathers rapidly in intensity from section three onwards and reaches a sort of climax or finale with the massed images of destruction at the end of section four: 'Noyons-la . . . Brûlons ce Capitole . . . Détruisons ses honneurs . . .'

The plan is clearly an old man's dream, a gigantic piece of wishful thinking. It is also in a sense the apex of the tragedy. Mithridate is thirsting to make his comeback; he does it in imagination and his morale reaches its highest point during the unfolding of the plan in which images of defeat are replaced by images of recovery, reaching a personal climax in the idea that he will arrive in Rome not as the prisoner they were expecting (this is the meaning of 'où j'étais attendu'), but as a conqueror and will purge his name of the disgrace now attached to it amid the ruins of Rome.

6

The scene is a turning point. From now on disillusion will set in and the imaginary comeback will be succeeded by a real decline and fall. The grandiose plan brings into the open the deep divisions between the parties which had previously been concealed, or partly concealed, and discussion is converted into action.

Pharnace's refusal to obey his father, his arrest and betrayal of Xipharès's 'secret' are together the first step in Mithridate's final defeat. His defiance and imprisonment lead to the uprising at the end of Act IV, and the disclosure of Xipharès's love for Monime to Mithridate's defeat in love in the scene immediately preceding the news of the uprising.

Xipharès protests that he has no designs on Monime, which given the couple's determination to put duty first is true. Mithridate assures him that he does not believe Pharnace, but the damage is done:

> Je ne le croirai point? Vain espoir qui me flatte!
> Tu ne le crois que trop, malheureux Mithridate.

The way in which he plans this conquest is revealing:

> Voyons, examinons. Mais par où commencer?
> Qui m'en éclaircira? Quels témoins? Quel indice? . . .

He at once resorts to subterfuge—to the kind of 'artifice' he used after the night battle:

> Le ciel en ce moment m'inspire un artifice.
> Qu'on appelle la Reine . . .
> S'il n'est pas digne de moi, le piège est digne d'eux.
> Trompons qui nous trahit. Et pour connaître un traître,
> Il n'est point de moyens . . . Mais je la vois paraître:
> Feignons; et de son coeur, d'un vain espoir flatté,
> Par un mensonge adroit tirons la vérité.

There is a parallel between this scene and the scene in which Mithridate announced his plan for the invasion of Rome. There is also a marked contrast between the styles used in the two scenes: between the confident forthright style of the man who knew what he was talking about and had worked out the details of his plan, and the uncertainty of the man who has been taken by surprise and sets to work quickly to try to find a way out of an impasse. Hesitation, indecision and perplexity about the method to be employed are conveyed by broken rhythms, the succession of questions, brief and sometimes unfinished sentences, the interruption caused by the sight of the queen. At the same time, the last part of the speech is dominated by a remarkable accumulation of words calculated to extract another party's 'secret': 'artifice', 'piège', 'trompons', 'feignons', 'mensonge adroit'. Mithridate has tried to bolster his own morale by what he realizes is a 'vain espoir'. He will now try to create the same 'vain hope' in the mind of the victim in order to induce her to give away her secret. A 'cunning lie' is to be the instrument of arriving at the 'truth'.

His meeting with Monime in Scene 5 is the first stage in what I have called the final battle between them. It is a splendid piece of dialectic—one of the finest in any of the plays—and has been the subject of a forty-page analysis by Gustave Rudler:[6]

> Enfin j'ouvre les yeux, et je me fais justice.
> C'est faire à vos beautés un triste sacrifice,
> Que de vous présenter, Madame, avec ma foi,
> Tout l'âge et le malheur que je traîne avec moi.
> Jusqu'ici la fortune et la victoire mêmes
> Cachaient mes cheveux blancs sous tente diadèmes.
> Mais ce temps-là n'est plus. Je régnais, et je fuis.
> Mes ans se sont accrus; mes honneurs sont détruits;
> Et mon front, dépouillé d'un si noble avantage,
> Du temps, qui l'a flétri, laisse voir tout l'outrage.

The first part of the speech is another example of the way in which Racine uses a combination of stylistic devices. Mithridate resumes the discussion at the point at which it had been broken off at the previous meeting and contrives to give the impression that, after thinking things over, he has come round to Monime's view that he is not a suitable husband for her. Nothing could be more disarming than the gentle, kindly, persuasive tone of the first four lines. Then comes one of those lovely single lyrical, or in the present context, elegiac, lines:

> Cachaient mes cheveux blancs sous trente diadèmes.

Next, the vigorous antitheses, reinforced by two strong caesuras and one other pause:

> Mais ce temps-là n'est plus. // Je régnais, / et je fuis.
> Mes ans se sont accrus; // mes honneurs sont détruits.

Finally, an accumulation of words describing physical decay which have obvious psychological implications: 'détruits', 'dépouillé', 'flétri', 'outrage'.

The attack is twofold. Mithridate tries to allay Monime's suspicions by the pretence of coming clean, abandoning his right to marriage: in fact, surrendering the 'altar'. At the same time, there is a covert appeal to her pity in the fresh portrait of the great warrior, now an old man, who is down on his luck—we observe the reappearance of the word 'fuis'. Although he is virtually certain that she is in love with Xipharès, he very ingeniously repeats the accusation that she is in love with the traitor who has since openly advocated a policy of appeasement. There is a deliberate reference back to his own first sentence in the lines,

> Cessez pourtant, cessez de prétendre à Pharnace.
> Quand je me fais justice, il faut qu'on se la fasse.

He goes on to make his specious offer: the throne and the hand of the son who is 'dear to me'. Monime is astonished:

> Xipharès! Lui, Seigneur?

Then she suddenly grows suspicious:

> Pourriez-vous approuver . . .
> Pourquoi, Seigneur, pourquoi voulez-vous m'éprouver?

This is the opportunity for which Mithridate has been working. Very well: she despises the good son and is obviously determined to have the traitor. He will marry her off to Pharnace at once. This gets right under Monime's defences. She is terrified, admits her love for Xipharès and realizes too late that she has been tricked:

> Seigneur, vous changez de visage.

The meeting is brought to an abrupt end. Mithridate says briefly that he is sending Xipharès to her.

Mithridate is shattered. 'Ils s'aiment.' But he has not yet finished:

> Dissimulons encor, comme j'ai commencé.

Monime's despair when she realizes what she has done provokes an incredulous comment from her confidant:

> Ah! traitez-le, Madame, avec plus de justice:
> Un grand roi descend-il jusqu'à cet artifice?

Phoedime may be one of the 'faceless' confidants, but on this occasion the effectiveness of the irony depends on her innocence; it is an unintentionally mocking echo of Mithridate's

> Le ciel en ce moment m'inspire un artifice,

as well as his 'je me fais justice'.

The effect of the revelation on the protagonists varies in a striking way. Although it places Xipharès's life in danger, he is delighted and regards it, a trifle unnecessarily, as confirmation of Monime's love for him. He urges her to mitigate the damage by going to the altar with Mithridate. But Mithridate's treachery has produced a dramatic change in Monime's attitude:

> Quoi? vous me demandez que j'épouse un barbare
> Dont l'odieux amour pour jamais nous sépare?

When Mithridate reappears, brushes aside the specious promise and orders her to the altar, she answers him with perfect courtesy and unshakable determination. His son is the greatest of men, but after him. She had triumphed over her 'fatal' love for Xipharès when a trick wrested her secret from her. Confidence between Mithridate and herself is impossible:

> Toujours je vous croirais incertain de ma foi;
> Et le tombeau, Seigneur, est moins triste pour moi
> Que le lit d'un époux qui m'a fait cet outrage,
> Qui s'est acquis sur moi cet cruel avantage,
> Et qui me préparant un éternel ennui,
> M'a fait rougir d'un feu qui n'était pas pour lui.

In spite of the courtesy, it is a powerful speech ending, as it does, with its accumulation of reproaches: 'outrage', 'cruel avantage', 'éternel ennui'. The final shot comes near the beginning of her second *réplique*:

> Mais le dessein est pris. Rien ne peut m'ébranler.

We recall at once Pauline in *Polyeucte*:

> ... il déchire mon âme et ne l'ébranle pas.

I have said that Xipharès and Monime are 'unbreakable'. 'Déchire' stands for the pain and confusion caused by the conflict; 'ébranler', used with a negative, for the knowledge that the character has triumphed over it and preserved an absolute integrity. The force behind the word in both dramatists is enormous.

Monime's reply to Mithridate invites one other comment. We saw that in speaking to Xipharès she used the words 'odieux amour'. They were followed in the exchange with Mithridate himself by the conjunction of 'tombeau' and 'lit'. The deepest reason for her resistance to Mithridate is naturally her love for Xipharès, but the appearance of the words I have mentioned shows that it is strengthened by a *physical* repugnance for the battered old man. She was, however, prepared to put everything aside and carry out her duty, including her 'conjugal duties', provided that he behaved tolerably. His trickery has completely discredited him. She is therefore perfectly correct in giving as the reason for her final refusal the breakdown in confidence caused by his subterfuges. We can go on to add that it is one of the signs of Monime's integrity that without saying so she evidently regards Mithridate's treachery as releasing her from what she once considered her duty.

Monime has triumphed, but in the last two acts we are aware of a growing disarray on all sides which is only dissipated by the *dénouement*.

Abandoned by Monime, Mithridate turns his dialectic on himself:

> Qui suis-je? Est-ce Monime? Et suis-je Mithridate?

This is not the only occasion, as we have seen, on which a protagonist asks himself in one of the later scenes who he is and what is happening to him. It seems to me to be a sign that the self has suffered irreparable damage, that the character is, indeed, 'ébranlé' rather than 'déchiré', and has begun to fall to pieces.

This view is supported by what follows. The agonized interrogation continues. There are moments when Mithridate is going to kill off everybody, beginning with Xipharès. Then, in a moment of lucidity, he sees the absurdity of killing the one person who can be relied on to help him with his plan for the invasion of Rome:

> J'ai besoin d'un vengeur, et non d'une maîtresse.[7]

Since Monime is lost to him for ever, would it not be better to give her up to the son whom he must keep?

> Cédons-la. Vains efforts, qui ne font que m'instruire
> Des faiblesses d'un coeur qui cherche à se séduire!
> Je brûle, je l'adore; et, loin de la bannir . . .
> Ah! c'est un crime encor dont je la veux punir.

The anguish and confusion of mind and feeling are brilliantly expressed in the ceaseless interrogation, the violent changes from one extreme to another, the staccato and broken sentences. Mithridate had been determined to achieve one of his two objectives before setting out for Rome. He has failed. It is ultimate defeat in the field of psychological warfare and the loss of the 'altar'. But, as the last line indicated, it will not prevent a half-hearted attempt at revenge.

Then, suddenly, dramatically, the battle switches from the private to the public sector: Arbate arrives with the news that Pharnace has escaped from prison and is leading a rebellion against his father. The marine imagery reappears in the account of the confusion caused by the uprising and the rebels' attempt to put a stop to the invasion of Rome:

> Les uns avec transport embressent le rivage,
> Les autres qui partaient s'élancent dans les flots,
> Ou présentent leurs dards aux yeux des matelots.

It is a vivid glimpse of the uprising described with Racine's usual conciseness. Troops who have not set sail cling to the shore to prevent a start; those in ships which have already set sail are either flinging themselves into the sea in order to get back or forcing the crews to turn back by threatening to kill them.

Arcas follows Arbate with even worse news. So far from Mithridate attacking Rome, the Romans have joined Pharnace and are attacking Mithridate on his home ground—a complete reversal of the plan outlined in the third act. 'All is lost', cries Arcas grimly.

Mithridate's last words are ominous. If he is going down, he will make sure that Monime goes down too:

> Du malheur qui me presse
> Tu ne jouiras pas, infidèle princesse.

The last act is characteristic. Although events move fast, all the ends are neatly tied together.

It opens with Phoedime's discovery of her mistress's unsuccessful attempt to commit suicide by hanging herself with the 'diadem' that Mithridate had given her to console her, as he imagined, for the delay in marrying her. The attempt was provoked by the conviction that Mithridate had murdered Xipharès out of jealousy and is evident in the anguished cry which is heard twice: 'Xipharès ne vit plus'. The faceless confidant is once again the instrument of Racine's irony:

> Ah! du moins attendez qu'un fidèle rapport
> De son malheureux frère ait confirmé la mort.

It looks back to Xipharès's 'fidèle rapport' and this time events are to demonstrate the confidant's good sense.

In spite of her toughness Monime is clearly distraught. She is in the middle of a denunciation of the 'diadem' for not helping her to end her life. Arcas arrives with a different kind of gift: a cup of poison. Monime welcomes it with a sort of ferocious glee as 'the dearest and most desired' of all Mithridate's presents to her. Arbate turns up in the nick of time to knock the cup out of her hand and announce that the king has countermanded the order. Monime is furious. But Arbate has a great deal more to say:

> Le Roi touche à son heure dernière . . .

The report of Xipharès's death was indeed a false report:

> Il vit chargé de gloire, accablé de douleurs.

In Arbate's first report of the uprising one phrase stands out:

> Le désordre est partout . . .

It recalls Mithridate's own account of the night battle:

> Le désordre partout redoublant les alarmes,
> Nous-mêmes contre nous tournant nos propres armes . . .

Although there is nothing to indicate that the rebellion takes place at night, there is an obvious connection between the two events. The uprising repeats the 'disorder' of the night battle, but this time the use of arms against one's own side is not accidental: it is the direct result of the treachery of the 'fils perfide' which was seen as a possible threat at the beginning of the play.

This is by no means the most important of the links between the night battle and the uprising. Mithridate's defeat in the night battle prompted the plan for a comeback by invading Rome. It was this plan which provoked the opposition of both Pharnace and Mithridate's defeated and defeatist soldiery. The first time he escaped with his life; the second time he loses it. The fact that he dies by his own hand takes on a significance of its own in the play. The suicide may have been prompted by still another false report or the mistaken belief that the uprising had succeeded. What seems quite certain is that Mithridate had come to realize that whatever the outcome of the latest battle he himself had suffered final defeat on both the military and the psychological planes. He had done his utmost according to his lights to bring order out of disorder by pursuing his twin objectives: Rome and Monime. He had failed signally on both counts. His death is really the logical outcome of his continual lamentation over his defeat and transforms the word 'vaincu' into a tragic reality. At the same time, we have the impression that a new and better order is emerging, and that its emergence is due to the elimination of the tyrant who for forty years has tried unsuccessfully to impose a highly personal order by eliminating the marauding Romans.

In the final scene the dying Mithridate, Xipharès and Monime are completely united. All their differences have been removed by force of circumstance and the king hands over his betrothed to his son—making good the specious promise he had never intended to keep. In inspires a magnificent gesture on the part of Monime:

> Vivez, Seigneur, vivez, pour le bonheur du monde,
> Et pour sa liberté qui sur vous seul se fonde;
> Vivez, pour triompher d'un ennemi vaincu,
> Pour venger . . .

There is an unintentional ambiguity about the reappearance of the word 'vaincu'. Monime is speaking of the defeat of Mithridate's enemies, but the word marks the final defeat of Mithridate himself and the removal of the person who was the real enemy of Xipharès and Monime. Her wish is no doubt misguided, but it shows true generosity. It reveals better than anything the chivalrous qualities of Xipharès and herself. They are too clearsighted not to be aware of Mithridate's vices and too generous not to pay tribute to his virtues as a soldier. Monime's final tribute echoes Xipharès's tribute in his opening speech: they both emphasize what appear to them to be his unique qualities by the word 'seul'. 'For forty years you *alone* wore down all Rome's principal leaders . . . On you *alone* depend the happiness and freedom of the world.'

7

No one has ever claimed that *Mithridate* is one of Racine's supreme masterpieces and though it enjoyed a considerable success when first produced, becoming according to Dangeau Louis XIV's favourite 'comedy', it has not retained its popularity with the public. There have been reservations, too, on the part of the critics. For Raymond Picard it is 'perhaps the least tragic of Racine's tragedies' and Professor Knight thinks that Mithridate's repentance is 'perhaps the one thing that strikes us as really shocking'.[8]

We may feel that the neglect by the public and the reservations of the critics are signs of a failure to do justice to what seems to me an undoubted masterpiece. If it is true that *Mithridate* marks the beginning of a new phase in Racine's work and that his ingrained pessimism gives way for a time to a more optimistic view of life, then there is nothing surprising about the fact that it is less tragic than the other tragedies and nothing shocking about the king's repentance. We can only conclude that Racine is being criticized because he departed from his usual form and demonstrated once again—I am thinking of *Bérénice*—his versatility.

If some critics have reservations about the play as a dramatic work, others have singled out its poetry for special praise, claiming that in *Mithridate* Racine developed a new style. It seems to me that this is the right view and that the new phase extended to the poetry as well as the dramatist's attitude. Racine's music is never easy to analyse. All his poetry possesses a music of its own which has an incantatory effect on the audience and enables them to share his vision. Now though there is a basic music which is always present, there are variations in what may be described as the 'tune' or, using the word in a musical sense, the 'theme'. It is in this sense that the verse of *Mithridate* is new. It reveals a movement away from *Bajazet* and looks forward to further development in *Iphigénie* and *Phèdre*. The right word for the new note or theme is serenity. It can be heard even in a sad pronouncement like Xipharès's

> Je vous rappelle un songe effacé de votre âme,

where the effect depends to a considerable degree on the soft *l*-s and the contrast between the rich deep 'songe' and the airy 'effacé'.

Pharnace provides an even more striking example when he says to Monime:

> Prêts à vous recevoir, mes vaisseaux vous attendent,
> Et du pied de l'autel vous y pouvez monter,
> Souveraine des mers qui vous doivent porter.

Although Pharnace is the real villain of the piece, his words are a form of apotheosis which invests Monime with an aura of her own. We see her in imagination moving upwards from the altar to the ship and in the superb last line rising above everything, a royal figure dominating the seas.

These lines should be compared with the passage quoted earlier in which Mithridate describes flight by sea:

> Vaincu, persécuté, sans secours, sans États,
> Errant de mers en mers, et moins roi que pirate,
> Conservant pour tous biens le nom de Mithridate . . .

Seen together the two passages reflect the pattern of the play in a double sense. Monime, who described herself as 'esclave couronnée', rises in the world and becomes a genuine 'sovereign' while Mithridate, the king who had once enjoyed thirty crowns, moves steadily downward to destruction like a mere 'pirate' whose plots and plans have gone awry.[9] This is also reflected in the interweaving or alternation of the two musical themes: the notes of serenity and doom. The fact that in the end serenity prevails and the youthful couple enjoy the success they deserve gives the play its special place in the canon.

NOTES

[1] In *Nouvelles réflexions sur le théâtre*, 1959, pp. 176–7; *Cahiers de la Compagnie Madeleine Renaud Jean-Louis Barrault*, No. 10, 1955, pp. 58–9.

Charles Mauron put it a little differently:

'Nous allons ainsi, avec *Mithridate*, passer, semble-t-il, de la phase phallique, et de l'arrachement au prégénital, à l'oedipe, puis son inhibition' (*L'Inconscient dans l'oeuvre et la vie de Racine*, 1957, p. 107).

[2] Xipharès and Iphigénie both show the same loyalty to a misguided father.

[3] We shall find that the same style is used when Mithridate catalogues his own misfortunes in the later stages of the play.

[4] In view of the length of the speech we should notice that Mithridate's is much the longest role in any of the plays and contains 580 lines. The runners-up are Titus with 498 and Joad with 496 lines.

[5] Doubts have been expressed about the possibility of reaching the Danube in two days, but the naval critic quoted in an earlier chapter states that it was not impossible even for the 'ships of antiquity' (J. Rouch, *art. cit.*, p. 41).

[6] See *L'Explication française*, 9th ed., 1952, pp. 127–73.

[7] Compare:

> Contre mon propre honneur mon amour s'intéresse:
> Il faut venger un père et perdre une maîtresse.

> Nous n'avons qu'un honneur, il est tant de maîtresses.
>
>   (*Le Cid*, I, 6; III, 6.)

[8] See *O.C.*, I, p. 613 and *Racine et la Grèce*, p. 296.

[9] It brings home forcibly to us J. L. Barrault's image of the 'swimmer' making his way back to the surface.

'IPHIGÉNIE'
1674

Un père immole sa fille par ambition, et il ne faut pas
qu'il soit odieux. Quel problème à résoudre!
DIDEROT

Ces flottements du Roi, ses mensonges, ses démentis,
ses ruses, rien en sa conduite n'est digne d'un héros
... Ordre, contre-ordre, l'image du désordre.
LUCIEN DUBECH

CHAPTER 8

'IPHIGÉNIE'

1674

I

ALTHOUGH the story of the Trojan War is one of the most celebrated of all Greek legends and has proved immensely fascinating to writers from Homer to Jean Giraudoux, we can hardly avoid the feeling, particularly if we belong to a generation which has been through two world wars, that the story is an essentially frivolous one. The unsuccessful suitors for the hand of Helen used their pledge to protect her marriage to Menelaus against all comers as a pretext for launching an unjust war. It lasted for ten years, cost innumerable lives, ended in the complete destruction of Troy and the wholesale massacre of its inhabitants—all the horror and all the squalor of 'total victory'.

The popularity of the story with writers does not mean that their attitude to the war, or at any rate to the Greeks, has been uncritical. Racine's was far from that. His return to Greek legend in *Iphigénie* for the first time since *Andromaque* was probably due to a change in fashion which had begun in 1671 with the production by other writers of plays and operas based on Greek legend. There was a tendency on the part of dramatists like Quinault and Thomas Corneille, who had introduced the new fashion, to invest the Greeks with an imaginary grandeur. It is thought that Racine disapproved of their approach and was determined to show that he knew better and could do better than his contemporaries.

There may have been another reason, possibly an unconscious one, for Racine's own change. He may have decided to complete a diptych. For there is no doubt that in the canon of his plays *Andromaque* and *Iphigénie* form a pair.[1] In *Andromaque* he deals with the aftermath of the Trojan War; in *Iphigénie* with the prelude to it. The contrasts and resemblances between the two plays are instructive. We have seen that in *Andromaque* he cut the heroes down to life size. They are not gallant warriors chivalrously keeping the rules of the game and compelling our admiration by their courage and nobility. They triumphed in the Trojan War by brute force and did not disdain any trick which gave them an advantage over the enemy. We find precisely the same sort of people in *Iphigénie*. It is another study of weakness, treachery and corruption.

If the Trojan War is *re*-fought in miniature in *Andromaque*, it might be argued that in *Iphigénie* it is *pre*-fought in miniature in the clashes between

Agamemnon and his followers. The image of Troy in flames belongs to both plays. In *Andromaque* it stands for the disillusionment which follows war; in *Iphigénie* for the illusions which precede war. Their emptiness and folly are demonstrated by the contrast between the excitement of Achille, who cannot wait to set out on the expedition against Troy, and the guilty feelings of his son in *Andromaque*. There are, indeed, marked resemblances between father and son, as Oreste was careful to point out at his first meeting with Pyrrhus:

> Hector tomba sous lui, Troie expira sous vous.

That was the official view of the diplomat. What is much more interesting is the fact that the exploits of Achille in Lesbos are described, or rather denounced, by Agamemnon in much the same terms as those used by Hermione of the son's exploits in Troy. Achille has razed Lesbos to the ground in record time in order to give himself a little preliminary practice in warfare. It is a foretaste of what is to come.

2

'Nothing', said Racine in his preface, 'is more famous among poets than the sacrifice of Iphigenia. But not all of them are in agreement on the most important elements of the sacrifice.' He goes on to discuss three different versions of the legend. In all three the Greek armies and a score of monarchs were assembled in Aulis under the supreme command of Agamemnon to launch the attack on Troy. There was a sudden calm which made it impossible to set sail. It lasted for several months. Then the oracles spoke. The calm could only be ended and the invasion begun by the sacrifice on the altar of Diana of Iphigenia who was promptly identified with Agamemnon's daughter. In the best known version Agamemnon allows his daughter to be put to death which may help to explain his own murder by his wife and her paramour when he returned victorious from Troy. In the second version, which was adopted by Euripides, Agamemnon consents to the sacrifice, but at the last moment Diana performs a miracle and a doe is substituted for Iphigenia who is transplanted to Tauris. Racine did not care for the first version. It was, he thought, too savage. He rejected the second on the ground that French audiences had become too sophisticated to swallow that kind of miracle. His reasons are not entirely convincing. It can of course be argued that it was thirty-four years since Rotrou had used the second version in his *Iphigénie en Aulide* and that times had changed, but Racine's own play ends with a miracle or near-miracle. The truth of the matter is that he deliberately unearthed another version which was less well-known and offered more scope for his special interests. In the course of her adventures Helen had met and secretly married Theseus. They had a daughter named Iphigenia. She was farmed out to humble foster-parents, her name changed and her noble birth concealed. She turned up in Aulis as the prisoner of Achilles who had captured her in Lesbos. Calchas revealed that it was she and not Agamemnon's daughter who was the predestined victim.

3

In spite of unexplained or misleading elements in them, the oracles—those garrulous oracles—have spoken so fully that their pronouncements are almost a blueprint for the campaign. Provided that the sacrifice is offered and the gods appeased, the Greeks will triumph. Achille will be the star performer on the Greek side, but the cost is also known in advance. Although he is the offspring of one of Venus's periodical incursions into the beds of mortals, he will not be among the returning heroes: he will be cut off in the flower of his age and buried in foreign soil. If Agamemnon does not consent to the immolation of his daughter, the armies will disperse, the potential heroes will return home to lead humdrum, boring, domestic lives, deprived of the 'glory' that beckons them on—the certain bet.

As Racine's genius ripened, the family feud became increasingly the centre of the plays. Although the protagonists in *Andromaque* are brought into the most intimate contact and the most violent collision, they are not a *family*. They are rather a new generation, the scattered offspring of the families who were responsible for the war and are for the most part dead. The family unit is more complete in *Iphigénie* than in any of the other secular plays: father, mother, daughter, baby son—Oreste whom we naturally do not see—and prospective son-in-law.

The final decision between performing and not performing the sacrifice, between a glorious and inglorious future, rests with the father alone. Inevitably, it divides the family and their connections into two violently opposing factions. Agamemnon faces the conflict between private and public interest which in this case becomes the conflicting claims of the State and humanity. He is subjected to the strongest pressure by his fellow warriors to permit the ritual murder and the strongest opposition from his wife Clytemnestre who is a much more powerful character: a formidable matron who is determined to save her daughter or perish in the attempt. Iphigénie is a charming and obedient daughter who prefers to die rather than see her father's hopes of glory disappointed and who causes great anguish by siding with her father against her protectors.

On the family falls the impact of what might be termed the two 'outsiders': the warrior Achille who, once he learns the price, is determined to save Iphigénie even if it means wrecking the campaign against Troy and revolution in the army; and Ériphile who though mistakenly believing herself a Trojan falls in love with Achille and when she realizes that it is hopeless, spends her time plotting against the family, which introduces the favourite theme of jealousy.

For anyone who did not know the story, *Iphigénie* would rank as a drama of suspense with the spectator continually asking himself whether Agamemnon would stand firm and save his daughter or whether he would give way and allow her to be brutally put to death. Agamemnon is one of Racine's great creations. His vacillations are the mainspring of the play and, paradoxically, the source of its unity. We learn in the opening scene that he had begun by defying the gods. He had been browbeaten by the bullying Ulysse into agreeing to the sacrifice. He summoned his wife and daughter from Argos on the pretext that it was for the wedding of Iphigénie and Achille. At the beginning of the play he is overcome with re-morse and sends his confidant to intercept them and give Clytemnestre a letter ordering their return to Argos on the false pretence that Achille has changed his mind and intends to marry Ériphile. The trick miscarries. Arcas fails to intercept mother and daughter who arrive at the camp. Ulysse gets to work again. Agamemnon gives in. Arrangements are made for Iphigénie to go to the altar in the belief that she is to be married to Achille who will escort her there when in fact the priest will be waiting with the sacrificial knife. In the middle of Act III Arcas lets the cat out of the bag. Mother, daughter and Achille all tackle Agamemnon in turn and in their different ways. He changes his mind once again which causes the blow-up.

On the face of it, Agamemnon finds himself in a truly appalling situa-tion. He has to decide between the sacrifice of a beloved daughter and national disaster. The truth is rather different. When we study his own pronouncements and listen attentively to his protestations of love for his daughter, we feel instinctively that her safety is not his primary concern.

4

The setting is Agamemnon's tent in the Greek camp. It is the dead of night. The wretched leader is worried to death and cannot sleep. He wakes his confidant:

> Oui, c'est Agamemnon, c'est ton roi qui t'éveille.

Although the sleepy confidant is startled and doesn't quite know what is happening, it is clear from his reply that *poetically* he is pretty quick on the draw:

C'est vous-même, Seigneur! Quel important besoin
Vous a fait devancer l'aurore de si loin?
A peine un faible jour vous éclaire et me guide.
Vos yeux seuls et les miens sont ouverts dans l'Aulide.
Avez-vous dans les airs entendu quelque bruit?
Les vents nous auraient-ils exaucés cette nuit?
Mais tout dort, et l'armée, et les vents, et Neptune.

It is an impressive example of Racine's new style: a vivid picture of the characters' physical environment. The softness and stillness of the night are beautifully conveyed by the *l*-s, the *c*-s of 'devancer' and 'exaucés', the murmur of voices by the nasals of 'besoin' and 'loin', the *i*-s of 'guide', 'Aulide', 'bruit' and 'nuit'. Then all sound fades in the 'tout dort' of the celebrated last line.

It is in no sense a piece of decoration. The implications of 'aurore' and 'faible jour' are complex. Agamemnon is struggling to find the light which will enable him to make his escape from the dark: the psychological darkness of a seemingly impossible situation; the physical darkness that brings bad dreams in which the gods appear to denounce the delays over the sacrifice as 'sacrilegious'. In spite of the difficulties, the darkness is somehow not the sinister darkness of other plays. There is a faint gleam of light; the 'dawn' is distant, but nevertheless a symbol of hope. Although in the end light will come in a totally unexpected manner, the passage will be a rough one. At the close of the scene he remarks hopefully:

Déjà le jour plus grand nous frappe et nous éclaire . . .

On this occasion the escape is an illusion, a movement from one form of darkness to another. He catches sight of Ulysse and Achille approaching and knows that they are going to put more pressure on him to do what they want.

Agamemnon's whispered reference to the happy lot of simple people living obscure lives unburdened by the 'yoke' from which he suffers prompts the innocent Arcas to describe what seems to him to be the king's fortunate position:

Roi, père, époux heureux, fils du puissant Atrée . . .

It is of course exactly the opposite of the real situation. But it provides Agamemnon with his cue. He proceeds to put both confidant and audience in the picture and to arrange for the interception of mother and daughter who are on their way to the camp. In the course of his revelations, he says of Ulysse:

Il me représenta l'honneur et la patrie,
Tout ce peuple, ces rois à mes ordres soumis,
Et l'empire d'Asie à la Grèce promis:
De quel front immolant tout l'État à ma fille,
Roi sans gloire, j'irais vieillir dans ma famille!

Moi-même (je l'avoue avec quelque pudeur),
Charmé de mon pouvoir, et plein de ma grandeur,
Ces noms de roi des rois et de chef de la Grèce
Chatouillaient de mon coeur l'orgueilleuse faiblesse.

The contrast between 'roi sans gloire' and 'roi des rois', the use of the word 'charmé'—the equivalent here of 'fasciné' or 'ensorcelé'—and 'grandeur' show, in spite of the coy reference to 'pudeur', where his real interests lie. 'Orgueilleuse faiblesse' is both a summing-up and a perfect description of the grievous shortcomings of the 'roi des rois'.

Although Arcas's first speech introduced the theme of the calm, he regards it as a minor misfortune which will soon come right. Agamemnon explains the true position and we have one of the poetical highlights of the play:

Tu te souviens du jour qu'en Aulide assemblés
Nos vaisseaux par les vents semblaient être appelés.
Nous partions; et déjà par mille cris de joie
Nous menacions de loin les rivages de Troie.
Un prodige étonnant fit taire ce transport:
Le vent qui nous flattait nous laissa dans le port.
Il fallut s'arrêter, et la rame inutile
Fatigua vainement une mer immobile.

First there is the spectacle of the Greek fleet setting forth, the excited cries of the soldiers thirsting to fling themselves into the attack on a target which is so tantalizingly visible on the other side of the water. We can hear the swish of the ships gliding through the sea and the flap of eager sails in the consonants of 'souviens', 'assemblés', 'vaisseaux', 'semblaient', 'vents', 'partions', 'menacions', 'rivage' and 'Troie'. There is a sudden silence. The cheering dies away. All movement stops. It is brilliantly expressed by the use of imperfects describing movement and the past definites describing the cessation of movement, almost in fact putting a stop to it. The sense of frustration is brought home by the *f*-s and the staccato verbs: 'fit', 'laissa', 'fallut', 'fatigua'. The *m*-s and *r*-s of 'rame' and 'mer', the 'vainement' and the heavy rhyme, 'inutile/immobile', transmit the sound of the useless oars battering away at the leaden mass of water.

The image of the calm, the sense of an irremovable barrier between individuals and their goal imposed by some supernatural power—'un prodige étonnant', 'ce miracle inouï'—dominates the play. It is the very element in which and with which the characters live and it determines their psychology. In *Andromaque* the eyes of the characters are fixed on the past which casts a heavy shadow over the present. In *Iphigénie* they are turned towards a future which seems beyond their reach. This means that time itself appears to be standing still, that they are caught in a perpetual present in which nothing can move forward, make progress, that individuals are seized with a feverish activity which is constantly frustrated and until the last act gets them nowhere. The sea is potentially the path to glory, the road to victory, but inexplicably remains closed.

This accounts for the importance of the images of paths which are continually turning up: 'chemin', 'sentier', 'route', 'course', 'passage' and 'voie'.

The image of the path is reinforced and elaborated by other images and words. There are 'open' and 'closed' paths, 'right' and 'wrong' paths, deviations from the right path expressed by the words 'écarter' and 'égarer'—all threatening disaster of one kind or another—as well as internal deviations corresponding to the external ones and indicated by the words 'détours' and 'artifice'.

The paths divide into three distinct but interrelated groups. The main path is naturally the sea route leading from Aulis to Troy which is closed by the gods' decree:

> Ces vents depuis trois mois enchaînés sur nos têtes
> D'Ilion trop longtemps vous *ferment le chemin.*[2]

> O ciel! pourquoi faut-il que ta secrète envie
> *Ferme* à de tels héros *le chemin* de l'Asie?

> Tandis qu'à nos vaisseaux *la mer toujours fermée*
> Trouble toute la Grèce et consume l'armée. . . .

The last example is of particular interest. The operative word is 'consume' read in conjunction with 'la mer toujours fermée'. 'Consume' refers to the frustration, the disintegrating effect on the army of the 'closed sea' which turns them into an ingrowing community, all bent on their own interests while the words 'glory', 'honour', 'fatherland', 'interests of State' and 'legitimate' (applied to the intended murder of Iphigénie) are bandied from mouth to mouth.

According to the oracles, the one way of opening up the main path is for Iphigénie to follow another path—the path to the altar. This path gives rise to every kind of ambiguity. Once again the altar is the place of love and death, marriage and murder, as it was in *Andromaque*. The word is used 34 times in *Iphigénie*, thirteen of them in Act III which points to rising tension in the middle of the play. Iphigénie and her mother believe, until Arcas gives away the secret, that the path to the altar leads to marriage with Achille: Agamemnon knows that it leads to the priest with the sacrificial knife in his hand. The path can only be opened to Iphigénie by making sure that it is closed to her mother who is to know nothing until the deed is done. Speaking of the supposed marriage to Achille, Agamemnon says to Clytemnestre

> Vous voulez que Calchas l'unisse à ma famille;
> Vous pouvez à l'autel envoyer votre fille . . .
> M'en croirez-vous? Laissez, de vos femmes suivie,
> A cet hymen, sans vous, marcher Iphigénie.

The stiffness of the syntax in the last two lines gives the impression of the victim being frogmarched to the place of execution.

It should be pointed out that in the standard versions of the legend Calchas is simply an astrologer and that his priesthood is an invention of Racine's. It is a highly relevant invention for his handling of the theme. It means that Calchas is invested with a duel role: he is the priest who may either conduct the marriage ceremony or perform what is supposed to be a religious sacrifice at the altar.

Attempts to bar Clytemnestre's path to the altar lead to a series of vigorous protests:

> Il me fait de l'autel refuser le *passage*.

> D'où vient que d'un soin si cruel
> L'injuste Agamemnon *m'écarte* de l'autel?

When she learns the truth:

> Je ne m'etonne plus de cet ordre cruel
> Qui m'avait interdit l'*approche* de l'autel.

They are examples of the way in which 'artifice' and 'détours' are used to divert a person from what is for her the 'right' path.

The ambiguity also produces some remarkable strokes of Racinian irony. Iphigénie is discussing the sacrifice with her father, but never for a moment dreams that the intended victim is a human being, least of all herself:

> IPHIGÉNIE
> Verra-t-on à l'autel votre heureuse famille? . . .

> AGAMEMNON
> Vous y serez, ma fille.
>
> Adieu.

In a bitter exchange with Agamemnon in Act IV Achille, who is now in the secret, says:

> On dit que sous mon nom à l'autel appelée,
> Je ne l'y conduisais que pour être immolée . . .

Later in the same scene Agamemnon retorts with the words:

> Mon coeur pour la sauver vous *ouvrait une voie*;
> Mais vous ne demandez, vous ne cherchez que Troie.
> Je vous *fermais le champ* où vous voulez courir.
> Vous le voulez, partez: *sa mort va vous l'ouvrir*.

It is a shocking answer with its play on 'open' and 'closed' paths which reflects in macabre fashion Agamemnon's vacillations. He has tried, or so he pretends, to save Iphigénie for Achille by 'closing' the way to Troy. Now the choice of a different path leading to Iphigénie's death is going to 'open' the way to Troy which, he suggests maliciously, is all that Achille really cares about. What adds to the horror is that Agamemnon is very unjustly imputing to Achille his own unworthy views.

In addition to the paths to Troy and to the altar there is a criss-cross of other paths, all playing a part in the drama: the paths leading in and out of the camp or to and from Argos. Agamemnon gives the most careful instructions to Arcas in order to make sure that he succeeds in intercepting Clytemnestre and her daughter on the way back from Argos:

> Prends cette lettre; cours au-devant de la Reine;
> Et suis sans t'arrêter *le chemin de Mycène* . . .
> . . . ne *t'écarte* point: prends un fidèle guide.
> Si ma fille une fois met le pied dans l'Aulide,
> Elle est morte.

When the plan goes awry it is reported in these words:

> La Reine, dont ma *course* a devancé les pas,
> Va remettre bientôt sa fille entre vos bras.
> Elle approche. Elle s'est quelque temps *égarée*
> Dans ces bois qui du camp semblent *cacher l'entrée.*

It is the same path which brings Ériphile, the dangerous 'outsider', to Aulis, ironically in the company of Clytemnestre and Iphigénie. Still another path brings Achille hot from his supposed triumph in Lesbos.

There are a number of other things that strike us about the images of paths. Although they divide into three closely related groups, until the last act only those belonging to the third group are actually used. The second path will be used by nearly everybody in the last act, but though the *dénouement* opens the first path it will not of course be used until the play is over. We also observe that the camp like the palaces of other plays is a 'prison', that 'access' to it, as the last quotation showed, is almost as complicated and exit impossible. Although ironically they are nearly saved by taking the 'wrong' path, the path which brings mother and daughter to the camp turns out to be another 'trap'. The daughter appears to be the 'captive' whose life is in terrible danger and in the end is only saved by the sacrifice of the other, or rather the real, 'captive'.

Finally, the paths are the direct translation into physical terms of Agamemnon's psychological vacillations. The arrivals, the abortive departures, the hesitation and confusion over the choice of the 'right' path, the pressure to take the middle path, the uncertainty about what lies at the end, the horrified recoil when the truth becomes known—all these things are the tangible and visible signs of Agamemnon's moral disarray and underline the importance of the images for the development of the drama.

5

Iphigénie is the first play since *La Thébaïde* with a definite religious motif and as the oracles exercise a determining influence on the minds of the protagonists, we must look at the concept of religion underlying the play.

We know that in the matter of religion Racine was not a free agent and that the kind of religion we find in *Iphigénie* was conditioned by his choice of fable. Greek religion is not exactly impressive at the best of times; in *Iphigénie* it is seen at its worst. Although they possess supernatural powers, the gods strike us as little more than larger-than-life human beings. They share many of the more undesirable traits of their victims such as Agamemnon's tyrannical inclinations and his trickery. We know from other sources that though they can hardly compete with biblical monarchs like Solomon, Jupiter and Venus are best remembered for exploits which are basically human and are represented as frivolous characters merrily fornicating with human beings like the performances of bank holiday crowds in the bushes of some public park.

Although the action of the play is dictated by divine decree there is nothing numinous about the gods, or at any rate not until the very last scene, and no religious devotion on the part of the characters—only irritation and fear. What the gods represent is first and foremost *authority*. They are divine: therefore they can close the path to Troy by fiddling with the weather. They are free to impose their own terms. The authority is a capricious one, reminding us in a way of Kafka's *Trial*. There is nothing comparable to Jehovah putting Abraham's faith to the test by ordering the sacrifice of Isaac or to the Christian doctrine of vicarious suffering. For no apparent reason the gods demand the sacrifice of a human being. If it is expiatory, nobody knows what wrong or what sin is being expiated; if it is to appease the gods, the grounds for their wrath are equally unknown. In short, the gods operate like an absolute but capricious monarch who fetters the freedom of his subjects, imposes taxes and threatens penalties if even his most unreasonable orders are not obeyed.

Although these criticisms apply to Greek religion in general, there is one obvious difference between the legends of Oedipus and Iphigenia. In the Oedipus legend Thebes is visited by a devastating plague. It is a punishment from the gods because one of its citizens has murdered Laïus. The plague only comes to an end when the actual culprit is identified and pays the penalty for his crime. If Agamemnon had been told to sacrifice his daughter in order to save a people from disaster, even if it were punishment for another person's crime, his conduct might have been excusable. Instead of that, the only penalty for refusing to obey the gods' command is the prevention of an unnecessary war or, given the Greek attitude, the cancellation of a sporting event. The fact that he seriously contemplates the sacrifice of his daughter in order to ensure that, instead of the peace for which most people pray, the unnecessary and unjust war will take place is a devastating comment on the wrongness of both his values and those of the gods. If the gods had disapproved of the war against Troy and put a permanent ban on it, or even if they had demanded the sacrifice of a human being as a punishment for planning such a disgraceful campaign, their action would have been understandable. They do the reverse. They deliberately encourage it. Their demand for the sacrifice of Iphigénie cannot be divorced from the reward they offer or, more appropriately, the carrot they dangle in front of the Greek aggressors: 'gloire'.[3]

We are about to see that, as used in this play, it is a decidedly hollow word which makes things worse.

6

The pronouncements of the oracles, as we know, divide the protagonists. The drama lies in the variety of the pressures which are brought to bear on Agamemnon and his reactions to them. Although every scene fits perfectly into the whole, the structure depends to a considerable degree on the principal encounters between the parties and the way in which they are balanced against one another. They begin when Agamemnon is confronted in Act I by Achille and Ulysse who are, or claim to be, the representatives of public interest; they conclude with what can only be described as the concerted attack in Act IV by the representatives of private or human interests: Iphigénie, Clytemnestre and Achille who by this time has naturally changed sides.[4]

Agamemnon and Achille get on badly from the start. It is the inevitable friction between the strong man and the weak or, to use a familiar expression, each finds the other *antipathique*. In the opening scene Agamemnon remarks of Achille:

> Mais qui peut dans sa course arrêter ce torrent?
> Achille va combattre, et triomphe en courant . . .

The distaste is obvious. We also suspect an element of fear in view of what is happening and probably of jealousy. At the same time it is an illuminating glimpse of a dynamic character expressed with Racinian conciseness. 'Torrent' had been used by Créon in the first play to describe the violence of the brothers and in the second to describe the impression

created by Alexandre on the battlefield. It is equally effective in conveying
the impression made by Achille—there will be a practical demonstration
in Act V—and is reinforced by 'courant', suggesting a man who is always
on the move, who is never still for a moment.

Achille has smashed Lesbos and is thirsting to get at the Trojans. He
learns, without knowing the reason, that Agamemnon is thinking of calling
off the expedition and protests. Agamemnon replies with a spiteful reminder that though Achille would have been a star performer the price
would have been death and burial in foreign soil. It cuts no ice. Achille
uses words which recall those used by Agamemnon himself to Arcas in
the first scene:

> Mais, puisqu'il faut enfin que j'arrive au tombeau,
> Voudrais-je, de la terre inutile fardeau,
> Trop avare d'un sang reçu d'une déesse,
> Attendre chez mon père une obscure vieillesse,
> Et toujours de la gloire évitant le sentier,
> Ne laisser aucun nom, et mourir tout entier?

There is nothing uplifting, nothing public spirited, nothing in the least
subtle about this conception of 'gloire'. It is as personal—I emphasize the
word in view of what will be said later—and as selfish as Agamemnon's.
They are, indeed, the words of a young man who must always be on the
move.

He gets no change out of Agamemnon and in spite of some respectful
references to his leadership departs in a defiant mood, leaving Ulysse to
try his hand again.

Ulysse's comment on his behaviour is worth noticing:

> Seigneur, vous entendez: quelque prix qu'il en coûte,
> Il veut *voler* à Troie et poursuivre sa *route*.

It is evident that Achille has made the same impression on Ulysse as on
Agamemnon. He, too, finds Achille *antipathique* and was snubbed by him
during the meeting. This, however, does not prevent him from using the
young man's violence as an argument against calling off the campaign, as
we see from this couplet.

In some ways Agamemnon's position as commander-in-chief resembles
that of a high official or senior executive: the weak man equally appalled
by the price of obedience and disobedience, wondering whether he can
find some way of circumventing his masters' orders without losing his
job. His initial reaction to the gods' decree was violent:

> Je condamnai les Dieux, et, sans plus rien ouïr,
> Fis voeu sur leurs autels de leur désobéir.

Many high officials have felt the same and reacted in the same way in the fastness of their offices, but they usually manage to avoid outbursts in the presence of the masters or putting their thoughts down in a memorandum.

Ulysse is also a high official. He is not so high as Agamemnon, but he has his position to consider. If Agamemnon defaults he will lose his job too. He is much given to specious argument and after all his son is not in danger, as Agamemnon points out to him. He must therefore find a way of keeping Agamemnon up to the mark in order to safeguard his own job. He has already accused him of sacrificing the State to his family or, in bureaucratic terms, the interests of the 'organization' to private interests. He returns to the charge and rings the changes with a shrewdness that fixes unerringly on Agamemnon's weaknesses. There is the moral argument:

> Songez-y. Vous devez votre fille à la Grèce . . .

Then there is the danger of a popular uprising:

> Gardez-vous de réduire un peuple furieux,
> Seigneur, à prononcer entre vous et les Dieux.

Next, the threat to Agamemnon's position from his rivals:

> Que ses rois qui pouvaient vous disputer ce rang
> Sont prêts, pour vous servir, de verser tout leur sang,
> Le seul Agamemnon, refusant la victoire,
> N'ose d'un peu de sang acheter tant de gloire?

In short, 'glory' is such a marvellous thing and Agamemnon's position as commander-in-chief so precarious, that it is surely worth a drop of blood even if the blood happens to be your own daughter's!

The badness of the argument and the falseness of the implied analogy between the blood of warriors shed on the battlefield in a worthy cause and the blood of an innocent daughter sacrificed in an ignoble cause are obvious. The contrast between the devious Ulysse and the forthright impetuous Achille, who in any case was unaware of the stake, explains the antipathy which I mentioned a few moments ago.

The debate is interrupted by the appearance of a servant with the news that Agamemnon's 'artifice' has miscarried and that mother and daughter have just arrived at the camp.

Ulysse assumes a very sympathetic tone which prepares the way for the final assault:

> Je suis père, Seigneur. Et faible comme un autre . . .
> Pleurez ce sang, pleurez; ou plutôt, sans pâlir,
> Considérez l'honneur qui doit en rejaillir.
> Voyez tout l'Hellespont blanchissant sous nos rames,
> Et la perfide Troie abandonnée aux flammes,
> Ses peuples dans vos fers, Priam à vos genoux,
> Hélène par vos mains rendue à son époux.

Voyez de vos vaisseaux les poupes couronnées
Dans cette même Aulide avec vous retournées,
Et ce triomphe heureux qui s'en va devenir
L'éternel entretien des siècles à venir.

We observe the illogical switch at 'ou plutôt, sans pâlir' to what one feels inclined to call the 'hearty' tone. For Ulysse seems to be treating the war as a sporting event. He is oblivious like all the Greeks of the cost in human lives of the divine 'carrot'. His mind is fixed on the victory of his own and the defeat of the other side. The restitution of Helen to her husband, which is the official aim of the war, is mentioned almost casually in a single line between the images of destruction—Troy in flames, its citizens in chains, their sovereign on his knees at the conqueror's feet—and the triumphant return of the Greeks to Aulis for all the world like a team of footballers with their supporters bringing back some petty trophy after a local success.

I have spoken of the hollowness of the Greek conception of 'gloire'. It is well brought out by Ulysse's last line. The destruction of Troy will simply give people something to gossip about in the centuries to come which is more or less what Achille meant when he spoke of the victorious Greeks sharing the immortality—in the circumstances a very dim immortality—of the gods.

Although it is anything but impressive, with the help of the bad news of the arrival of mother and daughter Ulysse's performance succeeds. Agamemnon cracks and surrenders:

Seigneur, de mes efforts je connais l'impuissance.
Je cède, et laisse aux Dieux opprimer l'innocence.

It's not his fault that the trick didn't come off. All he asks is Ulysse's help in keeping his formidable wife away from the altar until it is all over.

In the next two acts the friction and the confusion grow. Agamemnon feels guilty and is embarrassed when he finds himself in the presence of his daughter. His determination to keep his wife in the dark, as we know, produces clashes. There are misunderstandings between Iphigénie and Achille and a teenage tiff between Iphigénie and Ériphile. The moment that Arcas, in a state of desperation, leaks the truth about Agamemnon's activities Achille, as we should expect, wants to rush into action against him, but is persuaded by Iphigénie to let her mother and herself try to reason with the father before the fiancé enters the field.

7

The meeting between father, mother and daughter begins with a savage 'swipe' by the mother:

Venez, venez, ma fille, on n'attend plus que vous;
Venez remercier un père qui vous aime,
Et qui veut à l'autel vous conduire lui–même.

It is not until he hears these words and sees mother and daughter in tears that Agamemnon realizes that his secret is out and cries:

Ma fille, vous pleurez,
Et baissez devant moi vos yeux mal assurés.
Quel trouble! Mais tout pleure, et la fille, et la mère.
Ah! malheureux Arcas, tu m'as trahi.

It provides Iphigénie with an opening. She at once tries to comfort her father and goes on to make the first speech. Racine departs from the pattern adopted by Euripides and Rotrou who make the mother speak first. There was good reason for the change. In Rotrou both mother and daughter are openly hostile to Agamemnon. Clytemnestre is naturally a much stronger character. She therefore delivers her attack first. It is reinforced by her daughter's which though less vigorous is equally bitter. There has been some controversy about Iphigénie's plea to her father in Racine, but whatever the correct interpretation it is ostensibly affectionate and gentle and is delivered in an entirely different tone from Clytemnestre's. We shall find in comparing them that its effect on the audience and its latent effect on Agamemnon could not have been the same if she had followed instead of preceding her mother.

Charles Péguy remarked on the continual use in *Iphigénie* of the word 'cruel' and on what appeared to him to be the special cruelty of the devoted daughter's exchanges with her father in this scene.[5] Iphigénie certainly says some very wounding things, but I am not convinced that 'cruel' is the right word. It implies a deliberate intention to cause pain and I do not believe that she has any such intention. I think that it is a fair inference that Racine unconsciously injected some of his own innate cruelty into her speech and that it is the combination of her extreme gentleness and the hard sayings that makes it so damaging.

Although it is comparatively brief, it divides like many of the most important *tirades* into three carefully planned and closely linked sections. The first is a declaration of submission:

Mon père,
Cessez de vous troubler, vous n'êtes point trahi.
Quand vous commanderez, vous serez obéi.
Ma vie est votre bien. Vous voulez le reprendre:
Vos ordres sans détour pouvaient se faire entendre.
D'un oeil aussi content, d'un coeur aussi soumis
Que j'acceptais l'époux que vous m'aviez promis,
Je saurai, s'il le faut, victime obéissante,
Tendre au fer de Calchas une tête innocente,

> Et respectant le coup par vous-même ordonné,
> Vous rendre tout le sang que vous m'avez donné.

She begins in the kindest possible manner by trying to persuade her father, somewhat illogically, that he has not been betrayed by his servant when he clearly has. She addresses him as 'Mon père' instead of the 'Seigneur' she had used in earlier scenes. Line 3 is an unqualified promise of obedience. 'Commanderez' is matched by 'serez obéi', 'ordres' by 'soumis'. Submissiveness is pushed to extremes in the theory that as Agamemnon gave his daughter life he has an absolute right to take it away again and in the statement that she will 'if necessary'—the qualification is important in view of what is to come—go to the altar to be sacrificed with the same readiness that she would have gone there to marry the man whom her father has promised her as a husband. This is already sufficient to place the father in an uncomfortable position. Péguy may complain that every word Iphigénie utters 'puts the adversary (the father) in the wrong', but we all know that he has in fact been in the wrong from the start.

The qualifications are introduced in the last four lines and undermine nearly everything she has said. Her 'Je saurai, s'il faut', naturally makes any reasonable hearer ask himself whether the killing of a daughter could possibly be 'necessary'. Worse still, 'obéi' becomes '*victime* obéissante' and is reinforced by 'tête *innocente*'—both simple statements of fact which bring out the inherent wrongness of Agamemnon's proposal. The hardest thrust comes in the two closing lines. She will offer her 'head' to Calchas, but only because the 'blow' has been 'ordered' by her father which stamps him as the real killer. Calchas was intending to stab her. The reference to 'head' transforms what was supposed to be a religious rite into execution. At the same time it reduces the human victim to an animal which is to be slaughtered by having its head chopped off.

The process is continued in the second section by a succession of 'if-s' which add to the hearer's doubts and revulsion:

> *Si* pourtant ce respect, *si* cette obéissance
> Paraît digne à vos yeux d'une autre récompense,
> *Si* d'une mère en pleurs vous plaignez les ennuis . . .

The implication of course is that he is bound to see that her 'respect', her 'obedience', her 'innocence' deserve a very different reward—deserve, indeed, 'reward' instead of punishment. There follows the timid and moving suggestion that it would be pleasanter if, in spite of her father's 'rights', her life were not being 'snatched away' so near its beginning:

> J'ose vous dire ici qu'en l'état où je suis
> Peut-être assez d'honneurs environnaient ma vie
> Pour ne pas souhaiter qu'elle me fût ravie,
> Ni qu'en me l'arrachant un sévère destin
> Si près de ma naissance en eût marqué la fin.

> Fille d'Agamemnon, c'est moi qui la première,
> Seigneur, vous appelai de ce doux nom de père;
> C'est moi qui si longtemps le plaisir de vos yeux,
> Vous ai fait de ce nom remercier les Dieux ...

The endearments, 'doux nom de père' and 'plaisir de vos yeux', which are contrasted with the harsh 'ravie' and 'arrachant', add to the painfulness.[6] But something worse is to come:

> Hélas! avec plaisir je me faisais conter
> Tous les noms des pays que vous allez dompter;
> Et déjà d'Ilion présageant la conquête,
> D'un triomphe si beau je préparais la fête.
> Je ne m'attendais pas que pour le commencer,
> Mon sang fût le premier que vous dussiez verser.

The respectful tributes to the beloved father—the idea that the great man would soon be celebrating 'instant' victory—lead to the final sally: the couplet which places the commander-in-chief's daughter among the 'enemies', making her the first casualty of the coming war.

We have seen the reference to her mother in the second section. In the third she takes it up, directing attention away from the victim to the unhappy mother and fiancé. It is a very effective way of completing her case and adds greatly to its force. Before doing so she sums up what she has said about 'respect' and 'obedience' with the words,

> Mon coeur, de votre honneur jaloux,
> Ne fera point rougir un père tel que vous ...

The fact that she will continue to the last to support her father seems to demonstrate the genuineness of this statement and confirms my view that there is no deliberate cruelty on Iphigénie's part.

Altogether it is a brilliant piece of dialectic and much more an appeal to her father's humanity than an attack on him. This does not alter the fact that it is filled with observations of the kind that get right under any normal person's skin. It is a sign of Agamemnon's weakness and corruption that its immediate effect on him is minimal. He can stand up to gentle speeches: it is the tough ones that rouse him. His reply is exactly what we should expect of a weak man. It is really the stiff-upper-lip speech of father to child:

> Ma fille, il est trop vrai. J'ignore pour quel crime
> La colère des Dieux demande une victime;
> Mais ils vous ont nommée.

He goes on to give an account of his attempts to save her, then invites her resignation:

> Ma fille, il faut céder. Votre heure est arrivée.
> Songez bien dans quel rang vous êtes élevée ...
> Montrez, en expirant, de qui vous êtes née:
> Faites rougir ces Dieux qui vous ont condamnée.
> Allez: et que les Grecs, qui vont vous immoler,
> Reconnaissent mon sang en le voyant couler.

The ending is a shocking piece of vainglory, but the speech as a whole is an excellent illustration of the insincerity that I have already mentioned. At bottom, Agamemnon is immensely relieved to find that she is 'going quietly', that his own job is safe.

At this point Clytemnestre enters the list. Her speech is as different as it could well be from her daughter's and demonstrates the importance of the variety of the assaults. She has no interest in sparing her husband's 'blushes' or appealing to his better nature; she delivers a frontal attack in which like Ulysse before her, she fixes unerringly on each of his weaknesses. But though her speech is a 'tirade' in the literal sense it is also a careful piece of logic. She begins with a sombre denunciation:

> Vous ne démentez point une race funeste.
> Oui, vous êtes le sang d'Atrée et de Thyeste.
> Bourreau de votre fille, il ne vous reste enfin
> Que d'en faire à sa mère un horrible festin.
> Barbare! C'est donc là cet heureux sacrifice
> Que vos soins préparaient avec tant d'artifice.

Her words are at once a refutation of Agamemnon's boastful reference to his 'blood' at the end of his reply to his daughter and an ironic echo of Arcas's 'fils du puissant Atrée' in the first scene of the play.

The denunciation continues for another ten lines, then logic enters. She throws doubts, which prove well-founded, on the reliability of the oracles:

> Un oracle dit-il tout ce qu'il semble dire?

Why should *her* daughter be made to pay for Helen's crime?

> Faites chercher à Sparte Hermione sa fille.
> Laissez à Ménélas racheter d'un tel prix
> Sa coupable moitié, dont il est trop épris.

She turns her attention to Helen:

> Cet objet de tant de jalousie,
> Cette Hélène, qui trouble et l'Europe et l'Asie,
> Vous semble-t-elle un prix digne de vos exploits?
> Combien nos fronts pour elle ont-ils rougi de fois!

Then she goes to the heart of the matter:

> Mais non, l'amour d'un frère et son honneur blessé
> Sont les moindres des soins dont vous êtes pressé.

Cette soif de régner, que rien ne peut éteindre,
L'orgueil de voir vingt rois vous servir et vous craindre,
Tous les droits de l'empire en vos mains confiés,
Cruel, c'est à ces Dieux que vous sacrifiez;
Et loin de repousser le coup qu'on vous prépare,
Vous voulez vous en faire un mérite barbare.
Trop jaloux d'un pouvoir qu'on peut vous envier,
De votre propre sang vous courez le payer,
Et vous voulez par ce prix épouvanter l'audace
De quiconque vous peut disputer votre place.

I may be prejudiced, I may share the male dislike of strong women, but I do not find Clytemnestre a sympathetic figure any more than Agrippine or Athalie. This should not prevent anyone from appreciating the cardinal importance of her role. She is in many respects the perfect foil for the weak Agamemnon. Her speech is truly crushing. She possesses Hermione's command of the fishwife's language, but it is combined with a relentless logic and unlike Hermione's her values are right from the start. The result is that every shot goes home with devastating effect. Helen is seen for what she is: a tiresome little 'pick-up', or perhaps a 'push-over', whose sexual adventures have been a constant embarrassment to the family. The idea that Agamemnon's aim is to restore an erring wife to a beloved brother is dismissed as an absurdity.

I compared Agamemnon earlier to an administrator or a bureaucrat. The truth is that a commander-in-chief is sometimes more of an administrator than a warrior. He shares their particular vices. What Clytemnestre is denouncing is in fact *corruption*; the sort of corruption that, as many of us know to our cost, is the occupational disease of the bureaucrat. In the last analysis, there is no difference between weakness and corruption: the corruption of the man who finds himself in a post for which he does not possess either the moral or the intellectual qualities and which offers him a far greater reward than he is worth. Of course Agamemnon doesn't care about Helen or Menelaus or his oath. The root of the trouble is his fear of losing his job, being made 'redundant', being replaced by one of the twenty kings who are all on the watch for the slightest sign of failure so that they can grab the commander-in-chief's post. Whether or not Agamemnon realizes it to the full, the loss of his daughter, of whom he is fond in his way, does not really count compared with the loss of his job. He is ready to sacrifice her not to the gods or to the supposed good of the State, but to his own private gods, to his obsession with position and power.

Clytemnestre dwells with horror on the spectacle:

Un prêtre, environné d'une foule cruelle,
Portera sur ma fille une main criminelle?
Déchirera son sein? Et d'un oeil curieux
Dans son coeur palpitant consultera les Dieux?

The religious cult, too, is reduced to a hideous absurdity: the priest surrounded by a goggling crowd anxious for sensation, laying a 'criminal hand' on Clytemnestre's daughter, then peering, with an 'oeil curieux', at the throbbing heart of the murdered girl, 'consulting the gods', trying to find an answer to the problem before them.

She has finished with denunciation and ends astutely with an emotional appeal:

> Et moi, qui l'amenai triomphante, adorée,
> Je m'en retournerai seule et désespérée?
> Je verrai les *chemins* encor tout parfumés
> Des fleurs dont sous ses pas on les avait semés?

It is an imaginary picture of what would have happened if she had been taken in by her husband's 'artifice'. She sees herself as the shattered mother who had escorted her daughter along the flower-strewn 'path' only to discover at the end of it that instead of leading her to an altar with a priest waiting to bless a marriage, she had led her to a scaffold with an executioner waiting to put her to death. The horror of the return journey is underlined by the knowledge that the flowers which she had taken for wedding bouquets were really funeral wreaths.

Mother and daughter depart leaving Agamemnon reeling under their combined blows:

> A de moindres fureurs je n'ai pas dû m'attendre.
> Voilà, voilà les cris que je craignais d'entendre.

In a matter of seconds Achille arrives on the scene. I do not share the views of those writers who have compared him to Xipharès. He is completely without Xipharès's particular kind of chivalry. He is as tough as they are made.[7] He finds the evasiveness of the old warriors and their attempts to delay his marriage 'because there's a war on' incomprehensible and also exasperating. When Ulysse calls his patriotism in question in Act I, he is roundly snubbed:

> Dans les champs phrygiens les effets feront foi
> Qui la chérit le plus, ou d'Ulysse ou de moi.

'Just wait and see who's going to be the star performer for the fatherland—you or I!'

When he meets Agamemnon in Act IV he feigns ignorance of the plot to kill his bride and begins disarmingly with the words:

> Un bruit assez étrange est venu jusqu'à moi,
> Seigneur; je l'ai jugé trop peu digne de foi.
> On dit, et sans horreur je ne puis le redire,
> Qu'aujourd'hui par votre ordre Iphigénie expire . . .

We saw in Act I that Achille is the sort of man who arouses the aggressiveness—an aggressiveness born of fear—which is part of the make-up of a weak individual like Agamemnon. His encounter with Agamemnon in Act IV is very different from that of mother and daughter. In spite of the unusual restraint that he displays when he puts the question to which he knows the answer, he is soon engaged in a frontal attack: a verbal duel in which Agamemnon is constantly in retreat, but which is always threatening to turn into a different kind of duel. Agamemnon admits the truth of the report but declares, haughtily, that it is none of Achille's business. 'What!' cries the furious Achille, 'None of my business that you are going to kill the daughter whom you promised to give me as my wife?' Every reply by Agamemnon produces an even more smashing blow from Achille. Now there is one marked difference between Achille's tirade and Clytemnestre's. She speaks with great heat but, as we saw, everything she says is governed by logic. No one could reasonably refute her arguments. Achille makes his points in a much more personal way. Indeed, egocentric would hardly be an inaccurate description of what he says. It is always what 'I' think, what 'I' want. When Agamemnon taunts him with not caring about anything except the invasion of Troy, the answer is:

> Votre fille *me* plut, *je* prétendis lui plaire;
> Elle est de *mes* serments seule dépositaire . . .
> *Je* ne connais Priam, Hélène, ni Paris;
> *Je* voulais votre fille, et ne pars qu'à ce prix.

He cares as little about the causes of war as he does about the prophecy of his own death: his primary aim is not to restore the wayward Aunt Helen to Uncle Menelaus's bed, but to get himself into Iphigénie's bed. We note the crude 'Je *voulais* votre fille'.

Agamemnon loses his temper completely and tells him to 'get out'. This provokes the most smashing blow of all:

> Rendez grâce au seul noeud qui retient ma colère.
> D'Iphigénie encor je respecte le père.
> Peut-être, sans ce nom, le chef de tant de rois
> M'aurait osé braver pour la dernière fois.

The different techniques used by the trio produce different reactions. The brief monologue which follows Achille's departure reveals an even deeper degree of corruption in Agamemnon than Clytemnestre's onslaught:

> Et voilà ce qui rend sa perte inévitable.

For a moment Agamemnon actually means to proceed with the sacrifice to pay Achille out. Then he changes his mind. He will save his daughter, but will take good care to see that she does not marry Achille.

This completes the picture of the weak man. We have seen that compared with his position the life of his daughter hardly counts. Why then
does he suddenly decide to save her? The answer is that the weak man is
always at the mercy of pressure groups, that if the pressure is strong
enough he will even abandon his own interests. Agamemnon throws in
his hand, for that is what it amounts to, simply because the combination of
wife, daughter and son-in-law is more powerful and more frightening than
Ulysse.

8

Tension has been rising steadily. In the last act, as we should expect, it
explodes in massive violent action. The explosion is caused by the impact
of the two 'outsiders' on an ingrowing community. The reason is that from
the first they are bent on action and determined to put an end to the impasse, to the feverish pointless activity of the insiders who have simply
been going round in circles and 'consuming' themselves in the process.

The 'outsiders' present an interesting contrast. Achille is the extrovert,
Ériphile the introvert. Achille makes ten appearances in all. He is never
alone or even alone with a confidant. He nearly always appears in scenes
with a member or members of Agamemnon's or Clytemnestre's parties.
There are only two meetings with the opposition: the clash with Agamemnon and Ulysse in Act II and with Agamemnon in Act IV. With the
exception of Act II, Sc. 7, when Achille is alone with Ériphile and her
confidant because Iphigénie has misunderstood his intentions and left in a
huff, his meetings are with mother and daughter or with Iphigénie. We
should observe that Ériphile and her confidant are present at two of
Achille's meetings with mother and daughter and one of his meetings with
Iphigénie. Ériphile's presence at these meetings as well as at others when
Achille is not there is important because this is the way in which she discovers their 'secrets' and fashions her plot accordingly.

Altogether Ériphile is present during thirteen scenes. In four of them
she is alone with her confidant; in the remaining nine she is with other
characters, but she does not always speak. Except for the teen-age clash in
Act II, Sc. 5, when Iphigénie accuses her of trying to steal her fiancé, her
relations with members of both parties appear to be friendly though in
reality she is the enemy of everybody. Her first appearance in Act II, Sc. 1,
is both introduction and exposition. She has never known her real parents.
Her childhood was unhappy—she describes herself very neatly two scenes
later as 'étrangère partout'—but in spite of her horror at the destruction
of Lesbos she has fallen in love with Achille and is bitterly jealous of
Iphigénie. The fact that she makes her first appearance one scene earlier

than Iphigénie is another example of the care with which Racine linked his scenes. It means that we do not see the prospective victim until we have been fully informed of all the dangers that threaten her.

The scene in which she first appears runs to 135 lines and enables us to have a good look at her. Her account of the *coup de foudre* caused by the meeting with Achille stamps her as a much more Racinian character than Iphigénie:

> J'entrai dans son vaisseau, détestant sa fureur,
> Et toujours détournant ma vue avec horreur.
> Je le vis: son aspect n'avait rien de farouche;
> Je sentis le reproche expirer dans ma bouche.
> Je sentis contre moi mon coeur se déclarer;
> J'oubliai ma colère, et ne sus que pleurer.

She goes on:

> Je me laissai conduire à cet amiable guide.
> Je l'aimais à Lesbos, et je l'aime en Aulide.
> Iphigénie en vain s'offre à me protéger,
> Et me tend une main prompte à me soulager:
> Triste effet des fureurs dont je suis tourmentée!
> Je n'accepte la main qu'elle m'a présentée
> Que pour m'armer contre elle, et sans me découvrir,
> Traverser son bonheur que je ne puis souffrir.

It is a brilliantly perceptive picture of a young woman being carried away, falling in love in spite of herself with a man whom she has good reason to detest and becoming violently jealous of the kindest of 'rivals'. The way in which the erotic instinct obliterates all other considerations is brought out in a single line:

> Je sentis contre moi mon coeur se déclarer ...

In view of what I said about the prospective 'victim' and the dangers that threaten her, we should also notice the ruthlessness with which Ériphile speaks of her jealousy:

> Je n'accepte la main qu'elle m'a présentée
> Que pour m'armer contre elle ...

The passages are important for another reason. Whatever their standing, all the characters in a tragedy by Racine except the confidants play an essential part in the drama. Ériphile is the only character in *Iphigénie* who uses the Racinian language of passion—her words actually look forward to the *aveux* in *Phèdre*—but she remains one of the lesser figures. This reveals a modification in the usual pattern. The principal interest of the play is of course the weakness and the vacillations of Agamemnon. Although it helps to bring about the *dénouement*, passion clearly plays a subordinate role.

Ériphile makes her last appearance in Act IV, Sc. 11. She is alone with Doris. She has all the information she needs. Doris starts to follow the protagonists. Her mistress calls her back:

> Suis-moi. Ce n'est pas là, Doris, notre *chemin*.

The confidant was, significantly, about to take the 'wrong' path. Ériphile is going to see Calchas, but not to consult him about the oracles, as she said earlier:

> A Calchas, je vais tout découvrir.

9

By the middle of the last act four of the characters have taken the centre path and are converging on the altar: Iphigénie to offer herself as a sacrifice and save her father's reputation in spite of the opposition of mother and fiancé; Achille to demolish what he regards the enemy; Ériphile to wreck everybody's chance of happiness; Agamemnon vacillating as usual and not knowing what will happen.

Racine, as we have seen, was something of a specialist in what may be described as the invisible character who is sometimes an individual like Hector or Amurat and sometimes 'the people'. We find both in *Iphigénie*: Calchas and the soldiery. Calchas's name is on everybody's lips and is mentioned 40 times in the play. He is high priest, the mouthpiece of the gods, the man who interprets the oracles, the man standing knife in hand ready to kill the charming Iphigénie, the man who arouses fear in most of the characters and a violent antipathy in some of them:

> Plus de pitié. Calchas seul règne, seul commande . . .

The moment Ériphile betrays the plan to remove Clytemnestre and Iphigénie from the camp, the soldiery are alerted and set to work to prevent their escape. We naturally do not see the violent action any more than in other plays. Events move with the same speed which adds to the excitement. A series of messengers arrive in rapid succession to tell Clytemnestre what is happening. First we hear that Achille is battling with the Greek troops, that the odds are so great that he has no chance of success. Then better news comes through:

> N'en doutez point, Madame, un Dieu combat pour vous.
> Achille en ce moment exauce vos prières;
> Il a brisé des Grecs les trop faibles barrières.
> Achille est à l'autel. Calchas est éperdu.
> Le fatal sacrifice est encor suspendu.
> On se menace, on court, l'air gémit, le fer brille.

The tables have been well and truly turned. Achille the hero faces Calchas, who has become the villain of the piece, at the altar. A few moments ago Calchas dominated everybody:

> Calchas seul règne, seul commande . . .

Now he shows signs of cracking and a peculiarly Racinian word is used to describe his state:

> Calchas est *éperdu*.

Nor should we miss the superb last line:

> On se menace, on court, l'air gémit, le fer brille.

In ten words Racine provides an extraordinary evocation of the fury and confusion of the battle.

The passage goes on:

> Achille fait ranger autour de votre fille
> Tous ses amis, pour lui prêts à se dévouer.
> Le triste Agamemnon, qui n'ose l'avouer,
> Pour détourner ses yeux des meurtres qu'il présage,
> Ou pour cacher ses pleurs, s'est voilé le visage.

There is a second confrontation. Achille's friends form a bodyguard round Iphigénie. The cowardly Agamemnon stands there with his face covered, a neutral figure trying to avoid seeing not so much the expected sacrifice, but what looks like the collapse of his position—a matching figure this time with the distraught Calchas.

A moment later there is even better news. Ulysse arrives to announce what seems to most of them a happy ending. Calchas has just had a fresh inspiration from the gods. The real victim has been identified as Ériphile. The unfortunate waif has not waited to be sacrificed: she has scrambled on to the altar, grabbed Calchas's knife and stabbed herself to death. Then the miracle happens. There is a roll of thunder; the winds rise; the sails fill. Everything is ready for the Greeks to set out on their unlovely expedition against Troy, knowing that success is guaranteed, but not knowing that the gods will make them wait ten years for the 'carrot':

> Les vents agitent l'air d'heureux frémissements,
> Et la mer leur répond par ses mugissements.
> La rive au loin gémit, blanchissante d'écume.
> La flamme du bûcher d'elle-même s'allume.
> Le ciel brille d'éclairs, s'entr'ouvre, et parmi nous
> Jette une sainte horreur qui nous rassure tous.

It is the most brilliant piece of virtuosity in the play. Nature comes to life again. In the 'frémissements', 'mugissements' and 'gémit' we hear three different sounds: the rising of the winds, the swirl of the sea and the waves breaking on a distant beach. The change comes when the nasals merge into the soft 'écume/allume'. It marks the advent of the supernatural. The scene is suddenly bathed in a benign light which fills the people with a sense of religious 'awe' and at the same time reassures them.

It is the sign, too, that Agamemnon though no doubt much the worse for wear has emerged from the 'darkness' of the first scene and found his way back to the 'light'.

The close of the play may look at first like something of an anti-climax. Instead of the logical unfolding of the plot, a genuine *dénouement*, it seems as though the knot has been cut in order to create an artificially happy ending. The gods have been playing a cat-and-mouse game with humanity. All the anguish, the bitter exchanges, the vacillations and intrigues are the result of the misunderstanding of a deliberately ambiguous oracle which is put right by a fresh utterance that brings the game to an end.

This is neither a fair nor a correct interpretation and in any case would apply to Euripides as much as to Racine. In spite of its label, *Iphigénie* is not a tragedy in the strict sense. A tragedy is a play which normally ends with the death of the hero, meaning the character who engages the sympathies of the audience to the full. *Iphigénie* is really the kind of play which in the seventeenth century was often called tragi-comedy. For linguistic reasons the term is not always properly understood in this country. It does not mean a play which is a mixture of tragedy and comedy: it means a serious play in which an important character other than the hero loses his life, which is precisely what happens in *Iphigénie*.[8]

The ending of *Iphigénie* is not merely right; it illustrates the perfection of the play's construction. An unusual calm places a tiny group of people under an immense strain and becomes the instrument for a far-reaching examination of their reactions to an apparently insoluble problem: the familiar Racinian problem of making or failing to make the right choice among desperate alternatives. We have seen that their anguish is reflected in their perpetual comings and goings, not knowing which path to take or what lies at the end of it. In the last act we find that four people with different intentions have chosen the same path. The result is the reverse of what one might have expected. It resolves all the problems, or rather the immediate problems. Once the unfortunate 'outsider' has been eliminated, the antagonisms vanish; the survivors are reunited. The unnatural calm is broken and the natural order is restored. Agamemnon's description of the calm in Act I is matched by Ulysse's announcement in Act V that the winds have risen and the waves are breaking. The choice of the path to the altar by what must be regarded as the 'right' person has opened the path that they believe to be the most important of all.

NOTES

[1] This does not affect the comparison I made between *Iphigénie* and *Mithridate* in the last chapter.

[2] Compare:

> J'en rends grâces au ciel, qui m'arrêtant sans cesse
> Semblait m'avoir *fermé le chemin de la Grèce.*
>
> (*Andromaque*, I, 1.)

[3] The position is unaltered by the fact that the victim turns out to be a different Iphigénie. The gods have demanded an innocent victim and get one.

[4] It bears a marked resemblance to the method used in Act IV of *Britannicus* except that Néron's advisers are pushing him in different directions.

[5] *Victor-Marie, Comte Hugo*, 1934, pp. 156–61.

[6] 'Ce doux nom de père' is a direct borrowing from Rotrou's *Iphigénie en Aulide*, but Rotrou's Iphigénie uses the words with a very different accent from Racine's. They come in a speech which opens with these lines:

> Grand prince, car d'oser vous appeler mon père,
> A votre intention ce titre est bien contraire,
> Et vous avez pour moi trop d'inhumanité
> Pour ne pas renoncer à cette qualité . . .

Although she consents to the sacrifice, it is clear that Péguy's strictures are much more applicable to Rotrou's Iphigénie than to Racine's.

[7] Ériphile and her confidant describe him between them as 'vainqueur homicide', 'l'impitoyable Achille' and 'ce destructeur fatal'.

[8] These observations also apply to *Mithridate*. Although Mithridate is the main protagonist and gives his name to the play, he is not the hero because the audience's sympathies are reserved for Xipharès and Monime.

'PHÈDRE'

1677

Pour moi, il suffit que je pense à n'importe quelle tragédie grecque ... pour que *Phèdre* m'apparaisse comme une pièce moderne, le drame de la sexualité.

ANDRÉ MALRAUX

Quand il décrit l'amour, cela ne va pas loin ... Le Désir, voilà son Royaume, Phèdre n'aime pas plus Hippolyte que Roxane Bajazet ou qu'Hermione Phyrrhus: c'est l'exigence d'une faim qui tend à l'assouvissement et qui cherche l'issue par le crime.

FRANÇOIS MAURIAC

CHAPTER 9

'PHÈDRE'

1677

I

Phèdre is the summit of Racine's achievement and one of the summits of European drama. This much is common ground among many of his admirers. It has proved less easy to define its unique quality. 'There is an element of terror in *Phèdre*,' said Mauriac.[1] 'No figure in world drama', added Pierre Brisson, 'gives away such dangerous secrets as Phèdre and none comes so close to the abyss.'[2] *Phèdre* is not simply greater, more 'profound' or more 'poetical' than the other masterpieces. We are aware in it of a new dimension: a sense of metaphysical gulfs opening to reveal strange depths which are not to be found in the rest of the tragedies either of Racine or his contemporaries and predecessors.

The new dimension is provided in part by religion. It accounts for the element of 'terror', the sense of the 'abyss' and the moral ethos which makes *Phèdre* unique among the secular tragedies. It is a reasonable assumption that these factors are a reflection of the crisis which the dramatist is believed to have experienced at the time of composition and which appears to have given him fresh insights that were not confined to human nature.

Although it permeates the entire play, we must distinguish between religion in the sense in which I have just used the term and the role of the gods. The world of *Phèdre* is dominated by the twin figures of Neptune and Venus. The classical divinities, as we know, were frequently projections and personifications of basic human impulses, which means that in *Phèdre* they belong to the realm of psychology rather than theology. Neptune stands for virility, manliness, martial virtues. Venus is a much more complex figure. It is hardly an accident that she gave her name to a disreputable disease. Goddess of love was a courtesy title. She was the goddess not of love, but of sexuality. She is clearly identifiable with the Freudian *libido* and all that it implies.

'Without knowing it,' said Charles Mauron, 'the most lucid of our writers modelled his work on an unconscious. He acquired an intuitive knowledge of it in the process of creation, but the knowledge itself remained unconscious.'[3] Although this may be true of all Racine's plays, as Mauron was convinced that it was, we are much more aware in *Phèdre* than in any of the other plays of the workings of the unconscious with its complexes, repressions and sense of guilt. We see it in the image of the Labyrinth and a collection of supporting images suggesting a combination of depth and darkness: 'fond des forêts', 'fond des flots', 'lieux profonds', 'profonde demeure', 'cavernes sombres', 'rivages sombres', 'empire des ombres'. The Labyrinth with its tortuous paths and its 'monster' is the unconscious with its devious ways and the 'monstrous' impulses which originate and are concealed in it.

The unconscious determines the conduct in varying degrees of all the characters. They either recognize from the outset like Phèdre, or become painfully aware like Hippolyte, that they are defenceless against Venus. They discover too late that they are in the grip of an irresistible urge which erupts in the depths of their being and forces its way into the open in spite of all attempts at repression.

The divinities not only dominate the world of *Phèdre*; they divide the characters into two groups which might be labelled 'Followers of Neptune' and 'Victims of Venus'. The play looks at first like the familiar contrasts between the different kinds of attachment: the untroubled, extrovert womanizing of Thésée; the 'passion' of Phèdre; the 'love' of Hippolyte and Aricie. The reality is rather different. The distinction I drew in my opening chapter between the 'passion' of the protagonists and the 'love' of the *jeunes premiers* cannot be applied without qualification to *Phèdre*. It is one of the signs of the new complexity that there are resemblances between them as well as differences. The erotic instinct is of course present in varying degrees in all intimate relations between the sexes. Although they sometimes give the impression of being chaste to the point of sexlessness, it is as true of the *jeunes premiers* of earlier plays as of the protagonists. In *Phèdre* Racine probes more deeply into human nature than in any of the previous plays. Whatever his intentions, he concentrates on a single impulse which is common to all the characters and is at the root of the attitude of three of them. That is why we are at least as conscious of their resemblances as their differences. The differences are the result of their reactions to the sexual impulse; their resistance to an impulse which is felt to be inherently dangerous.[4] The resemblances are more marked in Phèdre and Hippolyte who have been described as 'doubles'.[5] In spite of different circumstances they both suffer from the same guilty feeling about what is plainly sexual appetite which they stigmatize in turn as 'un fol amour'. Phèdre is trying to recover, Hippolyte to preserve, a state of 'innocence'. The position is evident from the fact that they speak the same language. It can be seen in Phèdre's

> Il n'est plus temps. Il sait mes ardeurs insensées.
> De l'austère pudeur les bornes sont passées,

and Hippolyte's

Je me suis engagé trop avant.
Je vois que la raison cède à la violence.

The similarities are not restricted to Phèdre and Hippolyte. Nearly all the characters speak a language which is a blend of the erotic, lightly concealed by the *bienséances*, and the moral with its insistence on innocence, purity and modesty.

Leo Spitzer called Thésée 'the most important character' in the play.[6] This is plainly an exaggeration, but it draws attention to the significance of a role which is a novelty in Racine and which does not always receive its due, particularly from people who claim that Phèdre is 'the only character' in the play. Thésée is the follower of Neptune who has spent his life in the destruction of 'monsters' and 'brigands' and the seduction of women. Whatever his shortcomings, and they are many, it is obvious that the opposing impulses are reconciled and achieve a balance in him. He is proud of his martial feats; he is totally devoid of any feeling of guilt over the women he has seduced and abandoned. We might conclude that he has exercised the arts of Neptune and the wiles of Venus without becoming one of her victims. We know, however, that the price he has to pay is a heavy one. In the end he will be let down by Neptune and involved in the ravages caused by the intrusion of Venus.

The other characters are united in condemning what they describe as the 'faiblesses' of Thésée, meaning his particular form of sexual urge which is largely sex without love. The opposition is strongest in his son. It is impossible to decide whether Thésée's amorous adventures are the cause of Hippolyte's revulsion against the sexual instinct or whether an ingrained puritanism combined with a special form of pride provokes his disapproval of his father's womanizing. Two things, however, are certain. Hippolyte's admiration for the warrior is unbounded; he is profoundly shocked by the behaviour of the amorist. The reconciliation between the two impulses achieved by Thésée is beyond his power with the result that he will become in spite of himself what might almost be described as a 'convert' to Venus.

It is right at this stage to take a closer look at the central image which I mentioned when discussing the unconscious. It is richer, more complex, more pervasive than the central image in any other play except *Athalie* and throws a revealing light on the impulses at work. It is used by nearly all the characters including the confidants, but most frequently by Phèdre and Hippolyte. It is the dual image of day and night, light and darkness, sunlight and shadow, standing for innocence and guilt, truth and error, life and death. When Phèdre says to Hippolyte,

Dans le fond de mon coeur vous ne pouviez pas lire,

she is naturally referring to the guilty impulse concealed in the 'darkness' of her heart. There is a striking contrast between this line and Hippolyte's splendid

> Le jour n'est pas plus pur que le fond de mon coeur.

'Jour' is not merely a symbol of innocence; it is equated with 'fond' which for once loses its 'darkness', becomes something that can be exposed to all the world, which is precisely the opposite of what Phèdre said about the 'depths' of her heart.

It is the attempts of Phèdre to recover and Hippolyte to preserve a state of innocence that give the image its dramatic power. It shows that the characters are caught between conflicting feelings and have reached a point where they do not know which way to turn. There are times when they shun darkness because it stands for guilt and seek light because it represents innocence. At other times they do the reverse: they are drawn towards darkness because it hides their guilt, or what they regard as their guilt, and shun the light because it exposes it to the world and themselves. The dilemma is evident in Phèdre's

> Je me cachais au jour, je fuyais la lumière.

It is expressed perfectly in a superb couplet from Hippolyte's declaration to Aricie:

> La lumière du jour, les ombres de la nuit,
> Tout retrace à mes yeux les charmes que j'évite.

Hippolyte is literally at a parting of the ways; neither 'light' nor 'darkness' can help him; the charms of Aricie are inescapable.

Two lines earlier Hippolyte said: 'Présente, je vous fuis'. We saw that Phèdre used the words, 'je fuyais la lumière'. When discussing the palaces as 'prisons', I commented on the prevalence of the verb 'fuir' and its variants. It is of special importance in *Phèdre*. It is used 38 times which is almost a quarter of the total for the tragedies. In the opening scene of the play we shall find that Hippolyte eventually admits that his real reason for leaving Trézène is 'flight' from Aricie. In the last act they plan a joint 'flight' from Trézène which has ceased to be 'aimable' and become horrifying. Ironically their flight is prompted by Hippolyte's angry father who in pronouncing the sentence of banishment uses 'fuir' in the sense of 'Get out!'

Finally, there is the line of Phèdre's which associates 'darkness' with punishment and death:

> Fuyons dans la nuit infernale.

Although Phèdre suffers from a strong feeling of guilt in other versions of the legend, the intensity of her feeling in Racine's tragedy remains

something of a mystery because she hasn't actually *done* anything wrong.
A possible clue is provided by the lines

> Grâces au ciel, mes *mains* ne sont point criminelles.
> Plût aux Dieux que mon *coeur* fût innocent comme elles!

This seems to me to be linked with Christ's words about the woman
taken in adultery in Matthew v, 27–28:

You have heard that it was said, Thou shalt not commit adultery. But I tell you that
he who casts his eye on a woman so as to lust after her has already committed adultery
with her in his heart.

Phèdre certainly 'lusts after' Hippolyte and though she hasn't actually
done anything, she has undoubtedly 'committed adultery with him in her
heart'. Nor of course should we overlook the possibility that Racine may
have projected a personal sense of guilt into Phèdre. It is, however, the
result that counts. Phèdre suffers from a phenomenal sexual craving—a
craving which is at least as violent as Roxane's. It is met by an immensely
powerful but completely ineffectual *moral* resistance which is something
that is not found in Roxane. It is precisely the strength of the two impulses, particularly the moral impulse, which gives Phèdre a greater
depth and a greater hold over us than any other single character of
Racine's.[7]

2

Although somebody has made the strange suggestion that *Phèdre* really
comes to an end with Act IV, it seems to me on the contrary to be the most
brilliantly constructed of all the tragedies. It is a series of *aveux* or confessions: lover to confidant; lover to beloved; son to father; wife to husband. They are not simply highlights of the play; they are the pillars
round which it is built.

Hippolyte's confession to Théramène in the opening scene is matched
by Phèdre's to Oenone in the third scene, and by Aricie's to Ismène in
Act II, Sc. 1, which is the sixth scene of the play. There is a marked rise
in temperature in the passage from Hippolyte's confession to Phèdre's and
a lowering of the temperature in Aricie's.

The false report of Thésée's death in Act I, Sc. 4 like the false report of
Mithridate's releases the characters' inhibitions and they go on to make
their confessions to the beloved. Hippolyte's confession to Aricie is
followed by Phèdre's to him. In both cases we find that the confessions are
forced out of them, that they cannot contain themselves.

The news of Thésée's safe return in Act III, Sc. 3 leads to a reversal of
the process, a move from confession to silence. Phèdre tells Thésée that

there has been trouble while he was away, but refuses out of fear to say what has happened; in other words, refuses to confess. Hippolyte does the same in the next scene, but he does so because he is unwilling to give Phèdre away. Oenone then tricks Phèdre into allowing her to accuse Hippolyte to his father of trying to seduce her. There is another reversal. Hippolyte is too chivalrous to accuse Phèdre. He simply denies the accusation and confesses his love for Aricie. Phèdre is about to correct Oenone's calumny, but she learns of Hippolyte's confession of his love for Aricie and in spite of the wrongness of her own love out of jealousy does nothing. This is naturally decisive.

We can see how carefully the scenes are linked, how confessions and silences balance one another. The process does not end there. It is extended not merely to the content of individual scenes, but to the pattern of the main *tirades*. Georges Le Bidois pointed out many years ago that all important scenes in Racine are complete in themselves, that each of them is a miniature drama with a beginning, a middle and an end.[8] This means that their effect is twofold. They offer an experience which is complete in itself and at the same time prepares the way for the next experience, which is also the next stage in the overall experience of the drama, so that together the scenes form part of a chain.

We have already seen in discussing the earlier plays that the principal *tirades* are usually the enactment or re-enactment of a decisive event in the life of one or other of the protagonists, and that they frequently divide into three phases. These correspond generally speaking to Le Bidois' beginning, middle and end, and account for the unity of individual scenes.

3

Phèdre opens characteristically in the middle of a conversation between Hippolyte and his confidant. It lasts for 144 lines. The ground covered is remarkable. It sets the scene, creates the atmosphere which pervades the play, contains a general statement on the activities of Venus, introduces the differences and resemblances between Thésée and Hippolyte, and includes of course the first *aveu*.

This brings us to another difference between *Phèdre* and some of the earlier plays. Instead of the 'aggressor' forcing 'secrets' out of the 'victim', it is the devoted servants who coax the secrets out of their masters and mistresses. Their intentions are no doubt admirable and spring from a desire to help, but they are not exactly beneficial in two of the cases. With Phèdre confession lowers morale, weakens resistance, becomes in fact the first stage in her downfall. And the effect on Hippolyte of confession is decidedly upsetting.

*   *   *

It is six months since Thésée left Trézène on a mysterious mission. There has been no news of him. Théramène has searched far and wide without discovering a trace. Hippolyte decides that it is his duty to undertake a personal search:

> Le dessein en est pris: je pars, cher Théramène,
> Et quitte le séjour de l'aimable Trézène.
> Dans le doute mortel dont je suis agité,
> Je commence à rougir de mon oisiveté.

'Aimable' evokes a charming sylvan landscape, but it will be the scene of the most appalling tragedy. 'Doute mortel' already suggests the contrast between the sunlit outer landscape and the dark inner landscape where doubts and fears arise. One suspects, too, that though he does not yet realize it, Aricie is the real source of Hippolyte's 'doute mortel' rather than his father's disappearance.

Théramène's suggestion that Thésée is absent on another of his womanizing expeditions and should be left in peace produces a shocked protest from Hippolyte:

> Cher Théramène, arrête, et respecte Thésée.

When he goes on to say

> Enfin en le cherchant je suivrai mon devoir,
> Et je fuirai ces lieux que je n'ose plus voir,

we see for the first time the workings of the unconscious. 'Je pars' is replaced, significantly, by 'je fuirai'. The first line is a statement of the moral, and the second a statement of the emotional reasons for leaving what Hippolyte has just called 'l'aimable Trézène'. Hippolyte is a dutiful son, but the reference to 'devoir' is an unconscious attempt to conceal the real reason which begins to appear in 'fuirai'.

Théramène is understandably incredulous at the idea of Hippolyte 'fleeing' from a place which he had loved since childhood. The unconscious plays its next trick when Hippolyte declares that everything has changed since the gods sent Phèdre to Trézène. Phèdre has tried to smother her guilty passion by persecuting her stepson. Théramène tries to dispose of the objection when, in two memorable lines, he says

> Une femme mourante et qui cherche à mourir?
> Phèdre, atteinte d'un mal qu'elle s'obstine à taire...?

Hippolyte tries to correct what is obviously an inaccurate statement, or rather a Freudian slip, by saying something which will end by giving him away to Théramène—and to himself. It is not Phèdre who is worrying him:

> Je *fuis*, je l'avoûrai, cette jeune Aricie,
> Reste d'un sang fatal conjuré contre nous.

Once again it is a mixture of truth and unconscious concealment. He is afraid of Aricie, but tries to explain his fear by a reference, which is plainly absurd, to the 'sang fatal conjuré contre nous'.

Théramène naturally has a complete answer:

> Jamais l'aimable soeur des cruels Pallantides
> Trempa-t-elle aux complots de ses frères perfides?
> Et devez-vous haïr ses innocents appas?

This is one of several occasions on which a word used casually by one person without any intention of catching another person out will act as a talisman, evade the mechanics of repression and lead to an *aveu*. So it is with Théramène's 'haïr'. Hippolyte answers in a flash:

> Si je la haïssais, je ne la *fuirais* pas.

The trusted servant at once begins to place his questions with the deadly efficiency of a first-rate counsel. 'Seigneur', he begins smoothly, using the conditional tense and fastening on the word 'fuir',

> Seigneur, m'est-il permis d'expliquer votre *fuite*?
> Pourriez-vous n'être plus ce superbe Hippolyte,
> Implacable ennemi des amoureuses lois,
> Et d'un joug que Thésée a subi tant de fois?
> Vénus, par votre orgueil si longtemps méprisée,
> Voudrait-elle à la fin justifier Thésée?

Then the direct question:

> Aimeriez-vous, Seigneur?

The reaction is violent:

> Ami, qu'oses-tu dire?

Hippolyte is badly shaken. The speech for the defence runs to 49 lines. It divides into three sections. In the first he tries to preserve the image of the 'superbe Hippolyte'. In the second, he sets out to show that he does not resemble, or even appear to resemble, what he considers to be the unfortunate side of his father's character. In the third, he stresses the political ban on marriage by Aricie which he affects to regard as valid.[9]

In spite of the show of logic, we can see that his approach is emotional. It is an attempt to persuade himself as much as Théramène that there is no substance in the charge that he is succumbing to love. In a question addressed more to himself than his confidant, he asks incredulously:

> Et moi-même, à mon tour, je me verrais lié?
> Et les Dieux jusque-là m'auraient humilié?

This clearly calls for the answer: 'Good heavens, no!'—and doesn't get it.

The close, which takes the form of still more questions, betrays a radical feeling of uncertainty about himself. In one of the references to his father's ban on marriage by Aricie, he asks

> Dois-je épouser ses droits contre un père irrité?
> Donnerai-je l'exemple à la témérité?
> Et dans un fol amour ma jeunesse embarquée . . .

The last line with its sudden break is arresting. When he speaks of 'un fol amour' he describes exactly what is happening to him, what has been going on in his unconscious.

Théramène's reply demolishes in the kindest possible way all Hippolyte's defences:

> Thésée ouvre vos yeux en voulant les fermer,
> Et sa haine, irritant une flamme rebelle,
> Prête à son ennemie une grâce nouvelle.

Hippolyte, who has always thought of himself as a dutiful son, finds himself branded as a 'rebel'. In this case, why not?

> Enfin d'un chaste amour pourquoi vous effrayer?

The rub comes with the reference to Venus:

> Quels courages Vénus n'a-t-elle pas domptés?

It is an important observation. It shows that the belief that Venus is irresistible is in no way confined to her immediate victims; it is taken for granted by everybody.

It is followed by something far more striking:

> Mais que sert d'affecter un superbe discours?
> Avouez-le, tout change; et depuis quelques jours
> On vous voit moins souvent, orgueilleux et sauvage,
> Tantôt faire voler un char sur le rivage,
> Tantôt, savant dans l'art par Neptune inventé,
> Rendre docile au frein un coursier indompté.
> Les forêts de nos cris moins souvent retentissent.

Théramène shows by a simple statement of fact that a sudden change has come over Hippolyte, that there has been a break with his usual manner of life, that he is, so to speak, in transit to Venus. There is a contrast between the 'domptés' of the previous quotation and the 'coursier indompté'. Hippolyte has neglected 'the art invented by Neptune' and instead of taming the wild horse he is in the process of becoming one of those people 'tamed' by Venus.

Then comes a parting shot:

> Chargés d'un feu secret, vos yeux s'appesantissent.
> Il n'en faut point douter: vous aimez, vous brûlez;
> Vous périssez d'un mal que vous dissimulez.

It is a vivid glimpse of a young man in love, lethargic and 'heavy-eyed' with desire. It is a good deal more than that. I compared Théramène's interrogation earlier to that of a first-class counsel. I feel more inclined at this stage to compare him to an analyst with his 'patient' stretched metaphorically on the consulting room couch. 'Feu secret' may be a conventional phrase, but it is used here to describe a situation which is hardly conventional. It stands for Hippolyte's desire for Aricie which has been extracted, in spite of considerable resistance, from the unconscious.

When we look at the last pregnant line, we suspect that we may be watching the workings of Théramène's own unconscious. Although a few moments ago he was advocating 'un chaste amour', he suddenly changes to a vocabulary which one is almost tempted to describe as psychoanalytic. Whether we call it 'passion' or 'love' or simply 'desire', Hippolyte's feeling for Aricie is labelled in three key-words as a grave malady that he is trying to hide. In view of what is to come, we should notice that not only the word 'mal', but the entire line looks back to Théramène's

> Phèdre, atteinte d'un mal qu'elle s'obstine à taire . . . ?

and forward to the nature of her sickness.

In the final line of his speech Théramène reverts to a milder language recalling his 'chaste amour':

> La charmante Aricie a-t-elle su vous *plaire*?

Hippolyte ducks, reaffirms his intention to go in search of his father, and like his confidant changes his language by reverting to the word that he had used in the first line of the play:

> Théramène, je *pars*, et vais chercher mon père.

Although Hippolyte appears to be returning to his starting point, it is plain that he is no longer the same person. We shall find, indeed, how effectively Théramène's interrogation has done its work when he makes his declaration to Aricie.

4

Hippolyte has agreed with some reluctance that, as it is a matter of 'duty', he will see Phèdre before leaving Trézène. In a brief transitional scene Oenone tells them that Phèdre is on the way, but explains that owing to her sickness she needs to be alone:[10]

> Un désordre éternel règne dans son esprit.
> Son chagrin inquiet l'arrache de son lit.
> Elle veut voir le jour; et sa douleur profonde
> M'ordonne toutefois d'écarter tout le monde . . .

The moment she appears, we see that Phèdre is indeed a sick woman. Her physical strength is ebbing; her eyes are dazzled by the sun; she staggers on to the scene:

> Je ne me soutiens plus, // ma force m'abandonne.
> Mes yeux / sont éblouis // du jour / que je revoi,
> Et mes genoux / tremblants // se dérobent / sous moi.

With Oenone's 'désordre' in mind, we realize at once that we are witnessing the physical symptoms of what is plainly mental disturbance. Phèdre is so absorbed by her passion and the inner conflict that she is only intermittently aware of the outer world. She gives the impression of being in a dazed condition which is reflected in her halting language and the pauses. What is more, her state resembles the trance in which she will make her *aveux*.

The transitional scene and the start of the present one, with their repeated references to light and darkness, demonstrate the pervasiveness of the central image. Oenone announced her mistress's arrival with the words, 'Elle veut voir le jour'. As soon as she saw it, Phèdre recoiled with the words

> Mes yeux sont éblouis du jour que je revoi . . .

Oenone takes her up:

> Vous-même, rappelant votre force première,
> Vous vouliez vous montrer et revoir la lumière.
> Vous la voyez, Madame, et prête à vous cacher,
> Vous haïssez le jour que vous veniez chercher?

It is a description of a sick woman caught, in a physical sense, between light and darkness, and preparing to shun the light she has been seeking. Phèdre yearns for a life represented by 'light' and 'sun', signifying freedom from guilt, but is afraid of both, or rather cannot stand up to them in her present condition. Her brief eulogy of the sun ends with the line,

> Soleil, je te viens voir pour la dernière fois.

Her mind turns towards darkness as a refuge:

> Dieux! que ne suis-je assise à l'ombre des forêts!

The image of the cool, leafy green of the forest provides a momentary sensation of relief and relaxation. When she says

> Quand pourrai-je, au travers d'une noble poussière,
> Suivre de l'oeil un char fuyant dans la carrière?

—we have a 'cinematic' glimpse of the lover hidden away in the shadow, eagerly watching the beloved flash by in his chariot in a cloud of dust. It looks like an extension of the central image. There is nothing innocent about the use of 'ombre' in the first of the three lines. 'Darkness' may on occasion be a place of refuge; it is also the place where guilty desires may be gratified as we can see from this passage and as we shall see again when we come to Phèdre's declaration to Hippolyte and her preoccupation with the Labyrinth.

Although the result is the same, Oenone is a much less considerate, much less respectful confidant than Théramène. She is the old nurse who has known Phèdre since birth, who has sacrificed everything to her service, and is highly indignant at Phèdre's refusal to disclose the nature of her trouble. Her manner is rough and bluff. She upbraids her mistress as though she were a naughty child:

> Mourez donc, et gardez un silence inhumain;
> Mais pour fermer vos yeux cherchez une autre main.

Phèdre is of course in a different position from Hippolyte. She knows only too well what is wrong. The chance mention of Hippolyte's name by Oenone in what might be called a non-erotic context produces a violent reaction:

> Malheureuse, quel nom est sorti de ta bouche?

When Oenone eventually names him as the beloved the name acts as another talisman. Phèdre cuts short her cry of horror. We suddenly find ourselves listening to one of the greatest descriptions of a *coup de foudre* in any language:

> Mon mal vient de plus loin. A peine au fils d'Égée
> Sous les lois de l'hymen je m'étais engagée,
> Mon repos, mon bonheur semblait être affermi,
> Athènes me montra mon superbe ennemi.
> Je le vis, je rougis, je pâlis à sa vue;
> Un trouble s'éleva dans mon âme éperdue;
> Mes yeux ne voyaient plus, je ne pouvais parler;
> Je sentis tout mon corps et transir et brûler.
> Je reconnus Vénus et ses feux redoutables,
> D'un sang qu'elle poursuit tourments inévitables.

The speech is at once a confession in the moral sense and an exposure, in the psychological sense, of the nature of Phèdre's sickness which demonstrates very effectively the distinction that I drew in my opening chapter between 'analysis' and 'insight'. It divides as a whole into three main sections and a brief epilogue: the *coup de foudre*, the unsuccessful remedies, the return to the present. We shall find on examination that there are a number of internal divisions, each of them distinguished by a word or a phrase showing the direction in which things are moving.

The speech is also a particularly striking example of the 'flashback' and the way in which a *récit* is incorporated into a confession. This lends a special importance to the tenses of the verbs. There are four which count: present, imperfect, past definite, past indefinite.

The bald opening sentence disposes of Oenone's idea that the trouble only began with the arrival of Hippolyte in Trézène; the torture has been going on for much longer than that which accounts for Phèdre's precarious condition. The present tense focuses attention on what is actually happening, on the anguished situation which is rapidly moving towards a climax. 'Mal' has the effect of gathering up everything that has been said during the prolonged exchanges between Phèdre and her confidant, concentrating on a single issue which is now being revealed.

The conflict between the desire to repress and the need to confess appears in the balancing of words suggesting control and words with an explosive connotation: 'lois', 'engagée', 'repos', 'affermi' on the one hand; 'trouble', 's'éleva', 'éperdue' on the other.[11] Phèdre's attempt to keep a hold on herself is apparent in the syntax of the first two lines with the inversion and the word 'engagée', following 'lois', thrust to the end of line 2:

> A peine au fils d'Égée
> Sous les lois de l'hymen je m'étais engagée . . .

In the second line there is a change from the present tense to a past indefinite. It is followed in the third by an imperfect which coupled with the verb used conveys an illusion of stability, a continuing state. It is demolished in the next line. The use of an active transitive verb in the past definite—'Athènes me montra'—conveys a shattering sensation of the 'enemy' flinging himself into an irresistible attack on a hopelessly unprepared victim, destroying at a single blow all the defences signified by 'repos', 'bonheur', 'affermi'. The immediate reactions of the victim are described with an almost clinical precision heightened by the succession of brief staccato past definites:

> Je le vis, je rougis, je pâlis à sa vue;
> Un trouble s'éleva dans mon âme éperdue . . .

The first line describes a rapid succession of physical shocks. In the second line there is a movement inward from the physical symptoms. 'Un trouble s'éleva' records a subterranean eruption which is leading to a momentary blackout. It is heightened by 'éperdue'; she 'doesn't know what has hit her'. There is a loss of control which has a series of physical repercussions which clearly exceed the shocks in the first line:

> Mes yeux ne voyaient plus, je ne pouvais parler;
> Je sentis tout mon corps et transir et brûler.

We note the change from the past definites to the imperfects in the first of these lines. Imperfects are used to describe either a continuing state or

a continuing action. In their present context they describe the actual process of momentary loss of sight and speech, a growing sense of confusion
which prevents Phèdre from seeing what is happening or speaking. The
process is completed by the past definite in the last line which marks the
temporary blackout: a sudden sensation of paralysis and violent heat. The
general feeling of stupefaction and numbness is intensified by the alternation of blunt and sharp sounds: the *m*-s and *i*-s in 'mal', 'affermi', 'montra', 'ennemi', 'vis', 'rougis', 'pâlis', 'sentis'. The stability which seemed to
mark the beginning of the marriage is revealed as a false stability and we
feel the sharp *i*-s penetrating inadequate defences. The *ou*-s bring out the
relation between physical and psychological changes, between changes in
appearance and the sounds of disruption going on in the depths of her
being: 'trouble', 'pouvais', 'poursuit', 'tourments', 'redoutables'.

   The mention of Venus and the reappearance of the present tense show
the gravity of the situation and prepare us for the account of the attempted
remedies:

> Par des voeux assidus je crus les détourner:
> Je lui bâtis un temple, et pris soin de l'orner;
> De victimes moi-même à toute heure entourée,
> Je cherchais dans leurs flancs ma raison égarée.
> D'un incurable amour remèdes impuissants!
> En vain sur les autels ma main brûlait l'encens:
> Quand ma bouche implorait le nom de la Déesse,
> J'adorais Hippolyte; et le voyant sans cesse,
> Même au pied des autels que je faisais fumer,
> J'offrais tout à ce Dieu que je n'osais nommer.
> Je l'évitais partout. O comble de misère!
> Mes yeux le retrouvaient dans les traits de son père.

   There is a switch or, more accurately, an attempted switch, from an internal to an external holocaust. The feverish, futile slaughter of the animals is an effort to use external fires to extinguish the internal fires or
'feux redoutables', but 'voeux *assidus*' are powerless against 'tourments
inévitables'. The answer is not the success hopefully suggested by 'dé-
tourner', but 'remèdes impuissants'. Instead of restoring order and bringing calm, prayer and sacrifice have the reverse effect; they aggravate the
state of the woman who by sacrificing *animal* victims to Venus becomes
even more helplessly Venus's *human* victim. The extent of the frenzy can
be seen in the line,

> Je cherchais dans leurs flancs ma raison *égarée*,

which is heightened by the desperate wail of 'remèdes impuissants'. The
imperfect shows the frantic nature of the sacrifices which sound as though
they continued night and day without a break. The element of trance

appears when she describes the obsessive presence of the image of Hippolyte, using more imperfects:

> Quand ma bouche implorait le nom de la Déesse,
> J'adorais Hippolyte . . .

The internal rhyme, 'implorais/adorais', links goddess and lover, and is
a sign of her erotic obsession. What she describes is first the confusion of
Hippolyte and Venus, then of Hippolyte and his father which will be her
principal method of attack, so to speak, when she makes her declaration
to Hippolyte in Act II. It is a decidedly unusual example of the phenomenon known to theologians as 'distraction in prayer'. Her mouth automatically invokes the name of the goddess; her hand is burning incense on
the altars, but the whole operation is confused and nullified by what is
plainly the sexual urge: sacrifices designed to placate the supposed goddess
of love turn into phallic rites in which she is really imploring the 'false'
god—the loved one—to take her and 'make her':

> Même au pied des autels que je faisais fumer,
> J'offrais *tout* à ce Dieu que je n'osais nommer.

The burnt offerings—animals and incense—are all projections of
Phèdre's own inner fire: the flames of desire which are devouring her.

Phèdre's efforts to solve her problem on what might be called the religious or supernatural plane have been a failure. She turns to the human
or practical plane. She has Hippolyte banished:

> Contre moi-même enfin j'osai me révolter:
> J'excitai mon courage à le persécuter.
> Pour bannir l'ennemi dont j'étais idolâtre,
> J'affectai les chagrins d'une injuste marâtre;
> Je pressai son exil, et mes cris éternels
> L'arrachèrent du sein et des bras paternels.

It produces a temporary respite:

> Je respirais, Oenone; et depuis son absence,
> Mes jours moins agités coulaient dans l'innocence.
> Soumise à mon époux, et cachant mes ennuis,
> De son fatal hymen je cultivais les fruits.

The relief appears in the imperfects, 'respirais', 'coulaient', 'cultivais'.
The gritty 'agités' in the second line is smoothed out, swallowed up by the
liquid *l* of 'coulaient' and the *c*-s of 'innocence'.

The words, 'Vaines précautions!' in the next line are the sign of another failure and the end of the respite. In the most famous couplet that
Racine ever wrote the change of tense describes her final return from the
illusory past to present misery:

> Ce n'est plus une ardeur dans mes veines cachée:
> C'est Vénus tout entière à sa proie attachée.

Instead of the image of a suffering woman putting up a desperate resistance, we see the 'prey' on the run, being pursued like some hunted animal, being overtaken and collapsing as the goddess swoops down on her, which puts her in much the same position as the animals she had sacrificed. The rhyme, 'cachée/attachée', where the sound supports the sense, marks the end of resistance. Phèdre is completely in the grip of a sexual frenzy which brings with it a crushing sense of guilt:

> J'ai conçu pour mon crime une juste terreur;
> J'ai pris la vie en haine, et ma flamme en horreur.
> Je voulais en mourant prendre soin de ma gloire,
> Et dérober au jour une flamme si noire.

The guttural *r*-s in 'terreur', 'horreur' and 'mourant' convey an almost painful sensation of tearing and ripping. There has been some controversy about 'une flamme si noire'. In its present context it stands out as a striking image: the application of a word implying moral condemnation to one of the commonest and most conventional of the seventeenth-century symbols of love. It gains power retrospectively through Oenone's reference to 'flamme ordinaire' after the false report of Thésée's death.[12]

The epilogue takes the form of a sharp injunction to Oenone:

> que tes vains secours cessent de rappeler
> Un reste de chaleur tout prêt à s'exhaler.

'Vains secours' emphasizes Phèdre's earlier 'Vaines précautions!': any form of help is useless. 'Un reste de chaleur' looks back to the different 'fires' which have played a considerable part in the confession: the implication is that life itself is on the verge of being extinguished, that Phèdre is 'burnt out'.

We have a complete picture of Phèdre's 'mal' and its cause from the moment it began to the present. When we look at it as a whole we see that the internal divisions of the three main phases reveal the different stages which have brought her to her present pass: the enormous impact of her first sight of Hippolyte; the physical and psychological repercussions; the way in which the 'mal' takes root in her, then becomes progressively more deeply rooted—this is the significance of the two references to Venus—and more agonizing in spite of the attempts to expel it which recall Oreste's endeavours to overcome his malady and show, incidentally, what a long way Racine has travelled since his first masterpiece. In addition to the references to Venus, the signposts of the different stages in the progress of the 'mal' are the words 'éperdue', 'tourments inévitables', 'raison égarée', 'incurable amour', 'remèdes impuissants', 'vaines précautions', ending with 'un reste de chaleur'.

We have been listening to a private confession by mistress to confidant who in this play with its pagan setting and its Jansenist aura performs the role of spiritual director or confessor. There are naturally a number of different ways of interpreting it in performance. The days are happily past when actresses screamed their heads off and brought audiences, or at any rate those members occupying the more modestly priced seats, to their feet with cheers. One of the most successful performances since the war was given by Maria Casarès. In his acting edition of the play Jean-Louis Barrault recommends a 'ton de confessional'.[13] It describes very well the muted note which distinguished Casarès's interpretation of this particular scene. There were naturally some variations of tone, but the text of the confession is governed, no doubt intentionally, by a succession of strong central caesuras. What one heard, what one can still hear in the recording, is a penitent listing her faults and her unsuccessful efforts to reform in a deliberately sober, colourless, monotonous voice.

5

Phèdre's confession is followed immediately by the false report of Thésée's death. Hippolyte promptly decides to revoke the law forbidding Aricie to marry which provides him with an excuse for going to see her, while Aricie herself feels free to discuss her feelings for him which was something that she had always avoided doing.

The action moves to a scene between Aricie and her confidant. Ismène makes no attempt to conceal the fact that for her mistress and herself the report of Thésée's death is decidedly good news:

> Préparez-vous, Madame, à voir de tous côtés
> Voler vers vous les coeurs par Thésée écartés.

Aricie cannot believe that the man whom she calls 'l'insensible Hippolyte' will prove any more human than his father. This gives the cheerful confidant her opening. She goes straight to the point. She has watched Hippolyte when he was in the presence of Aricie:

> Ses yeux, qui vainement voulaient vous éviter,
> Déjà pleins de langueur, ne pouvaient vous quitter.

Aricie has been described by some critics as the ideal young woman, the only character in the play without any hint of a moral flaw in contrast to Hippolyte whose love ranks as a minor flaw because it conflicts with his father's ban on marriage by Aricie. This view is not altogether correct nor is it sufficient to say, as I myself once did, that there is something of the minx about her.

Her reaction to Ismène's observation is immediate and revealing:

> Que mon coeur, chère Ismène, écoute avidement . . .

In this context 'avidement' clearly hints at sexual desire and is an indication of what is to come:

> Tu sais que de tout temps à l'amour opposée,
> Je rendais souvent grâce à l'injuste Thésée
> Dont l'heureuse rigueur secondait mes mépris.
> Mes yeux, alors, mes yeux n'avaient pas vu son fils.

Her attitude has a good deal in common with Hippolyte's. She had persuaded herself that she was opposed to love as such, showing that she shared his unconscious fear of sexual desire. It is promptly contradicted in her case by three references to 'eyes'—always the instruments of temptation—in two lines. Nor should we fail to notice that the ardour of 'Mes yeux, alors, mes yeux' is scarcely balanced by the rather weak attempt to excuse herself in

> Non que par les yeux seuls lâchement enchantée,
> J'aime en lui sa beauté, sa grâce tant vantée,

where the second line removes all the force of the denial in the first line.

The puritan comes out in the lines that follow. We have seen that Hippolyte's own attitude to sexual love is the sign of a one-sided view of life. When Aricie declares

> J'aime, je prise en lui de plus nobles richesses,
> Les vertus de son père, et non point les faiblesses,

it becomes clear that she is trying to label herself as an admirer of Neptune. The truth emerges in the last part of the speech:

> J'aime, je l'avoûrai, cet orgueil généreux
> Qui jamais n'a fléchi sous le joug amoureux.
> Phèdre en vain s'honorait des soupirs de Thésée:
> Pour moi, je suis plus fière, et fuis la gloire aisée
> D'arracher un hommage à mille autres offert,
> Et d'entrer dans un coeur de toutes parts ouvert.
> Mais de faire fléchir un courage inflexible,
> De porter la douleur dans une âme insensible,
> D'enchaîner un captif de ses fers étonné,
> Contre un joug qui lui plaît vainement mutiné:
> C'est là ce que je veux, c'est là ce qui m'irrite.
> Hercule à désarmer coûtait moins qu'Hippolyte,
> Et vaincu plus souvent, et plus tôt surmonté,
> Préparait moins de gloire aux yeux qui l'ont dompté.

The remarkable thing about these lines is that Aricie is really using the language of the 'aggressors' of other plays. She will not use their methods, but her attitude has a good deal in common with theirs as we shall see that it has a good deal in common with Phèdre's. She is out to secure her 'prey'. She wants the young man—the virginal young man—who is reputed to be hostile to love. The lines are full of tell-tale phrases:

'faire *fléchir* un courage inflexible'; 'porter la *douleur* dans une âme insensible'; 'enchaîner un *captif* de ses *fers* étonné'; 'vainement mutiné';
'joug amoureux'; 'dompté'. The two appearances of 'fléchir' (reinforced
this time by 'enchaîner', 'désarmer' and 'dompté') recall its triple use at
the end of the first scene of *Andromaque*. 'Captif de ses fers étonné' reminds us of Hippolyte's 'Et moi-même, à mon tour, je me verrais lié?'
'Porter la douleur' suggests that Aricie is not entirely free from the sadistic streak which we find in all the 'aggressors' and which is completely
absent from the declarations of a Junie or a Monime. None of this ex-
cludes the 'minx' who certainly peeps out in the last three lines. She is out
to get a man who will be more of a 'catch' and more of a feather in her cap
—this is the meaning of her 'gloire'—than Hercules who, compared to
Hippolyte, was a male 'push-over'.

Her confession is cut short by the appearance of Hippolyte himself. He
has come, he tells her, to release her from a law which was too strict. His
opening speech ends with words that hint at the *aveu* which is to come:

> Je vous laisse aussi libre, et plus libre que moi.

Aricie is greatly moved by his generosity. Without any ulterior motive
she uses the same word as Théramène in the opening scene:

> Vous-même en ma faveur vous voulez vous trahir!
> N'était-ce pas assez de ne me point haïr?

In spite of the negative use of the word, 'haïr' has the same electric
effect as it did in the earlier scene:

> Moi, vous haïr, Madame? . . .
> Quelles sauvages moeurs, quelle haine endurcie
> Pourrait, en vous voyant, n'être point adoucie?
> Ai-je pu résister au charme décevant . . .

Aricie's 'Quoi? Seigneur' brings him down to earth with a bump:

> Je me suis engagé trop avant.
> Je vois que la raison cède à la violence.
> Puisque j'ai commencé de rompre le silence,
> Madame, il faut poursuivre: il faut vous informer
> D'un secret que mon coeur ne peut plus renfermer.

Racine, as we know, only made one major change in the best known
versions of the legend. He gave Hippolyte a girl. This meant that he had
to show a man who was traditionally hostile to women, who was almost a
'woman-hater', falling in love. The result is naturally highly unusual.
Hippolyte's declaration is a mixture of the stilted ('il faut vous informer')
and the lyrical, opposition and surrender. The opening lines are a sign that
he is already 'lost', but it does not prevent a continual alternation of the

images of the man he once was and the man he is becoming with the first growing fainter and the second more vivid all the time:

> Moi, qui contre l'amour fièrement révolté,
> Aux fers de ses captifs ai longtemps insulté;
> Qui des faibles mortels déplorant les naufrages,
> Pensais toujours du bord contempler les orages;
> Asservi maintenant sous la commune loi,
> Par quel trouble me vois-je emporté loin de moi?

It is another effective use of marine imagery. The proud 'follower of Neptune' had once gazed, metaphorically, from the shore at the 'ship-wrecks' of his fellow men, had seen disaster overtaking them and reducing them to 'victims of Venus', while he remained convinced that nothing like that could ever happen to him. He now has to recognize that his detach-ment is a thing of the past, that he is made of the same stuff, is a 'prisoner' of the same 'law', and caught in the same 'storms' as they were. The un-successful resistance to the process, already suggested by 'fers' and 'captifs' which look back to Aricie's own use of the words, emerges most clearly in the last line with its emphasis on the distance between what one might call the 'old' and the 'new' Hippolyte:

> Par quel trouble me vois-je *emporté loin de moi*?

There is another change in the splendid passage from which I have already quoted:

> Présente, je vous fuis; absente, je vous trouve;
> Dans le fond des forêts votre image me suit;
> La lumière du jour, les ombres de la nuit,
> Tout retrace à mes yeux les charmes que j'évite;
> Tout vous livre à l'envi le rebelle Hippolyte.
> Moi-même, pour tout fruit de mes soins superflus,
> Maintenant je me cherche, et ne me trouve plus.

In spite of himself, in spite of 'fuis' and 'évite', in spite of the hovering between 'light' and 'darkness', there is an element of euphoria in the first four lines. We catch a glimpse of a young man, who is absorbed by the image of Aricie, wandering rapturously in 'the depths of the forests'.

He comes down to earth again at the close, as we can see from a com-parison between the first and last lines. He is 'fleeing' from Aricie. Her image 'follows' him. The result is: 'absente, je vous trouve'; 'je me cherche et ne me trouve plus' (echoing 'emporté loin de moi'). The 'image' of Aricie and all that it implies is contributing largely to the obliteration of the vanishing image of the 'proud Hippolyte'.

He goes on:

> Mon arc, mes javelots, mon char, tout m'importune;
> Je ne me souviens plus des leçons de Neptune;

> Mes seuls gémissements font retentir les bois,
> Et mes coursiers oisifs ont oublié ma voix.

We notice that Hippolyte has developed a habit of echoing words already used by Théramène. It is a sign that they have done their work, that it was Théramène who 'opened Hippolyte's eyes' to his changing condition rather than parental opposition to marriage by Aricie. At the same time we also notice that Hippolyte modifies the sense of Théramène's words. Although he regarded it as a symptom of being in love, Théramène treated the neglect of 'the art invented by Neptune' as a temporary and a partial lapse:

> Les forêts de nos cris *moins souvent* retentissent.

For Hippolyte it is far more serious and anything but temporary. His 'tout m'importune' is ambivalent. It stands for something like revulsion against Neptune combined with anguish at the loss. Théramène is answered—answered rather than echoed this time—by Hippolyte's

> Mes seuls gémissements font retentir les bois . . .

The enthusiastic shouts of the hunter, the 'follower of Neptune', have been replaced by the lamentations of a 'victim of Venus', which was what I meant when I described Hippolyte as becoming something like a 'convert' to her.

We should not overlook the way in which the confessions of Phèdre and Hippolyte are matched and at the same time contrasted. It is characteristic of Racinian dialogue that it sometimes produces changes in the psychology of the characters which take place in front of our eyes. It applies particularly to *Phèdre*. Although he was adamant in refusing to admit anything, we saw that this is what happened to Hippolyte in the opening scene. Phèdre's confession to Oenone revealed the passage from a state of false stability created by her marriage to the edge of the abyss. In the present scene Hippolyte seems at first to complete the passage, begun in the opening scene, from a state of supreme self-confidence to one of extreme confusion. Now his previous state was not false in the sense that Phèdre's was; the right word is probably artificial. Phèdre and Aricie both describe him as 'insensible'. 'Superbe' is used five times: twice by Hippolyte himself and three times by other characters. Although we do not see him until the change has begun to work, the truth is that there was something inhuman and aloof about the original Hippolyte which is shown by the way in which he speaks of himself. What the change means is that he literally 'comes to his senses', abandons his 'pride', his aloofness, his hostile attitude to women which were the result of a defence mechanism, and shows that the 'real' as distinct from the 'artificial' Hippolyte is just as human as everybody else. That is the true meaning of his 'Asservi maintenant sous la commune loi', with 'asservi' reflecting the reluctance of the admission! It will prove in the usual Racinian way to be his undoing. Phèdre realizes that at bottom he is the same as other men when she says

> Hippolyte est *sensible*, et ne sent rien pour moi!

Her rage at the discovery leads, as we know, to the postponement of her confession to Thésée and to Hippolyte's death.

6

It is a sign of the excellence of the play's construction that save for the briefest of transitional scenes, we move straight from the scene in which the innocent man makes his declaration to the innocent woman to the one in which the guilty woman makes hers to the innocent man.

There has been a change in the situation since the meeting between Phèdre and Hippolyte was first arranged. Phèdre's ostensible purpose is now to discuss the political complications caused by Thésée's reported death. She is trying hard to behave normally and to be conciliatory after her harsh treatment of her stepson. But there is almost an outburst when Hippolyte, mistaking her meaning as he constantly does, tells her that it is quite natural for a mother to be worried about her children's future and is met with the reply:

> un soin bien différent me trouble et me dévore!

The irony becomes savage when Hippolyte tries to console her with the idea that her husband may not after all be dead and adds, in a couplet which points unmistakably to his own death,

> Neptune le protège, et ce Dieu tutélaire
> *Ne sera pas en vain imploré par mon père.*

Phèdre is already in a form of trance, confusing Hippolyte and his father, and nearly gives herself away:

> Que dis-je? Il n'est point mort, puisqu'il respire en vous.
> Toujours devant mes yeux je crois voir mon époux.
> Je le vois, je lui parle, et mon coeur ... Je m'égare,
> Seigneur; ma folle ardeur malgré moi se déclare.

This is literally true, but once again Hippolyte misunderstands:

> Je vois de votre amour l'effet prodigieux.
> Tout mort qu'il est, Thésée est présent à vos yeux ...

This provides Phèdre with the perfect cue:

Oui, Prince, je languis, je brûle pour Thésée.
Je l'aime, non point tel que l'ont vu les enfers,
Volage adorateur de mille objets divers,
Qui va du Dieu des morts déshonorer la couche;
Mais fidèle, mais fier, et même un peu farouche,
Charmant, jeune, traînant tous les cœurs après soi,
Tel qu'on dépeint nos Dieux, ou tel que je vous voi.
Il avait votre port, vos yeux, votre langage,
Cette noble pudeur colorait son visage,
Lorsque de notre Crète il traversa les flots,
Digne sujet des vœux des filles de Minos.
Que faisiez-vous alors? Pourquoi sans Hippolyte
Des héros de la Grèce assembla-t-il l'élite?
Pourquoi, trop jeune encor, ne pûtes-vous alors
Entrer dans les vaisseau qui le mit sur nos bords?
Par vous aurait péri le monstre de la Crète,
Malgré tous les détours de sa vaste retraite.
Pour en développer l'embarras incertain,
Ma sœur du fil fatal eût armé votre main.
Mais non, dans ce dessein je l'aurais devancée:
L'amour m'en eût d'abord inspiré la pensée.
C'est moi, Prince, c'est moi dont l'utile secours
Vous eût du Labyrinthe enseigné les détours.
Que de soins m'eût coûtés cette tête charmante!
Un fil n'eût point assez rassuré votre amante.
Compagne du péril qu'il vous fallait chercher,
Moi-même devant vous j'aurais voulu marcher;
Et Phèdre au Labyrinthe avec vous descendue
Se serait avec vous retrouvée, ou perdue.

There has been a good deal of speculation about Phèdre's age. Thierry Maulnier is convinced that she is a young and 'inexperienced' woman. I feel that François Mauriac was nearer the mark when he spoke of 'ce penchant d'une femme déjà au déclin pour un jeune être intact'.[14] This appears to be supported by Phèdre herself. In one of the scenes that follow her rejection by Hippolyte she adopts the same device as Roxane and tries to buy her way into his bed with the offer of a crown, saying to Oenone,

Va trouver de ma part ce *jeune* ambitieux . . .

She is not a young girl like Aricie trying to make a conquest of a man of her own age who is reputed to be indifferent to women and only interested in sport. Compared with Aricie, she appears in this scene as the mature and experienced woman who has fallen for a man who is a good deal younger than herself. Her tactics may be different from Aricie's, but the source of the attraction is the same. Phèdre's senses have become jaded by age and experience; she may possibly regard this as a last chance. The result is that she is overwhelmed by Hippolyte's looks, his freshness, the fact that he is a virgin or, as Mauriac put it, 'un jeune être intact'.

All this combines to produce a stupendous piece of sexual fantasy expressed in marvellous poetry.[15] It is rather as though we were watching a close-up of a woman studying photographs in a family album, comparing pictures of her husband as a young man with later ones of him as a considerably older man and reflecting on the events which have taken place. 'I love Thésée,' she says, looking at the pictures. Then she corrects herself. 'I don't mean the old ram he is now. I mean the young man he once was.' 'Just look,' she goes on; 'he was like those paintings they do of the gods.' It suddenly strikes her that her husband must once have been like her handsome stepson. She glances up at him:

> ou tel que je vous voi.

The essence of the speech is of course the identification of father and son followed by replacement, in Phèdre's imagination, of husband by stepson. It divides into a series of carefully presented stages: Thésée's middle age; his youth; the resemblances between Hippolyte and the young Thésée; the assembling of the expedition against the Minotaur; the absence of Hippolyte from the vessels arriving in Crete which was the home of Phèdre and her sister Ariane; the adventure in the Labyrinth. The process, indeed, culminates in what might be described as Phèdre's reconstruction of the celebrated event with changes in the principal roles. Comparisons between Hippolyte and the young Thésée were fanciful; with the introduction of the Labyrinth Phèdre moves into a world of pure fantasy, into a region—the point is important in view of what is to come— which is completely separated from, which is somehow outside, the actual world in which she is living.

It is done with consummate art: the caressing sibilants, the liquid *l*-s, the alliteration which reflect the growing excitement as the pictures of youth efface the pictures of middle age and in turn are replaced by the vivid figure of the young man in front of her:

> Oui, Prince, je languis, je brûle pour Thésée.

There is a contrast between the smoothness and softness of the opening line, the nasals of the second and the dentals of the third and fourth lines which betray Phèdre's irritation against the 'old ram':

> Volage *a*dorateur *d*e mille objets *d*ivers,
> Qui va *d*u *D*ieu *d*es morts *d*éshonorer la couche . . .

Alliteration is also used to bring out the attractions of the young man:

> Mais *f*idèle, *m*ais *f*ier, et *m*ême un peu *f*arouche . . .

Excitement becomes still more pronounced in

> Il avait votre port, vos yeux, votre langage . . .

The tempo slows down as she thinks of the great expedition and asks, wonderingly,

> Que faisiez-vous alors? Pourquoi sans Hippolyte
> Des héros de la Grèce assembla-t-il l'élite?

The major change begins with the tremendous emphasis on 'vous' in

> Par vous aurait péri le monstre de la Crète . . .

The verb is the first of a succession of nine past conditionals which except for one imperfect is the only tense used in the second half of the speech. The past conditional describes events which might have, but have not in fact taken place. It is used to express what is plainly wishful thinking on Phèdre's part. The lines which follow illustrate the way in which the unconscious disguises or represses guilty feelings and the way in which guilty feelings sometimes escape, at any rate partially, the machinery of repression. With the help of Phèdre's sister, Thésée had penetrated the Labyrinth, tracked down the 'monster' by using the 'thread' and emerged safely only to abandon Ariane in the most callous possible way in favour of Phèdre. Phèdre imagines Hippolyte performing the feat in place of his father:

> Ma soeur du fil fatal eût armé votre main.

There is a startling change:

> Mais non, dans ce dessein je l'aurais devancée . . .

Phèdre, very unorthodoxly and very significantly, would have got in first, pushed her sister out and done the job herself. There is a desperate urgency in the repeated 'moi' when she says 'C'est moi, Prince, c'est moi . . .'

The tempo slows down again in the rapturous

> Que de soins m'eût coûtés cette tête charmante!

The last vestiges of disguise vanish in the line:

> Un fil n'eût point assez rassuré votre amante.

The thread is discarded; Phèdre would have been there in person. The husband has been eliminated. Phèdre describes herself openly as Hippolyte's 'lover'.

I have said in other places, I repeat here, that this is one of the very few instances in great literature where the Freudian symbols offer a complete explanation of the unconscious motives of the poet and his characters. The 'descent', the 'thread', the 'détours', the 'darkness' are all familiar sexual symbols. The significance of the Labyrinth is multiple. It is at once the unconscious with its 'devious' ways and its 'monstrous' impulses, the

female organ, a prison and a love nest. Phèdre is a prisoner in the labyrinth of her repressed desires. She is anxious to see Hippolyte trapped in
the same prison in order to make him fall in love with her or to show him
that, without knowing it, he is already in love with her. The partnership
would transform the prison into a love nest which, as I have already suggested, is a region outside the ordinary world: a place where the ordinary
taboos no longer apply and where illicit desires could be satisfied with
impunity.[16]

The rapt ecstatic note is heard all through the speech. Phèdre has been
in a trance. The closeness of the imagined association and the alternatives
before them are evident in the 'vous' which appears in each of the last
three lines, first on one then on another side of the caesura, and seems like
a metaphorical 'bedding':

> Moi-même *devant vous* j'aurais voulu marcher;
> Et Phèdre au Labyrinthe *avec vous* descendue
> Se serait *avec vous* retrouvée, ou perdue.

The trance comes to an end in the dying fall of 'perdue', which is also
a sign that Phèdre is lost. The return to reality is signalled by Hippolyte's
horrified

> Dieux! qu'est-ce que j'entends? Madame, oubliez-vous
> Que Thésée est mon père et qu'il est votre époux?

There is a haughty rejoinder:

> Et sur quoi jugez-vous que j'en perds la mémoire,
> Prince? Aurais-je perdu tout soin de ma gloire?

Hippolyte tries, blunderingly, to excuse a misunderstanding and to beat
a retreat. Phèdre cuts him short with a lightning retort and a change to
the second person singular:

> Ah! cruel, tu m'as trop entendue.

Phèdre realizes with a shock that the message has gone home and been
badly received. The haughty rejoinder was an attempt to defend herself;
the defences have now collapsed. Hippolyte's forthrightness, the way that
he crashes through all the reticences, intensify her anguish and her sense
of guilt. The declaration of love is followed by confession to the beloved
which produces some intensely moving poetry:

> J'aime. Ne pense pas qu'au moment que je t'aime,
> Innocente à mes yeux je m'approuve moi-même,
> Ni que du fol amour qui trouble ma raison
> Ma lâche complaisance ait nourri le poison.

The voice rises to a scream at 'poison'. There is a change to the sound
of lamentation:

Objet infortuné des vengeances célestes,
Je m'abhorre encor plus que tu ne me détestes . . .
Pour mieux te résister, j'ai recherché ta haine.
De quoi m'ont profité mes inutiles soins?
Tu me haïssais plus, je ne t'aimais pas moins.
Tes malheurs te prêtaient encor de nouveaux charmes.
J'ai langui, j'ai séché, dans les feux, dans les larmes.
Il suffit de tes yeux pour t'en persuader,
Si tes yeux un moment pouvaient me regarder.
Que dis-je? cet aveu que je te viens de faire,
Cet aveu si honteux, le crois-tu volontaire?

The force of the passage is heightened by the contrast with the softly voluptuous language of the declaration, the change from 'je languis, je brûle pour Thésée' to 'J'ai langui, j'ai séché, dans les feux, dans les larmes.' The eyes which once gazed rapturously on the young man are now turned once again on herself in condemnation: his eyes cannot even bear to look at her: 'Il suffit de tes *yeux* . . . Si tes *yeux* pouvaient me regarder'. And 'yeux' rhymes internally with 'aveu' and 'honteux'.[17]

The apologia turns into a paroxysm which makes it one of the most dramatic as well as one of the most violent moments in the tragedy: Phèdre's remorseless denunciation of herself and a call for punishment by Hippolyte:

Venge-toi, punis-moi d'un odieux amour . . .
Délivre l'univers d'un monstre qui t'irrite.
La veuve de Thésée ose aimer Hippolyte!
Crois-moi, ce monstre affreux ne doit point t'échapper.
Voilà mon coeur. C'est là que ta main doit frapper . . .
Frappe. Ou . . .
Au défaut de ton bras prête-moi ton épée.
Donne.

No one who has seen and heard a proper performance of this scene with its repeated 'monstre', the terrifying shriek of 'Donne' and the spectacle of Phèdre grabbing Hippolyte's sword, is likely to forget it in a hurry. We see in front of us a woman who is completely shattered by frustrated sexual passion and the overwhelming sense of guilt that goes with it, who has lost any semblance of control over herself, who seems to be exposing herself to a degree that one might have thought impossible. The formal language and the alexandrine represent a deeper and more stable moral standard than Phèdre's protests. For this reason the contrast between manner and matter adds considerably to the effect. Passion has been pushed to the last extreme, pushed beyond the point where it could have collapsed into incoherence—and would have done so in any other hands than Racine's.

7

The news of Thésée's safe return comes exactly halfway through the play. Its impact on the psychology of the characters and on the action is decisive. Phèdre's passion ceases by any standards to be 'ordinary' or normal; it becomes again both 'incestuous' and 'adulterous'. And with the appearance of what might be called the last protagonist the final pattern of the play begins to emerge.

I have spoken of the particular importance of Thésée's role. I now want to suggest that in spite of all his shortcomings—he is a very typical example of fallen human nature—he represents *normality* in a world which seems to be moving rapidly in the direction of the abnormal.[18]

This lends a special interest to his latest exploit. He has not been pursuing women, as Théramène imagined, or at any rate not on his own account. He was persuaded, reluctantly, to help a friend carry off the wife of 'the tyrant of Epirus'. They were apparently not so spritely as they used to be and were caught. The outraged husband killed the would-be seducer by throwing him into a private menagerie of 'monsters' which fed on human blood. He imprisoned Thésée which produces one of Racine's magnificently evocative couplets:

> Moi-même, il m'enferma dans des cavernes sombres,
> Lieux profonds, et voisins de l'empire des ombres.

It was six months before he managed to make his escape. He avenged his friend by throwing the injured husband to his own 'monsters'.

There are other versions of the legend in which Thésée is absent at the time of Phèdre's attempt to seduce his son. Racine's appears to be the only one in which 'monsters' are involved. He evidently introduced them deliberately in order to emphasize their importance for the play as a whole. I shall discuss their function presently. For the moment I merely wish to observe one difference between this and Thésée's previous exploits:

> D'un perfide ennemi j'ai purgé la nature;
> A ses monstres lui-même a servi de pâture.

It is a startling reversal of the usual procedure. Instead of 'purging' the world of 'monsters', Thésée has used 'monsters' to 'purge' nature of a human enemy, which clearly looks forward to the *dénouement*.

The normal man makes his appearance, or rather swaggers on to the stage. He is full of confidence; he's brought it off again:

> La fortune à mes voeux cesse d'être opposée,
> Madame, et dans vos bras met . . .

We do not know how he intended to describe himself because Phèdre cuts him short with her 'Arrêtez, Thésée'. What she says is unintelligible to him: 'Ne profanez point des transports si charmants . . . Je ne mérite plus . . . Vous êtes offensé . . . La fortune jalouse n'a pas . . . épargné votre épouse . . . Indigne de vous plaire . . . me cacher'. Then she turns tail and bolts.

The normal man is appalled by his extraordinary reception and by the atmosphere:

> Quel est l'étrange accueil qu'on fait à votre père,
> Mon fils?

More strongly, as the atmosphere does its work:

> Quelle horreur dans ces lieux répandue
> Fait fuir devant mes yeux ma famille éperdue?

Then, a little later:

> . . . moi-même, éprouvant la terreur que j'inspire,
> Je voudrais être encor dans les prisons d'Épire.

The reappearance of the word 'éperdue' is appropriate. The return of the man from the dead causes bewilderment, consternation, terror. Thésée feels them himself, but the mere sound of his voice freezes the rest of them:

> Où tendait ce discours qui m'a glacé d'effroi?

asks Hippolyte. Then, more significantly:

> Quel funeste *poison*
> L'amour a répandu sur toute sa maison!

Besides echoing Thésée's 'répandue', Hippolyte's words look back to Phèdre's words to him in Act II, Sc. 5:

> Ni que du fol amour qui trouble ma raison
> Ma lâche complaisance ait nourri le *poison*,

and forward to his own words to Aricie when planning the runaway marriage in Act V, Sc. 1:

> Arrachez-vous d'un lieu funeste et profané,
> Où la vertu respire un air *empoisonné* . . .

'Love' has plainly become associated with 'poison'. Hippolyte's words also look back to Thésée's

> D'un perfide ennemi j'ai *purgé* la nature . . .

and forward to his denunciation of his innocent son:

> Monstre, qu'a trop longtemps épargné le tonnerre,
> Reste *impur* des brigands dont j'ai *purgé* la terre . . .
> *Fuis*, dis-je; et sans retour précipitant tes pas,
> De ton horrible aspect *purge* tous mes États.

What we feel, what the characters themselves clearly feel, is that a marked deterioration is taking place in the already bad atmosphere. It is a moral deterioration which is so marked that it seems at moments to become almost physical in its contagiousness. I anticipate by saying that the tragedy is caused by Thésée's confusing his son with the 'monsters' and the 'brigands'—the human as distinct from the animal 'monsters'—and in fact 'purging' nature of him.[19]

The characters have nearly all said or done something which they wish unsaid or undone. They have got to face Thésée; they must cover up somehow. Intrigue begins. In spite of her devotion, Oenone sometimes appears like a projection of Phèdre's worst self. She always catches her mistress in her weakest moments and does not always give the right advice. She told her at one moment that her love was all wrong; at another that it was all right. Now it is all wrong again. She persuades her to let her go and tell Thésée the cock-and-bull story about Hippolyte, which means that she becomes the real 'poisoner'. It leads, as we know, to Phèdre's discovery that Hippolyte is in love with Aricie. This produces a fresh crisis and in the scenes which follow some particularly memorable poetry:

> Ah! douleur non encore éprouvée!
> A quel nouveau tourment je me suis réservée!
> Tout ce que j'ai souffert, mes craintes, mes transports,
> La fureur de mes feux, l'horreur de mes remords,
> Et d'un refus cruel l'insupportable injure
> N'était qu'un faible essai du tourment que j'endure.
> Ils s'aiment! Par quel charme ont-ils trompé mes yeux?
> Comment se sont-ils vus? Depuis quand? Dans quels lieux?
> Tu le savais. Pourquoi me laissais-tu séduire?

The mental and moral confusion is most evident in the fifth line. Hippolyte's refusal to respond to her guilty love was already regarded as 'cruel' and an 'insupportable injure', but hardly counted compared with the outrage of his love for Aricie!

The piling up of phrases in apposition in the first part of the passage, and the stream of brief staccato interrogations in the second, reflect at once Phèdre's frenzy and the sly, deceitful movements she wrongly attributes to the young lovers:

> Comment se sont-ils vus? Depuis quand? Dans quels lieux?

Then she turns on the wretched Oenone accusingly and very unjustly:

> Tu le savais. Pourquoi me laissais-tu séduire?

As though any knowledge, even if Oenone had possessed it, could possibly have prevented Phèdre from falling for her stepson!

Her sick imagination goes on brooding over their allegedly secret meetings, investing them with a sexiness that was certainly absent:

> De leur furtive ardeur ne pouvais-tu m'instruire?
> Les a-t-on vus souvent se parler, se chercher?
> Dans le fond des forêts allaient-ils se cacher?

Phèdre, we remember, once imagined herself hiding in 'the depths of the forests' and watching Hippolyte racing by in his chariot. Now she imagines the young lovers slipping off into 'the depths of the forests' to hide from her. Instead of providing a love nest for Hippolyte and herself, which was her dream, 'depths' becomes an impenetrable screen which conceals from her the love-making of a new Hippolyte who is very different, or so she believes, from the silent, stubborn, tactless man she knows.
She goes on:

> Le ciel de leurs soupirs approuvait l'innocence;
> Ils suivaient sans remords leur penchant amoureux;
> Tous les jours se levaient clairs et sereins pour eux.
> Et moi, triste rebut de la nature entière,
> Je me cachais au jour, je fuyais la lumière.

The central image creates here something like a dappled effect. Instead of a character hesitating between light and darkness, the world is divided into two: the world of the innocent and the guilty. Although they are about to plan their flight from Trézène, Phèdre now imagines the young lovers roaming in the open under the clear sunlit skies whose very brightness sets the seal of innocence on their love, while she is left crouching guiltily in the dark.
Oenone greets Phèdre's latest outburst with characteristic bluffness:

> Quel fruit recevront-ils de leurs vaines amours?
> Ils ne se verront plus.

They both know about Hippolyte's banishment, but the reply with its contemptuous reference to their 'vaines amours', which was intended to quieten Phèdre, has the reverse effect. It produces an immensely dramatic scream of despair:

> Ils s'aimeront toujours.

There is another violent outbreak of jealousy. 'Il faut perdre Aricie', she says, and actually talks of getting Thésée to do the job. Then she realizes the full horror of what she is saying:

> Mon époux est vivant, et moi je brûle encore!

It shows that in spite of her sense of guilt nothing can put an end to her passion as long as Hippolyte is alive. That is why I described it as a *phenomenal* sexual craving.

It might be said that in the end she 'gets' the young lovers, but the first victim is the unhappy Oenone. When the confidant tries to console her by saying that it's not as bad as all that, the gods themselves have sometimes been victims of 'feux illégitimes', she rounds on her savagely with the words:

Voilà comme tu m'as perdue.

It is the beginning of the final ruthless denunciation. The false accusation of Hippolyte makes it difficult to sympathize with Oenone. It turns out in fact to be the equivalent of her death sentence. There is no need for divine intervention to settle her account. The devoted servant throws herself into the sea—the first of Neptune's victims.

8

It is a strange, disturbing world: a world of gods, men and monsters. Venus turns a deaf ear to Phèdre's prayer to cure her of her guilty passion. Neptune is all too prompt in answering Thésée's prayer to punish his innocent son.

The word 'monster' occurs 18 times in the play. It is used in three separate but related senses: to describe physical monsters, to denounce the monstrous element in human nature, and as a word of mere and usually misguided abuse.

In this world the actual 'monsters' are a disruptive element. They are never precisely defined. They stand somewhere between the natural and the supernatural worlds: a symbol of abnormality and evil which acts as a constant reminder of the greatest 'monster' of all—the Minotaur. Thésée made his name as a slayer of real 'monsters', animal and human: the normal man trying to establish a normal order by 'purging' it of its abnormal beings which are a perpetual menace to mankind. We saw that the expedition to Epirus led to a reversal of the usual formula. We shall now see a god following the example of 'the tyrant of Epirus' by using a private 'monster' to punish Thésée's innocent son, but this time Thésée will be left without any means of redress.

The 'monsters' in the private menagerie of 'the tyrant of Epirus' have a further significance. We see an apparently normal man harbouring 'monsters' which eventually devour him. This might be called the essence of the tragedy. Phèdre harbours and is 'devoured' by a passion which is 'monstrous' or abnormal, as she recognizes when she uses the word 'monster' twice in quick succession of herself near the end of the great encounter with Hippolyte in the second act.

In this decidedly Jansenist play the sexual instinct is branded as the element which converts the human being into a 'monster'. It is directly responsible for the deaths of Phèdre, Hippolyte and Oenone, and the ruin of the two survivors.

Hippolyte's death is the greatest stroke of irony in the play, and the cruellest. It is not the god's private 'monster' which actually kills Hippolyte. Hippolyte kills the monster, emulating at last the feats of his father which has always been his ambition, and is killed by his own horses bolting in fright—the horses which he had tamed by 'the art invented by Neptune'.[20]

The 'récit de Théramène' has appeared, particularly to French critics, to be too long, too ornate and badly placed. I do not share this view which seems to me to involve some misunderstanding of the dramatist's intentions. Théramène's account of Hippolyte's death was not an invention of Racine's. It was used by other dramatists and was seldom short. My own view is that it plays an important part in *Phèdre* and is an impressive example of Racine's virtuosity, which is apparent from the start:

> Il suivait tout pensif le chemin de Mycènes;
> Sa main sur ses chevaux laissait flotter les rênes.
> Ses superbes coursiers, qu'on voyait autrefois
> Pleins d'une ardeur si noble obéir à sa voix,
> L'oeil morne maintenant et la tête baissée,
> Semblaient se conformer à sa triste pensée.

The first thing we notice is that Hippolyte's departure from Trézène has the air of a funeral procession. It is suggested by the meditative tone with its 'pensif/pensée' and the sight of the horses with their sad eyes and bent heads.

The change comes at once and is made more striking by the neutral background:

> Un effroyable cri, sorti du fond des flots,
> Des airs en ce moment a troublé le repos;
> Et du sein de la terre une voix formidable
> Répond en gémissant à ce cri redoutable ...
> Des coursiers attentifs le crin s'est hérissé.

Then comes the description of the emergence of the monster from the sea:

> Cependant sur le dos de la plaine liquide
> S'élève à gros bouillons une montagne humide;
> L'onde approche, se brise, et vomit à nos yeux,
> Parmi les flots d'écume, un monstre furieux.
> Son front large est armé de cornes menaçantes;
> Tout son corps est couvert d'écailles jaunissantes;
> Indomptable taureau, dragon impétueux,
> Sa croupe se recourbe en replis tortueux.

Ses longs mugissements font trembler le rivage.
Le ciel avec horreur voit ce monstre sauvage,
La terre s'en émeut, l'air en est infecté,
Le flot qui l'apporta recule épouvanté.

We have heard a good deal in recent years about baroque elements in the French classic dramatists. There can be no doubt about their presence in this passage, particularly in the last three lines. The animal with its 'yellowing' scales, its bellowings, its stench, the 'tortuous' folds of its flesh, its ponderous movements, its mouth belching fire, is a typical baroque monster. The virtuosity is evident in the compression, the versification, the language, particularly the choice of long, heavy, awkward words with nasals and alliteration to convey the bulk, the movements and the appalling sounds of the beast. Racine seldom uses words describing colour.[21] There are times, indeed, in reading the plays when we almost have the impression that we are watching a film in black and white. This is the only occasion in any of the plays on which he mentions 'yellow'. The 'écailles jaunissantes' stand out with quite extraordinary vividness. The pauses in the first three lines help to emphasize the sudden swelling of the surface of the sea described by 'montagne humide' contrasted with 'dos de la plaine liquide' and the sudden parting of the waves to reveal the monster.[22] The strong caesuras and the absence of lesser pauses in most of the last nine lines increase the effect of the language used to describe the unwieldy movements of the beast. Although it is only describing a detail—the piling up of the folds of the flesh on the monster's croupe—the sixth line is one of the best illustrations of the virtuosity of the passage on account of the choice of words, alliteration and pauses:

Sa croupe / se recourbe // en replis / tortueux.

It cannot be too strongly emphasized that there is nothing comic about the monster. It is a horrifying creature. It is also—this is its real importance—the most striking symbol of the monstrous passions at work and their effect which is literally shattering, as we can see from the description of the flight of Hippolyte's horses:

A travers des rochers la peur les précipite.
L'essieu crie et se rompt. L'intrépide Hippolyte
Voit voler en éclats tout son char fracassé;
Dans les rênes lui-même il tombe embarrassé.

The emergence of the monster from the depths of the sea and the havoc it causes is the translation into visible concrete terms of the eruption of the monstrous impulses in the depths of a human being and the tragedy which follows when they force their way into the open. Hippolyte's chariot is smashed to pieces with the piercing screech of 'l'essieu crie', the thump of things being wrenched apart in 'se rompt', and the sound of them falling all over the place in 'fracassé/embarrassé'. He himself is fatally entangled in the 'reins' as he has become, in spite of his uprightness, fatally entangled in Phèdre's machinations and false accusations. A corpse, significantly mutilated beyond recognition, points to the psychological mutilation from which all the characters have suffered. We are told of Aricie

> Elle voit . . .
> Hippolyte étendu, sans forme et sans couleur.

There remain Phèdre's final confession, her death, and the meaning of the play. The confession ends with these lines:

> Déjà / jusqu'à mon coeur // le venin / parvenu
> Dans ce coeur / expirant // jette un froid / inconnu;
> Déjà / je ne vois plus // qu'à travers / un nuage
> Et le ciel, / et l'époux // que ma présence / outrage;
> Et la mort, / à mes yeux // dérobant la clarté,
> Rend au jour, / qu'ils souillaient, // toute / sa pureté.

The slow cadences, the hesitations, the efforts reflected in the pauses express marvellously the way in which the poison is filling her veins and her life is ebbing away.

The fact that Phèdre commits suicide by poisoning herself is of prime importance. The *physical* poison of the last scene is clearly related to the *moral* and *psychological* poisons of earlier scenes. Physical poison by removing Phèdre puts an end to a moral order which was poisoned. It is a perfect ending. Phèdre's life ebbs away; the skies clear; 'purity', which in one way or another haunted them all, is restored in the splendid final use of the central image. It is heavily emphasized through being the last word that Phèdre utters. We might go on to say that order is re-established. It is, but in spite of its 'purity', it is a sadly impoverished order.[23]

Racine, as we know, put a good deal of himself into some of his characters. He did so in the manner of the classic dramatists. None of them is a 'portrait of the artist'; many of them contain marked personal traits. There is a good deal of him in Thésée; there is more of him in Phèdre and Hippolyte. Racine was thirty-seven. He had reached a turning point in his life. It was time to look back and take stock. He had presumably remained a practising Christian, but it is unlikely that religion played any very serious part in his private or his literary life between the writing of *La Thébaïde* and *Iphigénie*. *Britannicus*, as we have seen, sounded a deeper note than the plays that came before or after it which was probably connected with the death of Marquise du Parc. All the evidence suggests that there was some sort of deepening at the time of *Phèdre*, that he felt that his life had not been exactly edifying, and that it was time to make his peace with Port-Royal. What I think we see in the play is a backward glance. Hippolyte is the young and innocent Racine; Phèdre the guilty Racine, the lover of

Marquise du Parc and other women. Although Thésée is anything but virtuous, up to the time of his marriage to Phèdre he has been a success: a success with women, a success in his career as monarch and a slayer of 'monsters', as Racine himself has been a success with women and in his career in the theatre. Thésée is overtaken by disaster and he, too, is obliged to take stock. Through his eyes Racine sees himself both as the young innocent and the sinner. From the first Phèdre is a doomed woman and because he does not share her love Hippolyte is forced to share her doom. I have been reproached for once describing the deaths of Phèdre and Hippolyte as a 'suicide pact'. Yet it seems to me that, metaphorically speaking, it is so. Racine, the successful playwright, the man of the world, had driven the young and innocent Racine into the abyss. Thésée loses wife and son: Racine had lost Marquise du Parc and their child.[24] In the person of Thésée, Racine is left contemplating the wreckage. Thésée has to save what he can, to be a father to Aricie who is all that is left to him. Racine may well have felt that his own position was menaced. If he did there was something prophetic about it. He was to make a *mariage de raison*, abandon the theatre, which was his great passion, and settle down to the prestigious but boring job of historiographer royal.

Lastly, the ultimate meaning of the play. Racine's world is a microcosm. His tragic family is the human condition in miniature. The odds against them are too heavy; they have no chance. The repentant sinner's prayers go unanswered; grace is not vouchsafed. The unrepentant sinner's prayer is answered at once with disastrous results. Doom overtakes the righteous man as well as the sinner. They are both predestined and therefore equal. It is a very terrible equality. There is no mercy and no justice. Sin is punished; virtue goes unrewarded. We leave the unrepentant sinner and his protégée trying to make the best of their ruined lives. It is indeed a sombre finale.

NOTES

[1] *La Vie de Jean Racine*, 1928, p. 126.

[2] *Les Deux visages de Racine*, 1941, pp. 153–4.

[3] *Op. cit.*, p. 181.

[4] 'Les faiblesses de l'amour y passent pour de vraies faiblesses. Les passions n'y sont présentées aux yeux que pour montrer tout le désordre dont elles sont la cause ...' Preface.

[5] Paul Bénichou: *L'Écrivain et ses travaux*, 1967, p. 308.

[6] *Linguistics and Literary History*, 1948, p. 92.

[7] When Thésée is reported dead, Oenone tries to reassure her mistress by saying 'Votre flamme devient une flamme ordinaire', meaning that it was no longer 'incestuous' or 'adulterous'. According to Greek law this was entirely correct and if Thésée had in

fact been dead Phèdre would have been free to marry her stepson. In the play it does little or nothing to diminish Phèdre's sense of guilt. In her confession to Hippolyte she says, significantly,

La *veuve* de Thésée ose aimer Hippolyte!

[8] *La Vie dans la tragédie de Racine*, 1901, p. 288.

[9] It is not. Aricie is the last survivor of the ruling family of Athens who had been removed to make way for the usurping Thésée.

[10] It is a neat way of avoiding the difficulties which are sometimes caused by the unity of place. It is essential for the construction of the play that we should see Phèdre in the first act, that her confession to Oenone should come immediately after Hippolyte's to Théramène, and should precede his declaration to Aricie. There is only one place where it could happen and one way of doing it.

[11] This was what I had in mind when I spoke earlier of 'the two ways of life which offer themselves to the protagonists' in Racine. See p. 16 above.

[12] The 'dark flame', as I indicated in the Introduction, was not an invention of Racine's. The identical phrase occurs twice though in much less impressive contexts in La Pinelière's *Hippolyte* which was published in 1635. The first use is by Phèdre in the opening scene of the play; the second by Thésée in the final scene. In the same play La Pinelière uses the expression, 'noire pâleur', but this time the experiment can hardly be described as a success.

[13] *Phèdre* (Collection 'Mises en Scène'), 1946, 1959, p. 93.

[14] *Lecture de Phèdre*, new ed., 1967, p. 63. *La vie de Jean Racine*, p. 132. Compare: 'Phèdre est dans l'âge de cette puberté seconde dont elle porte toute l'étrangeté et tout l'ennui' (Paul Valéry, *Variété V*, 1945, p. 192).

[15] Jean-Louis Barrault describes it amusingly as 'le grand morceau étrange, voluptueux, et impudique' (*Nouvelles réflexions sur le théâtre*, p. 193).

[16] One point about what I called Phèdre's reconstruction of the celebrated event deserves comment. If Hippolyte had slain the monster, it would have meant that he had routed the 'monstrous' impulse which is pursuing him in the person of Phèdre and would have emerged like his father as a 'follower of Neptune' instead of a 'victim of Venus'.

[17] In the next scene we get an example of what might be called contagion. The horrified Hippolyte says to Théramène:

Je ne puis sans horreur me regarder moi-même.

[18] His role varies considerably in different interpretations or, better, adaptations of the legend. It applies particularly to two seventeenth-century Spanish *autos*: Tirso de Molina's *El laberinto de Creta* and Calderón's *El laberinto del mundo*. In Tirso, Theseus is a Christ-figure; Ariadne is Nature; Minos, the World and the Devil; the Minotaur, Sin. In Calderón, Theseus (who is called 'Theos' instead of the usual 'Teseo') is Christ Himself. Ariadne is Untruth; Phaedra, Truth; Minos again the World, and the Minotaur, Sin and the Devil. It is Phaedra who provides Theseus with the weapons that enable him to destroy the Minotaur.

[19] In view of what I said earlier about Thésée's use of the verb 'fuir', it is interesting to observe that in this context it is linked with 'purger'.

[20] It will be remembered that Hippolyte so admired his father's feats with the monsters that he regarded them as to some extent excusing the seductions: Neptune cancelling out Venus.

[21] For a discussion of Racine's use of colour, see pp. 350-51 below.

[22] We remember that in English poetry in the eighteenth century 'liquid plain' was used constantly for 'sea' and became a very tiresome cliché.

[23] The *final* ebbing away of Phèdre's life looks back, significantly, to the *temporary* blackout caused by the *coup de foudre* and described in the confession to Oenone. The

first leads logically to the second; the two mark the beginning and the end of the tragedy.

²⁴ Marquise du Parc died in tragic circumstances in 1668. Racine had a daughter by her named Jeanne-Thérèse. The dates are uncertain. Mme Dussane thought that she was born between the summer of 1666 and November 1667 and died at the end of 1674 or the beginning of 1675 (*Du nouveau sur Racine*, p. 13). Henri Guillemin, on the other hand, suggests that she was born in May 1668 and died some time before Racine became engaged to Catherine de Romanet which was April or May 1677 (*Éclaircissements*, 1961, pp. 9–23).

'ESTHER'

1689

CHAPTER 10

'ESTHER'

1689

I

ONE of Mme de Maintenon's most cherished interests was the Maison de Saint-Cyr, a school that she had founded a few miles from Versailles for the education of the daughters of the poorer members of the nobility. She wished to give the girls a broader training than was generally available at convent schools. The sixteenth-century custom of amateur theatricals was therefore revived for their benefit. The material was originally provided by the principal, Mme de Brinon; but though they were pious her works proved too insipid for their purpose. The pupils were then allowed to perform Corneille's *Cinna* and Racine's *Andromaque*. They were altogether too successful. The girls, who seem to have been a lively lot, threw themselves with immense enthusiasm into the roles of Oreste and Hermione. The patroness decided that another change was necessary. 'Our little girls,' she said in a letter to Racine, 'have just performed *Andromaque* so well that they will never perform it or any of your plays again.' She went on, paradoxically, to invite the dramatist to write for her, or rather for her pupils, 'some kind of moral or historical poem from which love should be entirely banished.'

We may think that in spite of the ban on love, this was exactly what was needed to break 'the twelve years' silence'. The silence after all had not been as complete as is sometimes imagined. Racine's appointment as historiographer royal had not entirely killed his interest in the theatre or in his works. He had revised the plays, admittedly in a somewhat desultory fashion, for the edition of 1687; he was to do the same for the edition of 1697, and had also written a libretto for an operatic work.[1] He did not, however, accept the invitation with the alacrity that one might have expected. He consulted Boileau who advised against acceptance. Whatever the feelings of the man and the writer, the courtier in Racine must have realized that it would be difficult and probably unwise to turn down the request, which may have been the deciding factor.

There were several reasons for his choice of Esther as his subject. It gave the courtier an opportunity of paying a compliment to Louis XIV and his prudish consort—it is the only one of the plays in which there is a genuinely happy marriage with the wife helping her husband through a difficult period—and of delivering a parting shot at her disreputable predecessor who seems to me to be clearly identified with 'l'altière Vashti'. Racine's choice may also have been influenced by a desire to play safe. The story of Esther was popular among writers. There had been Rivaudeau's *Aman* as long ago as 1566. It was followed by Pierre Matthieu's trilogy, *Esther*, *Vashti* and *Aman* in 1585–89, Montchrestien's *Aman ou La Vanité* in 1601, and Du Ryer's *Esther* in 1644. Its popularity was not confined to dramatists or to Frenchmen. Lope de Vega's delightful 'tragicomedia famosa', *La hermosa Ester*, was produced in 1613. The Italian, Ansaldo Cebà, published a poem called *La Reina Esther* in 1615 and Desmarets another poem in seven books in 1673.

Although all the writers took their material from the Book of Esther, the treatment varied and the emphasis did not always fall in the same places. Some writers like Matthieu in his trilogy and Lope in his single play told the whole story from the fall of Vashti to the punishment of Aman and the triumph of Esther. Racine, as one would expect, disposes of Vashti in a passing reference, uses a 'flashback' to describe the way in which Esther succeeded her, and then concentrates on the religious conflict.

Assuerus, King of Persia and lord of a hundred and twenty-seven provinces stretching from Ethiopia to India, was in the third year of his reign. He held a great feast to demonstrate his splendour and his power to the nobility. He then decided to hold feasts for the poorer people—the Bible describes them harshly as the 'rabble'—and summoned Queen Vashti to come and show herself to the nobility and the poor. She refused. The king dismissed her and instituted an elaborate search for a successor. He chose Esther without knowing that she was a Jewess and a member of a race which suffered grievous persecution in his realm. She was either the niece or the cousin of Mardochaeus who became her guardian after her parents had lost their lives in one of the Jewish massacres. Shortly after Esther had been made queen, Assuerus appointed Aman, a scheming foreigner, as his chief minister. Aman was incensed because Mardochaeus sat outside the palace gates and unlike everybody else refused to acknowledge his position or, indeed, to show him the least sign of respect. Aman persuaded Assuerus that the Jews were a danger to the realm and a day was fixed for their extermination. Esther was ordered by Mardochaeus to intercede with the king for her people. Her first request was simply for two private banquets—there is only one in Racine—at which both the king and Aman should be present. In the meantime Assuerus had remembered during a sleepless night that he had not rewarded the man who had informed him of a plot by two of his palace servants to assassinate him. The man was Mardochaeus. The king sent for Aman and without naming Mardochaeus asked what the reward should be for someone who had performed such a signal service to his king. Aman, certain that he was the man, said that he should ride through Susan, the capital, on one of the king's horses wearing royal purple and a crown, escorted by the first man in the country after the king. He is told, to his horror, to arrange for Mardochaeus to be paraded through the streets with himself as escort. He was in the process of erecting a huge gallows outside his house on which to hang the Jew. Esther exposes him to the king. He is hanged on the gallows intended for Mardochaeus. The king decides that the order for the massacre of the Jews is irrevocable, but gives instructions that they are to be warned and told that they can adopt any means they choose to resist their enemies. They kill five hundred of them, including the ten children of Aman, in Susan on the first day and three hundred on the second. The same resistance takes place throughout the realm. The total number of people killed by the Jews is seventy-five thousand. Everybody is so satisfied that the king decrees that the day shall be observed as a feast day every year. Mardochaeus succeeds Aman as chief minister and the savage story ends happily, at any rate by biblical standards.

Racine followed the Bible story closely, but though biblical sources offered even greater scope than classical legend for his innate love of violence, some changes in the barbaric story were necessary to make the play suitable for performance by schoolgirls and to satisfy his patroness. The introduction of a hymn-singing chorus played a considerable part in hiding or at least softening the ferocity of the biblical narrative and heightening the religious atmosphere. The process was extended by the way in which the dramatist dwelt on the youth, innocence and devotion of the girls belonging to Esther's entourage. There were also certain modifications in the story itself. At the end of the play Assuérus rescinds the order for the massacre of the Jews instead of telling them that the order is irrevocable and that they must resist as best they can. They are also declared to be equal in standing to the Persians and free to kill their enemies. This leaves us wondering whether Racine was in fact toning down the biblical story or whether he was making, possibly unconsciously, an indirect criticism of the Revocation of the Edict of Nantes which took place in 1685.

The account of the replacement of Vashti by Esther in the first scene contains a more amusing change. In telling her confidant how she got the job, Esther says that after driving Vashti 'from his throne as well as from his bed', Assuérus scoured many countries for a successor. Candidates chosen for their youth and beauty arrived from India, the Hellespont, Egypt, Parthia and Scythia. They engaged in every form of plotting and canvassing in the hope of winning the king. Then came Esther's turn to appear before the judge:

De mes faibles attraits le Roi parut frappé.
Il m'observa longtemps dans un sombre silence;
Et le ciel, qui pour moi fit pencher la balance,
Dans ce temps-là sans doute agissait sur son coeur.
Enfin avec des yeux où régnait la douceur:
'Soyez reine', dit-il; et dès ce moment même
De sa main sur mon front posa son diadème.

It sounds like a description of a competition in which Esther emerges as a beauty queen—'Miss Persia' or, more accurately, 'Miss World'—and is presented with the prize by a national celebrity. In the Bible the story is far otherwise. Assuerus assembles an army of young virgins who spend a whole year being groomed for the occasion. It is not a matter of appearing before a panel or even a single judge. The 'seeded' candidates are expected not merely to display their charms, but to demonstrate their competence on a temporary nuptial couch:

It was a full twelvemonth before a maiden's turn came, to be the king's bride; first she must add art to her beauty, anointing herself for six months with oil, and for six months with paints and powders . . . Each morning the bride of yesternight was escorted to a new home, where the chamberlain Susagazi, master of the royal concubines, had charge of her, nor might she ever find her way back to the king, save at his will and on his express summons.

No exception is made in favour of the pious Esther who undergoes the same tests as the other 'maidens' though she is able to console herself with the thought that she is doing God's will:

So the day came when it was the turn of Esther, Abihail's child, daughter now to Mardochaeus, to be the king's bride . . . It was in Tebeth, the tenth month, in the seventh year of Assuerus' reign, that she was escorted to the royal bed-chamber. More than all those others she won the king's heart, more than all she enjoyed his loving favour; on her head he set the royal crown, and made her his queen in place of Vashti.

We may speculate about the precise meaning of the words, 'more than all she enjoyed his loving favour', which seem to suggest that Esther enabled the king to achieve a higher score in a single night than any of the other candidates. There is no doubt, however, about the nature of the competition. Nor can anyone suppose that the training was confined to learning about 'oil', 'paints' and 'powders'. It was a trial marriage on a vast scale with a fresh virgin being deflowered on each occasion and the unsuccessful candidates being assigned to the royal harem for possible future use if the king grew tired of the 'top girl' and needed some variety.

Although Vashti was driven out in the third year of Assuerus's reign, Esther did not replace her until the seventh year. Assuerus appears as a somewhat gloomy figure in both the biblical narrative and the play. The four-year competition must have been hard work—think of all those maidenheads—but it cannot have been altogether unenjoyable.[2] Sainte-

Beuve became positively lyrical about the moral qualities of the play, speaking of 'une virginale simplicité . . . la décence prise au sens le plus exquis du mot, la ravissante convenance'.[3] Although love in the Racinian sense is certainly 'banished' from the play, there is something to be said for the rather different view put forward by one of the most entertaining of Racine's critics. Pierre Guéguen suggested that it is really a play about 'le concubinage royal' or 'un drame du sérail' lightly disguised as a 'divertissement d'enfants' (Racine's own description in the preface). He concludes that *Esther* is a *Bajazet* in a religious setting which enabled the dramatist to give the little girls a lesson in 'contemporary' as well as 'sacred' history.[4] And there is of course no gainsaying the fact that both Esther and Roxane were winners in an international competition, that the prize in both cases was a crown and that in spite of the marriage in *Esther* both of them became 'top girls' in a royal harem.

2

Esther is a religious play in the sense that the material is taken from the Bible and that the main events are governed by religious instead of erotic motives. Although we are supposed to be aware of the presence of God directing the action and guiding his servants through Mardochée, there is little in the play that can be fairly described as charismatic. What we find are many of the usual ingredients of a Racine play transposed into a religious setting. It is, indeed, the story of a palace revolution in which the issues are religious-political instead of sexual-political. The characters divide into two sharply defined groups: sacred and secular, the devout Jews and their pagan enemies.

Racine turns Mardochée into a symbolical figure. He is God's Judge who pronounces on the activities of the pagan plotters. He is less violent, less tyrannical and in one respect a more impressive character than Joad. Although Joad has a transcendental moment—the moment when he goes into a trance and utters his great prophecy—the politician and the blood-thirsty commander-in-chief of the Levites tend to obscure the priest. The direct impact of Mardochée is less powerful, his indirect impact more powerful. We see him through the eyes of Aman: the frightening, prophetic figure covered with sackcloth and ashes sitting silently outside the palace.

Whatever the limitations of *Esther* as a play, the relations between the protagonists are worked out with considerable subtlety and it is beautifully symmetrical. Mardochée is the leader of the religious party with Esther as his second-in-command; Assuérus ostensibly the political leader with Aman as his henchman. The king and his minister appear to have a good deal in common. They are both men who hold high office; they are both tormented by the precariousness of their positions and the dangers to which they are exposed. Assuérus has a terrifying nightmare which reduces him to a state of near-hysteria. Aman's whole life has become a nightmare. He is haunted by the sight of Mardochée whose open contempt plays on his fears and ruins his confidence in himself.

There is also one important difference between them. Assuérus is the pagan of good will, Aman the pagan of bad will—the evil counsellor who is on the way to bringing both sides to disaster. For a time Assuérus occupies an intermediate position. The action consists of the attempts of the religious party to win him over, to rescue him from the clutches of the pagan of bad will before it is too late. In short, it is the story of a successful attempt by the people of God to 'save' and possibly to 'convert' the good pagan.

3

The differences and resemblances between the characters are naturally reflected in the language of the play and in the word-patterns, some of them peculiar to *Esther*, others transplanted from the secular plays into the religious context.

Esther and her companions are a religious minority inside the palace, secretly opposed to the pagan policies and practices that they see in operation around them. When Mardochée suddenly arrives among them, wearing for the first time the sackcloth and ashes, to announce the terrible news of the massacre planned by Aman and authorized by Assuérus, she does not recognize him, suspects for a moment that one of the enemy has found his way into the pious stronghold and cries:

> Quel *profane* en ce lieu s'ose avancer vers nous?

'Profane' is one of the key-words which is used by members of Esther's party. It is taken up by Mardochée himself when, later in the same scene, he tells his protégée that she must intercede with the king:

> Ce Dieu ne vous a pas choisie
> Pour être un vain spectacle aux peuples de l'Asie,
> Ni pour charmer les yeux des *profanes* humains.

These are not the first uses of the word. In the opening scene Esther had described the formation of the religious party in these terms:

> Cependant mon amour pour notre nation
> A rempli ce palais de filles de Sion,
> Jeunes et tendres fleurs, par le sort agitées,
> Sous un ciel étranger comme moi transplantées.

> Dans un lieu séparé de *profanes* témoins,
> Je mets à les former mon étude et mes soins;
> Et c'est là que fuyant l'orgueil du diadème,
> Lasse de vains honneurs, et me cherchant moi-même,
> Aux pieds de l'Éternel je viens m'humilier,
> Et goûter le plaisir de me faire oublier.

In the last two quotations we observe the phrases 'vain spectacle' and 'vains honneurs' coupled with a disparaging reference by Esther to the 'diadème'. One of the visible signs of the secular or 'profane' party is its addiction to pomp and circumstance. Esther is much more explicit in her prayer at the end of Act I:

> Pour moi, que tu retiens parmi ces infidèles,
> Tu sais combien je hais leurs fêtes criminelles,
> Et que je mets au rang des *profanations*
> Leur table, leurs festins, et leurs libations;
> Que même cette *pompe* où je suis condamnée,
> Ce bandeau, dont il faut que je paraisse *ornée*
> Dans ces jours solennels à l'orgueil dédiés,
> Seule et dans le secret je le foule à mes pieds;
> Qu'à ces *vains* ornements je préfère la cendre . . .

We remember Phèdre's reference to 'vains ornements', but it is clear that she used the words in a different sense from Esther, that her elaborate dress and jewelry were a *psychological* and not a *spiritual* burden. In *Esther* 'profane' is not merely a term of condemnation of the pagan; it is the central word in a network which describes and condemns all ostentation as something belonging peculiarly to the enemies of the people of God. One cannot help suspecting at the same time that the nature of the Jews' isolation—Esther and her maidens are really a secret religious sect hidden away in the palace—and their decidedly puritanical attitude to any form of ostentation was prompted by Racine's own attachment to Port-Royal and the Jansenists.

In her condemnation of the ostentation of the 'profane' life Esther refers to the life apart or 'secret' life of her companions and herself. We have seen in earlier chapters that 'secret' was a key-word in several of the secular tragedies, forming part of a word pattern to characterize a situation which is common to most of them. It is arguable that it is at least as important in *Esther*. It occurs 11 times and is used to describe the intrigues of both parties; it is also applied to the designs of God which are made known to Esther by Mardochée. When Élise learns that Esther has become Queen of Persia she says to her:

> Par quels *secrets* ressorts, par quel enchaînement
> Le ciel a-t-il conduit ce grand événement?

Esther explains that it has been arranged by her uncle:

> A ses desseins *secrets* tremblante j'obéis.
> Je vins. Mais je *cachai* ma race et mon pays.
> Qui pourrait cependant t'exprimer les *cabales*
> Que formait en ces lieux ce peuple de *rivales*,
> Qui toutes disputant un si grand intérêt,
> Des yeux d'Assuérus attendaient leur arrêt?

Esther is speaking here of her candidature for the throne. It is clear that the word-pattern is constantly expanding. She has obeyed the 'secret' orders of Mardochée, 'concealed' her race and her country in face of parallel scheming or 'cabales' on the part of her competitors and is the first of Racine's characters to use the word 'rival' in a non-erotic sense.

Once she is installed, Mardochée keeps in touch with her 'in secret' and is instrumental in saving the king's life:

> Un père a moins de soin du salut de son fils.
> Déjà même, déjà par ses *secrets* avis
> J'ai découvert au Roi les sanglantes pratiques
> Que formaient contre lui deux ingrats domestiques.

The other party deals equally in 'secrets':

> AMAN
> Quel est donc le *secret* que tu me veux apprendre?

> HYDASPE
> Seigneur, de vos bienfaits mille fois honoré,
> Je me souviens toujours que je vous ai juré
> D'exposer à vos yeux par des avis sincères
> Tout ce que ce palais renferme de *mystères*.

The word is also used, as it is in the secular plays, to describe the hidden worries of those in high places:

> HYDASPE
> Votre âme, en m'écoutant, paraît toute interdite.
> L'heureux Aman a-t-il quelques *secrets* ennuis?

When he hears from Aman that the presence of Mardochée at the palace gates is preying on his mind he replies.

> Ce n'est donc pas, Seigneur, le sang amalécite
> Dont la voix à les perdre *en secret* vous excite?

Hydaspe is incredulous. He finds it almost impossible to believe that a man in Aman's position is worrying over the Jew's presence when he imagined that his restlessness was due to his impatience to get on with the massacre—to his 'secret' excitement at the prospect of the event.

It is a play then about religious-political intrigue at court in which both parties operate 'in secret'. It is also a play in which there are contrasts between what people are and what they pretend to be; between the false values or 'vain ostentation' of political life and true values which are the values of religion. In addition to the words already discussed, these contrasts are expressed by two other sets of words, one suggesting concealment, the other exposure: 'dissimuler', 'déguiser', 'trompeur', 'paré', 'dérober', 'cacher', 'flatter', 'imposture', 'artifice', while their opposites are 'exposer', 'éclater', 'clarté'.

The main drama takes place in the minds of the king and Aman. I have already suggested that in spite of his great position and his vast domains, the king appears as a tormented soul, not knowing what is going on about him or the extent to which he is being deceived by his servants. Hydaspe provides a glimpse of him on the verge of hysteria because of a nightmare:

> Le Roi d'un noir chagrin paraît enveloppé.
> Quelque songe effrayant cette nuit l'a frappé.
> Pendant que tout gardait un silence paisible,
> Sa voix s'est fait entendre avec un cri terrible.
> J'ai couru. Le désordre était dans ses discours.
> Il s'est plaint d'un péril qui menaçait ses jours:
> Il parlait d'ennemi, de ravisseur farouche;
> Mais le nom d'Esther est sorti de sa bouche.
> Il a dans ces horreurs passé toute la nuit.

The passage is an excellent example of the way in which by skilful placing Racine obtains the maximum effect from commonplace words like 'effrayant', 'frappé', 'terrible' and 'farouche'. We shudder at the 'songe effrayant', seem to hear the sound of a violent slap in 'frappé' and a piercing shriek in 'un cri terrible'. The elliptical fifth line gives a vivid picture of the bedroom scene. The servant comes running in and stops dead as he finds the king literally raving. Once again Racine invests the word 'désordre' with a personal aura: it describes the state of mind of a protagonist at a critical moment in the development of the play. The confusion becomes even plainer in the last four lines where Esther is somehow mixed up with 'péril', 'ennemi' and 'ravisseur farouche'. Then everything dissolves into the deliberately generalized

> Il a dans ces horreurs passé toute la nuit.

The inference that we are apparently intended to draw is that the king's nightmare was a divine warning and that Esther was in some way involved. The impression is confirmed by the first meeting of Assuérus and Esther in Act II, Sc. 7:

> Croyez-moi, chère Esther, ce sceptre, cet Empire,
> Et ces profonds respects que la terreur inspire,
> A leur pompeux éclat mêlent peu de douceur,
> Et fatiguent souvent leur triste possesseur.

The first four lines of the king's speech are a picture of the monarch sitting with bowed head, crushed by the burdens of his position which pile up in the words 'sceptre', 'Empire', 'profonds respects', 'terreur', 'pompeux éclat', and come together in 'fatiguent'.

There is a sudden change of tone in the splendid lines that follow:

> Je ne trouve qu'en vous je ne sais quelle grâce
> Qui me charme toujours et jamais ne me lasse.
> De l'aimable vertu doux et puissants attraits!
> Tout respire en Esther l'innocence et la paix.

We imagine the king looking up at his queen. The weary sighs of the first four lines change to an immense sigh of relief. The 'grâce', 'puissants attraits', 'innocence' and 'paix' are the antidotes to the burdens catalogued in the previous lines. The verbs 'charme' and 'respire' are the reply to 'inspire' and 'fatiguent', and the sign that the king is, so to speak, coming back to life. He is still more explicit in the next six lines:

> Du chagrin le plus noir elle écarte les ombres,
> Et fait des jours sereins de mes jours les plus sombres.
> Que dis-je? sur ce trône assis auprès de vous,
> Des astres ennemis j'en crains moins le courroux,
> Et crois que votre front prête à mon diadème
> Un éclat qui le rend respectable aux Dieux même.

The speech looks back to Hydaspe's description of the nightmare in the first scene of Act II. The sight of Esther, mentioned in the earlier scene, dissipates the 'noir chagrin'; the dark 'shadows' disperse and are replaced by images of light: the 'jours sereins' and the 'éclat' which removes the wearying burden of the crown. One feels tempted to call this the first stage in the king's 'conversion', and to suggest that without realizing it to the full—there is a certain ambiguity about 'grâce' in the middle passage— he is looking to Esther as his saviour. He is already beginning to realize that there are two sets of values: the 'pompeux éclat' which belongs to the office of king, the 'profonds respects' which are the product of the terror he inspires in his people, and the true values represented by Esther: 'grâce', 'innocence', 'vertu', 'paix', and 'éclat' used in a different sense from the 'pompeux éclat'. They are also the values of religion which make the crown 'respectable' in the sight of the 'Gods'.

Assuérus is the pagan of good will who through no fault of his own belongs to the 'profane' world and is in danger of becoming the tool of his evil counsellor. Aman, the pagan of bad will, fails to distinguish between true and false values, or rather he chooses the false values and is hated by the people:

> J'ai chéri, j'ai cherché la malédiction.
> Et pour prix de ma vie à leur haine exposée,
> Le barbare aujourd'hui m'*expose* à leur risée!

We notice the double use of the verb 'exposer'. In order to satisfy his overweening ambition Aman has 'exposed' himself to public hatred. He is now in danger of being 'exposed' by the defiance and contempt of Mardochée, described bitterly as 'ce barbare', to something still more dangerous —public derision. For laughter could in a moment destroy his position completely.

He admits that his position is founded on fraud and deceit:

> Je previns donc contre eux l'esprit d'Assuérus:
> J'inventai des couleurs; j'armai la calomnie;
> J'intéressai sa gloire; il trembla pour sa vie.
> Je les peignis puissants, riches, séditieux;
> Leur dieu même ennemi de tous les autres dieux.

The falseness of his values becomes clearest of all in the next two lines. Aman is quoting from his speech to the king in which he used a word which belongs peculiarly to the party he is denouncing:

> Jusqu'à quand souffre-t-on que ce peuple respire,
> Et d'un culte *profane* infecte votre Empire?

It is emphasized by his use of another word earlier in the same scene. He is describing Mardochée's disrespectful attitude towards himself:

> Lorsque d'un saint respect tous les Persans touchés
> N'osent lever leurs fronts à la terre attachés,
> Lui, fièrement assis . . .
> Présente à mes regards un front séditieux . . .

The disruptive effect of Mardochée on Aman is one of the most fascinating features of the play and his descriptions of the scene at the palace gates are particularly revealing:

> Son visage odieux m'afflige et me poursuit;
> Et mon esprit troublé le voit encor la nuit.
> Ce matin j'ai voulu devancer la lumière:
> Je l'ai trouvé couvert d'une affreuse poussière,
> Revêtu de lambeaux, tout pâle. Mais son oeil
> Conservait sous la cendre encor le même orgueil.

> Mais Mardochée, assis aux portes du palais,
> Dans ce coeur malheureux enfonce mille traits;
> Et toute ma grandeur me devient insipide,
> Tandis que le soleil éclaire ce perfide.

The repeated descriptions of Mardochée sitting outside the palace, the way in which Aman dwells on his attitude and appearance bring out the extraordinary nature of his obsession and its shattering effect on the evil counsellor. What I want to look at in these last quotations is the reappearance of the images of light and darkness, night and day.

At the beginning of the first passage there is a specific reference to the way in which the image of Mardochée sitting outside the palace haunts Aman's nights. It means that for Aman, Mardochée is associated with darkness and doom. His aim in going out before daybreak was presumably to avoid seeing Mardochée. In this he is foiled. The sight of Mardochée in sackcloth and ashes is even more frightening. What strikes Aman most forcibly, however, is the glint in his eye which is somehow intensified by the grimness of his apparel. In the second passage the same obsessive image of the Jew turns up again, but the crux is in the last two lines. The reference to the 'sun' has the effect of spotlighting Mardochée, switching the light away from Aman who remains in the shadow, in the dark. The use of the word 'insipide' marks a definite stage in Aman's disintegration: the sight of Mardochée lighted up by the sun suddenly makes him feel that his own dubious 'grandeur' has dissolved, melted away, which is what will happen when in a matter of minutes he is hoisted on to the gallows he erected to kill his enemy.

When we compare passages like these with the report of Assuérus's nightmare and his pronouncements to Esther, we see how ingeniously Racine has worked out the contrast between the king and Aman. One of the clearest signs that the good pagan is on the way to 'conversion' and escape from his mental torment is his description of himself moving out of the 'shadow' into the light and his use of words like 'sereins', 'paix' and 'éclat'. This is the reverse of what is happening to Aman. His obsession becomes more and more intense as he moves further and further into the dark. Assuérus's 'noir chagrin' has been dissolved in precisely the same way that Aman's imagined 'grandeur' has melted away.

It has been suggested that the scene between Aman and his wife in Act III, Sc. 1, is a sort of comic interlude which has no real relevance to the play. I find this view difficult to accept. There are two brief references to Aman's wife, Zares, in the Book of Esther. At one of the meetings she and various friends advise him to erect the gallows outside his house and hang Mardochaeus. At the next meeting 'he could get no comfort' from them. They tell him that Mardochaeus has 'begun to outmatch' him and that he will 'never get the better of him'. It is evident therefore that the first scene of Act III is very largely an invention of Racine's and it seems to me to have a definite place in the play. Although Zarès is an amiable wife who is desperately anxious to help her husband, the scene recalls the meeting between Clytemnestre and Agamemnon in the fourth act of *Iphigénie*. For in spite of the difference of manner Zarès does exactly the same as Clytemnestre: she tells her husband some vital home truths about himself which he has been too blind or too obstinate to discover for himself:

Seigneur, nous sommes seuls. Que sert de se flatter ?
Ce zèle que pour lui vous fîtes éclater,
Ce soin d'immoler tout à son pouvoir suprême,
Entre nous, avaient-ils d'autre objet que vous-même ?
Et sans chercher plus loin, tous ces Juifs désolés,
N'est-ce pas à vous seul que vous les immolez ?

Then comes the warning:

Où tendez-vous plus haut ? Je frémis quand je voi
Les abîmes profonds qui s'offrent devant moi.
La chute désormais ne peut être qu'horrible.
Osez chercher ailleurs un destin plus paisible.
Regagnez l'Hellespont . . .
La mer la plus terrible et la plus orageuse
Est plus sûre pour nous que cette cour trompeuse.

The words 'abîmes profonds', 'chute', 'mer la plus orageuse' are prophetic. In a sense they complete the imagery of light and darkness: Aman
will disappear into the 'abyss'. Ironically, Zarès is advising flight when it is
already too late. The scene is interrupted by the arrival of Hydaspe to
summon Aman to Esther's banquet. This produces another stroke of
Racinian irony. He announces that 'the wise men' have been consulted
about the situation:

Ils disent que la main d'un perfide étranger
Dans le sang de la Reine est prête à se plonger;
Et le Roi, qui ne sait où trouver le coupable,
N'impute qu'aux seuls Juifs ce projet détestable.

The other party have been so successful in 'hiding' the fact that Esther
is a Jewess that Aman has no idea that he is the 'foreigner' who is plotting
the death of the queen. It will be his final and horrifying discovery at the
banquet when the modest Esther will display a truly Racinian ruthlessness.

4

Racine attached great importance to the chorus in *Esther*. Music was
specially composed for the choruses in both *Esther* and *Athalie* by J. B.
Moreau, 'Maistre de Musique du Roy', and Racine rightly praises his
music highly in the preface to *Esther*. Although it represented a fresh departure for Racine, the appearance of a chorus in a play of the French
classical period was far from being a novelty. Choruses had been used
extensively by Racine's predecessors, particularly in the sixteenth century.
Their use had not been restricted to religious plays like Matthieu's and
Montchrestien's versions of the Esther story; it included secular plays

such as Garnier's *La Troade*, *Antigone* and *Hippolyte* which has two choruses: a chorus of hunters and a chorus of Athenians. They were popular, too, with the Spanish masters of the sixteenth and seventeenth centuries who enjoyed introducing musical interludes and seldom missed an opportunity in plays with a rural setting of turning the peasantry into a singing and dancing chorus with instrumental accompaniment.

It is generally believed that in the secular plays Racine had used the confidants as a substitute for a chorus in the Greek manner. Their functions were not dissimilar. The Greek chorus uttered warnings and commented on the events taking place. Racine's confidants, as we have seen, stand for the common sense view of life, are often the voice of 'the people' trying hard to stave off disaster by their sound advice to their masters or, in the case of a Narcisse or an Oenone, contributing to their downfall by their bad advice. The substitution of confidants for a chorus had decided advantages in the secular plays. It modified the ritual element and since the confidants were members of the cast permitted a greater degree of verisimilitude.

The chorus in *Esther* is rather more closely integrated into the play than the chorus in *Athalie*. It provides a commentary on events, looking back to what has already taken place and forward to what it hopes will happen. In short, in spite of the difference of ethos, its functions are not unlike those of a Greek chorus. In view of what I said in the last paragraph about confidants and verisimilitude, one or two features deserve attention. Racine's chorus is formed from the young girls, the Jewish companions, whom Esther has assembled in her own quarters in the palace and whom she describes in the opening scene in two of the most charming lines of the play as

> Jeunes et tendres fleurs, par le sort agitées,
> Sous un ciel étranger comme moi transplantées.

They are therefore members of the cast in the Spanish manner. It is significant that the chorus is present during thirteen out of a total of twenty-two scenes in the play, but that during eight of the thirteen they are silent onlookers. This gives them an opportunity of witnessing a major event like the announcement of the impending massacre and reacting appropriately in the choral scenes. The other point is that Élise fills the dual role of Esther's confidant and leader of the chorus.

At its first two vocal appearances in Act I, Scenes 2 and 5, the chorus strikes a note of alarm over the condition of the Chosen People:

> Déplorable Sion, qu'as-tu fait de ta gloire?

> Pleurons et gémissons, mes fidèles compagnes ...
>   O mortelles alarmes!
> Tout Israël périt. Pleurez, mes tristes yeux.

The Jews see themselves as

> Faibles agneaux livrés à des loups furieux.

There is a vision of future disasters:

> Quel carnage de toutes parts!
> On égorge à la fois les enfants, les vieillards ...

It is followed by a touching lamentation by the single voice of a young Israelite:

> Hélas! si jeune encore ...
> Je tomberai comme une fleur
> Qui n'a vu qu'une aurore.

The consternation, reflected in the repetition in Act I, Sc. 5, of the refrain, 'O mortelles alarmes', is caused by the announcement of the impending massacre. At this point there is a noticeable stiffening in the attitude of the chorus. Lamentation is followed by invocation:

> Le Dieu que nous servons est le Dieu des combats:
> Non, non, il ne souffrira pas
> Qu'on égorge ainsi l'innocence.

We should also observe the way in which the chorus echo the words of the protagonists: Mardochée when they speak of 'l'impie Aman' and Esther when they denounce pagan ostentation:

> Arrachons, déchirons tous ces *vains ornements*
> Qui parent notre tête.

In the last scene of Act II, after being present at the meeting of Esther and Assuérus, the chorus sounds a more optimistic note:

> Un moment a changé ce courage inflexible.
> Le lion rugissant est un agneau paisible.
> Dieu, notre Dieu sans doute a versé dans son coeur
> Cet esprit de douceur.

This is a reference to Assuérus. In view of what I have said about the 'good pagan', it will be seen how neatly it fits into the drama, that it is both a commentary and a forecast of what is to come. The chorus continues as a prayer to God to finish the job and open the king's eyes:

> Dieu d'Israël, dissipe enfin cette ombre.

'Ombre' echoes what Assuérus has just been saying to Esther in a passage on which I commented earlier.

The appearance of the chorus in this final scene of Act II closes on a note of high confidence—confidence in the destruction of the wicked by God and the peace to come:

> La gloire des méchants en un moment s'éteint.
> L'affreux tombeau pour jamais les dévore.

The chorus is heard twice in Act III: in Scenes 3 and 9. There is a ferocious denunciation of Aman whom they have seen on his way to the fatal banquet. It is divided among three young Israelites:

> On lit dans ses regards sa fureur et sa rage.
>
> Je croyais voir marcher la Mort devant ses pas.
>
> Je ne sais si ce tigre a reconnu sa proie . . .

The final chorus is a song of triumph. It is very long, presumably to make up for the rather brusque ending to the drama itself. God has touched the king's heart. The Jewish religion will be restored and the temple rebuilt. '[Dieu] nous fait remporter une illustre victoire'.

The choruses, particularly when they are performed, have a charm of their own. They are the voices of children resounding in this adult world, reflecting its hopes and fears and creating a pleasing contrast with the heavier and more formal speech of the protagonists. This gives the biblical plays not so much a greater as a different kind of variety from the secular tragedies.

I have dwelt on the virtues of the chorus, but there are certain reservations to be made. *Esther* contains a total of 1286 lines. Disregarding the brevity of many of the chorus's lines, this means that it is approximately 40 per cent shorter than any of the secular tragedies. 357 of these lines are either sung or recited which means that *in the text* the chorus occupies nearly 28 per cent of the play. *Performance* is a different matter. When I timed a performance on a gramophone record I found that the total playing time was 100 minutes and that approximately 40 minutes were taken up by the chorus.[5] Some parts of the chorus are recited, but they are only a comparatively small proportion of the whole. Most parts are sung with orchestral accompaniment. It will be apparent that Racine is at the opposite pole to the Spaniards in whose plays the choral scenes are essentially musical *interludes* and no more. This applies particularly to Lope de Vega who in *La hermosa Ester* assembles a few peasants and some rustic 'musicos' for a couple of scenes.

Nobody who in recent years has seen performances in London of Greek classics by visiting theatrical companies—I am thinking especially of the production of *Electra* in 1961—can have failed to be deeply impressed by the unaccompanied *chant* of the choruses which has a strangely haunting, strangely fascinating tone. The effect of the chorus in *Esther* is very different. Racine was so skilful in relating the words and moods of the chorus to those of the drama that one cannot avoid the feeling that if all the choral parts had been recited the effect would have been more memorable, or rather memorable in a different way. Moreau's music is, indeed, a delight and Racine was speaking the literal truth when he said in his preface that he could not do justice to it 'sans confesser franchement que ses chants ont fait un des plus grands agréments de la pièce'. It also has to be confessed that the chorus occupies such a large proportion of what is already a very short play and in performance the music is so abundant that it undoubtedly detracts from the dramatic force of the play as a play, comes in fact very close to swamping the drama. It is scarcely going too far to suggest that one's final impression of the performance is that of a religious oratorio with dramatic interludes.

We must conclude that the limitations of the play are largely the result of the space occupied by the chorus. Racine did not have room to develop the characters or elaborate their experiences in the way in which he was accustomed. We can see from the subtlety and insight he displayed that he could very easily have done it as he was to do it in *Athalie*. The fact remains that in *Esther* he did not do so. For all its merits therefore it is important primarily as an approach shot for *Athalie* and considered in itself the right verdict is 'slight'.

NOTES

[1] See Boileau's comments referred to on p. 37 above.

[2] It should be said in fairness that a footnote in my edition of the Bible suggests that Assuerus was away for part of the four years engaged in military campaigns. The Bible and the play also state that it took him some time to recover from the breach with Vashti—to get her out of his heart as well as his bed.

[3] *Port-Royal* (Pléiade Edition), III, 1955, p. 585.

[4] *Poésie de Racine*, pp. 297, 305–6.

[5] It must of course be remembered that in the musical accompaniment there are a considerable number of repetitions—it applies to both *Esther* and *Athalie*—which are not shown in the text of the play.

'ATHALIE'
1691

Athalie est peut-être le chef-d'oeuvre de l'esprit humain. Trouver le secret de faire en France une tragédie intéressante sans amour . . . c'est là ce qui n'a été donné qu'à Racine et qu'on ne reverra probablement jamais.

VOLTAIRE

'ATHALIE'

1691

I

THE success of *Esther* at the court was a triumph for Mme de Maintenon and Racine. They were both anxious to repeat it. Mme de Maintenon promptly invited him to write another play for her protégées. This time Racine had none of the doubts which assailed him when he received his first invitation. He set to work on *Athalie* with a will and put all his genius into it. We saw that in *Esther* he chose a subject which had already been treated by a number of professional dramatists. With *Athalie* he broke fresh ground. No professional had previously written a play on the subject. There had merely been two school plays, one in Latin, the other in French. It seems unlikely that Racine had read either of them, but he may have heard of their existence which could have suggested the subject to him.

Although *Athalie* is generally regarded as one of Racine's greatest masterpieces, he did not repeat the success that he had enjoyed with *Esther*. While he was busily immersed in biblical studies and the writing of the play, puritanical clergy were making vigorous protests to his patroness. They considered it wrong that the king should have spent all that money on Saint-Cyr for it to be turned into a theatre. They expressed fears about the effects on the pupils which were not altogether groundless.

The attacks were not restricted to ecclesiastics. Anonymous pamphlets were beginning to circulate in Holland which put matters much more crudely. One of them described Saint-Cyr as a 'harem which an elderly sultana had prepared for a modern Assuerus'.

On top of this, Mme de Maintenon was severely lectured by a narrow-minded priest from Saint-Sulpice, Godet de Marais, who at the end of the year 1690 was appointed Bishop of Chartres. It was hardly surprising that she capitulated. 'God knows,' she said, 'I wanted to install virtue at Saint-Cyr, but I have built on sand.'

Racine rehearsed the girls with the same care as for *Esther*. He was privately approved by the king and in December 1690 received the special honour of being made a Gentilhomme Ordinaire de la Chambre. It did not affect the issue. *Esther* had been remarkable for the richness and splendour of costumes and scenery. *Athalie* was produced on 5 January 1691 without scenery or costumes. It had a few other performances, one of them attended by the exiled James II of England, but the productions were so muted that they were commonly described in contemporary documents as 'rehearsals'. The puritanical spoil sports had got away with it.

2

Racine took his materials from IV Kings, 11–12, and II Paralipomena, 23–4.[1]

Athalia was the daughter of Ahab, King of Israel, and Jezabel of Tyre. Her brother, Joram, succeeded Ahab as King of Israel. She herself married another Joram who was King of Juda. Their son, Ochozias, became King of Juda on the death of his father. He had a son and heir named Joas.

The kingdoms of Israel and Juda had fallen on evil days. They had abandoned the worship of God and gone over to Baal. The prophet Elias was sent by God to anoint a soldier, Jehu, as King of Israel, and order him to stamp out the worship of Baal in both kingdoms. Jehu killed Joram, King of Israel, himself; Ochozias and Jezabel were killed on his instructions. He assembled all the priests of Baal on the pretext of holding a feast, had them all killed and the temple pulled down. He then retired to his kingdom where he later became slack in matters of religion and turned a blind eye to pagan cults which had not all been abolished.

Her son's death provided Athalia with her opportunity. She ordered the slaughter, and personally took part in it, of all the royal princes who might have succeeded Ochozias as King of Juda. She attempted to kill her grandson Joas, but without her knowing it, he was rescued by Josaba, wife of the High Priest and her own stepdaughter, and brought up in the temple by Joiada, the High Priest, and herself. Athalia made herself Queen of Juda, was a worshipper of Baal and a persecutor of the Jews. This continued for seven years.[2] Then a conflict broke out with the Jews, led by the High Priest, and the queen. Athalia was put to death at the order of the High Priest and the child Joas proclaimed king. He restored the temple, but later he was won over to paganism. There was a strong protest from Zacharias, the son of Joiada, who had succeeded his father as High Priest. He was killed on an order by the king. Joas himself was eventually murdered in revenge by his own servants.

Racine followed the events of the biblical story with the same care that he had shown in *Esther*. The way in which he interpreted them explains the special relevance of *Athalie* for our own time.

The scene is in the temple at Jerusalem. It is not a simple change from palace to temple to meet the requirements of a religious play. Racine presents us with a perennial situation. The temple and the palace of Athalie face one another. They stand for the conflict between two orders: one religious, the other secular; one based on divine 'law', the other on force bolstered up by superstition.

He drew on his imagination for the characters of Athalie, Joad, Josabet and Mathan who are much richer and more complex than the originals and give the play its highly individual nature. Abner, an important figure, does not appear in the biblical narrative and is an invention of Racine's. He gives Joad and Josabet a daughter named Salomith who is also his own invention and the leader of the chorus.

In the letter of dedication in *A Burnt-out Case*, Graham Greene describes his novel as 'an attempt to give dramatic expression to various types of belief, half-belief and non-belief'. It is an excellent description of one of Racine's achievements in *Athalie*. A religious-political conflict is bound to leave its mark on the beliefs of individual members of the parties. Instead of the biblical division into worshippers of God and followers of Baal, Racine sets out to study the different kinds and degrees of belief and unbelief. Joad is the militant believer who will stop at nothing, for whom no trick is too base, in order to destroy the heretical cult of Baal and punish its adherents. Athalie herself is not so much the unbelieving as the anti-religious tyrant who is haunted by fear of the God whom she has abandoned. Mathan is not merely the sceptical priest of Baal; he is the Apostate Priest—this is another of Racine's inventions—who has rejected the priesthood of Jehovah after some trivial quarrel with the High Priest over what would today be regarded as a liturgical point. He, too, like his sovereign is haunted by the religion he has deserted. Abner and Josabet are the waverers. They do not suffer from religious doubt in the ordinary sense; they doubt whether God will in fact come to the rescue of the Jews and give them victory over the tyrant. The picture is completed by the figure of Mathan's confidant. Nabal is a buffoon who 'serves neither Baal nor the God of Israel'; in other words, the crude unbeliever and the only one in the play.

'The great or rather the only character in *Athalie* from beginning to end,' said Sainte-Beuve, 'is God.'[3] A century later Pierre Guéguen took a somewhat different view. He described it as 'la plus terrible de ses tragédies, où Dieu même est attiré dans la disgrâce par un piège tendu en son nom'.[4]

There was a time when I felt inclined to subscribe to Sainte-Beuve's view. I must confess, however, to feeling some sympathy with those critics who have expressed misgivings about its particular form of violence which they find difficult to reconcile with religion, as well as with Péguy's reference to Racine's 'exécrables prêtres' which apparently brackets Joad and Mathan and is much easier to justify than branding Iphigénie as 'cruel'.[5] Nobody questions the fact that *Athalie* is a play about religion. What is at issue is the quality of the religion. With the exception of the chorus and possibly Joad's prophecy, religious feeling, in so far as it is present at all, is largely aggressive. There may be a supernatural element in the prophecy and in Athalie's dream, but in the main the drama consists of a head-on collision between a ruthless secular tyrant and an equally or an even more ruthless religious leader who eventually outwits the tyrant by what appears to be a purely human as distinct from a God-inspired ruse.[6]

Racine was of course dealing with a brutal story about primitive people. His God is not the God of Love of the New Testament; he is the Old Testament God of Vengeance. Yet it is a fair comment that instead of attenuating the brutality of the story as he had done in *Esther*, he underlines it; that in so doing he was using it as an outlet for something in his own make-up as he had done in the secular plays, particularly in *Bajazet*. The result is that though imaginatively, poetically and technically *Athalie* is indeed one of his greatest plays, it ranks with *Bajazet* as one of the two most brutal in the entire canon.[7]

I must glance briefly at the question of topical allusion in the play which has been the subject of learned discussion. The suggestion has been made that *Athalie* is a form of political allegory, that Racine used the biblical narrative to write a play about the English Revolution and that he was covertly attacking Louvois's policy of non-intervention. A great writer is naturally aware of what is happening in his own time, but while we cannot be certain that there are no references to the English Revolution in *Athalie*, I myself am not convinced by the theory of political allegory because the conflict in the play has remarkably little in common with events in England.[8] What strikes me as much more plausible is the view that there is a parallel between the situation of the Jews and the Jansenists, between the Jews who were the true believers in the Old Testament and the Jansenists who for Racine were an élite of true believers in the Church and who like the Jews suffered persecution because their religious position was regarded as a potential danger to the royal authority.

This view is strengthened by the figure of Abner. No creative writer, as we know, can avoid putting something of himself into his work. There seems to me to be a resemblance between Abner returning to the temple in a penitent mood and Racine making his peace with Port-Royal after leading a turbulent life which filled the Jansenists with horror; between Abner with his dual loyalty to God and his queen and Racine with his dual loyalty to Port-Royal and his king; or again between the doubting Abner's fears about the outcome of the conflict with Athalie and Racine's fears, which turned out to be well-founded, for the fate of Port-Royal.[9] We might go further and suggest that Racine identified himself to some extent with the orphaned Joas who had been brought up in the temple as the orphaned Racine was brought up at Port-Royal.

3

It is a Jewish feast day. Abner is paying one of his rare visits to the temple. The reasons for his visit are two. He has come to attend the religious ceremony and to warn Joad of the dangers threatening the Jewish people.

The feast, as we can see from Abner's opening speech, is the Feast of the Covenant which commemorates God's appearance to Moses on Mount Sinai, his declaration of the law and his covenant with the Chosen People. It was the sign of a fresh start—one of many fresh starts—by the Jews who were described by Aaron to Moses as a people 'whose whole bent . . . is towards wrongdoing'.[10] The Jewish feast corresponds to the Christian Pentecost.[11] It is the spring festival—the festival of rebirth and renewal. This introduces the principal theme of the play: the rebirth or another fresh start by the Chosen People which emerges from the struggle between the religious and secular orders. We shall find that it is reflected in the central image.

Abner is engaged in conversation with the High Priest:

> Oui, je viens dans son temple adorer l'Éternel.
> Je viens, selon l'usage antique et solennel,
> Célébrer avec vous la fameuse journée
> Où sur le mont Sina la loi nous fut donnée.
> Que les temps sont changés! Sitôt que de ce jour
> La trompette sacrée annonçait le retour,
> Du temple, orné partout de festons magnifiques,
> Le peuple saint en foule inondait les portiques;
> Et tous devant l'autel avec ordre introduits,
> De leurs champs dans leurs mains portant les nouveaux fruits,
> Au Dieu de l'univers consacraient ces prémices.
> Les prêtres ne pouvaient suffire aux sacrifices.
> L'audace d'une femme, arrêtant ce concours,
> En des jours ténébreux a changé ces beaux jours.
> D'adorateurs zélés à peine un petit nombre
> Ose des premiers temps nous retracer quelque ombre.
> Le reste pour son Dieu montre un oubli fatal,
> Ou même, s'empressant aux autels de Baal,
> Se fait initier à ses honteux mystères,
> Et blasphème le nom qu'ont adoré leurs pères.
> Je tremble qu'Athalie, à ne vous rien cacher,
> Vous-même de l'autel vous faisant arracher,
> N'achève enfin sur vous ses vengeances funestes,
> Et d'un respect forcé ne dépouille les restes.

It is the third of Racine's plays which begins with the word 'Yes'. It has greater force here than in the two previous plays because Abner is making what amounts to a profession of faith. We shall soon see that his faith is not of the quality demanded by Joad, but it is clear that in religion he belongs to the High Priest's camp.

The opening lines with the rhyming of 'Éternel/solennel' and the stream of inversions are an impressive example of the grand manner. Abner begins to speak in a tone of great enthusiasm. There is a sudden break at line 5:

> Que les temps sont changés!

We are aware of a contrast between the outer form and the internal vibrations. They are the sign of a deep-seated uneasiness, a fear that final destruction threatens the Chosen People. The speech as a whole will turn out to be a confrontation of the two opposing orders and we shall find that the uneasiness is not confined to the Jews.

Abner dwells for the moment on other and happier occasions when he visited the temple and the tone recovers its equilibrium. They were the great days when God's law was supreme, when there was a stable order, when vast crowds flocked to the temple bringing the first fruits of the soil as offerings to the Lord, when there were insufficient priests to minister to their needs. In line 10, which includes eight words of one syllable, we hear the footsteps of the faithful hurrying from every direction and converging on the temple.

The scene presented by Abner is a subtle blend of splendour and homeliness. Abstract words like 'loi' and 'ordre' are balanced by vivid concrete imagery. The splendour gives dignity to the homeliness and the homeliness tangible reality to the splendour. It is best illustrated by the sight of the faithful being shepherded into the temple in an orderly manner with their offerings, which is the visible sign of the practical operation in the human sphere of the divine 'order'.

The offering of the 'first fruits' of the land was one of the provisions of the Covenant.[12] It is the first use of the central image. Abner's comparison between past and present is a comparison between the days when the Jews were enjoying the benefits of rebirth which they owed to the Covenant and their present eclipse.

The real change comes in lines 13 and 14 which bring Abner back to the present. It is preceded in performance by a very marked pause at the end of line 12:

> L'audace d'une femme, arrêtant ce concours,
> En des jours ténébreux a changé ces beaux jours.

Racine's art can be seen in the smallest details. The inversion and the placing of 'jours ténébreux' in front of 'beaux jours' creates the impression of a dark shadow spreading across the scene and obliterating the brightness of 'beaux jours'. The disruptive effect is stressed by the rugged *r*-s of 'arrêtant' and 'ténébreux', followed by the boom of 'nombre' and 'ombre' in the next lines. Compared with the passive 'changés' in line 5, the second 'changé' is a strong, active verb. The bold, aggressive action of a woman upset the 'order' mentioned in line 9 and reduced the crowd of believers to a few stragglers furtively making their way to the temple on feast days; the rest have gone over to Baal or simply 'lapsed'. The word 'audace' is important for its sound and its meaning. Its sharpness is increased by the soft *ou*-s of other lines: we feel it cutting through and somehow demolishing the solid, or apparently solid, splendour of the past, casting a deepening shadow over the present. It looks forward to Athalie's boldness in thrusting her way into the temple during a religious ceremony and becoming involved in violent exchanges with Joad. This brings Abner to the most urgent reason for his visit to the temple. He wants to warn Joad that open conflict is imminent, that Athalie is actually assembling her troops in order to snatch him away from the very altar and destroy the temple. The danger, the incipient violence, is felt in the harsh sound of 'arracher'.

At the conclusion of the first part of Abner's speech Joad asks a question which only takes one line:

> D'où vous vient aujourd'hui ce noir pressentiment?

It looks like a straightforward invitation to Abner to explain his fears, but we detect already in 'noir pressentiment' a note of reproach which Joad will develop in his reply.

Abner responds with the words:

> Dès longtemps votre amour pour la religion
> Est traité de révolte et de sédition.

This is the first direct reference to the connection between religion and politics, to the invariable opposition of an absolute ruler to any form of religion which seems a challenge to his political authority. More than that, 'révolte' and 'sédition' turn the practice of religion into a political activity.

Abner is used in the customary Racinian manner to prepare the way for the appearance of the two principal enemies. The method employed on this occasion is outright denunciation. He begins with the renegade priest:

> Mathan d'ailleurs, Mathan, ce prêtre sacrilège,
> Plus méchant qu'Athalie, à toute heure l'assiège;
> Mathan, de nos autels infâme déserteur,
> Et de toute vertu zélé persécuteur . . .
> Ce temple l'importune, et son impiété
> Voudrait anéantir le Dieu qu'il a quitté.

The violence is explained partly by the fact that Mathan is encouraging Athalie to adopt fresh measures against the Jews, but it is also another sign of Abner's uneasiness. It is followed by something approaching a close-up of Athalie herself:

> Enfin depuis deux jours la superbe Athalie
> Dans un sombre chagrin paraît ensevelie.
> Je l'observais hier, et je voyais ses yeux
> Lancer sur le lieu saint des regards furieux;
> Comme si dans le fond de ce vaste édifice
> Dieu cachait un vengeur armé pour son supplice.
> Croyez-moi, plus j'y pense, et moins je puis douter
> Que sur vous son courroux ne soit prêt d'éclater,
> Et que de Jézabel la fille sanguinaire
> Ne vienne attaquer Dieu jusqu'en son sanctuaire.

In view of what I have already said about the doubters in both parties, we should notice particularly the references to religion in 'Ce temple l'importune' and 'Dieu cachait un vengeur'. They are a clear indication that members of both parties suffer from the same feeling of uneasiness, the same sense of impending crisis. We should also notice in the passage on Athalie the contrast between 'sombre chagrin' and 'fille sanguinaire'. It is our first glimpse of the conflict which divides the public figure from the private person.

Comparisons between past and present play much the same part in *Athalie* as they did in *Andromaque*. Certain incidents such as the killing of Jezabel, who is mentioned in this passage for the first time, and the attempted murder of Joas like the deaths of Hector and Priam have made a profound impression on the characters belonging to both parties and will play an important part, psychologically, in the unfolding of the drama.

Abner gets a mixed reception from the High Priest. Joad thanks him politely for his warning, then proceeds to treat his fears as a sign of the poor quality of his faith:

> Je vois que l'injustice en secret vous irrite,
> Que vous avez encor le coeur israélite.
> Le ciel en soit béni. Mais ce secret courroux,
> Cette oisive vertu, vous en contentez-vous?
> La foi qui n'agit point, est-ce une foi sincère?

His words brand Abner, in spite of protests which are firmly brushed aside, as a waverer. His 'secret' faith is compared unfavourably with Joad's which is naturally open, avowed, defiant:

> Je crains Dieu, cher Abner, et n'ai point d'autre crainte.

He then says with characteristic arrogance:

> Voici comme ce Dieu vous répond par ma bouche . . .

And God's 'mouth' is made to complete Joad's homily:

> Rompez, rompez tout pacte avec l'impiété.

It is an invitation to abandon any form of loyalty to his queen.

The homily is followed by something which looks like a slightly odd form of religious instruction. In order to dispose of Abner's doubts, Joad asks enthusiastically:

> Et quel temps fut jamais si fertile en miracles?

What is remarkable is that God's miracles are nearly all violent acts of punishment or vengeance and reflect in a striking manner the general atmosphere of the play:

> Faut-il, Abner, faut-il vous rappeler le cours
> Des prodiges fameux accomplis en nos jours?
> Des tyrans d'Israël les célèbres disgrâces,
> Et Dieu trouvé fidèle en toutes ses menaces;
> L'impie Achab détruit, et de son sang trempé
> Le champ que par le meurtre il avait usurpé;
> Près de ce champ fatal Jézabel immolée,
> Sous les pieds des chevaux cette reine foulée,
> Dans son sang inhumain les chiens désaltérés,
> Et de son corps hideux les membres déchirés;
> Des prophètes menteurs la troupe confondue . . .

Words of destruction pile up: 'détruit', 'immolée', 'foulée', 'déchirés', 'confondue', 'sang'—the spilt blood of Ahab drenching the land he had usurped and the 'sang inhumain' of Jezabel being lapped up by the thirsty dogs. The death of Jezabel is described in detail in preparation for Athalie's dream. This singularly horrible death ranks as one of God's 'miracles': it is something to be thrown in the faces of the enemy and it undoubtedly plays an important part in the moral disintegration of Athalie.

Joad's catalogue of God's miracles proceeds in descending order. He has dealt with the downfall and deaths of the tyrants and the confusion of the lying prophets; he goes on to the flame coming down on to the altars, Elijah speaking to the elements 'en souverain'—and producing a three-year drought! The only miracles which are not destructive are those of Elisha bringing the dead back to life. They occupy precisely one line:

> Les morts se ranimants à la voix d'Élisée.

If we place this beside the spectacle of 'Jézabel immolée', we can see the difference in the power of the two images, but both actions count as God's miracles.

The most striking thing is not so much the list of disasters overtaking the wicked as the relish with which Joad recalls them: the satisfaction of 'Dieu trouvé fidèle en toutes ses menaces', the way in which he positively gloats over the sight of Jezabel being ripped to pieces by the ferocious dogs. It looks forward to the way in which Joad will play his cards and have Athalie slaughtered like an animal. We may think, too, that it gives substance to Péguy's 'prêtres exécrables'.

Abner remains unconvinced. Joad neatly manoeuvres him into declaring that if by any chance the true heir to the throne has escaped the fury of Athalie, he would be among the first to recognize him. Joad has no intention of revealing his 'secret' at this stage; he drops a hint and refuses to explain. He knows now that Abner will be his ally when Joas is proclaimed king and arranges for him to return to the temple during the next twenty-four hours.

His parting words are important:

> Allez: pour ce grand jour il faut que je m'apprête,
> Et du temple déjà l'aube blanchit le faîte.

For Joad the 'grand jour' has lost none of its splendour. The spectacle of 'dawn' lighting up the roof of the temple is the answer to Abner's 'jours ténébreux' and what Joad called his 'noir pressentiment'. It is also symbolic. Abner is afraid that the Jews are facing final disaster. Joad is convinced that the present feast marks the 'dawn' of a new era and the triumph of the Chosen People over their enemies.

This takes me back to the central image. It has the same force and complexity, the same pervasiveness, as the image of light and darkness in *Phèdre*. It is another dual image: rebirth and death, fertility and decay, triumph and disaster.

Joas is the last of David's descendants. If he dies without issue, the prophecy that the Messiah will be born of David's line will not be fulfilled. Abner believes that he is dead. Joad knows that he is alive. He regards him as the human saviour of his people and the forerunner of the divine Saviour.

The fact that everybody except Joad and Josabet is convinced that Joas is dead contributes largely to the effectiveness of the play's ending. The totally unexpected reappearance of Joas almost gives the other characters the impression that he has been reborn. The death of Athalie which follows completes the pattern of rebirth and death.

We know that Joad's optimism is only partially justified, that the rebirth signified by 'dawn' will be no more than a temporary religious revival and that the Jews will suffer further disasters before the advent of the Saviour. We also know that rebirth in nature is treated as a symbol of spiritual rebirth. The ambivalence of the situation appears in the use of the mixed images of fertility and decay which, as I have said, is one of the forms of the central image. We saw that the first direct reference to rebirth occurred in Abner's opening speech, that it was something which belonged to the past and had come to a stop. Towards the end of the first scene the doubter asks:

Ce roi fils de David, où le chercherons-nous?
Le ciel même peut-il réparer les ruines
De cet arbre séché jusque dans ses racines?
Athalie étouffa l'enfant même au berceau.

Joad dodges with his 'Je ne m'explique point'. Abner must put his trust in God and God's mouthpiece.

Joad himself echoes Abner's words though with a different emphasis when speaking to Josabet in the second scene:

Grand Dieu, si tu prévois qu'indigne de sa race,
Il doive de David abandonner la trace,
Qu'il soit comme le fruit en naissant arraché,
Ou qu'un souffle ennemi *dans sa fleur a séché*

When he reveals the secret of Joas's rescue in Act IV, Joad prefaces the announcement with the words:

De *cette fleur si tendre et sitôt moissonnée*
Tout Juda, comme vous, plaignant la destinée,
Avec ses frères morts le crut enveloppé.

The image of the 'flower', which stands for the infant Joas surrounded by mortal dangers, is taken up by the chorus:

Triste reste de nos rois,
Chère et dernière fleur d'une tige si belle,
Hélas! sous le couteau d'une mère cruelle
Te verrons-nous tomber une seconde fois?

We can see from these examples that the mixed images of fertility and decay or fertility and destruction like 'arbre' and 'séché', 'fleur' and 'moissonnée', as well as the references to 'racines' and 'tige', are prophetic. They indicate that something will go wrong with the 'roots' or the 'stem' which is what will happen. Ironically, the enemy will not be responsible for the trouble; it will be caused by the fact that Joas does indeed prove 'indigne de sa race'.

Abner departs in order to attend the religious ceremony for all the world like a Catholic going off to mass on a holiday of obligation. Josabet appears and Joad proceeds to deal with the second of his waverers in a scene which matches the meeting with Abner. For Joad is busy assembling his troops. He begins by announcing that the time has come to reveal the great secret. Although she is better informed about the situation and prospects than Abner, it places a considerable strain on her trust in God and she exposes herself to the same reproaches as Abner:

Quoi? déjà votre foi s'affaiblit et s'étonne?

She answers meekly:

A vos sages conseils, Seigneur, je m'abandonne.

But it is not as easy as all that. Like Abner she produces a series of difficulties. The expression of her doubts is used to continue the exposition. It is our first knowledge of the 'secret' and of the fact that Joad is actually mustering his troops. We are also given a succinct account of the events which have placed the Jews in their present position and a vivid picture of Athalie's attempted murder of Joas.

Joad deals firmly with his wife's doubts, as he had done with Abner's. She, too, gets ready to attend the ceremony. Her words to the chorus, with their contrast between past and present, are an echo of Abner's opening words to Joad. They bring out the similarity between the doubters and the gap which separates them from Joad gazing at the 'dawn' with his mind fixed on the future:

> Enfants, ma seule joie en mes longs déplaisirs,
> Ces festons dans vos mains et ces fleurs sur vos têtes
> Autrefois convenaient à nos pompeuses fêtes.
> Mais, hélas! en ce temps d'opprobre et de douleurs,
> Quelle offrande sied mieux que celle de nos pleurs?

In this first act Racine not only gives an admirably lucid exposition of the main issues; he contrasts Joad's granite-like faith with that of his two doubters. In addition, the way has been prepared for the entry of Athalie and Mathan and a tentative connection has been sketched between the waverers in both camps.

4

In Act II the first clash takes place between Joad and Athalie who had forced her way into the temple. It is vividly reported by Zacharie in Scene 2. When we meet Athalie in Scene 3 she is clearly the worse for wear. We shall find, however, that the damage was not due to Joad's violence, but to her first glimpse of Joas. This prompts the appeal to Abner and Mathan and the famous account of the dream, but before going on to examine it we must take a look at Athalie herself.

With one exception, Athalie's role is the shortest of any of Racine's protagonists with a mere 235 lines.[13] She makes only two appearances and takes part in a total of seven scenes: five consecutive scenes in Act II and two in Act V. In spite of this, she is the dominant character and by far the most interesting one in the play. There is a world of difference between the simple biblical figure who is struck down by the servants of an avenging God and the complex modern woman whom Racine studies with such insight and who clearly belongs to the sisterhood of the secular plays.

I have suggested that there are two separate images of Athalie corresponding to the public and private view of her. The most memorable image that we have been given of the public figure is a line of Josabet's at her meeting with her husband in Act I:

> Un poignard à la main, l'implacable Athalie . . .

It was qualified in advance by Abner's

> Enfin depuis deux jours la superbe Athalie
> Dans un sombre chagrin paraît ensevelie.

In Act III her henchman, Mathan, will go further than this:

> Ami, depuis deux jours je ne la connais plus.
> Ce n'est plus cette reine éclairée, intrépide,
> Élevée au-dessus de son sexe timide,
> Qui d'abord accablait ses ennemis surpris,
> Et d'un instant perdu connaissait tout le prix.
> La peur d'un vain remords trouble cette grande âme:
> Elle flotte, / elle hésite; // en un mot, / elle est femme.

We see that both Abner and Mathan are referring to a crisis, a sudden and totally unexpected change which has taken place in the past 'two days'. The hard, indomitable qualities of 'implacable', 'superbe', 'intrépide' dissolve into 'sombre chagrin', 'vain remords', 'trouble' and the confusion suggested by 'flotte' and 'hésite'. The practical effect is emphasized by the heavy wording of Mathan's sixth line which gives the impression of someone crumpling under the weight of her troubles, and the pauses in the last line which bring out the hesitation and uncertainty.

Abner's words coupled with his 'fille sanguinaire' and Josabet's 'implacable Athalie' announce, while Mathan's underline, the change which is enacted in Athalie's account of the dream.

It is one of the minor complications of the unity of place that, somewhat inappropriately, Athalie rejects her confidant's advice to go and relax in her palace and relates her dream in the vestibule of the High Priest's quarters in the temple!

The greatest speech in the play is 80 lines long and is only interrupted once by a brief exclamation from Abner. It divides into three sections. The first section is Athalie's apologia. It is delivered in her haughtiest manner. Its purpose is twofold: to boost her own morale after the shock caused by the dream and its aftermath, and to justify herself in the eyes of her followers. The first line is not a request to advisers; it is a command addressed to subordinates:

> Prêtez-moi l'un et l'autre une oreille attentive.

She goes on in the same tone:

> Je ne veux point ici rappeler le passé,
> Ni vous rendre raison du sang que j'ai versé.

Her doubts about his loyalty probably explain the next line which is addressed specifically to Abner:

> Ce que j'ai fait, Abner, j'ai cru le devoir faire.

This may also be the explanation of an argument which sounds strange on the part of an anti-religious tyrant. Whatever the 'insolent' Jews may have said,

> Le Ciel même a pris soin de me justifier.

Her real argument appears in the next lines. It is the argument favoured by all tyrants: *political* success carries with it its own *moral* justification:

> Sur d'éclatants succès ma puissance établie
> A fait jusqu'aux deux mers respecter Athalie.

The strong, resonant words, 'éclatants', 'puissance' and 'établie', are used in an attempt to convey an impression of stability which will turn out to be an illusion. She looks back to what might be called the religious argument when she claims that

> Par moi Jérusalem goûte un calme profond.

This is followed by a catalogue of her military and political successes. She has crushed the Arab and the Philistine who were traditional enemies of the Jews. She has done even better in Syria:

> Le Syrien me traite et de reine et de soeur.

She shows signs of agitation when she mentions Jehu, the man who had wiped out the leading members of her family and whom she calls 'de ma maison le perfide oppresseur', but she seems satisfied that as a result of her intervention he is under the thumb of neighbouring states:

> Jéhu, le fier Jéhu, tremble dans Samarie.

She ends this part of the speech boastfully:

> Il me laisse en ces lieux souveraine maîtresse.
> Je jouissais en paix du fruit de ma sagesse ...

When studied closely, Athalie's apoligia seems like an elaborate panto-mime which has profound psychological implications. She describes *physical* victories in an attempt to exorcize *psychological* fears which she has not yet named. In spite of the haughty tone, the effect of the first twenty-one lines is to create in the spectator's mind the impression of a decidedly precarious peace.

The defences begin to collapse in the lines that follow. Athalie has come to the thing that is really worrying her. The rage and boasting give way to hesitation. The crumbling of the precarious peace is heard in the grating *r*-s when she says

Mais un trouble / importun // vient, / depuis quelques jours,
De mes prospérités // interrompre / le cours.

When she actually mentions the dream she seems for a moment to forget her listeners and to be speaking to herself:

Un songe / (me devrais-je inquiéter / d'un songe?)
Entretient / dans mon coeur // un chagrin / qui le ronge.

The caesura is virtually eliminated in the first line and the pauses place the emphasis on the repeated 'songe', balancing each other at the beginning and end of the line. The pauses and the contrast between the soft s-s of 'songe' and the rugged r-s are very effective, as they were in the previous couplet, in underlining Athalie's hesitation, but the most striking thing of all is the rhyme. The 'songe/ronge' indicates precisely what is happening. The psychological rot has set in, is literally 'gnawing' away her self-confidence, undermining her entire position.

I have spoken of contrasts between past and present in *Athalie*. There seems to me to be a parallel between Abner's opening speech and Athalie's apologia. Abner was horrified by the present wretchedness of God's people, turned his eyes towards past splendour and only returned to the present when forced to do so by the need to warn Joas of the danger threatening the people. With Athalie the process is reversed. She puts the past behind her ('Je ne veux point ici rappeler le passé . . .') and concentrates on the present. This explains her choice of tenses. They consist mainly of present tenses and past indefinites. It is part of the attempt to bolster up her morale. The present tenses are intended to emphasize what she regards as the stability of her position, the past indefinites the steps by which it was achieved. The imperfect in line 21, 'Je jouissais', prepares us for the coming change. It is not introduced, as frequently happens, by a past definite. She retains present tenses, but instead of describing a continuing state of calm, they describe a continuing state of anxiety. The dream belongs not to the past, but to the present and we have 'un trouble importun *vient*', 'un songe . . . *entretient*', 'un chagrin qui le *ronge*' 'Je l'*évite* partout, partout il me *poursuit*'.

This brings us to the dream:

C'était pendant l'horreur d'une profonde nuit.
Ma mère Jézabel devant moi s'est montrée,
Comme au jour de sa mort pompeusement parée.
Ses malheurs n'avaient point abattu sa fierté;
Même elle avait encor cet éclat emprunté
Dont elle eut soin de peindre et d'orner son visage,
Pour réparer des ans l'irréparable outrage.
Tremble, m-a-elle dit, *fille digne de moi.*
Le cruel Dieu des Juifs l'emporte aussi sur toi.
Je te plains de tomber dans ses mains redoutables,
Ma fille. En achevant ces mots épouvantables,

Son ombre vers mon lit a paru se baisser;
Et moi, je luis tendais les mains pour l'embrasser.
Mais je n'ai plus trouvé qu'un horrible mélange
D'os et de chair meurtris, et traînés dans la fange,
Des lambeaux pleins de sang, et des membres affreux,
Que des chiens dévorants se disputaient entre eux.

These seventeen lines are among the most arresting that Racine ever wrote. The celebrated first line focuses our whole attention on the dream, gathers up the emotion of the previous twenty lines (in much the same way as in the account of Phèdre's *coup de foudre*) and fixes it on a single point. The imperfect conveys an impression of prolonged suffering. The passage itself is a masterly example of Racine's power of condensation and of his dramatic sense. It robs the material triumphs, sedulously catalogued in the first section, of their reality. For the rest of the play it is the dream world which is the reality, the shadow world of the supernatural which breaks through Athalie's armour and destroys her. The terror and darkness suggested by the long, heavy syllables of 'profonde nuit' extend over everything. The 'calme profond', for which Athalie had been fighting desperately, changes into another sort of 'calme'—a silence in which terror reigns. Suddenly, the fantastic figure of 'the painted Jezabel' surges upwards, spotlighted in the midst of darkness. Athalie makes no attempt to conceal the facts or the artifices. It is Jezabel as she appeared on the day of her death. She has lost none of her arrogance; she has spared no pains to conceal the ravages of the years by a lavish use of cosmetics: 'pompeusement parée', 'éclat emprunté', 'peindre', 'orner'. It is all in vain. She is a hideous, revolting and essentially evil old hag. She utters the terrible warning:

Le cruel Dieu des Juifs l'emporte aussi sur toi,

which will be echoed in Athalie's despairing cry in the last act:

Dieu des Juifs, tu l'emportes!

The next line with the sharp nasals, the internal rhyme, 'plains/mains', and the *enjambement* ends in a wail:

Je te plains de tomber dans ses mains redoutables,
Ma fille.

One of the things which makes the passage so telling is the *speed* of the process of disintegration. The painted Jezabel is presented in six lines: six lines that convey a sickening feeling of collapse. There is a pause; the grotesque figure hangs suspended in the darkness illuminated by a harsh, crude light which reveals its battered appearance, reinforced by the sound of lamentation in 'l'irréparable outrage'. The warning is uttered; 'fille digne de moi' links the fate of mother and daughter. Then the figure leans dramatically towards Athalie. We see Athalie rising in her bed, stretching out her arms to embrace her mother and possibly like a child to seek refuge in her arms. The actual movement, conveyed by the imperfect, 'tendais', is cut short by the past indefinite. Athalie does not see what happens; she simply finds herself staring at the ferocious dogs fighting for a share of the torn and bleeding remains. It is an image which has branded itself as firmly in the minds of the characters as the image of Troy in flames in *Andromaque*.

It is a sign of moral and physical disintegration: the same moral and physical disintegration to which Athalie herself will succumb. For it is clear that mother and daughter are identified, that Jezabel is not simply Jezabel, that she is Athalie too. She has replaced the image, or the illusion, of the proud and independent Athalie which was built up in the first section. The unreal, painted Jezabel is Athalie in her precarious and un-real security. The re-showing of her death points to what is to come.

At the end of the dream there is a horrified 'Grand Dieu!' from Abner. Athalie goes on:

> Dans ce désordre à mes yeux se présente
> Un jeune enfant couvert d'une robe éclatante,
> Tels qu'on voit des Hébreux les prêtres revêtus.
> Sa vue a ranimé mes esprits abattus.
> Mais lorsque revenant de mon trouble funeste,
> J'admirais sa douceur, son air noble et modeste,
> J'ai senti tout à coup un homicide acier,
> Que le traître en mon sein a plongé tout entier.

If the power of the second section is increased by contrast with the first, the third section derives much of its power from contrast with the second. The process reminds me of a cinematic 'mix' or 'dissolve'. The spectacle of the dogs fighting over the mangled flesh and the streams of blood melts away and the figure of an unknown child dressed in 'dazzling white' emerges. It is of the essence of the process that we see both figures at the same time and that the second gradually obliterates the first, which is brought out by Athalie's '*Dans* ce désordre à mes yeux se présente . . .' It is a good illustration of the pervasiveness of the image of rebirth. One order is destroyed; another is reborn from the disorder which follows the collapse of the first order. The dramatic difference between the 'painted' Jezabel and the child in his simple white robe—we shall see later that the reference to the robes of 'Hebrew priests' is of some importance—stands for the difference between order and disorder, innocence and corruption.

I do not think there can be any doubt that the Joas of the dream is in-tended to suggest the Christ-Child. For the process of rebirth that we are witnessing is twofold. Joas stands for the temporary rebirth of a local order. But he is the direct ancestor of the Founder of Christianity whose mission is world-wide rebirth and the mitigation of the disorder caused by the Fall of man.

Athalie is disarmed by his gentleness; then by some sleight of hand she is stabbed by him. This part of the dream is twice repeated. Athalie tries to convince herself that it is the result of some 'sombre vapeur'. She fails. She rushes to the temple of Baal. Then she has the idea of appeasing the God of the Jews. Her account of her arrival in the temple reinforces Zacharie's report and the confusion she causes is brilliantly reflected in the elliptical language:

> J'entre. Le peuple fuit. Le sacrifice cesse.

The climax, or rather the second climax, is reached when she comes face to face with Joas and recognizes him as the child of the dream:

> Le grand prêtre vers moi s'avance avec fureur.
> Pendant qu'il me parlait, ô surprise! ô terreur!
> J'ai vu ce même enfant dont je suis menacée,
> Tel qu'un songe effrayant l'a peint à ma pensée.
> Je l'ai vu: son même air, son même habit de lin,
> Sa démarche, ses yeux, et tous ses traits enfin.
> C'est lui-même. Il marchait à côté du grand prêtre . . .

The passage might be described as an extension of the central image. The dream is being translated into reality. There was a symbolical rebirth in the dream. The dream-child has now become a real person, has been reborn into the real world. It is an intermediate stage. The final stage will be reached when the child undergoes another transformation and becomes king.

The moment her account is finished, Athalie asks Mathan for his advice. In the discussion that follows Abner and Mathan naturally express contradictory views. Abner, the believer, argues against the murder of the child on purely human grounds. Mathan, the apostate priest, at once invokes the wisdom of heaven which is supposed to be a warning against what he later describes as a 'monstre naissant':

> Le ciel nous le fait voir un poignard à la main:
> Le ciel est juste et sage, et ne fait rien en vain.
> Que cherchez-vous de plus?

What strikes us at once is the image of the child with a dagger in his hand. Although the dagger was not actually *seen* in the dream, I do not think that there can be any doubt that Racine deliberately matched the images of the child with a dagger and Athalie, 'un poignard à la main', trying, unsuccessfully, to kill the infant Joas. It suggests that the process has been reversed, that the initiative has gone over to the other side. It also seems to confirm what I said about the dream being translated into reality. The symbolical stabbing is replaced by the sight of the High Priest and

Joas together, lined up, as it were, against Athalie. It is another indication of what is to come. She will naturally not be killed by Joas, but she will be killed on his account and partly as a revenge for the attempted murder.

The immediate effect of the dream is quite different from Mathan's first suggestion. It starts a series of attempts by Athalie to reach a compromise. At her meeting with Joas and Josabet, she tries to persuade Joas to leave the temple and go and live with her in her palace. She is roundly snubbed and leaves in a rage, little knowing that Joas will indeed go and live in the palace, but not with her.

5

A substantial part of Act III is occupied by Mathan's visit to the temple. He has been sent by Athalie to see whether he can succeed where she has failed. He is to tell Josabet that Athalie will leave the Jews in peace and their temple intact provided that they hand over Joas to her.

Mathan is accompanied by his confidant. Nabal chooses this moment to announce that he 'serves neither Baal nor the God of Israel' and is only interested in the reward which has been promised him for participation in the negotiations. His declaration of unbelief prompts Mathan's own confession.

One writer has compared Mathan to Narcisse in *Britannicus* and described him as a stage villain in a religious setting. It has been suggested that his confession, which is at the same time a self-portrait, is overlong and only convincing if we regard the play as a parable rather than tragedy or drama.[14]

These views seem to me to do less than justice to Racine's stagecraft and the variety of interests that he introduces. Comedy does not exclude villainy as we know from *Tartuffe* and *Dom Juan*. Mathan is certainly a villain. It would be going too far to describe him as a comic character like his confidant, but he is surely a brilliantly ironical creation.

It is important to remind ourselves that though *Athalie* is a portrait of an individual, it is also a study of a political situation with far reaching implications. Racine places the tyrant in her proper milieu. One of the most impressive things about the play is the moral deterioration of her entourage and its influence on her policies. It would have been impossible to represent them adequately without Mathan's confession which is an essential factor in the drama. It divides like Athalie's dream into three sections. I shall begin by looking at the first two:

> Ami, peux-tu penser que d'un zèle frivole
> Je me laisse aveugler pour une vaine idole,

> Pour un fragile bois, que malgré mon secours
> Les vers sur son autel consument tous les jours?
> Né ministre du Dieu qu'en ce temple on adore,
> Peut-être que Mathan le servirait encore,
> Si l'amour des grandeurs, la soif de commander
> Avec son joug étroit pouvaient s'accommoder.

Although Mathan describes himself as being 'born a minister of the God whom they worship in this temple', meaning that he was born a Levite, he is a well-known type who is always with us: the man who enters the priesthood not because he has a vocation or, for that matter, any deep religious feeling, but because it appears to offer an easy way of winning a position in the world. When he finds that things are not working out as expected, that the discipline of the priesthood is too tight for him to satisfy his ambitions, which are described lusciously as 'l'amour des grandeurs, la soif de commander', he uses a petty squabble with the High Priest as a pretext to leave the priesthood of God and try the priesthood of Baal. He has no illusions about Baal. His comments, indeed, are more damaging than the thunder of Joad. They are a mixture of flippancy and cynicism as we can see from the tone of these eight lines with the image of the worms eating away the idol and the use of the words 'frivole' qualifying 'zèle', 'vaine idole' and 'fragile bois'. His contempt for Baal gives a retrospective irony to Athalie's apology to him for rushing off to the temple to try to placate the God of Israel after the dream:

> Pontife de Baal, excusez ma faiblesse.

He goes on:

> Qu'est-il besoin, Nabal, qu'à tes yeux je rappelle
> De Joad et de moi la fameuse querelle . . .
> Vaincu par lui, j'entrai dans une autre carrière,
> Et mon âme à la cour s'attacha toute entière,
> J'approchai par degrés de l'oreille des rois,
> Et bientôt en oracle on érigea ma voix.
> J'étudiai leur coeur, je flattai leurs caprices,
> Je leur semai de fleurs le bord des précipices.
> Près de leurs passions rien ne me fut sacré;
> De mesure et de poids je changeais à leur gré.
> Autant que de Joad l'inflexible rudesse
> De leur superbe oreille offensait la mollesse,
> Autant je les charmais par ma dextérité,
> Dérobant à leurs yeux la triste vérité,
> Prêtant à leurs fureurs des couleurs favorables,
> Et prodigue surtout du sang des misérables.

Mathan, as we see, did not go straight over to Baal. He began by ingratiating himself with the ruling class, turned himself into a sycophantic courtier. It was his hold over them, as he explains later, that induced

Athalie to make him high priest of Baal when she adopted the cult. This turned him into another type who was by no means unknown in Racine's day: the priest-courtier.

Subterranean influences undermining the integrity of the ruling class are an important factor in the play. There is a close connection between the image of the dream 'gnawing' away Athalie's peace of mind, the worms 'consuming' the idol and Mathan taking advantage of the moral 'softness' —it is really corruption—of the rulers to lead them astray. His methods of insinuating himself into their confidence are similar to that of the 'worms' and the results are equally disastrous: the sovereign becomes by implication a 'vaine idole'.

We can only appreciate Racine's range to the full if we place the second section of Mathan's confession beside some lines from Joad's warning to Joas on the dangers of absolute power in Act IV:

> Loin du trône nourri, de ce fatal honneur,
> Hélas! vous ignorez le charme empoisonneur.
> De l'absolu pouvoir vous ignorez l'ivresse,
> Et des lâches flatteurs la voix enchanteresse.
> Bientôt ils vous diront que les plus saintes lois,
> Maîtresses du vil peuple, obéissent aux rois . . .
> Ainsi de piège en piège, d'abime en abime,
> Corrompant de vos moeurs l'aimable pureté,
> Ils vous feront enfin haïr la vérité,
> Vous peindront la vertu sous une affreuse image.
> Hélas! ils ont des rois égaré le plus sage.

It strikes us at once as a remarkably bold speech; an outright condemnation of Athalie and her entourage and to later generations at all events a very outspoken criticism of the policies of Louis XIV. On the last point there must be certain reservations. It cannot be assumed that Racine was deliberately attacking his king. We know, however, from other plays that he was decidedly hostile to tyranny. We also know from other plays, particularly from Phèdre's final onslaught on Oenone, which drives her to her death, that Racine was bitterly antipathetic to sycophantic advisers and confidants who led their masters and mistresses astray.[15] It seems a fair assumption therefore that the creative writer's mind, as I suggested earlier, is unconsciously shaped by personal experience and that Racine is here giving expression to dangers of which he had become aware while living under an absolute monarchy.

Whatever Racine's intention, Joad's speech is admirably 'democratic' and a brilliantly concise account of the way in which sovereignty degenerates into dictatorship. It is wholly constructive because it leads to Joas taking the solemn oath to put God first and accept him as 'judge'. Next, we observe that it is an almost point by point commentary on Mathan's speech. Mathan's 'flattai leurs caprices', 'semai de fleurs le bord des

précipices', 'changeais à leur gré', 'charmais par ma dextérité', 'dérobant
. . . la triste vérité', 'prêtant à leurs fureurs des couleurs favorables' are
answered by Joad's 'charme empoisonneur', 'des lâches flatteurs la voix
enchanteresse', 'les plus saintes lois . . . obéissant aux rois', 'de piège en
piège, d'abîme en abîme', 'haïr la vérité', 'peindront la vertu sous une
affreuse image' as well as 'corrompant' and 'égaré'.

The effect of Joad's words are evident. The flowers strewn on the edges
of precipices, the 'couleurs favorables' which hide uncomfortable truths
are cleared away; the full rottenness of the situation is exposed and
judged.

We must look now at the closing lines of Mathan's confession:

> Par là je me rendis terrible à mon rival,
> Je ceignis la tiare, et marchai son égal.
> Toutefois, je l'avoue, en ce comble de gloire,
> Du Dieu que j'ai quitté l'importune mémoire
> Jette encore en mon âme un reste de terreur;
> Et c'est ce qui redouble et nourrit ma fureur.
> Heureux si sur son temple achevant ma vengeance,
> Je puis convaincre enfin sa haine d'impuissance,
> Et parmi les débris, le ravage et les morts,
> A force d'attentats perdre tous mes remords!

Mathan's description of what might be called his religious position
looks back to Abner's statement in the opening scene. 'L'importune
mémoire', echoing Abner's 'Ce temple l'importune', betrays the profound
uneasiness which has haunted him ever since his apostacy and undermines
the 'comble de gloire' which becomes something purely external that conceals his real state of mind. There is genuine fear in the 'reste de terreur'.
It is fear, too, which inspires the rage of the last five lines. 'Convaincre
enfin sa haine d'impuissance' can only mean 'convince myself that the
God of Israel does not exist'. His anxiety to see the temple smashed and
the reference to 'les débris, le ravage et les morts' looks forward, ironically,
to his own fate and the fate of the temple of Baal. Mathan's fears underline the parallel between the waverers on both sides. If Abner and Josabet
are afraid that God will not intervene to save the Jews, Mathan is secretly
afraid that he will and there is nothing he can do to put an end to his fears.

Mathan emerges therefore as an agnostic who cannot rid himself of the
last vestiges of belief. In this he resembles his mistress. Athalie and her
minion are both apostates and agnostics. They have abandoned one
system to beliefs because it was an obstacle to their ambitions. They have
set up in its place an alien system in which they do not really believe because they think that a religion of some sort may help them to consolidate
their position by rooting out the old religion without itself introducing
fresh obstacles. For the one essential thing about the new religion, as we

can see from the earlier parts of Mathan's speech, is that it shall never be a challenge to the royal authority, that on the contrary it will not merely countenance, but will lend an appearance of morality to the ruler's most outrageous actions.

Although Mathan's mission ends with his being hounded out of the temple by the furious High Priest, the effect of his visit on Josabet demonstrates the insidious way in which his influence works. Her doubts suddenly become more acute. She shocks her husband by telling him in language which recalls that of the inhabitants of the palaces in the secular plays that she knows of a secret way of escape from the temple—'une secrète issue' —and begs him to let her use it in order to save Joas. She gets short shrift:

> Quels timides conseils m'osez-vous suggérer?

The act ends with the High Priest's celebrated prophecy. Peter France has observed that 'the introduction of music and song into a scene of spoken dialogue' helps to pick out the scene as 'the culminating point of the play'.[16] The prophecy is remarkable in several ways. It relates only to events taking place after the end of the play. They are, however, essential for a proper interpretation of it as a whole and, as we shall see, they give it a range and finality which are not to be found in any other play.[17] It is closely integrated into the play and has certain affinities with Athalie's dream. It would be an exaggeration to describe Athalie as being in a trance during the re-enactment of the dream, but she is clearly in the grip of forces, whether supernatural or psychological, which have a trance-like effect. The prophecy is delivered by Joad in what is plainly a trance. It seems highly unlikely that he knows what he is saying or that it is understood by his hearers; it is equally unlikely that once he has finished either he or his followers have any recollection of what was said or what 'happened' to him.[18] Athalie's dream, as we know, is also prophetic. She does not forget it for a moment, but though it is a sign of psychological defeat she maintains her stand against Joad and until the last moment seems confident of reaching a settlement or, failing that, of crushing the Jews by force of arms. Joad of course is full of confidence, but he has no idea that what appears to be a complete triumph—the crowning of Joas and the execution of Athalie—is a prelude to another disaster, another eclipse of the worship of God and the Chosen People.

The effectiveness of the prophecy depends not only on the introduction of music and singing into a scene of spoken dialogue, but also on the variations in both versification and language. It strikes a lyric note which perhaps recalls the *stances* in *Polyeucte* and in Racine's first play, but much more obviously the language of the chorus. It is divided into two sections.

The first deals with the impending disasters and the second with ultimate triumph, or what appears to be ultimate triumph. We shall find that the theme is death and rebirth, corresponding to the images of fertility and decay discussed earlier.

The three opening lines, beginning with the words 'Cieux, écoutez ma voix', serve as an introduction to the prophecy as a whole. The first part consists of twelve alexandrines, two decasyllabics and one six-syllable line; the second part consists of nine alexandrines, six octosyllabics and one decasyllabic.

The first part opens with six alexandrines which place the disasters vividly before us:

> Comment en un plomb vil l'or pur s'est-il changé?
> Quel est dans le lieu saint ce pontife égorgé?
> Pleure, Jérusalem, pleure, cité perfide,
> Des prophètes divins malheureuse homicide.
> De son amour pour toi ton Dieu s'est dépouillé.
> Ton encens à ses yeux est un encens souillé.

The splendid opening line, with the arresting contrast between 'gold' and 'squalid lead', strikes a note of surprise. In spite of all that God has done for them, the Chosen People have gone wrong again with the high priest being slaughtered in the temple on the instructions of the king— the king who was to have been the saviour of his people. There is a change after the sixth line and Racine uses a single decasyllabic line to describe the people being led into captivity:

> Où menez-vous ces enfants et ces femmes?

There follow three more alexandrines, all with the same rhyme, describing God's vengeance on the Holy City:

> Le Seigneur a détruit la reine des cités.
> Ses prêtres sont captifs, ses rois sont rejetés.
> Dieu ne veut plus qu'on vienne à ses solennités.

The destruction is reflected in the sharp é-s which link it to 'changé/ égorgé'; it is the result of the change from good to evil, from 'gold' to 'lead'.[19]

The next line, an alexandrine, looks like a description of a final holocaust and rhymes with the decasyllabic line:

> Temple, renverse-toi; cèdres, jetez des flammes.

It closes with a dirge: another decasyllabic line, two rhyming alexandrines, and fades away in a six-syllable line:

> Jérusalem, objet de ma douleur,
> Quelle main en un jour t'a ravi tous tes charmes?
> Qui changera mes yeux en deux sources de larmes
>   Pour pleurer ton malheur?

The second part is preceded by more music and a couple of lines by the chorus. There is a sudden change from dirge and lamentation to an ecstatic note: it is the vision of rebirth:

> Quelle Jérusalem nouvelle
> Sort du fond du désert brillante de clartés,
> Et porte sur le front une marque immortelle?
> Peuples de la terre, chantez.
> Jérusalem renaît plus charmante et plus belle.
> D'où lui viennent de tous côtés
> Ces enfants qu'en son sein elle n'a point portés?
> Lève, Jérusalem, lève ta tête altière.
> Regarde tous ces rois de ta gloire étonnés.
> Les rois des nations, devant toi prosternés,
> De tes pieds baisent la poussière;
> Les peuples à l'envi marchent à ta lumière.
> Heureux qui pour Sion d'une sainte ferveur
> Sentira son âme embrasée!
> Cieux, répandez votre rosée,
> Et que la terre enfante son Sauveur.

The images of destruction and squalor vanish and are replaced by positive images with an aura of splendour: 'égorgé', 'perfide', 'homicide', 'dépouillé', 'souillé' and 'détruit' by 'clartés', 'lumière', 'ferveur', 'embrasée' and 'rosée'. In the first two lines a new order—'Jérusalem nouvelle' is of course the Christian Church—emerges from the ruins of the old order, reminding us of the image of Joas emerging from 'disorder' in the third section of the dream. Instead of kings being 'rejected' and the people marched away into captivity, the process is reversed. We see the kings of the earth converging on the Holy City and prostrating themselves before God with the people surging towards the 'light' which stands for the conversion of the Gentiles to Christianity. There is a change from 'pleure', 'pleurer' and 'larmes' to a joyful 'chantez'.

> Pleure, Jérusalem, pleure, cité perfide,

is answered by

> Lève, Jérusalem, lève ta tête altière.

Since *Athalie* is a play about rebirth, we should notice specially the line describing the destruction of Jerusalem,

> Le Seigneur a détruit la reine des cités,

and the matching line in the second part:

> Jérusalem *renaît* plus charmante et plus belle.

It will also be apparent that the words expressing religious fervour and illumination lead up to three words which are deliberately placed last: 'enfante son Sauveur'.

The first part of the prophecy describes what will in effect be a *revanche*. Athalie's curse in Act V will come home to roost: the violence inflicted on her will be repeated by the violence which overtakes the Chosen People. Equally, the note of triumph on which the play ends will be repeated when the 'new Jerusalem' emerges from the 'desert' of darkness and destruction, and David's line gives birth to the divine Saviour who is compared by implication to the fallible human saviour who fails to save— King Joas.

There is one point which should not be overlooked. For all their beauty, there is a hint of fragility, possibly even of 'repository' art, in the images of rebirth. This no doubt looks forward to the vicissitudes of the Christian Church, but we shall find that it is also a reflection of something personal in the attitude of the dramatist.

Finally, it is worth comparing the way in which the imagery changes in the prophecy and in Athalie's dream. In the prophecy, as we have seen, it is a straight change from images of destruction to images of rebirth. In the first two sections of the dream there is a change from positive images— images of apparent stability—to images of destruction and death. The last section is composed largely of images of rebirth, but they are a sign of disaster for Athalie.

6

The first three acts alternate between past, present and future, particularly in Abner's opening speech, Athalie's dream, Mathan's account of his career and Joad's prophecy. In the last two all the characters concentrate on the immediate present, on action: the proclamation of Joas as king, the assembling of the forces of resistance and the destruction of the tyrant. Joad becomes the commander-in-chief whose task it is to rally his troops. He presents the Levites with their king and proceeds to address them in terms which are even more ruthless than any of his earlier pronouncements.

That ruthlessness is evident is the repeated use of the word 'blood' in lines like these:

> Dieu sur ses ennemis répandra sa terreur.
> Dans l'infidèle sang baignez-vous sans horreur.

He goes on to remind them of the way in which they acquired their present privileged position. Their ancestors made their name by slaughtering their nearest and dearest relations who had gone over to idolatry during the captivity in Egypt:

> De leurs plus chers parents saintement homicides . . .

'Homicide' is a word which occurs on a number of occasions in the play, usually to describe or denounce the activities of Athalie. 'Sainte- ment homicides' is a striking example of Racine's oxymoron.[20]

The slaughter of the Levites' near relations is extolled as a 'noble exploit'.[21] They are told that on the present occasion they must not spare any Israelites who have gone over to Baal.

This must be seen in relation to the lines in which Joad presents the king to the Levites and his homilies to both on the 'law(s)':

> Roi, voilà vos vengeurs contre vos ennemis.
> Prêtres, voilà le roi que je vous ai promis.

There is a conjunction here of king and priests which is important for what follows.

In the homilies 'roi(s)' and 'loi(s)' are made to rhyme on three separate occasions. This brings us to one of the great problems of Racine's age. The conjunction of 'priests' and 'king' leads to the conjunction of what was to become known as 'throne' and 'altar'. The conflict in *Athalie* springs from the separation of sacred and secular or 'throne' and 'altar'. The danger lies in the subjection of religion to the secular power. It is overcome for a time by the union of the two in Joas. The only way of achieving a proper balance and running state and people in the right way is for the king to set an example by rejecting flatterers and submitting himself to the strict law of God. The clergy's job is to help him.

Without realizing what she was doing, by trying first to inveigle Joas into exchanging the temple for the palace, then to persuade Joad and Josabet to hand him over to her, Athalie was working for a separation of 'throne' and 'altar' and the subjection of the sacred to the secular. That was my reason for emphasizing Athalie's reference to the robes of 'Hebrew priests' which was followed later by the mention of Joas's 'habit de lin'. The fact of the matter is that he was a sort of 'altar-boy' and looked like an embryo priest when Athalie first met him.

The opening scene of Act V serves as a brief prologue to what is about to happen. Zacharie provides his sister with up-to-the-minute news about the military situation and invokes the frightening picture of Athalie:

> Cependant Athalie, un poignard à la main,
> Rit des faibles remparts de nos portes d'airain.
> Pour les rompre, elle attend les fatales machines . . .

This appears to be a deliberate repetition of the public image of Athalie. It concentrates our attention on Athalie as she will appear when she makes her final entry in Scene 5. In spite of her private anguish, she is putting a brave face on things again and is leading her troops with the fearful dagger clutched in her hand.

Joad's role is now a triple one: he is High Priest, commander-in-chief and in this act a sort of impresario who exploits to the full the dramatic possibilities of the situation. Abner has been imprisoned by Athalie who has released him so that he can repeat Mathan's offer: peace on condition that Joad hands over Joas and the mythical 'treasure of David'. When it comes to tricks nobody can compete with the High Priest. His reply to Abner is an incredible piece of cunning. He deliberately confuses Joas and the non-existent *material* treasure in order to inveigle Athalie into his 'trap':

> Il est vrai, de David un trésor est resté ...
> Que mes soins vigilants cachaient à la lumière.
> Mais puisqu'à votre reine il faut le découvrir,
> Je vais la contenter, nos portes vont s'ouvrir.

Abner departs to carry out his mission. The bloodthirsty Joad cries out gloatingly:

> Grand Dieu, voici ton heure, on t'amène ta proie.

'Proie' is used occasionally in the secular plays in a baldly sexual sense with the aggressor aching to get his 'victim'. Here Joad becomes an aggressor aching to get at the political enemy and the sinner, to order his minions to lead the 'prey' off to execution—another unlovely 'blood' sacrifice to the Lord which reminds us of Zacharie's description in Act II of his father offering to God:

> entre *ses mains sanglantes*
> Des victimes de paix les entrailles fumantes.

Athalie's own performance in the last act has won her a good deal of sympathy from the critics. The moment she appears, we see that outwardly she is the Athalie whom her followers admire and her enemies fear. Her opening words are a violent attack on the High Priest:

> Te voilà, séducteur,
> De ligues, de complots pernicieux auteur,
> Qui dans le trouble seul a mis tes espérances,
> Éternel ennemi des suprêmes puissances.
> En l'appui de ton Dieu tu t'étais reposé.
> De ton espoir frivole est-tu désabusé?
> Il laisse en mon pouvoir et son temple et ta vie.
> Je devrais sur l'autel, où ta main sacrifie,
> Te ... Mais du prix qu'on m'offre il faut me contenter.
> Ce que tu as promis, songe à l'exécuter.

It is Racine's irony at its best—and its cruellest. The dream has done its work. Her offer of a compromise peace was genuine, but owing to Joad's trickery it is leading to her downfall and death.

All the rest of the tricks are Joad's too. The drawing of the curtain hiding Joas—the real 'treasure of David'—the invitation to Athalie to recognize him from the wound inflicted by her dagger, the spectacle of

Abner throwing himself at the feet of his lawful sovereign are a splendid piece of showmanship and extremely effective dramatically.

We see the other Athalie. Her call to her soldiers to rescue her from Joad's trap is answered by Joad's priest-warriors swarming from their hiding places and Joad's triumphant

> Tes yeux cherchent en vain, tu ne peux échapper.

Events move fast. Another cry from Athalie to her soldiers is answered by the arrival of Ismaël with the news that God has scattered her army, that the Jews, or most of them, have declared for Joas and that the attack by the people on the temple of Baal has begun. He ends with the staccato

> Mathan est égorgé.

This produces Athalie's celebrated last speech beginning,

> Dieu des Juifs, tu l'emportes!

Admission of defeat is underlined in the middle of the passage by the superb

> Impitoyable Dieu, toi seul as tout conduit.

This may be the recognition of the existence of an all-powerful God, but Athalie maintains an attitude of defiance. The passage closes with the curse which will be tragically fulfilled, as we know from Joad's own prophecy:

> Qu'il règne donc ce fils, ton soin et ton ouvrage . . .
>   . . . j'espère
> Qu'indocile à ton joug, fatigué de ta loi,
> Fidèle au sang d'Achab, qu'il a reçu de moi,
> Conforme à son aïeul, à son père semblable,
> On verra de David l'héritier détestable
> Abolir tes honneurs, profaner ton autel,
> Et venger Athalie, Achab et Jézabel.

The linking of Athalie's curse and Joad's prophecy is an impressive example of the way in which in this, as in the secular plays, Racine always ties up all the threads at the end of his tragedies. The process extends in *Athalie*, as it does in *Andromaque*, to the language used. Athalie's curse is a form of prophecy. The words, 'indocile à ton joug', 'fatigué de ta loi', 'profaner ton autel' are a precise description of what will happen.

At Joad's command she is marched out of the temple by his men. In a few moments a Levite appears to announce that justice has been done. Joad, now the priest again, utters a brief epilogue:

> Par cette fin terrible, et due à ses forfaits,
> Apprenez, roi des Juifs, et n'oubliez jamais
> Que les rois dans le ciel ont un juge sévère,
> L'innocence un vengeur, et l'orphelin un père.

Apart from the chorus and Joas's meeting with Athalie, the last three words are the only reference in the play to a loving God. They seem pale beside the 'juge sévère' and 'l'innocence un vengeur' which are more accurate descriptions of the God of this savage play.

Racine has been criticized for not bringing the chorus back at the end of Act V. We may be sure that this was deliberate, that he felt in the circumstances that the gruff, sober ending was preferable to the long musical ending of *Esther*.

7

I think it will be agreed that even if it does not happen to be our favourite play, *Athalie* possesses a greater range than any of the other plays and illustrates better than any of them what I have called the relevance of Racine. I make no excuse for emphasizing that the three principal themes, which are superbly interwoven, are perennial and their implications multiple. The religious-political conflict is the unending conflict between the Church and the world, between the anti-religious dictator and the church in a particular country or even the political dictator in conflict with a liberal minority where the issues may not be specifically religious. 'Rebirth' means the religious 'revivals' which come and go, periods remarkable for their ardent and widespread devotion among a section of the population alternating with periods of religious decline which is what we see and what is foretold in *Athalie*. In spite of changes in the setting, the different kinds and degrees of belief remain—a point brought home to us by *A Burnt-out Case*.

It follows from this that we should not be misled by the apparent triumph of the ending of *Athalie* or overlook the importance that Racine personally attached to Joad's prophecy. Racine does not offer a panacea or a facile solution of a major problem. In this play he looks back a trifle wistfully to a time when he imagined that a stable order was an established fact. He believes that the order has been preserved in a fragmentary condition by one section of the community and considers the means of extending it to the rest of society. He comes to the conclusion that the one solution, the only guarantee of 'law', lies in the union of throne and altar with the altar acting as a 'brake'—'frein' is an important word in the Racinian vocabulary—on the absolute power against which we are warned in the play. But though he was writing at a time when Louis XIV and his court had become pious, it is evident that he had very little hope of the union coming about or very little confidence in its efficacity if it did. He suffered after all from the same doubts as Abner and they are reflected, as we have seen, in the close of the prophecy. The Saviour had come, but he had not put an end to the difficulties; the tension between Port-Royal and the throne was there to demonstrate it. For this reason the vision which informs the great religious play is as pessimistic as the vision which informs the secular plays. Its pessimism has been amply justified. We may think that the bad relations between Port-Royal and the throne were a very minor affair. No doubt this was so, but they were a pointer to what was to come: the virtual disappearance of thrones in east and west and their replacement by dictators whose 'implacability' makes Athalie's appear almost mild by comparison and the replacement of the grotesque Baal by far more sinister substitutes for religious faith.

It remains to take a final look at the style. In his essay on *Athalie* the Abbé Bremond drew a distinction between what he called the *cantique* of the religious and the *chant* of the secular plays, suggesting that the religious plays belong to a different genre and are written in a different language from the secular plays. He appeared to regard the genre as inferior and clearly preferred the *chant* of the secular plays.[22] One of the most striking things about *Athalie* is the variety of its style or what I am inclined to call unity in diversity. Athalie's own speeches are unquestionably *chant* and underline her affinities with the protagonists of the secular plays. They differ from the more religious speeches of some of the other characters which ranked as *cantique* for Bremond. But when we recall the speeches of Joad in his capacity as commander-in-chief of the Levites, we see that Athalie does not have the monopoly of *chant*. I have mentioned Athalie's meeting with Joas in Act II, but have not quoted from it. We shall see later that it is of particular interest in demonstrating the adaptability of the alexandrine which reproduces brilliantly the tone of a conversation between grandmother and infant grandson.[23]

With the exception of the chorus, the prophecy is the most obvious example of *cantique* in the whole play. We saw that the way in which Racine introduced it into the body of the play is one of the more striking stylistic innovations and its virtuosity has been examined in some detail. It is unnecessary to comment at length on the chorus itself, but comparisons with *Esther* are not without interest. Its functions are similar. It offsets to some extent the brutality of the play, contains fine and moving poetry and pertinent observations on the development of the action. It might be argued that in one respect it is more functional than the chorus is *Esther*; it is after all the temple chorus which resembles a modern church choir and not simply a chorus composed of the companions of one of the principal characters. On the other hand, it seems less closely integrated into the play, as we can see from its omission from the final act. It also occupies a good deal less space, presumably because Racine was determined to ensure that it did not dominate the drama as it does in *Esther*.

It is present in 15 out of 35 scenes compared with 13 out of 22 in *Esther*. *Athalie* is 1,816 lines in length of which 260 are by the chorus. This is slightly under 15 per cent of the text. The performance on record lasts approximately 2 hours 18 minutes of which 43 minutes are occupied by choral singing and recitation, representing 31 per cent of the total performance time. It will be remembered that the corresponding figures for *Esther* are 31 per cent of the text and 40 per cent of the performance time. The reasons, or one of them, for the gap between text and performance time were explained in the chapter on *Esther* and naturally apply to *Athalie*.

NOTES

[1] Racine summarises the Bible story in his preface because he considered it important for an understanding of the play. He also wanted to defend minor divergences on his part.

[2] Racine argues in his preface that the conflict took place in the eighth year of Athalia's reign and that Joas was nine or ten when he was proclaimed king.

[3] *Port-Royal* (Pléiade Edition), III, p. 589.

[4] *Poésie de Racine*, p. 329.

[5] *Victor-Marie, Comte Hugo*, p. 155.

[6] The prophecy and the dream were both inventions of Racine's.

[7] When pushed to its logical conclusion, as it is by Raymond Picard, Sainte-Beuve's view can detract considerably from the greatness of the play. For M. Picard the divine presence turns the characters into 'God's puppets' whose psychology is dominated by a 'few very simple traits' and who possess a 'sort of sculptural beauty' without any real depth (*O.C.*, I, p. 887).

[8] The argument has been pushed a long way. Athalie has been identified with William III, her Tyrian troops—another of Racine's inventions—with William's Dutchmen, Joad with Bancroft, the Archbishop of Canterbury who organized resistance against William, Mathan with William's Protestant adviser, Burnet, and Joas with the little Prince of Wales.

[9] Port-Royal was closed by royal decree in 1705 and razed to the ground in 1710.

[10] Exodus, XXXII, 22.

[11] Racine associates the two feasts in his preface and appears to have been the first person to do so.

[12] Exodus, XXXIV, 26.

[13] The exception is Andromaque with 228 lines. Athalie's role is also a good deal shorter than Esther's which even in a play of greatly reduced length has 312 lines, and is less than half the length of Joad's 496 lines.

[14] P. France in his edition of *Athalie*, 1966, p. 169.

[15] We recall his description of Narcisse in the preface to *Britannicus* as 'cette peste de cour'.

[16] In his edition of *Athalie*, p. 173.

[17] Some of the secular plays end on what can only be called a mark of interrogation. It is the result of changes made by Racine in legend or history which shows that his real interest was the stage production as a dramatic experience. The obvious examples are *Andromaque* and *Mithridate*. We can hardly help wondering what will become of the Trojan woman who has been crowned Queen of Epirus or her son who is King of Troy.

The same question arises over the prospects of Xipharès and his divided country in the war against Rome.

[18] This has given rise to a good deal of discussion. It is summarized by Mrs. Annie Barnes in 'La Prophétie de Joad' in *The French Mind*, 1952, pp. 90–108.

[19] According to the Bible narrative, Joas was a good king for thirty years, then went to pieces like Jehu.

[20] Other, less striking examples are 'un encens idolâtre', 'un téméraire encens' and 'heureux larcin'.

[21] In fairness, it must be pointed out that Moses told them that they had 'earned the Lord's blessing' (Exodus, XXXII, 29).

[22] See '*Athalie* poème religieux' in *Racine et Valéry*, 1930, pp. 209–230.

[23] See pp. 346–7 below.

VERSIFICATION AND LANGUAGE

Racine n'était qu'un très bel esprit à qui j'ai appris à
faire difficilement des vers faciles.

BOILEAU

Il rase la prose, mais avec des ailes.

ANON.

Je ne louerai pas, tout le monde l'a fait, cette forme
qui accomplit la synthèse de l'art et du naturel, semble
ignorer ses chaînes prosodiques dont elle se crée, au
contraire, un ornement, et comme une draperie sur le
nu de la pensée.

PAUL VALÉRY

CHAPTER 12

VERSIFICATION AND LANGUAGE

I. Versification

General

'Why,' asked a Cambridge lecturer in English literature, 'did Shakespeare use blank verse?' 'He used it,' he replied, 'because it was easy to write.' Although it was a rhetorical question intended to impress a first year audience, there is an element of truth in the answer. One of the main problems that faced the authors of poetic drama in the seventeenth century was to find a way of combining the flexibility necessary for the spoken word with the dignity proper to tragedy. It was not confined to one country. It was common to English, French and Spanish dramatists.

Shakespeare's blank verse is a wonderfully supple instrument which is capable of expressing in dramatic form the most prosaic and the most exalted sentiments. It was 'easy to write' in two senses. It was extremely close to the spoken word and the dramatist was not hampered by a collection of rigid rules which affected writers in other countries. It does not matter if lines sometimes have a syllable too many or too few, it does not matter if a line breaks off in the middle and is left unfinished. If the dramatist grew tired or found himself in a situation in which he needed greater freedom or greater variation than that offered by blank verse, there was nothing to prevent him from changing to prose.

The Spanish dramatists did not leave their lines unfinished or change over to prose. They had another method of avoiding monotony. It was their metrical variety or what is known as 'polymetric'. Their use of it is highly professional. 'The criterion which determines the choice of this or that metre,' said Francisco Ruiz Ramón in his admirable history of the Spanish theatre, 'is essentially dramatic.'[1] In *El castigo sin venganza* Lope employs ten different metres which reflect perfectly the changing moods of the tragedy.

One of the greatest difficulties of French classical tragedy has always been its versification. There have been two main criticisms of the alexandrine. The first came from Ronsard in the sixteenth century. 'Les alexandrins', he wrote, 'sentent trop la prose très facile, sont trop énervés et flasques . . .'[2] The other is its supposed inflexibility. Foreigners have long concentrated on the second of these criticisms. Compared with English blank verse or even the Spanish metres, the French alexandrine appears to the untutored Englishman to be frigid, stilted and unwieldy: a rigid metal frame imposed on the dramatist's language. There are no unfinished

335

lines and no prose. Metrical variety in a formal sense is extremely rare. Racine used *stances*—a borrowing from Corneille—in his first play, but except for the letters in *Bajazet* and the prophecy in *Iphigénie*, there are no other metrical variations until we come to the choruses in the last two plays and Joad's prophecy in *Athalie*. The only form of external variety is his practice of breaking up the alexandrine in the more violent exchanges between the characters and dividing a single line among as many as three or, in one instance, four speakers.

Nobody denies that French seventeenth-century dramatists were expected to conform to some very strict and often highly artificial rules, but before going on to examine the methods they employed to reduce their nuisance value, two things need to be said. In the hands of the masters the formalism of the alexandrine, which can be very wearisome in the work of minor dramatists, is a positive advantage. In the first place it possesses what must be described as a moral value. It creates in a subtle way a standard by which the actions of the characters are seen in perspective and judged. In the next place it reflects the shape of the society which brought it to perfection. It was the product of a society which though outwardly stable was inwardly rent by many kinds of conflict. It is precisely the contrast between the regularity of the medium and the violence of the emotions simmering just below the surface and constantly erupting that makes Racine's handling of his instrument peculiarly effective.

Count of the Syllables

The origins of French versification are not without interest. It developed like the French language from Latin and is said to have been a combination of the formal Latin hexameter and Latin popular poetry.[3] The alexandrine made its first appearance in an eleventh-century poem, *Le Pèlerinage de Charlemagne*. The name, however, came from a very long twelfth-century epic called the *Roman d'Alexandre*, but was not actually used to describe the twelve-syllable line until the fifteenth century.

For the dramatists the rule became not merely the twelve-syllable line in rhyming couplets, but couplets which ended alternately with masculine and feminine rhymes. A masculine rhyme is an end-rhyme which can be heard either because it is a consonant or an accented syllable. A feminine rhyme is an end-rhyme with a mute *e*. The rule is to some extent theoretical. If a line ends with a past participle in the masculine gender like 'pensé' it is a masculine rhyme, but if a participle is feminine or the substantive 'pensée' is used it is classified as a feminine rhyme because the final *e* is mute. Equally, if it ends with the third person plural of a verb, which might be 'demandent', it is feminine because a final unaccented *e* is mute.

The count of the syllables is strict, but there is one curious artifice. The mute *e* always counts as a syllable except when it comes at the end of a line in a feminine rhyme or when its pronunciation would create a hiatus, as it would in this line from *Phèdre*:

Tout vous livr(e) à l'envi le rebell(e) Hippolyte.

It is an artifice because whatever the theorists may think, the *e* is only heard on the stage today (apart from the choruses in the last two plays) in a few rare instances when the performer is anxious to give special emphasis to a particular word. It is common therefore to find lines with two mute *e*-s, both of which count as syllables and neither of which is actually pronounced. There are also plenty of lines with three mute *e*-s, reducing the alexandrine to a nine-syllable line, or what Souriau calls a 'véritable faute de quantité', which the artist might, but only might, contrive to extend by dwelling on some of the other pauses.[4] *Phèdre* again provides an example:

La Rein*e* touch*e* presque à son term*e* fatal.

The strictness of the count led to other devices. For one thing it meant padding which may or may not appear obvious. We continually come across phrases like 'cher Osmin', 'cher Théramène' or 'cher Abner', and the repeated use of words like 'enfin' or 'ici'. There are also circumlocutions. Instead of 'Titus vient', or something of the kind, we are told: 'Titus porte vers nous ses pas'. When Oenone wants to remind her mistress that she hasn't slept for three nights, she says:

Les ombres par trois fois ont obscurci les cieux
Depuis que le sommeil n'est entré dans vos yeux.

It is one thing to find an extra syllable or two in order to complete a line; there is nothing to be done when one needs more space. It is impossible to read Hermione's ecstatic reference to Pyrrhus's feats in the Trojan War,

T'es-tu fait raconter
Le nombre des exploits ... Mais qui les peut compter?

without feeling that the sense really calls for 'le nombre de *ses* exploits'.

Rhyme

Souriau remarked that 'the great poets are nearly always mediocre rhymers and Racine is not an exception to the rule'.[5] He was followed many years later by J. G. Cahen who said that 'far from enriching his vocabulary, the necessity of rhyming was rather the cause of impoverishment'.[6] There are not only rhymes which are inclined to become wearisome owing to their frequency or banality like 'gloire/victoire'; there are many cases of false rhymes like 'princesse/Grèce', or rhymes which are merely visual like 'Pyrrh*us*/confus' or 'Josab*et*/secret' where the first *s* and the first *t* are pronounced and the seconds are not. In a celebrated line, Racine actually distorts a verb in order to produce a visual rhyme:

> Vaincu, chargé de fers, de regrets consumé,
> Brûlé de plus de feux que je n'en allum*é* . . .

There are two reservations to be made. I have confined myself here to commenting on one or two of the weaknesses of Racine's rhymes, but we have seen in discussing individual plays that there are occasions when his rhymes are remarkably effective. The other reservation is that though we can hardly fail to be struck by these artifices when studying the text of a play, they are far less noticeable on the stage, which is what really matters.

The Caesura

We come next to the much more complicated question of caesuras and pauses.

> It was [writes Grammont of the alexandrine] a *syllabic* form of verse composed of two members or hemistiches. In the beginning these two members were sharply divided from one another by a pause or caesura. But when the caesura had become, as a result of a series of weakenings, a mere *coupe*, the line could include other *coupes* which were just as sharp as the caesura and other accents which were just as powerful as, and sometimes even more powerful than, the one at the sixth syllable.[7]

It is a concise summary which calls for some elaboration. There is a firm rule that every line must be divisible at the sixth syllable with a less important pause, sometimes called a second caesura, at the end of the line. The division must come at the end of a word: no word can begin in the first hemistich and end in the second, which means that no word of more than six syllables could ever have been used in an orthodox alexandrine.[8]

There are a number of minor or supporting rules. The central caesura, or *césure médiane*, must not separate the article from its substantive, a preposition from the word or phrase that it governs or, except in special circumstances, an adjective from its noun.

Grammont speaks of the gradual relaxation of the rule of the central caesura. I want to take a closer look now at the methods used by Racine to bring this about. I deliberately described the alexandrine as being divisible at the sixth syllable or the hemistich. The fact that it is *divisible* does not mean that it is invariably *divided* at the hemistich. We have seen that in Racine the force of the caesura varies considerably and that in some cases it is virtually eliminated without any indication that a particular line ceases to be divisible. While the rule about divisibility is basic, dramatists enjoyed a good deal of freedom inside the hemistich, and the additional or alternative pauses which they introduced played an important part in the provision of variety and the avoidance of monotony.

Although we are concerned for the moment with the loosening of the rules, it would be a mistake to overlook the value of the strong central caesura. Racine was equally good at taking advantage of the rules when it suited his purpose and modifying them when it did not. We can summarize the position by saying that he employs a succession of strong caesuras in *récits* describing the march of events—the '*récit* de Théramène' is an excellent example—in the more violent *tirades*, in confessions and in declarations of love in order to increase the drive of the alexandrine. He does the same in individual or isolated lines in order to give the maximum effect to categoric statements, commands and decisions, or to fix the attention of other characters and the audience on a particular issue which is to be the subject of a discourse by a protagonist, which is what happens when Mithridate outlines his plan for the invasion of Rome to his sons. The effect is usually achieved by a combination of syntax and punctuation.[9] An obvious example is the opening of *Bérénice*:

> Arrêtons un moment. La pompe de ces lieux,
> Je le vois bien, Arsace, est nouvelle à tes yeux.

The first short sentence mimics the action of the characters. They march on to the stage and come to a halt. Antiochus proceeds to describe the essential features of their surroundings which, as we have seen, are of great importance in the play.

Racine uses the same method to attenuate or to efface the central caesura and to put the main emphasis in another place. We remember that the one inescapable fact which dominates Mithridate's mind is his defeat in the night battle. He therefore begins his account of it to Arbate with the staccato

> Je suis vaincu. Pompée a saisi l'avantage . . .

Titus's contrast between 'living' and 'reigning' is achieved by a mere comma:

> Mais il ne s'agit plus de vivre, il faut régner.

In both lines the alexandrine remains 'divisible', but the entire effect depends on the fact that it is not divided at the hemistich.

When Phèdre says to Hippolyte

> J'aime. Ne pense pas qu'au moment que je t'aime,
> Innocente à mes yeux je m'approuve moi-même,

the strong pause after the second syllable places the emphasis on the fact of illicit love and prepares the way for the hysterical apologia which follows: a stream of lines delivered at great speed with pauses reduced to a minimum.

On the face of it, we may feel that it does not greatly matter whether the main pause comes after the second, fourth or eighth syllable. In fact, the examples I have given do a very important thing. In addition to the avoidance of monotony, they give the alexandrine a sort of naturalness by bringing it closer to everyday speech.

It is generally accepted that the standard pattern of the alexandrine is the line divided into four sections by a central caesura and pauses after the third and ninth syllables. It is certainly the commonest form and once again it is not unusual for the divisions to be emphasized by the punctuation:

> Je le vis, / je rougis, // je pâlis / à sa vue...

> Mais tout dort, / et l'armée, // et les vents, / et Neptune.

> Je vous vois / sans épée, // interdit, / sans couleur?

The next commonest pattern is the line divided into four sections by the central caesura and pauses after the second and eighth syllables:

> Mon arc, / mes javelots, // mon char, / tout m'importune.

This pattern is capable of a number of variations. Instead of 2–4–2–4, we may have 4–2–2–4:

> Mais fidèle, / mais fier, // et même / un peu farouche.

And 2–4–4–2:

> Ces Dieux / qui se sont fait // une gloire / cruelle
> De séduire le coeur ...

The two commonest forms are often combined in the same line: 2–4–3–3:

> Toujours / devant mes yeux // je crois voir / mon époux.

One of the functions of the caesura, as we know, is to place emphasis on a particular word, to balance or bring out the antithesis between two contrary words. It is also a function of a pause near or at the end of a line, as we can see from 'mon époux' in the last line quoted which gains further emphasis through being balanced with 'toujours' after the initial pause.

The need for emphasis produces other variations:

> Fier / de votre valeur, // tout, / si je vous en crois ...

This is a fresh pattern: 1–5–1–5.

In other cases we find a blend of the standard or near-standard hemistich with one of the less common forms:

> Et comptez-vous / pour rien // Dieu / qui combat pour nous?
> Dieu, / qui de l'orphelin // protège / l'innocence ... (4–2–1–5)
> (1–5–3–3)

The lines I have quoted are no more than samples and are naturally in no sense exhaustive. They are merely offered as an indication of the variety of Racine's rhythmical patterns.

There has been a good deal of argument among French authorities about what are known as the *dimètre* and the *trimètre*. The *dimètre* is the standard line divided into two hemistiches by the central caesura. The *trimètre* is a line divided by two caesuras of equal strength into three sections consisting usually, but not invariably, of four syllables each. It became common form in the poetry of the Romantics when they were trying to refurbish the classical alexandrine. In the seventeenth century it was a rarity. There is only one line in any major tragic dramatist which everybody is agreed in describing as a *trimètre*. It comes from Corneille's *Suréna*:

> Toujours aimer, // toujours souffrir, // toujours mourir.

We can see at once that the line could not be scanned in any other way. According to Grammont this is the one absolute test of the genuine *trimètre*.[10] He has asserted categorically that though there may be one or two *trimètres* in *Les Plaideurs*, there is not a single one in any of Racine's tragedies and he has been active in exposing what he calls the 'faux *trimètre*'. A different view has been taken by other writers on versification who claim to have discovered a number of genuine *trimètres* in Racine's tragedies.[11] Although I am convinced by some of their examples, I do not propose to examine them. It is evident that, as I have already said, the *trimètre* was a rarity in the seventeenth century. It is therefore sufficient in a short discussion of Racine's versification to define and illustrate the term without going into further detail.

Enjambement

The steps taken by dramatists to reduce the strength of the less important pause at the end of a line brings us to *enjambement* and the *rejet*. Malherbe, Boileau and the teachers at Port-Royal were at one in condemning *enjambement* absolutely, at any rate in serious poetry. This is Grammont's definition of the terms:

> When a proposition which has begun in one line ends in the next without filling it completely, we say that there is *enjambement* and that the end of the proposition which appears in the second line is the *rejet*.[12]

An example illustrates the tightness of the definition:

> Mais tout n'est pas détruit, et vous en laissez vivre
> Un . . . Votre fils, Seigneur, me défend de poursuivre.
> > (*Phèdre*, V, 3).

Je suis vaincu. Pompée a saisi l'avantage
D'une nuit qui laissait peu de place au courage.
                                        (*Mithridate*, II, 3).

According to Grammont's definition, the first couplet counts as *en-jambement* because the break prevents the end of the proposition from filling the second line completely; the second couplet does not rank as *enjambement* because the end of the proposition does in fact fill the second line.[13]

Although he argues that as the central caesura weakened less attention was paid to the pause at the end of the line, Grammont maintains that in the whole of Racine's tragedies as distinct from his only comedy there are only one or two genuine *enjambements*. Souriau takes a rather broader view, but though he thinks that there are a considerable number of *en-jambements* in the tragedies, the examples he quotes consist of couplets like the one from *Phèdre* where there is a break in the formulation of the proposition or where the *rejet* is simply a mode of address which is carried over to the second line.[14] Suberville takes a similar view to Souriau, but adds a third type of *enjambement*: the addition of a relative clause which completes the second line and in his opinion 'conceals the *rejet*'.[15] The following are examples of the three different forms:

La douceur de sa voix, son enfance, sa grâce,
Font insensiblement à mon inimitié
Succéder . . . Je serais sensible à la pitié?
                                        (*Athalie*, II, 7).

Et sur quoi jugez-vous que j'en perds la mémoire,
Prince?
                                        (*Phèdre*, II, 5).

Songez combien de fois vous m'avez reproché
Un silence / témoin de mon trouble caché.
                                        (*Bajazet*, V, 4).

The first with its double *enjambement* is clearly the most impressive of the three examples. It is clear, however, that in all of them the alexandrine becomes more supple, closer to a conversational tone. I feel inclined to add that the accepted definition as stated by Grammont strikes me as too narrow, that the important thing is the carrying over of an unfinished proposition from one line to another and not whether it fails to fill the second line completely or not. This means that the couplet from *Mithridate* really fulfills the same function as the others I have quoted.

Inversion

With the exception of a very brief section in Souriau, none of the writers on French versification has much to say about inversion. There is or has been a general tendency to assume that it is one of the penalties of the alexandrine and is generally used to make the number of syllables or the rhyme come right. This certainly happens on occasion. I recall one unfortunate example which is the only flaw in Paulin's great speech in *Bérénice*, Act II, Sc. 2:

> De l'affranchi Pallas nous avons vu le frère,
> Des fers de Claudius Félix encor flétri,
> De deux reines, Seigneur, devenir le mari . . .

In spite of this kind of lapse, inversion performs definite and necessary functions. Its principal aims are to give the verse a lift, to introduce or underline the formal element in what are otherwise colloquial or even prosaic exchanges between the characters, and to place special emphasis on particular words.

One of the best examples, as we have seen, is the opening speech in *Athalie*. Its effectiveness is underlined by a strangely insensitive comment by Louis Racine. He remarks of the first line of all,

> Oui, je viens dans son temple adorer l'Éternel,

that it would have been 'more poetical' to do away with the inversion and write:

> Oui, je viens adorer l'Éternel dans son temple.[18]

Anyone can see of course that the change wrecks the line which loses its poetry, its dignity and the strong emphasis that inversion deliberately places on 'l'Éternel'.

The Spoken Word

Nobody who has read some of the leading works on French versification will have failed to notice that even among experts there are differences of opinion about the correct scansion of a particular line. I am now going to suggest that, short of attending a drama school, the only really practical way of appreciating Racine's versification is to listen to long-playing records of some of the tragedies in the quiet of the study with the text in one's hands.

One or two things should be borne in mind. There can be no definitive interpretation of every line that Racine wrote. The tragedies naturally leave plenty of room for differing personal interpretations which may be equally valid. I am not saying therefore that a performer's interpretation of a given line is the only one or is necessarily the best one. What I am saying is that in general it is likely to be more reliable than one's own and a useful corrective to it. What I am also saying is that an ample use of gramophone records gives us a much better understanding than we can hope to gain from occasional visits to the theatre of the working not merely of pauses, but of the versification as a whole.

The point is illustrated by a remark of Grammont's. 'A *coupe*,' he said, 'is not a pause or a stop: it is simply a passage from one section of a line to another.'[17] This clearly calls for some qualification. It is obvious to everybody that in any performance of the tragedies there are a large number of actual, physical pauses, that they vary in length and that many of them conform to accepted metrical schemes while others do not. Grammont, however, is perfectly correct in saying that by no means all the *coupes* are actual, physical pauses. With the exception of the divisibility of the alexandrine at the hemistich, the pauses are not a matter of hard and fast rules; they are something which has been deduced from the writings of the dramatists, something which emerged of its own accord in the course of the dramatists' search for the right rhythm. This brings me to the most important point of all. What the caesuras and other pauses really add up to is an underlying pattern or rhythm which gives the plays their tone, their symmetry, their shape. The great value of listening to gramophone records is that they do make us acutely aware of the existence and effectiveness of this pattern.

Flexibility

I have suggested more than once that one of the great virtues of Racine's style is the way in which he strikes a balance between the formality of the alexandrine and everyday speech. It happens, as we have seen, when a character suddenly breaks off or 'dries up' in the middle of a speech owing to excitement, anger, surprise or fear, as Hermione does when speaking of Pyrrhus's martial feats, as Pyrrhus himself does in the scene of 'black comedy', or as Athalie does at her first meeting with Joas and her last with Joad.[18] We find a similar effect when one character angrily cuts another short in the middle of a speech and takes over the rest of the alexandrine, as Clytemnestre does in the clash with her husband at the beginning of the third act of *Iphigénie*:

AGAMEMNON
Vous n'êtes point ici dans le palais d'Atrée.
Vous êtes dans un camp . . .
CLYTEMNESTRE
Où tout vous est soumis,
Où le sort de l'Asie en vos mains est remis . . .

I want to look now at one or two other ways of obtaining the same kind of effect: the use of colloquial or prosaic language and the division of a single alexandrine among several characters.

When Antiochus says to his confidant:

De son appartement cette porte est prochaine,
Et cette autre conduit dans celui de la Reine,

the second line might be described as 'rasant la prose'. The purely prosaic
statement is balanced by the inversion in the first line and the formal rules
of the alexandrine which give it its effectiveness.

When Arcas discloses Agamemnon's secret plan to sacrifice his daughter,
his hearers react in this way:

ARCAS
Il l'attend à l'autel pour la sacrifier.

ACHILLE
Lui!

CLYTEMNESTRE
Sa fille!

IPHIGÉNIE
Mon père!

ÉRIPHILE
O ciel! quelle nouvelle!

It will be seen that Achille is given one syllable, the mother three, the
daughter two, and Ériphile a whole hemistich to herself. The way in
which their reactions vary is interesting and is well brought out by the
division of the alexandrine. They are all profoundly shocked, but the
warrior Achille's 'Lui!' is primarily an expression of violent hostility towards an enemy who is unnamed and whose status is unmentioned. The
mother's mind fixes on the potential victim; the daughter's not so much
on the danger to herself as on her father's incredible decision. The outsider's reaction is a decidedly ambiguous one. She, too, is astonished, but
the announcement may already have begun to cast a sudden light on the
possibilities of her own position.

There are two other examples which I can only mention briefly. One is
the announcement of the death of Bajazet in the penultimate scene of the
play which produces another break-up of the alexandrine and the division
of a single line between three different speakers. The other is the conversation between Athalie and Joas in Act II, Sc. 7 of the play. The difference
between the child's voice and adult voices is naturally an important factor
in production. What I want to suggest is that Racine chooses words,
rhythm and tone with such skill that even before seeing or hearing a performance, a reading of the text is sufficient to convey something of the
contrast between the motherly tone adopted by Athalie and the childlike
tone of Joas. The effect is increased by Joas's language which is a mixture
of innocence and childish pomposity. It is apparent in the boldness of his
comparison between his God and Athalie's, in the way in which he spon-
taneously shrinks at the idea of exchanging 'such a father' (meaning Joad)

for 'such a mother' when Athalie invites him to come and live with her in her palace and promises to treat him as a son. The childish pomposity comes out in a line like

> Le bonheur des méchants comme un torrent s'écoule,

which sounds as though he is quoting from a ceremony or a sermon heard in the temple.[19]

Conclusion

A useful way of ending a discussion of Racine's versification is to look at a piece of contemporary evidence. Nearly forty years ago the late Béatrix Dussane discovered an anonymous document describing Racine's own views on the way in which his verse should be spoken on the stage. Although the author is anonymous, there is no reason to doubt the veracity of his statement. He tells us that 'he had the honour of seeing M. Jean-Baptiste Racine every day during a period of several years and up to the date of his death.' His account is so convincing that it is fair to assume, as Mme Dussane did, that his information was derived from Jean-Baptiste's own discussions with his father:

> Il n'approuvait point la manière trop vraie de réciter établie dans la troupe de Molière. Il voulait qu'on donnât aux vers un certain ton qui, joint à la mesure et aux rimes, se distingue de la prose; mais il ne pouvait supporter ces tons outrés et glapissants qu'on veut substituer au beau naturel, et qu'on pourrait pour ainsi dire noter comme de la musique.

The writer goes on to tell us that, 'shocked by the bad taste which was beginning to spread,' Racine went one day to see a troupe of his actors. He announced solemnly that he had brought them some bad news: their theatre was going to be closed. When the horrified artists asked why, he replied:

> Pourquoi? C'est que vous devez savoir que Lully a seul le privilège de faire chanter sur son théâtre, et on s'aperçoit que fort mal à propos vous chantez sur le vôtre.[20]

We must agree with Mme Dussane that it is a fascinating document. Racine was always extremely sensitive about the way in which his works were performed. The reference to Molière reminds us that it was almost certainly his early dissatisfaction with the methods used by his company that led to his disgraceful behaviour over *Alexandre*. He not only coached the actresses playing leading parts in the tragedies and directed the productions of *Esther* and *Athalie* at Saint-Cyr; he was greatly admired for the way in which he read his plays to private audiences. The document published by Mme Dussane confirms the impression that in performances of his plays Racine's aim was a middle way, a form of naturalness which would avoid alike stiltedness, ranting and chanting.

We might perhaps summarize Racine's handling of the alexandrine in this fashion. The framework that it provides is constant, but its functions are positive and organic. It is in no sense an unwieldy form imposed on the poet's material: it is a discipline which enables him to maintain a certain level of elevation combined with a large measure of suppleness and variety. It is, indeed, the suppleness and variety, which are geared to changes of mood, the rise and fall of emotion, and to the speaking voice, that make his instrument a living thing.

Although I used it as one of the epigraphs for this chapter, I naturally have no sympathy with Boileau's description of Racine as being no more than a 'très bel esprit' or with his claim to have taught him to 'faire difficilement des vers faciles'. The process may have been more difficult than Racine admitted: there can be no doubt about the significance of 'faciles' which is almost a shorthand summary of the virtues which we have examined individually. There is one point, however, on which we must be clear. The merits of Racine's alexandrine are not the result of technical devices invented by him. We find exactly the same changes of emphasis, the same variations in the force of the caesura and the same degree of variety in the other pauses in the works of the minor dramatists of the seventeenth century. Yet the effect is in no sense the same. In the work of the minor dramatists the monotony is inescapably there. For the most part theirs is not a *living* drama. We continually have the impression that the dramatists failed to identify themselves sufficiently closely with their characters. The speeches read like a succession of set pieces placed in the mouths of the characters from without instead of somehow originating inside them.[21] What Racine offers, what any great dramatist must offer, is a fully integrated work in which all the elements combine. It is only when this is achieved that we find what is known as *vraisemblance*. It has nothing to do with the modern cult of 'realism' nor does it mean that Racine's tragedies are like 'everyday life': one of their great merits is that they are certainly not. It means that the formula works, that it produces the kind and degree of naturalness mentioned above, that we are drawn more and more deeply into the conflict as it develops on the stage.[22]

II. Language

There are considerable differences between the French of the sixteenth and seventeenth centuries. In the sixteenth century it was not less inventive, less rich in earthy concrete images or narrower in vocabulary than other European languages. In the seventeenth century it underwent what its authors were pleased to describe as a process of purification. It began with the controversy between Malherbe and Desportes in which the principal target was Ronsard. Malherbe, we are told, wished to purify the language as well as imposing a new form of versification. His aim was the removal of Latinisms, baroque elements and archaisms. He proscribed 'dirty' words like *barbier* and 'low' words like *poitrine*.[23] He was followed by the grammarian, Vaugelas, who declared in his *Remarques* (1647) that the French language 'must be cleansed of the *ordures* it has contracted'.[24] The grammarians were supported by the poets, or some of them. 'The word *sueur*,' said Boileau, 'can never be agreeable in French and leaves an unpleasing impression on the mind.'[25] Corneille classified *lavement* (Louis XIV used the word *remède*) as belonging to the *mots déshonnêtes*, and Racine added that *cochon* was a word of *la dernière bassesse*.[26]

We can hardly avoid the impression that there is a certain primness about these observations which produced marked changes in the language of seventeenth-century dramatists. A glance at Garnier's plays illustrates some of them. The most revealing examples are to be found in *Hippolyte*, which appeared in 1573, because they invite direct comparisons with Racine's *Phèdre*.[27]

Garnier's Nourrice is a much more robust figure than Racine's Oenone and her language is much more forthright. Although she ends by trying to act as a sort of procuress for Phèdre, she begins by reproaching her passion for Hippolyte in terms which would have been unthinkable for Racine:

> Voulez-vous que la mère avec son enfant couche,
> Flanc à flanc accouplez en une même couche ?[28]

This is her description of the physical symptoms of Phèdre's sickness:

> La force à ses genoux défaut en se levant.
> Elle chancelle toute, et ses bras imbéciles
> Battant à ses cotez lui pendent inutiles,

which is a good deal more vivid—particularly the 'bras imbéciles'—than Oenone's description of Phèdre in Act I, Sc. 2 of Racine's tragedy, or Phèdre's own reference to her 'genoux tremblants' in the next scene.

When Garnier's Phèdre compares the young and the middle-aged Thésée, she speaks of the 'beautez de Thésée'

> Telles qu'il les avait lors que bien jeune encor
> Son menton cotonnait d'une frisure d'or ...

A comparison with Racine's

> Charmant, jeune, traînant tous les coeurs après soi,
> Tel qu'on dépeint nos Dieux, ou tel que je vous voi,

is a practical demonstration of what seems to me a serious loss. It is the disappearance from seventeenth-century tragedy of descriptions of the physical appearance of people. Racine's abstractions also underline the peculiar charm of Garnier's second line and the creative use of the homely 'cotonnait'.

The next passage comes from the Messenger's account of Hippolyte's death:

> les chevaux ardans le traînent contre terre
> A travers les halliers et les buissons touffus,
> Qui le vont deschirant avec leurs doigts griffus.
> La teste luy bondist et ressaute sanglante.
> Des ses membres saigneux la terre est rougissante,
> Comme on voit un limas qui rampe advantureux
> Le long d'un sep tortu laisser un trac glaireux.
> Son estomac, ouvert d'un tronc pointu, se vuide
> De ses boyaux traînez sous le char homicide.

We may feel that the image of the snail is a little too homely in this context, but the absence of the earthy, concrete detail from the corresponding lines in the 'récit de Théramène' is the sign of another loss suffered by the seventeenth century.

There are some lines in two of Garnier's later tragedies which deserve a glance. The first comes from *Antigone* (1580):

> Moi, j'ai toujours l'amour cousu dans mes entrailles.

'Entrailles' does not appear to have been among the words banned by the purists, but it can hardly have been very popular in the seventeenth century. Racine only uses it four times in the plays, but though they include an unlovely reference to the 'entrailles fumantes' of the animals sacrificed on the altar in *Athalie*, he uses a more genteel word in Clytemnestre's onslaught on her husband in the fourth act of *Iphigénie*. When she speaks of Calchas slitting open her daughter's chest in order to 'consult the gods', it is on her 'heart' and not on her 'entrails' or 'guts' that he is expected to fasten his 'oeil curieux'. What is most striking about Garnier's line, however, is not the word 'entrailles', but the way in which he relates it to the homely 'cousu'. It brings out the close connection between a character's emotions and his body far more vividly than Racine's use of the words 'brûler' and 'dévorer'.

The other passage comes from *La Troade* which appeared a year before *Antigone*. It is the description of the preliminaries of the execution of Priam's daughter, Polyxène, by the Greeks at the end of the Trojan War:

> Elle fendit sa robe avec sa blanche main,
> Et jusques au nombril se découvrit le sein;
> Sa poitrine fut veue avec ses mammelettes,
> S'enflant également comme rondes pommettes . . .

'Poitrine', as we know, was rated by Malherbe as a 'low' word. 'Nombril' and 'mammelettes' would presumably have been branded as 'dirty'.

The adjective that he would have chosen for the faintly comic and at the same time moving comparison of 'mammelettes' and 'pommettes' can only be a matter of speculation. What we should notice is the remarkable vividness and concreteness of the picture in which nearly every word from 'blanche main' to 'pommettes' plays an effective part.

It is right to add that one of the most useful ways of appreciating what was happening is to look at some of the changes that Corneille made in the later editions of his early plays which show the process actually at work. The best example is probably *Mélite*, his first play, which was produced in 1629 and published in 1633. There were six further editions between 1644 and 1668. Changes were made in all of them, but by far the largest number occurred in the edition of 1660 and only minor changes in those appearing after 1668. What we find is that all words and expressions branded by the purists as 'dirty', 'low' or vulgar are steadily eliminated and that by the time we reach the definitive edition have disappeared completely.

In the chapter on *Phèdre* I referred briefly to the absence of colour in Racine and suggested that the plays were rather like black and white films. His use of words describing colour throws an interesting light on the question of abstract and concrete language. We begin by finding that there is a dearth even of black and white. 'Noir' and its variants occur 46 times in the plays. The surprising thing is that there are only three occasions when the word is actually used to describe physical colour: 'noirs Africains', 'cheveux noirs' (in *Les Plaideurs*), and 'une flamme si noire'.[29] All its other uses are abstract: 'noirs pressentiments', 'noir chagrin', 'noire fureur' and the like.[30] 'Blanc' is used only 4 times; the uses are all concrete. In view of what has been said about the change in Racine's style in the later plays, it is worth observing that out of the four uses of the word, or rather its variants, one appears in *Mithridate*, two in *Iphigénie* and one in *Athalie*. They have all been quoted, but there is no harm in reminding ourselves of the special beauty of two of them:

> Cachaient mes cheveux blancs sous trente diadèmes.

> Voyez tout l'Hellespont blanchissant sous nos rames.

'Or' is used 11 times. Although it always conveys an impression of colour, we find that in five instances it stands for wealth or money rather than physical colour. Something of the same is true of 'pourpre'. It is used 5 times. The emphasis is plainly on colour when Bérénice speaks of 'Cette pourpre, cet or' in her account of Titus's accession to the imperial throne, but in all other cases the emphasis falls primarily on purple as a symbol of royalty e.g. 'la pourpre de nos rois', 'la pourpre des Césars', 'de la pourpre habillé'.

'Rouge' is the most curious example of all. Out of a total of 52 uses, 5 describe redness caused by the spilling of blood; the remainder are all references to blushing![31] Except for 'jaunissantes', there are no other references to colour: no blue or green or brown.

This prompts me to look again at Garnier. There is no dearth of words describing physical colour in his plays. In the first act of the play to which he gives his name, Hippolyte describes the dawn. In the space of eight lines he uses the words 'vermeil', 'jaunir' and 'brunette'. In the next line there is another example of the creative use of the homely or unexpected word when he addresses Phoebus as 'O grand dieu *perruquier*'.

Although there may have been something to be said in favour of the purists' desire to restore the dignity of the language of poetry, nothing can alter the fact that the price was altogether excessive. It led to a drastic impoverishment of the language of creative writers which was not cured until the nineteenth century. In the case of Racine there were compensations.

> The essential quality of Racine's style [said Charles Bruneau] is simplicity ... In no circumstances does the word assume a predominant value ... In the scenes in which violence reaches a paroxysm the vocabulary is simpler than ever.[32]

Racine's simplicity is a positive virtue. This does not alter the fact that it was largely the result of the problems created by the purists. Bruneau was clearly right in stating that in his work 'the word is never predominant'. When we turn to the nineteenth century, we find that a number of treatises have been written on the special use by individual authors of different parts of speech: adjectives in Balzac, verbs in Flaubert, substantives in Zola, the Goncourts and Daudet. There is no sign of this form of inventiveness in the writers of the seventeenth century and comparisons with Garnier have demonstrated that the creative use of homely or unexpected words practised in the sixteenth century was largely a thing of the past. We know that Racine made some use of oxymoron, but neither this nor any of his other uses of particular parts of speech is likely to provide material for a doctoral thesis.

What he does, as I have tried to show, is to create patterns by the recurrent use of certain words. He does not give them fresh meanings in themselves; he simply places his personal seal on them so that they acquire a special significance in a given play which contributes largely to its ultimate meaning.

It is right to stress the fact that these words are essentially commonplace words in order to appreciate the inhibiting effect of the rules and the way in which Racine triumphed in spite of them. For what the rules and the purification of the language did between them was not simply to ban vulgar, 'low' or 'dirty' words, but to exclude a substantial number of words which would have added greatly to the vividness of the language and compelled Racine to rely on a decidedly conventional terminology in his greatest achievements. The simplicity which results and which Bruneau rightly commends is a positive virtue because it is responsible for the tremendous impact of the great *tirades*, the clarity of the expositions and the ease with which the action can be followed.

Although some words like 'feu', 'flamme', 'funeste', 'fatal' and 'hymen', which were already conventional in Racine's time, have acquired a period air, and though others like 'étonner', 'charme', 'ennui' and 'triste' have lost most of their original force, it would be a mistake to exaggerate the difficulty that this presents for present day audiences. Bruneau regarded the first half of the seventeenth century as the period in which 'modern French' developed. He pointed out that there are 'few differences between seventeenth-century and modern syntax' and that 'after three centuries Racine's vocabulary only contains a small number of words which have become obsolete'.[33] This has special implications for foreigners. What it adds up to is that the gap between Racine's language and modern French is a good deal narrower than that between Shakespeare's language and modern English. This means that all we need to do is to accustom ourselves to the 'palace style' which is part of the method of 'access', then surrender ourselves as completely as possible to the poetry.

I have insisted throughout this book that the determining factor is the poetry. The truly astonishing thing about Racine, the thing that places him in a class by himself among French dramatists, is not merely that he succeeded as a dramatic poet in spite of the obstacles, but that he also managed to produce some of the greatest poetry in the French language. It was done in a variety of ways: the brilliant placing of simple, ordinary words and the evocative power with which he invested them; the different forms of 'rhetoric'; the drive, the persuasiveness, above all the music of the Racinian alexandrine.

NOTES

[1] *Historia del teatro español* . . . p. 158.

[2] Quoted by M. Grammont, *Le Vers français, ses moyens d'expression, son harmonie*, 3rd ed., 1923, p. 8.

[3] See G. Lote, *Histoire du vers français*, I, 1949, pp. 2–51.

[4] M. Souriau, *L'Évolution du vers français au dix-septième siècle*, 1893, p. 145.

[5] *Ibid.*, p. 425.

[6] *Le Vocabulaire de Racine*, 1946, p. 175.

[7] *Petit traité de versification française*, 14th ed., 1952, p. 47.

[8] Comparisons with English practice are instructive. In the heroic couplet the caesura continually varies between the fourth, fifth and sixth syllables. In Shakespeare's blank verse, as we should expect, the changes are a good deal more varied.

[9] Modern editors have made some changes in punctuation. In the examples which follow the punctuation corresponds to that used in the edition of 1697 which can be regarded as Racine's own punctuation.

[10] *Petit traité*, p. 63; *Les Vers français*, pp. 70–73.

[11] Souriau, *Op. cit.*, pp. 448–50; J. Suberville, *Histoire et théorie de la versification française*, Nouvelle édition revue et complétée, 1946, pp. 19, 61–2.

[12] *Petit traité*, pp. 20–21.

[13] *Ibid.*, p. 111.

[14] *Op. cit.*, pp. 451–60.

[15] *Op. cit.*, pp. 72–3.

[16] Quoted, Souriau, *Op. cit.*, p. 467.

[17] *Le Vers français*, p. 10.

[18] See pp. 70, 75–6, 326 above.

[19] Raymond Picard uses the word 'mièvre' which I take to mean 'affected' in the present context (*O.C.*, I, p. 1189).

[20] *Du nouveau sur Racine*, pp. 6–7. Mme Dussane explains that she discovered the document six or seven years before publishing it in her booklet in 1941.

When Racine spoke of 'privilège', he was referring to the monopoly granted by the king to Lully for the production of opera. There was evidently a strong element of sour humour in his poker-faced announcement to the artists which he presumably had no intention of carrying out.

[21] They also illustrate what Ronsard had in mind when he complained that alexandrines were 'trop énervés et flasques'.

[22] The faults that I have noted are by no means confined to minor dramatists in France. They are frequently found in English Restoration tragedy. Although I observed earlier that the placing of the caesura continually varies in the English heroic couplet, there is an inescapable monotony about Restoration tragedy in which rhyming couplets are used. We might also observe that translation of Racine into English involves transposition into one of the two corresponding English metres: the heroic couplet or blank verse. I find that the use of the heroic couplet gives the translation exactly the same monotony as Restoration tragedy. The only two genuinely successful translations of Racine into English are in blank verse. They are by John Cairncross and Samuel Solomon who have both managed to catch the beat of English blank verse.

[23] C. Bruneau, *Petite histoire de la langue française*, I, 1958, pp. 144, 145.

[24] *Ibid.*, p. 159.

[25] and [26] *Ibid.*, p. 221.

[27] I have used the word 'appeared' because it still seems to be uncertain whether Garnier's plays were staged in his lifetime.

[28] 'Flanc(s)' is used 14 times in the tragedies. On eight occasions it means 'womb'. On the remaining six it is divided between descriptions of wounds in battle and sacrifices of animals.

[29] It might be argued that 'une flamme si noire' is as much of an abstraction as 'noires amours' and the other examples which follow. The answer is that the application of a colour adjective to the seventeenth-century 'flamme' has converted the abstraction, at any rate for modern audiences, into a *visual* image.

[30] We should not, however, overlook the fact that 'ombre' and its variants are used 37 times. On some 13 occasions the word is the equivalent of 'darkness' or 'blackness' e.g. in Hippolyte's 'La lumière du jour, les ombres de la nuit.'

[31] In view of what I said about 'ombre', I should perhaps mention 'pâle' and its variants. They are used 18 times in the plays, but in every instance the reference is either to complexion or the state of a person's skin.

[32] *Op. cit.*, pp. 222, 224.

[33] *Op. cit.*, pp. 188, 224.

CONCLUSION

ALTHOUGH I said in the chapter on *Mithridate* that it would be a mistake to try to discover in Racine's work a formal pattern in which every play has its particular place, I want to conclude by taking a brief glance at the plays as a whole to see whether anything in the nature of a general pattern emerges. In order to do so I shall have to repeat the points that I made about the individual plays.

The first two plays are the work of a talented apprentice, but they show fairly clearly where the dramatist's main interests lay and what he was likely to choose as his subjects when he matured.

Andromaque has made a greater impression on the public at large than any other play except *Phèdre*. It stamped Racine as the dramatist of irresistible passion. He was prompt to react against this view. In *Britannicus* love-interest is rigorously subordinated to politics. It is the only one of the secular plays of Racine's maturity in which this happens. There was an unexpected change from one of the most violent to the gentlest play of all. If I am right in thinking that Racine's subject was chosen for him, it would suggest that in *Bérénice* he was muzzled. This would explain why the gentlest play in the canon was followed by the toughest, why Racine went out of his way in *Bajazet* to choose a subject which would provide the greatest scope for his personal inclinations. The contrast between the plays is absolute and is as marked in the difference in style as in every other feature.

The change from violence to gentleness and from gentleness back to violence that we find in these three plays looks like an alternation between extremes. The view is encouraged by the next two plays. *Mithridate* and *Iphigénie* are not free from violence, but they are both plays with something like a 'happy ending' and (leaving aside the apprentice works) they both reveal a more optimistic outlook than any of the previous plays.

In *Phèdre* there is a move in the opposite direction. It seems at first to confirm the impression originally created by *Andromaque*: that Racine is primarily the dramatist of irresistible passion. What distinguishes them is the presence in *Phèdre* of the powerful moral element and a much more profound vision. There is at the same time a very marked difference be-

354

tween *Phèdre* and the two plays which immediately preceded it. The glimmer of a more optimistic view of life which we saw in *Mithridate* and *Iphigénie* has been completely extinguished. Although *Phèdre* is in some respects the most moral of all the tragedies, it presents the gloomiest picture of the human condition to be found in any of them.

While *Esther* is not without attraction, it is clear that it was primarily an approach shot for *Athalie*. What we find in *Athalie* is a transformation of the processes at work in *Andromaque*, *Britannicus*, *Bajazet* and *Mithridate*. Religion has taken the place of sexual passion. The tyrant is still there, but her interests are purely political; the 'aggressor's' intended 'victim' is a religious community instead of an unwilling lover. She is matched by a religious fanatic or what one might almost describe as a religious 'aggressor'. In *Esther*, which was not devoid of violence, the dictator underwent something like 'conversion'; in *Athalie* she is of course destroyed.

The conclusion I reach is that though the plays have many common features, there is no sign of a consistent general pattern. The alternation of violence and gentleness as well as the other changes were the result of circumstance: criticism in the case of *Britannicus*, patronage in the case of *Bérénice*, changes in the dramatist's own outlook in the last three secular plays, and patronage again when we come to the religious plays. What is particularly striking is that *Athalie* is at least as violent as the most violent of the secular plays and that religion is used as a mask to conceal or perhaps to justify what is plainly one of the most marked characteristics of the plays.

Finally, we might observe that between them *Phèdre* and *Athalie* present us with Racine's testimony. Passion plays havoc in a secular society, but even in a religious community where it is directed towards a positive end there are no grounds for an optimistic view of life on earth.

BIBLIOGRAPHY

In the absence of a contrary indication, books in English are published in London and books in French in Paris.

I. EDITIONS

1. Collected Works
   Oeuvres ('Les Grands Écrivains de la France'), ed. P. Mesnard, 8 volumes and 2 albums, Hachette, 1865–73.
   Oeuvres complètes (Bibliothèque de la Pléiade), ed. R. Picard, 2 volumes, Gallimard, 1950. (I have used this edition for all quotations in the book.)

2. Single Plays
   La Thébaïde de Racine, ed. M. Edwards, Nizet, 1965.
      (Texts of original and definitive editions)
   Andromaque (Les Classiques du Peuple), ed. A. Ubersfeld, Éditions Sociales, 1961.
   Britannicus, ed. P. Butler, Cambridge University Press, 1967.
   Bérénice, ed. C. L. Walton, Oxford University Press, 1965.
   Athalie, ed. P. France, Oxford University Press, 1966.
      (All five editions specially recommended for their introductory essays.)

3. Acting editions
   Bajazet, X. de Courville, 1947.
   Phèdre, J. L. Barrault, 1946, 1959.
   Athalie, G. le Roy, 1952.
      (All three plays were published in the collection 'Mises en Scène', Éditions du Seuil, and contain detailed commentaries by distinguished producers.)

II. GENERAL

ADAM, A., *Histoire de la littérature française au XVIIe siècle*, 5 volumes, Domat, 1948–56. (Racine, IV, pp. 255–377; V, pp. 39–57.)

—, *Le Théâtre classique* ('Que sais-je?' No. 1414), Presses Universitaires de France, 1970, 128 pp.
   (Everything that Professor Adam writes on the seventeenth century is indispensable reading.)

BÉNICHOU, P., *Morales du Grand Siècle* (Bibliothèque des Idées), Gallimard, 1948, 231 pp. (Outstanding.)

BORGERHOF, E. B. O., *The Freedom of French Classicism*, Princeton University Press, 1950, xi + 266 pp.

BOULENGER, J., *Le Grand Siècle*, Hachette, 1911, 1924 (revised), 424 pp.

BRAY, R., *La Formation de la doctrine classique en France*, Nizet, 1927, vi + 389 pp.

CRUICKSHANK, J. (Editor), *French Literature and its Background*, 2. The Seventeenth Century, Oxford University Press, 1969, vi + 234 pp.

GAIFFE, F., *L'Envers du Grand Siècle*, Albin Michel, 1924, xxiv + 366 pp.

GUTH, P., *Histoire de la littérature française*, I. Des Origines épiques au siècle des lumières, Fayard, 1967, 621 pp. (Entertaining history of French literature by well-known comic novelist.)

LANCASTER, H. C., *A History of French Dramatic Literature in the Seventeenth Century*, 9 volumes, Baltimore: John Hopkins Press, 1929–42.

— (Editor) *Le Mémoire de Mahelot, Laurent et d'autres décorateurs de l'Hôtel de Bourgogne et de la Comédie Française au XVIIe siècle*, Champion, 1920, 158 pp.

LOUGH, J., *Paris Theatre Audiences in the Seventeenth and Eighteenth Centuries*, Oxford University Press, 1957, 293 pp.

MONGRÉDIEN, G., *La Vie littéraire au dix-septième siècle*, Jules Talladier, 1947, 443 pp.

MORNET, D., *Histoire de la littérature française classique* 1660–1700, 3e éd. Armand Colin, 1947, 427 pp.

NURSE, P. H., *Classical Voices*. Corneille-Racine-Molière-Mme de Lafayette. Harrap, 1971, 230 pp. (Excellent.)

PICARD, R., *Two Centuries of French Literature* (World University Library), Tr. J. Cairncross, Weidenfeld and Nicolson, 1970, 254 pp.

REYNOLD, G. DE, *Le XVIIe siècle: le Classique et le Baroque*, Montreal: Éditions de l'Arbre, 1944, 280 pp.

RUIZ RAMÓN, F., *Historia del teatro español desde sus origenes hasta mil novecientos* (El Libro de Bolsillo), Madrid: Alianza Editorial, 1967, 503 pp.

SAINTE-BEUVE, C. A., *Port-Royal* (Bibliothèque de la Pléiade), 3 volumes, Gallimard, 1955. (Racine, III, pp. 535–602.)

SCHERER, J., *La Dramaturgie classique en France*, Nizet, 1954, 427 pp.

STEINER, G., *The Death of Tragedy*, Faber and Faber, 1961, viii + 356 + Index xii pp.

VALBUENA PRAT, A., *Historia del teatro español*, Barcelona: Editorial Noguer, 1956, 708 pp.

III. BOOKS ON RACINE

BARTHES, R., *Sur Racine*, Éditions du Seuil, 1963, 171 pp.

BAUDOUIN, C., *Jean Racine l'enfant du désert* (Collection: 'La Recherche de l'Absolu'), Plon, 1963, 190 pp.

BIERMANN, K. H., *Selbstentfremdung und Missverständnis in den Tragödien Jean Racines*, Bad Homburg: Berlin: Zürich: Verlag Max Gehlen, 1969, 150 pp. (Interesting study of characters' reactions to one another.)

BRERETON, G., *Jean Racine, A Critical Biography*, Cassell, 1951, xii + 362 pp. (Excellent biography.)

BRISSON, P., *Les Deux visages de Racine*, 1944, 245 pp.

BUTLER, P., *Classicisme et baroque dans l'oeuvre de Racine*, Nizet, 1959, 349 pp. (Valuable study and much wider than suggested by the title.)

CLARK, A. F. B., *Jean Racine* (Harvard Studies in Comparative Literature, Vol. XVI), Cambridge (Massachusetts): Harvard University Press, 1939, 1969, xiv + 354 pp. (Good general study of the dramatist and his work.)

CLAUDEL, P., *Conversation sur Jean Racine*, Gallimard, 1956, 49 pp.

COENEN, H. G., *Elemente der Racinischen Dialogtechnik* (Forschungen zur Romanischen Philologie, Heft 10), Münster: Aschendorfsche Verlags-buchhandlung, 1961, 145 pp.

DELTOUR, F., *Les Ennemis de Racine au XVIIe siècle*, Hachette, 1898, 393 pp.

DESCOTES, M., *Les Grands rôles du théâtre de Racine*, Presses Universitaires de France, 1957, 208 pp.

—, *Racine* (Collection: 'Tels qu'en eux-mêmes'), Bordeaux: G. Ducros, 1969, 190 pp.

DUBECH, L., *Jean Racine politique*, Grasset, 1926, 320 pp. (Interesting.)

DUSSANE, B., *Du Nouveau sur Racine*, Le Divan, 1941, 16 pp.

EIGELDINGER, M., *La Mythologie solaire dans l'oeuvre de Racine*, Neu-châtel: Faculté des Lettres; Geneva: Droz, 1969, 157 pp.

ELLIOTT, R., *Mythe et légende dans le théâtre de Racine* (Collection: 'Situations'), Minard, 1969, 284 pp.

FUBINI, M., *Jean Racine e la critica delle sue tragedie*, Turin: Sten, 1925, 291 pp.

GIRAUDOUX, J., *Racine*, Grasset, 1930, 80 pp. (Also in *Littérature*, Grasset, 1941, pp. 27–55.)

GOLDMANN, L., *Racine* ('Les Grands Dramaturges', 13), L'Arche, 1956, 159 pp.

GUÉGUEN, P., *Poésie de Racine*, Éditions du Rond-Point, 1946, 343 pp. (One of the most attractive and entertaining studies of Racine so far written. Unfortunately, out of print and unobtainable.)

HUBERT, J. D., *Essai d'exégèse racinienne : Les Secrets témoins*, Nizet, 1956, 278 pp. (Good study of Racine's symbolism.)

JASINSKI, R., *Vers le vrai Racine*, 2 volumes, Armand Colin, 1958, I, xxviii + 491 pp.; II, 563 pp. (The most elaborate and determined attempt so far made to identify the 'originals' of Racine's characters.)

KNIGHT, R. C., *Racine et la Grèce* (Études de Littérature Étrangère et Comparée, No. 23), Boivin, 1951, 467 pp.

—, *Racine, Convention and Classicism*, University College of Swansea, 1952, 31 pp.

— (Editor) *Racine* (Modern Judgements), Macmillan, 1969, 239 pp. (Fourteen studies by English, American, French and German critics previously published in books and magazines. All foreign studies in English translation.)

LACRETELLE, P. DE, *La Vie privée de Racine* (Collection: 'Les Vies Privées'), Hachette, 1949, 255 pp.

LE BIDOIS, G., *La Vie dans la tragédie de Racine*, 1901, 336 pp. (Chapters on structure and style particularly good.)

LAPP, J. C., *Aspects of Racinian Tragedy*, Oxford University Press, 1955, xii + 195 pp. (Excellent study.)

LEMAITRE, J., *Jean Racine*, Calmann-Lévy, 1908, 328 pp.

MASSON-FORESTIER, A., *Autour d'un Racine ignoré*, Mercure de France, 1910, 442 pp. (Biased but influential.)

MAULNIER, T., *Racine*, Gallimard, 1936, 269 pp.

MAURIAC, F., *La Vie de Jean Racine* ('Le Roman des Grandes Existences', No. 15), Plon, 1928, new ed., 1962, 255 pp. (Still the most imaginative life of the dramatist.)

MAURON, C., *L'Inconscient dans l'oeuvre et la vie de Racine*, Gap: Éditions Ophrys, 1957, 350 pp. (Entertaining psychoanalytical study.)

MERCATON, J., *Racine* ('Les Ecrivains devant Dieu'), Brussels–Paris: Desclée de Brouwer, 1966, 142 pp.

MOREAU, P., *Racine l'homme et l'oeuvre* ('Connaissance des Lettres' No. 13), 1943, nouvelle éd., 1968, 192 pp. (Good introduction.)

MORNET, D., *Jean Racine*, Aux Armes de France, 1943, 224 pp.

MOUGUES, O. DE, *Racine or The Triumph of Relevance*, Cambridge University Press, 1967, 171 pp.

—, *Autonomie de Racine*, Corti, 1967, 200 pp. (Revised and translated version of the English work.)

ORCIBAL, J., *La Génèse d'Esther et d'Athalie*, Vrin, 1950, 152 pp. (Standard work on the origins of the two religious plays.)

PICARD, R., *La Carrière de Jean Racine* (Bibliothèque des Idées), Gallimard, 1956, 1961, 708 pp.

—, *Corpus Racinianum*, Les Belles Lettres, 1956, 395 pp.

—, *Supplément au 'Corpus Racinianum'*, Les Belles Lettres, 1961.

POMMIER, J., *Aspects de Racine*, Nizet, 1954, xxxviii + 465 pp.

SCHMID, R., *Der dramatische Stil bei Racine*, Aarau: Verlag H. R. Sauer-länder, 1958, 158 pp. (Stimulating essay on Racine's stagecraft.)

SEGOND, J., *Psychologie de Jean Racine*, Les Belles Lettres, 1940, 225 pp.

TRUC, G., *Le Cas Racine*, Garnier, 1921, vi + 200 pp.

—, *Jean Racine, l'oeuvre, l'artiste, l'homme et le temps*, Garnier, 1926, 314 pp.

VAUNOIS, L., *L'Enfance et la jeunesse de Racine*, del Duca, 1964, 253 pp. (Good piece of research into the origins of the family and Racine's early years.)

VINAVER, E., *Racine et la poésie tragique*, Nizet, 1951, 253 pp. Eng. tr., P. M. Jones, Manchester University Press, 1955.

VOSSLER, K., *Jean Racine*, Munich: Hüber, 1926, 189 pp. 2nd ed., Baden: Bühl, 1948. (Both German editions of this important study are out of print, but it is still available in a Spanish translation in the Colleción Austral, Buenos Aires: Espasa-Calpe, S.A., 1946.)

WEINBERG, B., *The Art of Jean Racine*, University of Chicago Press, 1963, xiv + 355 pp.

WEINRICH, H., *Tragische und komische Elemente in Racines 'Andromaque'*. Eine Interpretation. (Forschungen zur Romanischen Philologie, Heft 3), Münster: Aschendorfsche Verlagsbuchhandlung, 1958, 18 pp.

WHEATLEY, K. E., *Racine and English Classicism*, Austin: University of Texas Press, 1956, xi + 345 pp.

IV. BOOKS DEALING PARTLY WITH RACINE, STUDIES PUBLISHED IN REVIEWS, ETC.

AUERBACH, E., 'Racine und die Leidenschaften', pp. 196–203, *Gesammelte Aufsätze zur Romanischen Philologie*, Munich and Berne: Francke Verlag, 1967, 384 pp.

AZORIN, *Racine y Molière*, Madrid: 'La Lectura', 1924, 88 pp. (Racine pp. 11–25.)

BARKO, I. P., 'La Symbolique de Racine: Essai d'interprétation des images de lumière et de ténèbres dans la vision tragique de Racine', pp. 353–77, *Revue des Sciences Humaines*, Fasc. 115, Juillet-Septembre, 1964.

BARNES, A., 'La Prophétie de Joad', pp. 90–108, *The French Mind*, Oxford: Clarendon Press, 1953.

BARRAULT, J. L., *Nouvelles réflexions sur le théâtre*, Flammarion, 1959, 252 pp. ('De la Diction (A Propos de *Phèdre*)' pp. 55–64; 'Le Récitatif', pp. 65–71; 'Essai de Portrait', 165–85 (Also in *Cahiers*, No. 10, 1955); 'Les

Mouvements Symphoniques de *Phèdre*', pp. 186–200. Nobody interested in Racine as dramatist can afford to neglect anything that Barrault has written about him.)

BEGUIN, A., 'Phèdre Nocturne', pp. 115–22, *Poésie de la présence*, Éditions du Seuil, 1957.

BÉNICHOU, P., *L'Écrivain et ses travaux*, Corti, 1967, 362 pp. (*Andromaque*, pp. 207–36; *Phèdre*, pp. 237–323).

BLANCHET, A., 'Phèdre entre le soleil et la nuit', pp. 61–84, *La Littérature et le spirituel*, II, Aubier, 1960, 287 pp.

BLANCHOT, M., 'Le Mythe de Phèdre', pp. 84–90, *Faux pas*, Gallimard, 1943, 366 pp.

BREMOND, H., '*Athalie* poème religieux', pp. 209–30, *Racine et Valéry*, Grasset, 1930, 255 pp. (Important essay.)

DUSSANE, B., *Le Comédien sans paradoxe*, Plon, 1933, 255 pp. ('Les Héroines de Racine', pp. 113–214.)

FERGUSSON, F., '*Bérénice*: the Action and Theatre of Reason', pp. 42–67, *The Idea of a Theater*, Princeton: Princeton University Press, 1949, 240 pp.

GOLDMANN, L., *Le Dieu caché* (Bibliothèque des Idées), Gallimard, 1955, 454 pp. Eng. tr. T. Thody, Routledge and Kegan Paul, 1964. (Racine, pp. 347–451.)

GRACQ, J., 'A Propos de *Bajazet*', pp. 183–202, *Préférences*, nouvelle ed., Corti, 1961, 253 pp. (Remarkable essay.)

GUILLEMIN, H., 'Racine en 1677', pp. 9–23, *Éclaircissements*, Gallimard, 1961.

HOOG, A., 'Notre Mère Phèdre', pp. 21–78, *La Littérature en Silésie*, Grasset, 1944, 311 pp.

JOUVET, L., *Tragédie classique et théâtre du XIXᵉ siècle*, Extraits des cours de Louis Jouvet au Conservatoire (1939–40), Gallimard, 1968, 272 pp. (What I said about Jean-Louis Barrault applies to Jouvet's writings, and to these notes taken by somebody who was present at his course on Racine.)

MAULNIER, T., *Langages*, Éditions du Conquistador, 1946, 279 pp. (Good studies of the first three plays, pp. 79–171.)

MAURIAC, F., *Journal*, II, Grasset, 1937, 230 pp. (Racine, pp. 115–19; 141–5.)

—, *Journal*, III, Grasset, 1940, 218 pp. (Racine, pp. 202–11.)

—, 'La Querelle de Racine', pp. 119–22, *Cahiers de la Compagnie Madeleine Renaud Jean-Louis Barrault*, No. 11, 1955.

(Mauriac's contribution to the controversy mentioned in my opening chapter.)

MAY, G., *Tragédie cornélienne, tragédie racinienne*: Étude sur les sources de l'intérêt dramatique, Urbana: University of Illinois Press, 1948, 255 pp. (Racine, pp. 116–91.)

MERIAN-GENAST, E., 'Die Kunst Racines', pp. 135–51, *Die Neureren Sprachen*, Band XL, Heft 3, 1932. (Brilliant essay on Racine's construction.)

OTT, K. A., 'Uber die Bedeutung des Ortes im Drama von Corneille und Racine', pp. 341–65, *Germanisch-Romanische Monatsschrift*, Neue Folge, Band XI, 1961.

PÉGUY, C., *Victor-Marie, Comte Hugo*, Gallimard, 1934, 241 pp. (Racine, pp. 154–98).

POULET, G., *Études sur le temps humain*, Edinburgh University Press, 1949, 407 pp. (Racine, pp. 138–53).

—, *Mesure de l'instant*, Plon, 1968, 379 pp. ('Racine, Poète des Clartés Sombres', pp. 55–78.)

RAYMOND, M., 'Le Discours Poétique de Racine', pp. 116–23, *Génies de France* (Les Cahiers du Rhône, No. 4), Neuchâtel: Éditions de la Baconnière, 1942, 248 pp.

RIVIÈRE, J. and FERNANDEZ, R., *Moralisme et littérature*, Corrêa, 1932, 203 pp. (Rivière on Racine, pp. 26–41.)

ROUCH, J., 'Le Thème de la Mer dans Racine', pp. 29–47, *Comité des Travaux Historiques et Scientifiques: Bulletin de la Section de Géographie*, Tome LXIII, Années 1949 et 1950.

SAINTE-BEUVE, C. A., *Oeuvres* (Bibliothèque de la Pléiade), I, Gallimard, 1949. (Racine, pp. 721–58; 'Sur le Reprise de *Bérénice*', pp. 759–69.)

SPOERRI, T., 'Trieb und Geist bei Racine', pp. 60–89, *Archiv für das Studium der neureren Sprachen*, Band 163, Heft 1 and 2, März, 1933. (Important essay. Abridged version in English translation in *Racine* (Modern Judgements). See above.)

STAROBINSKI, J., 'Racine et la Poétique du Regard', pp. 69–90, *L'Oeil vivant*, Gallimard, 1961, 262 pp.

STRACHEY, G. L., *Landmarks in French Literature*, Williams and Norgate, 1912, 256 pp. (Racine, pp. 89–110.)

—, *Books and Characters*, Chatto and Windus, 1922, 306 pp. (Racine, pp. 3–27.)

TAINE, H., *Nouveaux essais de critique et d'histoire*, 3e éd., Hachette, 1880. (Racine, pp. 171–223.)

VALÉRY, P., 'Sur Phèdre Femme', pp. 185–96, *Variété V*, Gallimard, 1945, 325 pp.

VARIOUS, *Cahiers de la Compagnie Madeleine Renaud Jean-Louis Barrault.*

—, No. 8, 1955. Special number on Racine.

—, No. 40, Novembre, 1962, Special number, 'Connaissance de Racine'.

—, *Europe*, No. 453, Janvier, 1967. Special number, 'Pour le Tricentenaire d'*Andromaque*'.

—, *Jeunesse de Racine*, La Ferté-Milon; diffusion, Minard, 1958 —.

VIVIER, R., *Et la poésie fut langage*, Brussels: Palais des Académies, 1954, 232 pp. (Racine, pp. 123–61.)

ZIMMERMANN, E. M., 'La Lumière et la Voix: Étude sur l'unité de *Britannicus*', pp. 169–83, *Revue des Sciences Humaines*, Fasc. 130, Avril-Juin, 1968.

V. MONOGRAPHS ON INDIVIDUAL PLAYS

Andromaque

MORNET, D., *Andromaque de Racine*. Étude et Analyse (Les Chefs-d'Oeuvre de la Littérature Expliqués), Mellottée, 1947, 309 pp.

Britannicus

MOORE, W. G., *Racine: Britannicus* (Studies in French Literature, I), Edward Arnold, 1960, 48 pp.

Bérénice

MICHAUD, G., *La Bérénice de Racine*, Société Française d'Imprimerie et de Librairie, 1907, xiii + 355 pp.

Bajazet

SCHERER, J., *Racine: Bajazet* ('Les Cours de Sorbonne'), Centre de Documentation Universitaire, 1958, 310 pp.

VAN DER STARRE, E., *Racine et le théâtre de l'ambiguité*. Étude sur *Bajazet*, Universitaire Pers Leiden, 1966, 236 pp.

Phèdre

DÉDÉYAN, C., *Racine et sa Phèdre*, Société d'Édition d'Enseignement Supérieur, 1965, 302 pp.

MAULNIER, T., *Lecture de Phèdre*, Gallimard, 1943, nouvelle éd., revue et augmentée, 1967, 171 pp.

MAURON, C., *Phèdre*, Corti, 1968, 188 pp. (A pendant to his study of the unconscious in Racine. See above.)

Athalie

MONGRÉDIEN, G., *Athalie de Racine* (Les Grands Événements Littéraires), Sfelt, 1946, 177 pp. (Useful on background. Not a critical work.)

VI. VERSIFICATION AND LANGUAGE

BRUNEAU, C., *Petite histoire de la langue française*, I, Armand Colin, 1958, 284 pp. (Best work of its kind for anybody whose interests are primarily literary.)

CAHEN, J. B., *Le Vocabulaire de Racine*, Droz, 1946, 251 pp.

CRESSOT, M., 'La Langue de *Phèdre*', pp. 169–82, *Le Français Moderne*, Tome X, 1942.

ELWERT, W. T., *Traité de versification française des origines à nos jours* (Bibliothèque Française et Romane), Klincksieck, 1965, 210 pp. (Author's own translation of *Französische Metrik*, Munich: Hüber, 1961.)

FRANCE, P., *Racine's Rhetoric*, Oxford: Clarendon Press, 1965, 256 pp.

FREEMAN, B. C. and BATSON, A., *Concordance du Théâtre et des Poésies de Jean Racine*, 2 volumes, New York: Cornell University Press, 1968, 1,483 pp. (A computerized concordance which supersedes any previous work of the same kind and is invaluable to anybody making a close study of Racine. Strange to say, it did not appear to have reached the Bibliothèque Nationale when I was last there in August 1970 or the British Museum by October 1971.)

GRAMMONT, M., *Le Vers français, ses moyens d'expression, son harmonie*, 3e éd., Champion, 1923, 510 pp. (Remains the standard work in spite of reservations expressed by other prosodists.)

—, *Petit traité de versification française*, 14e éd., Armand Colin, 1952, 162 pp. (In my opinion still the best introduction to the subject.)

GUIRAUD, P., *Essais de stylistique* (Initiation à la Linguistique, Série B, No. 1), Klincksieck, 1969, 285 pp. (Analysis by one of the best known authorities on linguistics of two of the most famous *tirades* in *Phèdre*, pp. 151–71.)

—, *La Versification* (Collection 'Que sais-je?' No. 1,377), Presses Universitaires de France, 1970, 128 pp.

GUIRAUD, P., HARTLE, R. W. and BANDY, W. T., *Index du vocabulaire du théâtre classique: Racine*, I–XI, Klincksieck, 1955–64. (Useful, but much less detailed than the Freeman-Batson concordance mentioned above.)

LE HIR, Y., *Analyses stylistiques* (Collection U), Armand Colin, 1965, 302 pp. (*Mithridate*, pp. 38–54; *Phèdre*, pp. 55–64.)

LOTE, G., *Études sur le vers français*, 3 volumes, Éditions de la Phalange, 1913–14, I, xix + 368 pp.; II, pp. 369–719; III, vi + 215 pp.

—, *Histoire du vers français*, 3 vols., Boivin, I, 1949, xxxv + 362 pp.; II, 1951, 316 pp.; III, 1955, 375 pp. (Author unfortunately died before completing this last work which does not go beyond the middle ages.)

RUDLER, G., *L'Explication française*, Armand Colin, 9ᵉ éd., 1952, 251 pp. (*Mithridate*, pp. 127–73.)

SOURIAU, M., *L'Évolution du vers français au dix-septième siècle*, Hachette 1893, xiv + 494 pp. (Racine, pp. 402–91.)

SPITZER, L., 'Die klassische Dämpfung in Racines Stil', pp. 135–268, *Romanische Stil- und Literaturstudien*, I, Marburg a. Lhan: N. G. Elwert' sche Verlagsbuchhandlung, 1931, 301 pp.

—, *Linguistics and Literary History*, Princeton University Press, 1948; New York: Russell & Russell, 1962, vii + 236 pp. (Impressive defence of the 'Récit de Théramène', pp. 87–134.)

SUBERVILLE, J., *Histoire et théorie de la versification française*, Les Éditions de 'L'École', nouvelle éd. revue et complétée, 1946, 253 pp.

VII. GRAMOPHONE RECORDS

1. COMPLETE PLAYS

Andromaque: Jean Deschamps (Oreste), Jean-Pierre Aumont (Pyrrhus), Éléonore Hirt (Andromaque), Maria Mauban (Hermione), Fernand Ledoux (Phoenix), Pierre Vaneck (Pylade). Réalisation: Georges Hacquard. L'Encyclopédie Sonore, 2 disques, 320 E 834–5. Hachette, n.d.

Britannicus: Robert Hirsch (Néron), Paul-Émile Deiber (Burrhus), Michel Bernardy (Britannicus), François Chaumette (Narcisse), Annie Ducaux (Agrippine), Danièle Ajoret (Junie). Mise en scène, Michel Vitold. Comédie Française. 3 disques. Stéréo. Pathé, CPTA 323–5. 1963.

Bérénice: Jean Deschamps (Titus), Maurice Escande (Antiochus), Paul-Émile Deiber (Arsace), Jean Marchat (Paulin), Annie Ducaux (Bérénice). Comédie Française. 2 disques. Pathé, DTX 240–1. 1957

Phèdre: Marie Bell (Phèdre), Jacques Dacqmine (Thésée), Henriette Barreau (Oenone), Raymond Gérome (Théramène), Claude Giraud (Hippolyte), Danielle Volle (Aricie). Mise en scène, Raymond Gérome. 'Théâtre du Gymnase—Marie Bell.' 3 Disques Adès, TS 30 LA 600–02. 1965.

Esther: Catherine Sellers (Esther), Pierre Blanchar (Mardochée), Michel Bouquet (Aman), Jean Deschamps (Assuérus), Éléonore Hirt (Élise). Réalisation, Georges Hacquard. Musique de J. B. Moreau. L'Encyclopédie Sonore, 2 disques, 320 E 839–40. Hachette, n.d.

Athalie: Maria Mériko (Athalie), Jean Deschamps (Joad), Maria Mauban

(Josabet), Michel Bouquet (Mathan), Didier Haudepin (Joas). Réalisation, Georges Hacquard. Musique de J. B. Moreau. L'Encyclopédie
Sonore, 3 disques, 320 E 862–4. Hachette, n.d.

2. EXTRACTS

Iphigénie: Nelly Borgeaud (Iphigénie), Geneviève Casile (Ériphile), Jean
   Topart (Agamemnon), Jean Négroni (Achille), Maria Mériko (Clytemnestre). Réalisation, Alain Barroux. Sélections Sonores Bordas, 122.
   n.d.

Phèdre: Maria Casarès (Phèdre), Germaine Kerjean (Oenone), Michel
   Ruhl (Hippolyte), Pierre Ollivier (Thésée). Réalisation, Alain Barroux.
   Sélections Sonores Bordas, 106. n.d.

INDEX